MW00803897

# Scripture, Texts, and Tracings in Galatians and 1 Thessalonians

# SCRIPTURE, TEXTS, AND TRACINGS
## IN PAUL'S LETTERS

# Scripture, Texts, and Tracings in Galatians and 1 Thessalonians

## Edited by

A. Andrew Das
B. J. Oropeza

LEXINGTON BOOKS/FORTRESS ACADEMIC
*Lanham • Boulder • New York • London*

Published by Lexington Books/Fortress Academic
Lexington Books is an imprint of The Rowman & Littlefield Publishing Group, Inc.
4501 Forbes Boulevard, Suite 200, Lanham, Maryland 20706
www.rowman.com

86-90 Paul Street, London EC2A 4NE, United Kingdom

Copyright © 2023 by The Rowman & Littlefield Publishing Group, Inc.

*All rights reserved.* No part of this book may be reproduced in any form or by any electronic or mechanical means, including information storage and retrieval systems, without
written permission from the publisher, except by a reviewer who may quote passages
in a review.

British Library Cataloguing in Publication Information Available

Library of Congress Cataloging-in-Publication Data Avaiable

ISBN 9781978716056 (cloth : alk. paper) | ISBN 9781978716063 (epub)

# Contents

# Abbreviations

| | |
|---|---|
| AB | Anchor Bible |
| ABG | Arbeiten zur Bibel und ihrer Geschichte |
| *ABR* | *Anglican Biblical Review* |
| AcBib | Academia Biblica |
| ALGHJ | Arbeiten zur Literatur und Geschichte des Hellenistischen Judentums |
| AnBib | Analecta Biblica |
| *ANET* | *Ancient Near Eastern Texts Relating to the Old Testament.* Edited by James B. Pritchard. 3rd ed. Princeton: Princeton University Press, 1969. |
| *ANRW* | *Aufstieg und Niedergang des römischen Welt: Geschichte und Kultur Roms im Spiegel der neueren Forschung.* Edited by H. Temporini and W. Haase (Berlin, 1972–) |
| ASNU | Acta Seminarii Neotestamentici Upsaliensis |
| AT | Authorized Translation |
| ATD | Das Alte Testament Deutsch |
| BDAG | Danker, Frederick W., Walter Bauer, William F. Arndt, and F. Wilbur Gingrich. *Greek-English Lexicon of the New Testament and Other Early Christian Literature,* 3rd ed (Chicago: University of Chicago Press, 2000) |
| *BBR* | *Bulletin of Biblical Research* |
| BECNT | Baker Exegetical Commentary on the New Testament |
| BNTC | Black's New Testament Commentaries |
| BrillDAG | *The Brill Dictionary of Ancient Greek.* Ed. Franco Montanari, Madeleine Goh, and Chad Schroeder (Leiden: Brill, 2015) |
| *BTB* | *Biblical Theology Bulletin* |
| BThSt | Biblisch-Theologische Studien |
| BTS | Biblical Tools and Studies |
| BZNW | Beihefte zur Zeitschrift für die Neutestamentliche Wissenschaft |
| CBQMS | Catholic Biblical Quarterly Monograph Series |

| | |
|---|---|
| *CurBR* | *Currents in Biblical Research* |
| CCF | Commentaries for Christian Formation |
| CCSS | Catholic Commentary on Sacred Scripture |
| *CIL* | *Corpus Inscriptionum Latinarum.* Berlin, 1862– |
| CSB | Christian Standard Bible |
| *DPL²* | *Dictionary of Paul and His Letters.* Second Edition. Ed. Scot McKnight, Lynn H. Cohick, and Nijay Gupta (Downers Grove, IL: InterVarsity Press, 2023) |
| EBTC | commentary series for Harmon Lexham |
| *EDNT* | *Exegetical Dictionary of the New Testament.* Edited by Horst Balz and Gerhard Schneider. ET, 3 vols. (Grand Rapids: Eerdmans, 1990–1993) |
| EJL | Early Judaism and Its Literature |
| ESBT | commentary series for Harmon IVP |
| ESV | English Standard Version |
| EKKNT | Evangelisch-Katholischer Kommentar zum Neuen Testament |
| FRLANT | Forschungen zur Religion und Literatur des Alten und Neuen Testaments |
| HCOT | Historical Commentary on the Old Testament |
| HThKNT | Herders Theologischer Kommentar zum Neuen Testament |
| *HTLS* | *Historical and Theological Lexicon of the Septuagint.* Volume 1. Edited by Eberhard Bons and Jan Jooste (Tübingen: Mohr Siebeck, 2020) |
| *HTR* | *Harvard Theological Review* |
| ICC | International Critical Commentary |
| ITC | International Theological Commentary |
| *JBL* | *Journal of Biblical Literature* |
| *JGRChJ* | *Journal of Greco-Roman Christianity and Judaism* |
| *JRS* | *Journal of Roman Studies* |
| *JSJ* | *Journal for the Study of Judaism in the Persian, Hellenistic, and Roman Periods* |
| *JSNT* | *Journal for the Study of the New Testament* |
| JSNTSup | Journal for the Study of the New Testament Supplement Series |
| *JSOT* | *Journal for the Study of the Old Testament* |
| JSOTSup | Journal for the Study of the Old Testament Supplement Series |
| *JSP* | *Journal for the Study of the Pseudepigrapha* |
| *JTI* | *Journal of Theological Interpretation* |
| *JTS* | *Journal of Theological Studies* |
| LNTS | Library of New Testament Studies |
| LPS | Library of Pauline Studies |
| *M-AJT* | *Mid-Atlantic Journal of Theology* |

| | |
|---|---|
| NAC | New American Commentary |
| NCB | New Century Bible |
| NET | New English Translation |
| NETS | New English Translation of the Septuagint |
| NICNT | New International Commentary on the New Testament |
| NICOT | New International Commentary on the Old Testament |
| *NIDB* | *New Interpreters* |
| NIGTC | New International Greek Testament Commentary |
| NIVAppC | NIV Application Commentary |
| NRSV | New Revised Standard Version |
| NSBT | Harmon IVP |
| NTL | New Testament Library |
| *NTS* | *New Testament Studies* |
| *NovT* | *Novum Testamentum* |
| NTAbh.NF | Neutestamentliche Abhandlungen; Neue Folge |
| NTOA | Novum Testamentum et Orbis Antiquus |
| OBT | Overtures to Biblical Theology |
| *OHPS* | *The Oxford Handbook of Pauline Studies.* Ed. Matthew V. Novenson and R. Barry Matlock (Oxford: Oxford University Press, 2022) |
| PAST | Pauline Studies, Brill |
| PCS | Pentecostal Commentary Series |
| *PRSt* | *Perspectives in Religious Studies* |
| PW | *Paulys Real-Encyclopädie der Classischen Altertumswissenschaft.* New edition by Georg Wissowa and Wilhelm Kroll. 50 vols, in 84 parts |
| RRA | Rhetoric of Religious Antiquity |
| RSV | Revised Standard Version |
| *SBJT* | *Southern Baptist Journal of Theology* |
| SBLDS | Society of Biblical Literature Dissertation Series |
| SBLSymS | Society of Biblical Literature Symposium Series |
| SEG | inscriptions in Heilig |
| SemeiaSt | Semeia Studies |
| *SJT* | *Scottish Journal of Theology* |
| SNTSMS | Society of New Testament Studies Monograph Series |
| SPhiloA | Studia Philonica Annual |
| StBibLit | Studies in Biblical Literature |
| VTSup | Supplements to Vetus Testamentum |
| *TAPA* | *Transactions of the American Philological Association* |
| *TDNT* | *Theological Dictionary of the New Testament.* Edited by Gerhard Kittel and Gerhard Friedrich. Translated by Geoffrey Bromiley. 10 vols. (Grand Rapids; Eerdmans, 1964–1976) |

| | |
|---|---|
| THKNT | Theologischer Handkommentar zum Neuen Testament |
| TSAJ | Texte und Studien zum Antiken Judentum |
| *TynBul* | *Tyndale Bulletin* |
| UTB | Uni-Taschenbücher |
| *VF* | *Verkündigung und Forschung* |
| *VT* | *Vetus Testamentum* |
| VTSup | Vetus Testamentum Supplements |
| WBC | Word Biblical Commentary |
| *WTJ* | *Westminster Theological Journal* |
| WUNT | Wissenschaftliche Untersuchungen zum Neuen Testament |
| *ZNW* | *Zeitschrift für die neutestamentliche Wissenschaft* |

# Preface

The editors wish to express their appreciation to Neil Elliott at Lexington Books/Fortress Academic for the opportunity for a planned series of four books on the use of Scripture in Paul's undisputed letters. Volume One addressed the topic of Scripture, Texts, and Tracings in 1 Corinthians. The second volume was on Romans, and the third on 2 Corinthians and Philippians. This fourth volume focuses on Scripture, Texts, and Tracings in Galatians and 1 Thessalonians.

Paul's engagement with Scripture has long been a contentious debate with many unresolved issues. Despite the variety of interpretative approaches that have been proposed, a lack of scholarly consensus persists. Although comparative approaches sometimes may result in attributing textual differences to Paul's creativity, it is important that scholars not overlook the rich biblical and extra-biblical tradition-history in which Paul stands. The contributors of this volume take seriously the sources behind Paul's letters; such sources may extend beyond the Scriptures to other texts, and hence the title for this volume, *Scripture, Texts, and Tracings in Galatians and 1 Thessalonians*.

Eleven of the twelve papers for this volume were delivered at the 2021 and 2022 SBL national meetings in the Scripture and Paul Seminar. Thanks to all who participated in the seminar for the very fruitful and stimulating conversations. All the papers have been extensively revised in light of the discussions, critiques, and further reflection.

# Introduction

## Scripture, Texts, and Tracings in Galatians and 1 Thessalonians

### A. Andrew Das and B. J. Oropeza

Paul's interplay with Scripture has become a matter of intense interest in recent decades due in no small part to Richard B. Hays's pivotal work, *Echoes of Scripture in the Letters of Paul*.[1] Many New Testament scholars were introduced to the "figure of an echo" and started to pay closer attention to *unmarked* references from Jewish Scripture. Likewise, more thorough examinations of Paul's *marked* quotations assisted in understanding the apostle's use of Scripture in relation to the Septuagint, Old Greek, Masoretic, Qumran scrolls, and other early translations and interpretations of Scripture.[2]

This volume's chapters advance the work on marked and unmarked Scripture references in Galatians and 1 Thessalonians. The collection originates from exceptional, invited papers presented at the Scripture and Paul Seminar at the annual Society of Biblical Literature conferences in 2021 and 2022. The previous volumes in the series tackled 1 Corinthians,[3] Romans,[4] and 2 Corinthians and Philippians.[5] Galatians, another *Hauptbrief*, enjoys its fair share of Scriptural quotations, allusions, and echoes. First Thessalonians, like Philippians, has fewer—thus forming a manageable tandem with Galatians. Also, many consider 1 Thessalonians Paul's earliest letter. Although most place Galatians in the time frame of Paul's letters to the Corinthians and Romans, a significant minority contend for Galatians as the earliest.[6] Some might say, then, that this series is ending at the beginning.

We recognize that even though our contributors cover significant texts in Galatians and 1 Thessalonians, this modest, one-volume monograph cannot possibly cover all potential Scripture references in these letters. The intent of this collection is, in the words of the seminar's program unit description, "to work toward the resolution of scholarly gridlock concerning the way the apostle Paul interpreted and applied the Jewish Scriptures" in Galatians and 1 Thessalonians. As the fourth volume in a series, the reader should also consult the array of methodological and textual approaches in the first three volumes for a comprehensive survey of the contemporary scholarly scene on these questions.

A word about our title for the series is in order. By "Scripture" we mean the Jewish sacred writings that Paul and other early followers of Jesus the Messiah read, studied, and obeyed. This collection is later identified as the "Old Testament" and in Paul's day consisted of the Law, Prophets, and Writings. With the majority of scholars today, we recognize that the apostle mostly uses texts compatible with the LXX. At the same time, we are quite aware that Paul's quotes often are not exactly the same as any extant source, whether Greek or Hebrew. By a citation or quotation of Scripture, which we use interchangeably for this series unless otherwise stated, we mean a recognizable set of words that is signaled by a marker such as, "It is written" or by indirect markers such as γάρ or ὅτι, or that is otherwise set apart from the immediate context so as to be commonly recognized as a text reference.

By "Texts" we mean any ancient source that might inform Paul or his auditors inclusive of but not limited to the Jewish Scriptures. Such sources include the vast array of Second Temple and Greco-Roman literature. Along with classical literature, source texts may include ancient papyri documents, inscriptions, numismatics, maxims, and so forth. This is all to say that we recognize the social, cultural, and ideological world of the first century informed both Paul and his recipients implicitly and explicitly.

By "Tracings" we mean Scripture or other texts that are alluded to rather than quoted by Paul. In other words, a tracing is any external text presence that is not from a quotation. We use "tracings" synonymously with allusions.[7] For our purposes, then, a tracing is an indirect reference of a pre-text that has one or more agreements with the Pauline text. The agreements may include the same or similar word(s), whether verbatim, conceptual, structural, topical, thematic, and/or referring to a person, place, action, or event. How the tracings are detected by scholars today prompt the same explanations of how allusions are detected—normally, with rigorous argumentation or criteria comparable with or the same as the sevenfold model of Richard Hays.[8] Our expectation through this volume is that the reader will be provoked and challenged with new insights from Scripture in Galatians and 1 Thessalonians.

To that end, Jeremiah 16:14–15 and 23:7–8 both identify God not as "the one who brought Israel up out of Egypt" as in prior texts but as the one who restored the people from exile. Matthew S. Harmon contends that this promised "reidentification" is interwoven with several other motifs in a network of ideas connected to: raising up a righteous Davidic ruler, return from exile, resurrection, forgiveness of sins, the gift of the Spirit, and fulfillment of the promises to the patriarchs. Since these ideas arguably figure in Paul's Letter to the Galatians as well, it is likely that they stand behind Paul's reidentification of God as the Father who raised Jesus from the dead in Gal 1:1.

Interpreters struggle with Gal 2:18, especially its relation to 2:17, and yet the almost universal consensus is that the Mosaic law is being broken down and reconstituted, whether wholly or in some part, aspect, or function. As Nicolai Techow explains, Isa 5:2, Let. Aris. (Letter of Aristeas) 139, and Eph 2:14–15 do not serve as useful parallels supporting the law as that which is broken down and built up in Gal 2:18—language rarely associated with the law. Rather, Paul's language echoes Jeremiah's: God is tearing/breaking down sinful people and their sin in order to build them back up as a new people, all through the mission and activity of the prophet. In Paul's case, were he to rebuild the same sinners and sin that he had broken down, he would be a transgressor of his God-given calling and mission. That mission is patterned after his own death with Christ crucified under the law's curse and judgment, and it is patterned also after his resurrection with Christ to new life. Thus the "I"/Paul is no longer the same. Christ does *not*, then, promote indifference to sin.

B. J. Oropeza seeks to rectify the lack of attention to the Holy Spirit in Pauline soteriology in Galatians, especially with respect to life and justification. Scripture, revelation, and the Jesus traditions inform Paul's understanding. Even the Galatians' experience of the Spirit demonstrates that they have been righteoused by trust and not by works of law (Gal 2:16–3:5). Their experience of the Spirit and suffering recall Paul's own power-in-weakness revelation from the Lord Jesus (experienced earlier but later written in 2 Cor 12:1–10). The promise of the Spirit in Gal 3:14 is in both the Jesus tradition and prophetic discourse—from John the Baptist, to Jesus, to the disciples, and finally to Paul and the Galatians—and it is anticipated in the prophetic Scriptures, especially in the echoes of Ezekiel that Oropeza traces through Galatians. For Paul, the righteous by trust *live* through union with Christ in the Spirit.

Craig S. Keener analyzes Gal 3:8–14 on the basis of the shared and contrasting terms that link the verses. The blessing of Abraham sandwiches the section and stresses how the promised blessing of Abraham is experienced through the Spirit (3:5, 14) and is available to all the families of the earth. Within this section is the curse for those who do not obey the law, but Jesus exhausted his people's curse in their place on the tree of the cross. This is appropriated by faith and not by law-works. In the process, the apostle reframes his opponents' Scriptural texts.

Scholars have overlooked how the repeated phrase ἐκ πίστεώς (*ek pisteos*) serves as a shorthand reference to the Old Greek of Hab 2:4, a verse Paul explicitly cites in Gal 3:11. Roy E. Ciampa explains that Paul also rewrites Hab 2:4 with expressions *other* than ἐκ πίστεως, including διὰ πίστεως, πίστει, forms of πίστευω, combined with terms from the δικαι- root. Ciampa therefore seeks to trace the contribution of Hab 2:4 throughout Galatians, including 2:16, 20; 3:7; 3:8; 3:9; 3:12; 3:14; 3:22; 3:24; 3:26; 5:5 (and possibly in 3:2, 5). Since Paul understands ἐκ πίστεως in relation to Christ Jesus, Ciampa asks whether πίστις (πίστις Χριστοῦ) refers to faith in Christ (or faithfulness to Christ) or to Christ's own faithfulness. Relying on Teresa Morgan, Ciampa maintains that πίστις is always double-ended, incorporating both trust and trustworthiness, faithfulness and good faith. Nevertheless, Greek and Latin sources shy away from expressing those relations reciprocally in cases of unequal social relations. Paul therefore is usually referring to faith in Christ (or faithfulness/allegiance to Christ) rather than Christ's own faithfulness, although some of the texts may be intentionally ambiguous. Readers should also consult Ciampa's chapter in this regard on Romans: "Habakkuk 2:4 in Romans: Echoes, Allusions, and Rewriting" in *Scripture, Texts, and Tracings in Romans*, edited by A. Andrew Das and Linda Belleville (Lanham, MD: Lexington/Fortress Academic, 2021), 11–29.

Mark A. Seifrid revisits Paul's appeal to the story of Hagar and Sarah and their two children as it appears in Gal 4:21–31, arguing that the proper translation of Gal 4:24 is "these things are spoken allegorically" (ἅτινά ἐστιν ἀλληγορούμενα). Paul does not say that he is interpreting the text allegorically, as is often maintained. He signals that the text itself is speaking allegorically. This hermeneutic finds a parallel in Philo, who like Paul, understands the Scripture to speak allegorically, albeit out of a differing premise. According to Paul, already in the Abraham narratives the Scripture was proclaiming the gospel of Jesus Christ. Hagar and Sarah thus serve to contrast two differing peoples, respectively determined by law and promise, flesh and Spirit, slavery and freedom. Paul correspondingly reads the Isaianic promise to the desolated Jerusalem (Isa 54:1) as reflective of the Genesis allegory as it now has been fulfilled in Christ, the gift of the Spirit, and belonging to the new creation. The hermeneutic of the apostle implicitly challenges any and all interpretive paradigms that give priority to the insight and skill of the interpreter.

Ernest Clark compares Paul's allegorical method and rationale in Gal 4:21–31 with those of his Jewish contemporary Philo. He then analyzes Paul's distribution of the weight of his argument between allegoresis and exegesis, which suggests that Paul distrusts allegoresis. Ultimately, Paul impugns the hermeneutical validity of scriptural allegoresis but exploits it in 4:21–31 for its rhetorical value: he listens to the law allegorically in order to dismiss hearing the law allegorically. Paul is opposing teaching like Philo's: allegorical readings of scriptural narratives to promote practicing the law in order to gain life, righteousness, and the inheritance. Paul writes exegetically to confront this sort of teaching since it is by faith, through the Spirit, that he and his brothers and sisters wait for righteousness in hope (Gal 5:6).

"Peace" and "mercy" in Gal 6:16 alludes to Isa 54:10. A. Andrew Das contends that the allusion supports identifying the "Israel of God" as ethnic Christ-believing Jews. The unusual syntax favors the identification, and Paul's regular distinction between Jews and gentiles, circumcised and uncircumcised in the letter is likewise supportive. As for the role of gentiles in Isaiah, scholars have abandoned the view that Isaiah envisions the gentiles converting. Isaianic scholars favor either that the gentiles/nations will enjoy God's salvation as *gentiles* or will be subject to Israel with diaspora *Israelites* as those streaming to Zion. In effect, Isaiah did not envision gentiles becoming part of Israel. The Septuagintal Isa 54:15 is a unique Second Temple text in possibly describing gentile conversion. Terence Donaldson does not think it supports gentile proselytism after all, but others think the Septuagint may attest to a Second Temple tradition in favor of gentile conversion, a position that would have been shared by Paul's rivals. Donaldson describes four patterns of gentile universalism in the Second Temple period: conversion (Paul's rivals' approach), gentile sympathizing, ethical monotheism, and eschatological salvation. Paul envisions more than ethical monotheism and denies the need for gentiles to convert. That leaves gentile sympathizing and eschatological salvation as potential Second Temple parallels for Paul's message. In both patterns, the gentile remains a gentile and does not become a member of Israel. Second Temple understandings of the gentiles' eschatological salvation maintain the distinction between Israel and the nations, paralleling the distinction in the Hebrew text of Isaiah. The "Israel of God" is best taken, then, as referring to ethnic Jews who agree with Paul's "rule" in Gal 6:16.

Channing Crisler tracks the motif of suffering throughout Galatians as one of the alternative marks to circumcision of the righteous. Paul therefore draws on patterns of lament from Israel's Scriptures. Justification in Christ is a *painful* experience. As Paul calls God's curse upon the rivals (1:6–9), he draws on the language of the imprecatory lament. Deuteronomy 13:1–18 calls upon the Israelites to slaughter actively those who teach idolatry, and the lament Psalms draw on this language in prayer for God to intervene (e.g., Ps 68:23–24 LXX). Galatians 2:11–14 draws on the language of answered lament since the withdrawal from the table at Antioch echoes the righteous from Hab 2:4 LXX whose soul does not "shrink back"; cf. Hab 2:4 in Gal 3:11. Paul draws on Ps 142:2 LXX in Gal 2:16, another instance of answered lament as the Psalmist calls on God for deliverance. Likewise, Gen 15:6 in Gal 3:6 and Hab 2:4 in Gal 3:11 are instances of answered lament, following

Paul's mention of the Galatians' suffering in 3:4. In Gal 3:11 Paul is warning against the curse of 3:10. The vision of redemption is fulfilled in the crucified Christ alone. Galatians 3:16 draws on the language of messianic lament in Ps 88:39 LXX (with σπέρμα and Χριστός). Finally, Gal 4:1–20 is an instance of human-divine participation in lament even if lacking specific echoes of pre-texts. The lament language helps provide a theological framework to understand that justification in Christ can be painful.

Christoph Heilig tackles imperial counter-narratives in Galatians. Unfortunately, Richard Hays's criteria for detecting allusions are problematic, and John Barclay has raised objections to identifying anti-imperial motifs in Galatians. Heilig evaluates the proposal of Hardin that the persecution of Gal 6:12 should be connected with a refusal to participate in the imperial cult. Christians may have been stressing continuity with Judaism to avoid the uncomfortable consequences of their rejection of imperial and other pagan cults, whether or not Gal 6:12 may be rightly construed along these lines. Galatians just does not provide evidence that pressure to participate in imperial cults was the determining factor behind advocating circumcision in the Galatian churches. Nevertheless, one need not argue for hidden code for Paul to allude to the imperial context (e.g., 2 Cor 2:14). For instance, Paul's language of co-crucifixion with Christ would be comforting in the face of Roman power, especially since Paul is crucified to the (Roman?) world in 6:14. Finally, Heilig proposes a possible allusion to Rome if Galatians is written later in the mid-50s and reflects in 4:1–7 Nero's accession as Claudius's adopted heir. Even though somewhat speculative, ultimately such proposals are useful in furthering historical reconstruction.

Although 1 Thessalonians contains no explicit citation of the Scriptures and was written to gentiles, Jeffrey A. D. Weima contends that Paul's thinking and expression remain indebted to those Scriptures. The Scriptures ground the apostle's conviction that the predominantly gentile Jesus-followers in Thessalonica are included among God's end-time people and so possess the gifts of holiness, the Holy Spirit, and divine instruction—all anticipated blessings of the new covenant in the messianic age. Since Weima limits himself in his chapter to OT allusions found in 1 Thess 4:1–12, contemporary readers will benefit from consulting Weima's comprehensive coverage in "1–2 Thessalonians," in the *Commentary on the New Testament Use of the Old Testament*.[9] As for 1 Thess 4:1–12 and its ethical exhortations, the admonitions to be holy in sexual conduct and to love others echo the Jewish Scriptures and suggest that Paul views this as the fulfillment of eschatological promises to Israel. The Thessalonian gentiles are *no longer* "gentiles who do not know God" but are members of the renewed, covenant people of Israel with all the ethical expectations that this new status entails as those taught of God.

Nijay K. Gupta takes as his starting point *not* a collation of Scriptural echoes and allusions in 1 Thessalonians, but rather Jewish religious discourse influenced by the Septuagint and how that discourse would have been understood by the Romanized Thessalonians. Paul was catechizing his pagan-turned-Jesus-followers on how to honor the divine in a distinctively (Hellenistic) *Jewish* way: they are called to consecration to God through Jesus. A Jewish conception of holiness was more comprehensive and required a deeper level of personal purity, made possible by the indwelling of God's own Spirit. Thus, the Thessalonians are to be a priestly people in their sexual behavior and in how they treat others.

## NOTES

1. New Haven: Yale University Press, 1989.

2. E.g., Dietrich-Alex Koch, *Die Schrift als Zeuge des Evangeliums: Untersuchungen zur Verwendung und zum Verständnis der Schrift bei Paulus,* BzHT 69 (Tübingen: Mohr Siebeck, 1986); Christopher D. Stanley, *Paul and the Language of Scripture: Citation Technique in the Pauline Epistles and Contemporary Literature,* SNTSMS 74 (Cambridge: Cambridge University Press, 1992).

3. Linda L. Belleville and B. J. Oropeza, eds., *Scripture, Texts, and Tracings in 1 Corinthians* (Lanham, MD: Lexington/Fortress Academic, 2019).

4. Linda L. Belleville and A. Andrew Das, eds., *Scripture, Texts, and Tracings in Romans* (Lanham, MD: Lexington/Fortress Academic, 2021).

5. A. Andrew Das and B. J. Oropeza, eds., *Scriptures, Texts, and Tracings in 2 Corinthians and Philippians* (Lanham, MD: Lexington/Fortress Academic, 2022).

6. See the discussion in A. Andrew Das, *Galatians,* Concordia Commentary (St. Louis: Concordia, 2014), 31–47.

7. Allusion in this instance also includes echoes. We recognize that certain scholars prefer to use the terms synonymously, whereas others make distinctions between them. For assessments, see B. J. Oropeza, "Quotations, Allusions, and Echoes: Their Meaning in Relation to Biblical Interpretation," in *Practicing Intertextuality: Ancient Jewish and Greco-Roman Exegetical Techniques in the New Testament,* ed. Max Lee and B. J. Oropeza (Eugene, OR: Cascade, 2021), 17–26; and A. Andrew Das, *Paul and the Stories of Israel: Grand Thematic Narratives in Galatians* (Minneapolis: Fortress, 2016), 4–13.

8. See Hays's list in *Echoes of Scripture,* 29–32; idem, *The Conversion of the Imagination* (Grand Rapids: Eerdmans, 2005), 34–45. These criteria include: (1) availability; (2) volume; (3) recurrence/clustering; (4) thematic coherence; (5) historical plausibility; (6) history of interpretation; and (7) satisfaction. For a sample critique, see Stanley E. Porter, "The Use of the Old Testament in the New Testament: A Brief Comment on Method and Terminology," in *Early Christian Interpretation of Israel: Investigations and Proposals,* ed. Craig Evans and James A. Sanders, JSNT-Sup 148/SSEJC 5 (Sheffield: Sheffield Academic, 1997), 79–96, esp. 83–88. Despite

criticisms, Hays's criteria are still valued today by a number of scholars—see Christopher D. Stanley, "What We Learned—And What We Didn't," in *Paul and Scripture: Extending the Conversation,* ECIL 9 (Atlanta: SBL Press, 2012), 321–330.

9. "1–2 Thessalonians," in the *Commentary on the New Testament Use of the Old Testament*, ed. G. K. Beale and D. A. Carson (Grand Rapids: Baker Academic, 2007), 871–89.

# PART I

# Paul's Engagement with Scripture in Galatians

## Chapter 1

# Divine Identity and the Resurrection in Galatians 1:1

## *An Exploration of the Intertextual Matrix Underlying Paul's Redefinition of God's Identity*

### Matthew S. Harmon

Paul's careful description and elaboration of his identity as an apostle in Gal 1:1 has long been scrutinized. What has been less frequently explored is the way that Paul speaks of the divine identity,[1] referring to "God the Father, who raised him [i.e., Jesus] from the dead" (Gal 1:1). In the OT, God repeatedly identifies himself as "the one who brought Israel up out of Egypt" (e.g., Exod 20:2; Lev 26:13; Deut 5:6; Ps 81:10, etc.). But two OT prophetic texts anticipate a day when God will no longer primarily be identified this way; instead, he will be identified as the one who restored his people from exile (Jer 16:14–15; 23:7–8).[2] This promised "reidentification" is interlocked with several other themes/motifs that form a broader network of ideas. This network promises a change in Yahweh's name connected with raising up a righteous Davidic ruler, return from exile, resurrection, forgiveness of sins, the gift of the Spirit, and fulfillment of the promises to the patriarchs.

To trace the logic behind this redefinition of God's identity in Gal 1:1, we will first briefly summarize Gal 1:1 within its immediate context. Second, we will look at the question of divine identity in the OT and its promised redefinition by focusing on two key texts from Jeremiah that promise this redefinition in connection with an interlocking network of several themes. Third, we will look at the presence of several themes from this network within Galatians, other Pauline letters, and Acts in connection with God's identity as the one who raised Jesus from the dead.

## BRIEF SUMMARY OF GALATIANS 1:1

After identifying himself as an apostle (Gal 1:1), Paul qualifies this statement with three prepositional phrases that stress the divine origin of his apostleship:

1. "not from men" (οὐκ ἀπ' ἀνθρώπων)
2. "nor through a man" (οὐδὲ δι' ἀνθρώπου)
3. "but through Jesus Christ and God the Father" (ἀλλὰ διὰ Ἰησοῦ Χριστοῦ καὶ θεοῦ πατρὸς)

The reference to "God the Father" at the conclusion of this final explanatory prepositional phrase leads Paul to further identify him as the one "who raised him [i.e., Jesus Christ] from the dead" (τοῦ ἐγείραντος αὐτὸν ἐκ νεκρῶν).[3] Identifying God the Father as the one who raised Jesus from the dead is more than a historical statement. This identification draws on a deep OT tradition of God defining himself based on epoch-shifting redemptive acts as a way of revealing his identity to his people. More specifically, Paul is drawing on a network of OT promises and motifs that had anticipated a redemptive act of such significance that it would redefine the way that his people would describe the identity of God himself.

## THE BACKGROUND OF PAUL'S REDEFINITION
## OF THE DIVINE IDENTITY

Central to the revelation of God's identity is his name. So in order to understand Paul's redefinition of the divine identity we need to first look at God's revelation and explanation of his special memorial name Yahweh.

### The Divine Name and It's Promised Redefinition

A good place to begin when discussing the divine identity within the OT is God's revelation of himself to Moses at the burning bush (Exod 3:1–4:17). God reveals his name to Moses as "I AM WHO I AM [אֶהְיֶה אֲשֶׁר אֶהְיֶה]" to which he then adds "Say this to the people of Israel: 'I AM [אֶהְיֶה] has sent me to you'" (Exod 3:14). God then further clarifies by saying, "Say this to the people of Israel: 'The LORD [יְהוָה], the God of your fathers, the God of Abraham, the God of Isaac, and the God of Jacob, has sent me to you.'

This is my name forever, and thus I am to be remembered throughout all generations" (Exod 3:15). Scholars have long debated the precise nuance of the Hebrew phrase rendered "I AM WHO I AM" and its implications for the meaning of the divine name, but it seems safe to conclude that part of what it means is that Yahweh defines who he is through self-revelation.[4] In addition to explicit descriptions of his character (e.g., Exod 34:6–7), this self-revelation comes through his actions within human history and the subsequent explanation of those actions through those to whom and through whom he reveals his words. Thus the "acts of God and the character description of God combine to indicate a consistent identity of the one who acts graciously towards his people and can be expected to do so."[5] Therefore, even though God had revealed his name Yahweh to the patriarchs and they even spoke to him using that name (e.g., Gen 15:8), they could not understand the meaning and significance of that name because it was so intimately connected with an act that had not occurred yet—redeeming his people from their slavery in Egypt (Exod 6:2–8). Yet this redemptive act is rooted in Yahweh's promises to the patriarchs (Exod 6:3–4, 8). What the patriarchs only knew dimly the nation of Israel knew more fully.

Given that God links the significance of his memorial name with the fulfillment of his promises to the patriarchs through the exodus, it should come as no surprise that he begins to regularly identify himself as Yahweh "who brought you ought of the land of Egypt" (e.g., Exod 6:7; 16:6; etc.).[6] Perhaps the most noteworthy example is the opening words of the Ten Commandments: "I am the LORD your God, who brought you out of the land of Egypt, out of the house of slavery" (Exod 20:2). From that point forward in the biblical narrative, God repeatedly identifies himself as the one who delivered his people from their Egyptian bondage as a reminder of the definitive act of redemption he accomplished for his people.

Against this backdrop two passages from Jeremiah stand out. The first is Jer 16:14–15. In verses 1–13 Yahweh tells Jeremiah not to marry, have children, or enter the house of mourning or the house of feasting because judgment is coming for Judah's covenant unfaithfulness, a judgment that culminates in exile. But all hope is not lost, as Yahweh announces in verses 14–15:

> "Therefore, behold, the days are coming, declares the LORD, when it shall no longer be said, 'As the LORD lives who brought up the people of Israel out of the land of Egypt,' but 'As the LORD lives who brought up the people of Israel out of the north country and out of all the countries where he had driven them.' For I will bring them back to their own land that I gave to their fathers."

Yahweh is so committed to restoring his people from exile that he will send out fishers and hunters to gather them regardless of where they are (Jer

16:16–17; cp. Matt 4:18–22).[7] He wants his people to "know my power and my might, and they shall know that my name is the LORD" (Jer 16:21). Yet the significance of the name Yahweh will shift dramatically in light of this new redemptive act. Previously the exodus had been the definitive act that revealed God's identity; now it would be restoring his people from exile, an act rooted in Yahweh's original promise to the fathers and his initial redemption of Israel from Egypt.

This promise of Yahweh's name being redefined on the basis of restoring his people from exile is picked up again in Jer 23:1–8. After condemning Judah's current shepherds (23:1–2), Yahweh promises to bring his people back to the land and put shepherds over them who will care for them (23:3–4). He expands on this promise by stating:

> "Behold, the days are coming, declares the LORD, when I will raise up for David a righteous Branch, and he shall reign as king and deal wisely, and shall execute justice and righteousness in the land. In his days Judah will be saved, and Israel will dwell securely. And this is the name by which he will be called: 'The LORD is our righteousness.' Therefore, behold, the days are coming, declares the LORD, when they shall no longer say, 'As the LORD lives who brought up the people of Israel out of the land of Egypt,' but 'As the LORD lives who brought up and led the offspring of the house of Israel out of the north country and out of all the countries where he had driven them.' Then they shall dwell in their own land." (Jer 23:5–8)

In wording similar to Jer 16, God promises a name redefinition rooted in bringing his people out of exile and restoring them to the land he gave to their fathers. But this name redefinition rooted in restoration from exile is associated with several other notable themes.

The first is the promise of a Davidic king, described in multiple ways. He is a "Branch [צֶמַח]," a term that consistently refers to a descendant of David in whom the covenant promises made in 2 Sam 7 will find their fulfillment.[8] More specifically, Jeremiah likely draws on language from Isa 4:2–6, where God promises a coming day when "the branch [צֶמַח] of the LORD shall be beautiful and glorious" (4:2) in connection with redeeming the faithful remnant of God's people.[9] As a result, God will dwell with his people. This promise is then expanded in Isa 11, where God promises to bring forth "a shoot [חֹטֶר] from the stump of Jesse and a branch [נֵצֶר] from his roots" (11:1).[10] This Spirit-empowered Branch will rule with justice and righteousness (11:2–5) over a transformed creation permeated by knowledge of Yahweh (11:6–9). This "root [שֹׁרֶשׁ] of Jesse" will be "a signal for the peoples" (11:10), and "In that day the Lord will extend his hand yet a second time to recover the remnant that remains of his people" (11:11) through a new exodus (11:11–16).

Zechariah 3 further develops the promise of the Branch as a messianic figure and weds it to another messianic motif. Yahweh promises, "Behold, I will bring my servant the Branch [צֶמַח] . . . and I will remove the iniquity of this land in a single day" (Zech 3:8–9). The prophet appears to have wedded the promises of Jeremiah's Branch and Isaiah's Servant together as the hope of the postexilic remnant struggling for survival in the land.[11]

Righteousness is the second notable theme related to Yahweh's name redefinition related to restoration from exile. Not only is the branch himself "righteous [צַדִּיק]" but he will "execute . . . righteousness [צְדָקָה]" (Jer 23:5). Indeed, his very name will be "Yahweh our righteousness [יְהוָה צִדְקֵנוּ]" (23:6 AT).[12] In Jer 33:14–26, God expands on this initial promise of a righteous Branch from David's line by noting that when God saves Judah and Jerusalem through this Davidic descendant, the city of Jerusalem itself will be called "Yahweh our righteousness [יְהוָה צִדְקֵנוּ]" (33:16). In other words, through the work of the Branch, who is the embodiment of Yahweh's righteousness, those whom he redeems will share in Yahweh's righteousness because they are identified with the Branch. This emphasis on righteousness ties into the promise of Isa 11:4–5 that this Davidic descendant would judge the poor "with righteousness [בְּצֶדֶק]" and that "Righteousness [צֶדֶק] shall be the belt of his waist."

Before leaving Jer 23:5–8, we must revisit the specific language of the opening clause of what God promises to do. He promises to "raise up [וַהֲקִמֹתִי] for David a righteous Branch" (23:5). Although the Hebrew verb קוּם has a wide range of uses, it should be noted that it occurs in Isa 26:19 to depict the future resurrection of God's people: "Your dead shall live; their bodies shall rise [יְקוּמוּן]. You who dwell in the dust, awake and sing for joy! For your dew is a dew of light, and the earth will give birth to the dead."[13] The NT authors were not ignorant of this usage. They regularly use the equivalent LXX verb ἀνίστημι to describe Jesus's resurrection (as well as that of his people) in connection with OT texts they see as fulfilled in Jesus.[14]

In summary, these two texts from Jeremiah anticipate a day when the primary redemptive act that explicates the name of Yahweh will shift from Israel's exodus out of Egypt to their restoration from exile. This restoration from exile is explicitly linked to God raising up a Davidic descendant who not only rules in righteousness but is the embodiment of Yahweh's very own righteousness. Through this Davidic descendant God's people will be saved and dwell securely in the land that God promised them. This promised redefinition of God's name is not a replacement so much as an expansion. Since restoration is rooted in his promise to Abraham (Gen 12:1–3; 15:1–20; 17:1–21; 22:15–18; etc.) to give the land to him and his descendants (Jer 16:15; 23:8). It is this same promise to Abraham, Isaac, and Jacob that motivated God to bring Israel out of Egypt (Exod 2:24–25; 3:15). So this promise in Jeremiah of a new redemptive act that will become the primary revelation of Yahweh's name is less a replacement of the exodus than it is the latest and most definitive expression of his name in fulfillment of the original promise to Abraham.

## Resurrection and Restoration from Exile

Within the OT, restoration from exile is described from a variety of different angles. Most noteworthy for our purposes is the portrayal of restoration from exile as a resurrection from the dead. In Ezekiel 37, the Spirit of Yahweh gives the prophet a vision of a valley full of dry bones (37:1–3). He instructs Ezekiel to prophesy over them that God will put sinews, flesh, and skin on them when he breathes life into these bones, so that his people will know that he is Yahweh (37:4–6). When Ezekiel does what Yahweh commands, the bones come to life and stand on their feet (37:7–10). Yahweh then explains that these bones represent the whole house of Israel, whom he will raise from their graves and place them in the land (37:11–12). Because of this resurrection and the gift of his Spirit to dwell in them as they live in the land, they will know that he is Yahweh (37:13–14).

The surrounding context reveals further important insights. In Ezek 36:22–38, Yahweh promises to bring his people out of exile and back into the land. He will cleanse them from their idolatry (36:25), give them new hearts and spirits (36:26), and put his Spirit in them to cause them to obey (36:27). Throughout this oracle, Yahweh emphasizes that he is acting for the sake of his name. He will vindicate the holiness of his name before Israel and the nations so that both will know that he is Yahweh (36:22–23, 36, 38). Ezekiel 37:15–28 contains another restoration oracle. Yahweh promises to reunite Judah and Israel into one land with one king ruling over a people cleansed from their idolatry (37:15–23). This king will be "my servant David" (37:24, 25) and will rule over an obedient people in the land Yahweh gave to their fathers as part of an everlasting covenant with them (37:24–26). Yahweh will dwell in their midst so that he will be their God and they will be his people (37:27). His ultimate purpose is that the nations will know that he is "Yahweh who sanctifies Israel" (37:28).

Taken together, Ezekiel 36–37 anticipate a day when God will restore his people from exile by raising them from the dead. This restoration will result in a Davidic descendant ruling over a cleansed, transformed, and obedient people who have Yahweh's own Spirit dwelling inside of them. Yahweh will do all this to both preserve the holiness of his covenant name and make it known to Israel and the nations.[15]

## Synthesis

What emerges from these texts is a network of overlapping texts and motifs.[16] This network contains at least seven elements. The first is the promise of a Davidic ruler, variously described as a Branch, king, prince, or shepherd. Second is the association of righteousness language with this Davidic ruler. This language can be applied to the character of the Davidic ruler, how he will rule, or the manifestation of Yahweh's own righteousness. Third is the name of Yahweh, whether it takes the form of vindication, proclamation, praise, or redefinition of that name. The fourth element is restoration from exile, a restoration that is closely associated with resurrection from the dead. Fifth is the forgiveness of sins, which also is linked with restoration from exile in numerous prophetic texts. The sixth element is the gift of the Spirit, who not only empowers the Davidic ruler but also cleanses God's people from their sin. The final element is the fulfillment of God's promises to the patriarchs, with particular emphasis placed on the promise of land.

The presence or absence of these elements in each of the texts discussed is summarized in table 1.1.

While it is true that not every text has every element, the overlap of specific language and themes confirms the presence of this larger network of associated ideas within the OT itself. The question we must now turn to is whether there is evidence of this network behind Paul's identification of God the Father as the one who raised Jesus from the dead in Gal 1:1.

**Table 1.1. Proposed Network**

|  | *Jer 16:14–15* | *Jer 23:1–8* | *Jer 33:14–26* | *Isa 11:1–16* | *Ezek 36–37* | *Zech 3:1–10* |
|---|---|---|---|---|---|---|
| Davidic ruler |  | X | X | X | X | X |
| Righteousness |  | X | X | X |  |  |
| Yahweh's name | X | X | X |  | X |  |
| Restoration from exile // resurrection | X | X | X | X | X |  |
| Forgiveness of sins // cleansing |  |  |  |  | X | X |
| Spirit |  |  |  | X | X |  |
| Promises to the patriarchs | X | X | X |  | X |  |

## SUPPORTING EVIDENCE

If indeed Paul draws upon this network of OT promises described above, it is reasonable to expect to see evidence of these associated motifs elsewhere.

### Galatians

Within the immediate context of Gal 1:1–5 we see other elements of the proposed network in addition to the explicit reference to God raising Jesus from the dead. The title "Christ" (1:1, 3) is inherently linked to the expectation of a Davidic ruler (see Ps 2:1–12 and its use in Romans 1:3–4). Jesus is also described as the one "who gave himself for our sins" (1:4), language that alludes to the work of the Suffering Servant giving himself for the sins of his people (Isa 53:6, 10, 12).

Throughout the remainder of Galatians Paul mentions several of the thematic elements of this proposed network. First, and most prominently, is the presence of righteousness/justification language.[17] Words from the δικ- family occur thirteen times in the letter.[18] In 2:16–17 Paul contrasts two possible means of justification—works of the law or faith in Jesus Christ (cp. 3:24). The fact that Christ had to die makes it clear that righteousness cannot come through the law (2:21; cp. 3:21). Abraham's faith being counted to him as righteousness is a paradigm for all who believe in Jesus, but especially Gentiles, since God's original promise to Abraham in Gen 12:3 anticipated this (Gal 3:6–9). Describing the posture of the believer, Paul writes, "For through the Spirit, by faith, we ourselves eagerly wait for the hope of righteousness" (5:6).

The second is the gift of the Spirit.[19] As the definitive blessing of the new creation kingdom (3:1–5), he is given to all who believe in Jesus regardless of ethnicity (3:14). Indeed, the Christian life begins by the Spirit (3:2; 4:29) and is continuously lived by the Spirit (3:5; 5:25). Because believers are united to Jesus the Son of God by faith, God has given them the Spirit of his Son as the initial part of their promised inheritance (4:4–7). Just as Ezek 36:26–27 and Isa 32:15–20 had promised, the Spirit transforms the lives of God's people to produce fruit (Gal 5:22–23). The Spirit also empowers believers to eagerly wait for the hope of righteousness when Christ returns (5:5) and live in a way that sows to the Spirit in anticipation of reaping eternal life on the last day (6:8).

Third, although often not explicit, there is a steady undercurrent of sin-exile-restoration motifs running through Galatians.[20] In 3:10–14, the curse that rests upon those who rely on works of the law is expressed in language borrowed from Deuteronomy 27–30.[21] Christ's redemption of his people by becoming a curse is framed as a new exodus that restores humanity from their exile away from God's presence and results in the fulfillment of the Abrahamic promise and the gift of the Spirit. In 4:1–7, Paul uses new exodus typology to describe the work of Christ. Through this second exodus believers have been freed from their slavery to the elementals and the resulting exile from God himself. They are now sons who have the Spirit of the Son dwelling in them. Galatians 4:21–5:1 also contains sin-exile-restoration motifs. The citation of Isa 54:1 signals that the work of Jesus has restored God's people from their exile and fulfilled the promises to Abraham.[22]

Speaking of the promises to Abraham, that is a fourth element of the proposed network present in Galatians.[23] The central argument of the letter (3:1–5:1) has as its thesis the claim that all who are "of faith" (regardless of their ethnicity) are justified sons of Abraham who receive the blessing he was promised (3:6–9). Through his curse-bearing death Christ redeems his people from the curse so that the blessing of Abraham can come to the Gentiles (3:13–14). Christ is also the singular seed of Abraham who inherits the promised blessing (3:15–18), and all who are joined to him by faith (regardless of ethnicity, gender, or socioeconomic status) are Abraham's offspring (3:25–29). They are sons of Sarah the free woman whose true home is the heavenly Jerusalem, children of the promise who are born of the Spirit and live in the freedom that Christ has freed them to experience (4:21–5:1).

Finally, although David is not explicitly mentioned, note should be made of the sonship language in Gal 4:4–7.[24] Within the OT Adam (Gen 5:3; cp. Luke 3:38), Israel (Exod 4:22–23; Jer 31:9; Hos 11:1), and the Davidic king (2 Sam 7:14; Ps 2:1–12; 89:25–29) are all designated as sons of God. In Gal 4:4–7 Paul describes Jesus's identity and work by bringing together the Abrahamic promises and Davidic covenant.[25] "Because Jesus is the Son of God from David's line who redeems his people from their exile through a new exodus, his redeemed people are adopted as sons of God and given the Holy Spirit. As adopted sons they experience the presence of God's Spirit in their lives and receive the inheritance promised to Abraham's seed."[26]

Returning to our chart summarizing this proposed network, we can now compare it to what we have found in Galatians (see table 1.2).

The presence of each element of this proposed network and its interrelated themes bolsters the possibility that this network lies behind Paul's redefinition of God the Father's identity as the one who raised Jesus Christ from the dead. The resurrection of Jesus is the climactic redemptive act that now defines the name of God.

**Table 1.2. Proposed Network**

|  | Jer 16:14–15 | Jer 23:1–8 | Jer 33:14–26 | Isa 11:1–16 | Ezek 36–37 | Zech 3:1–10 | Galatians |
|---|---|---|---|---|---|---|---|
| Davidic ruler |  | X | X | X | X | X | X |
| Righteousness |  | X | X | X |  |  | X |
| Yahweh's name | X | X | X |  | X |  | X |
| Restoration from exile // resurrection | X | X | X | X | X |  | X |
| Forgiveness of sins // cleansing |  |  |  |  | X | X | X |
| Spirit |  |  |  | X | X |  | X |
| Promises to the patriarchs | X | X | X |  | X |  | X |

## Other Pauline Letters

Further evidence for this network of texts and themes can be found other places within the Pauline corpus. At the conclusion of his presentation of Abraham as a model of faith for those who are not circumcised (Rom 4:1–25), Paul parallels the faith of Abraham with that of believers. Just as God counted Abraham's faith to him as righteousness, so too . . .

> It will be counted to us who believe in him who raised from the dead Jesus our Lord, who was delivered up for our trespasses and raised for our justification. (Rom 4:24–25)

Paul identifies God as the one who raised Jesus from the dead in connection with: (1) the promises made to Abraham; (2) forgiveness of sins ("delivered up for our trespasses"); and (3) righteousness language ("justification"). Near the beginning of his argument, Paul highlights David as someone who experienced the blessing of having righteousness counted to him apart from works (Rom 4:6–8, citing Ps 32:1–2). The expression "delivered up for our transgressions" is also an allusion to the servant of Yahweh giving himself as an offering for sin described in Isa 53:6, 10, 12.[27] This allusion to Isa 53 is especially noteworthy in light of the allusion to Isa 53:6, 10, 12 in Gal 1:4, where Paul describes Jesus as the one "who gave himself for our sins."[28]

Paul uses a slightly different version of this modified divine identity in Rom 8. He contends that believers are not "in the flesh but in the Spirit, if in fact the Spirit of God dwells in you" (Rom 8:9). Those who have Christ dwelling in them have the Spirit producing life in them because of God's gift of righteousness by faith given to believers through their union with Christ (Rom 8:10). This reference to the Spirit prompts Paul to write:

> If the Spirit of him who raised Jesus from the dead dwells in you, he who raised Christ Jesus from the dead will also give life to your mortal bodies through his Spirit who dwells in you. (Rom 8:11)

God's identity as the one who raised Jesus from the dead is explicitly tied to the Spirit, to the extent that instead of referring to the "Spirit of God" Paul can refer to "the Spirit of him who raised Jesus from the dead." This connection between the Spirit and resurrection echoes Ezek 37:1–14, where the Spirit is the one who brings life to the dead bones representing Israel and their exile.[29] The larger context links the work of the Spirit to a transformed life (language that is consistent with the promise of Ezek 36:25–27) and believers' identity as sons of God (language that has strong Davidic associations in addition to its association with Israel) with an inheritance (8:14–17). This identity is rooted in the new exodus that God has accomplished through the risen Jesus Christ.

In addition to these texts that connect God's identity as the one who raised Jesus from the dead with a similar network of motifs in Galatians, Paul explicitly cites a key OT Branch text. To prove his contention that Christ became a servant to confirm God's promises to the patriarchs and cause the Gentiles to glorify God for his mercy, Paul cites four OT texts united around the theme of the Gentiles praising or rejoicing in the Lord (Rom 15:8–13).[30] The last text cited is Isaiah 11:10, which asserts that

> The root of Jesse will come, even he who arises [ὁ ἀνιστάμενος] to rule the Gentiles; in him will the Gentiles hope. (Rom 15:12, citing Isa 11:10)

Several features deserve to be highlighted. First, the description of the root of Jesse "arising" (ἀνίστημι) harkens back to Paul's description of Jesus as the Son of God descended from David according to the flesh but declared "to be the Son of God in power according to the Spirit of holiness by his resurrection [ἀναστάσεως] from the dead" (Rom 1:3–4). Second, the raising up of this root of Jesse to rule the Gentiles is reason for them to praise the name of Yahweh. The citation of 2 Sam 22:50/Ps 18:49 in Rom 15:9 portrays David praising and singing the name of Yahweh among the nations. Third, Paul transitions from this citation of Isa 11:10 to a concluding prayer wish that emphasizes the power of the Holy Spirit to enable believers to abound in hope, joy, and peace in believing (Rom 15:13). So here in Rom 15:8–13 Paul brings together the resurrection of a Davidic descendant, the nations praising the name of Yahweh, and work of the Spirit as the fulfillment of God's promises to the patriarchs.

## Acts

Acts 13:13–52 recounts Paul's redemptive-historical sermon in the synagogue at Pisidian Antioch and the fallout from it.[31] Luke summarizes Paul
portraying Jesus as the fulfillment of the OT hope and in particular the fulfillment of God's promises to David. Paul notes that, after the failed reign
of Saul, God "raised up [ἤγειρεν] David to be their king" (13:22). Paul then
claims that Jesus is the promised descendant of David, sent to be Israel's
Savior (13:23). After describing the ministry of John the Baptist (13:24–25)
and the unjust crucifixion of Jesus (13:26–29), Paul asserts that "God raised
[ἤγειρεν] him from the dead" (13:30). Indeed, this is the heart of the good
news Paul preaches, "that what God promised to the fathers, this he has
fulfilled to us their children by raising [ἀναστήσας] Jesus" (13:32–33). This
claim is supported by a citation of Ps 2:7 ("You are my Son, today I have
begotten you"). The fact that God "raised [ἀνέστησεν] him from the dead"
never to see corruption is supported by citing Isa 55:3 ("I will give you the
holy and sure blessings of David") and Ps 16:10 ("You will not let your
Holy One see corruption"). Whereas David's body remained in the tomb,
"God raised up [ἤγειρεν]" Jesus so that he "did not see corruption" (13:36).
Through the resurrection of Jesus forgiveness of sins is available to all who
believe in him (13:38–39). When Paul and Barnabas are kicked out of the
synagogue the following week for continuing to preach about the risen Jesus,
they explain their decision to focus their ministry on the Gentiles by citing Isa
49:6 ("I have made you a light for the Gentiles, that you may bring salvation
to the ends of the earth").

Several elements of the network of OT texts and motifs that stand behind
Gal 1:1 are present in Acts 13:13–52. Most notable is the connection between
God "raising up" David as king and "raising" Jesus his descendant from the
dead. This connection demonstrates how Paul could have read texts where
God promised to raise up a righteous Branch for David (e.g., Jer 23:5) as
anticipating the resurrection of Jesus. Second, raising Jesus from the dead
is presented as God fulfilling his promises not only to David, but also to
the fathers (cp. Jer 16:15; 23:8; Ezek 36:28; 37:27). Third, raising Jesus the
Davidic descendant from the dead results in the forgiveness of sins. Ezekiel
36–37 in particular connects God cleansing his people from their sin with
resurrection from the dead (i.e., restoration from exile) and the reign of a
Davidic descendant as king over them. Finally, proclaiming the good news
about the risen Jesus among the nations brings salvation to the ends of the
earth. This emphasis, here drawn from Isa 49:6 and its surrounding context,
resonates with the emphasis in Ezek 36–37 that God is acting for the sake
of his name being known among the nations, as well as the promise that

God's act of restoring his people from exile will result in a new definition of God's name.

## CONCLUSION

Paul's redefinition of God's identity as the one who raised Jesus Christ from the dead is rooted in a network of OT texts and themes that anticipated a day when God's name would be redefined on the basis of a climactic redemptive act—restoring his people from exile. This network of OT texts includes a number of closely associated themes: a righteous Davidic ruler, resurrection, forgiveness of sins, the gift of the Spirit, and the fulfillment of the promises to the patriarchs. The presence of this network elsewhere in Paul's writings, as well as in Acts 13, provides supporting evidence for its presence in Gal 1:1.

## NOTES

1. The language of divine identity can have several different meanings; see the helpful discussion in Kevin J. Vanhoozer, "Does the Trinity Belong in a Theology of Religions? On Angling in the Rubicon and the 'Identity' of God," in *The Trinity in a Pluralistic Age: Theological Essays on Culture and Religion*, ed. Kevin J. Vanhoozer (Grand Rapids: Eerdmans, 1997), 41–71. In this chapter I am using it in the sense articulated by Richard Bauckham: "Reference to God's identity is by analogy with human personal identity, understood not as a mere ontological subject without characteristics, but as including both character and personal story (the latter entailing relationships). These are the ways in which we commonly specify 'who someone is'"; see Richard Bauckham, *Jesus and the God of Israel: God Crucified and Other Studies on the New Testament's Christology of Divine Identity* (Grand Rapids: Eerdmans, 2008), 6n5.

2. The original "seed" from which this chapter grew was the observation by Roy Ciampa that referring to God as the one who raised Jesus from the dead "suggests that the new climactic act of salvation has displaced deliverance from Egypt, the house of bondage, as the defining act which identifies the God of redemption"; see Roy E. Ciampa, *The Presence and Function of Scripture in Galatians 1 and 2*, WUNT 2/102 (Tübingen: Mohr Siebeck, 1998), 46. He goes on to link this observation to Jer 16:14–15; 23:7–8. In one sense, then, this chapter is an attempt to establish more firmly his observation.

3. Unless otherwise noted, all Scripture references are taken from the English Standard Version (ESV). References marked AT indicate my own translation. Since the ESV is based on the MT, any significant differences between the MT and the LXX that bear on our discussion will be noted.

4. For a helpful discussion of the meaning of the divine name, see W. Ross Blackburn, *The God Who Makes Himself Known: The Missionary Heart of the Book of Exodus*, NSBT 28 (Downers Grove, IL: InterVarsity, 2012), 34–41.

5. Bauckham, *Jesus and the God of Israel*, 8.

6. While the precise wording of the expression can vary slightly, this expression is nearly ubiquitous in the OT; see, e.g., Exod 6:6–7; 20:2; 29:46; Lev 11:45; 19:36; 22:33; 25:38; 26:13; Num 15:41; Deut 5:6; 6:12; 8:14–15; 13:5, 10; 20:1; Josh 24:17; 1 Kgs 9:9; 2 Kgs 17:36; 2 Chr 7:22; Ps 81:10, Isa 63:11; Jer 2:6; Dan 9:15; Hos 12:9; 13:4 (list adapted from Ciampa, *Presence and Function*, 46n36). On this expression as a standard designation for God in the OT, see Sylvia C. Keesmaat, *Paul and His Story: (Re)-Interpreting the Exodus Tradition*, JSNTSup 181 (Sheffield: Sheffield Academic Press, 1999), 34–48.

7. In passing it should be noted that the LXX of Jer 16:16 uses the verb ἀποστέλλω to depict God sending out these fishermen, from which the noun ἀπόστολος comes.

8. For a helpful summary of Second Temple Jewish expectations surrounding this Branch, see John J. Collins, *The Scepter and the Star: The Messiahs of the Dead Sea Scrolls and Other Ancient Literature* (New York: Doubleday, 1995), 49–73.

9. On Jeremiah's use of Isaiah, see especially Ute Wendel, *Jesaja und Jeremia: Worte, Motive und einsichten Jesajas in der Verkündigung Jeremias*, BThSt 25 (Neukirchener-Vluyn: Neukirchener-Verlag, 1995).

10. On the nuances between the terms used in this passage, see Gordon H. Johnston, "Messianic Trajectories in Isaiah," in *Jesus the Messiah: Tracing the Promises, Expectations, and Coming of Israel's King*, ed. Herbert W. Bateman, Darrell L. Bock, and Gordon H. Johnston (Grand Rapids: Kregel, 2010), 149. He further notes that related terms in surrounding cultures had royal connotations as well.

11. On the blending of texts and motifs from Isaiah and Jeremiah as the background to Zech 3, see Meredith G. Kline, *Glory in Our Midst: A Biblical-Theological Reading of Zechariah's Night Visions* (Eugene, OR: Wipf and Stock, 2001), 120–21. This combination may have been facilitated by observing that the suffering servant would "act wisely [שׂכל]" (Isa 52:13) just as the Branch would "deal wisely [שׂכל]" (Jer 23:5).

12. This name is likely a play on the name of the King of Judah at the time—Zedekiah [צִדְקִיָּה], which means "Yah my righteousness." This future king will be a "righteous branch" not only in the sense of his character and conduct, but also in the sense that he will fully embody the ideals of the Davidic king, in contrast to Zedekiah's wickedness and treachery (J. A. Thompson, *The Book of Jeremiah*, NICOT [Grand Rapids: Eerdmans, 1980], 489).

13. The LXX renders the verb קוּם with a form of ἀνίστημι, a verb that the NT regularly uses to describe the resurrection of Jesus. Interestingly, the opening lines of Isa 26:19 (LXX) are rendered "the dead ones will rise [ἀναστήσονται] and the ones in the tombs will be raised [ἐγερθήσονται]" (AT). The interchangeable use of these two verbs to describe resurrection anticipates the same dynamic in the NT (see discussion of Acts 13:13–52).

14. This is especially true in Acts (e.g., 2:24, 32; 3:22, 26; 7:37; 10:41; 13:33–34; 17:3) but also found in Paul (Rom 15:12; 1 Cor 10:7; Eph 5:14).

15. A similar constellation of promises also occurs in Ezek 39:25–29, where God promises to restore his people from exile by planting them back into the land and pouring out his Spirit upon them. Yahweh does this out of jealousy for his holy name (39:25) and a desire to vindicate the holiness of that name in the sight of the nations (39:27). As a result, "Then they shall know that I am the LORD their God" (39:28).

16. I am using the term network in a broad sense that allows for the connections between these texts and motifs to be based on exegesis and/or similarity of themes. For thoughtful discussion of textual networks within the OT, see Gary Edward Schnittjer, *Old Testament Use of the Old Testament: A Book-by-Book Guide* (Grand Rapids: Zondervan, 2021), 873–87. He distinguishes between networks (internally connected texts based on exegesis and interpretation of previous texts) and constellations (texts that are linked by the use of catchwords, phrases, and thematic similarities that do not involve the exegesis of earlier texts). While such distinctions have a place within discussions of Scripture's use of Scripture, they are unnecessary for our purposes here.

17. On righteousness language in Galatians, see further Douglas J. Moo, *Galatians*, BECNT (Grand Rapids: Baker, 2013), 48–62; and Matthew S. Harmon, *Galatians*, EBTC (Bellingham, WA: Lexham, 2021), 440–52.

18. Paul uses the verb δικαιόω (Gal 2:16 [3x], 17; 3:8, 11, 24; 5:4), the noun δικαιοσύνη (2:21; 3:6, 21; 5:5), and the adjective δίκαιος (3:11).

19. On the Spirit in Galatians, see further Harmon, *Galatians*, 418–19.

20. On this motif in Galatians, see further Scott J. Hafemann, "Paul and the Exile of Israel in Galatians 3–4," in *Exile: Old Testament, Jewish, and Christian Conceptions*, ed. James M. Scott (Leiden: E. J. Brill, 1997), 329–71; Matthew S. Harmon, *Rebels and Exiles: A Biblical Theology of Sin and Restoration*, ESBT (Downers Grove, IL: Intervarsity, 2020), 120–22; Harmon, *Galatians*, 387–403.

21. More specifically Paul appears to cite a combination of Deut 27:26 and 28:58.

22. Two additional passages where the sin-exile-restoration motif is likely present are Gal 5:16–26 (the Spirit leads his people just as he did in the original exodus) and 6:15 (new creation as the culmination of God restoring his people from exile).

23. The importance of Abraham in Galatians has often been noted; see, e.g., G. Walter Hansen, *Abraham in Galatians: Epistolary and Rhetorical Contexts*, JSNTSup 29 (Sheffield: JSOT Press, 1989); and Bruce W. Longenecker, *The Triumph of Abraham's God: The Transformation of Identity in Galatians* (Nashville: Abingdon Press, 1998). What follows here is a summary of Harmon, *Galatians*, 382–86.

24. On the Davidic background to sonship language here, see further James M. Scott, *Adoption as Sons of God: An Exegetical Investigation into the Background of ΥΙΟΘΕΣΙΑ in the Pauline Corpus*, WUNT 2/48 (Tübingen: Mohr, 1993), 178–86.

25. Paul explicitly connects Jesus's sonship with his descent from David and the resurrection in Rom 1:3–4.

26. Harmon, *Galatians*, 461.

27. On this allusion, see further Shiu-Lun Shum, *Paul's Use of Isaiah in Romans: A Comparative Study of Paul's Letter to the Romans and the Sibylline and Qumran Sectarian Texts*, WUNT 2/156 (Tübingen: Mohr Siebeck, 2002), 189–93; and Matthew S. Harmon, *The Servant of the Lord and His Servant People: Tracing a Biblical Theme through the Canon*, NSBT 54 (Downers Grove, IL: InterVarsity, 2020), 167–69.

28. On this allusion, see Matthew S. Harmon, *She Must and Shall Go Free: Paul's Isaianic Gospel in Galatians*, BZNW 168 (Berlin: de Gruyter, 2010), 56–66.

29. On this echo see further J. W. Yates, *The Spirit and Creation in Paul*, WUNT 2/251 (Tübingen: Mohr Siebeck, 2008), 143–51.

30. For an excellent treatment of these citations within the context of Romans, see J. Ross Wagner, *Heralds of the Good News: Isaiah and Paul in Concert in the Letter to the Romans* (Leiden: Brill, 2003), 307–40. In order the texts are 2 Sam 22:50 (= Ps 18:49); Deut 32:43; Ps 117:1; and Isa 11:10. Citing texts from the Torah, Prophets, and the Writings suggests Paul sees his claim rooted in the entire OT revelation. All four texts describe the Gentiles joining with Israel to praise Yahweh, with the first three using various terms for worship/praise and the fourth using the term hope (Wagner, *Heralds*, 311).

31. The historical reliability and value of Acts in reconstructing the early Christian movement in general and Paul's life in particular remain hotly disputed issues that cannot be resolved here. I am persuaded that Acts contains independent and reliable information about Paul and his ministry. For a helpful summary of the scholarly discussion, see Craig S. Keener, *Acts: An Exegetical Commentary*, 4 vols. (Grand Rapids: Baker, 2012–2015), 1:221–57.

## BIBLIOGRAPHY

Bauckham, Richard. *Jesus and the God of Israel: God Crucified and Other Studies on the New Testament's Christology of Divine Identity*. Grand Rapids: Eerdmans, 2008.

Blackburn, W. Ross. *The God Who Makes Himself Known: The Missionary Heart of the Book of Exodus*. NSBT 28. Downers Grove, IL: InterVarsity, 2012.

Ciampa, Roy E. *The Presence and Function of Scripture in Galatians 1 and 2*. WUNT 2/102. Tübingen: Mohr Siebeck, 1998.

Collins, John J. *The Scepter and the Star: The Messiahs of the Dead Sea Scrolls and Other Ancient Literature*. ABRL. New York: Doubleday, 1995.

Hafemann, Scott J. "Paul and the Exile of Israel in Galatians 3–4." In *Exile: Old Testament, Jewish, and Christian Conceptions*. JSJSup 56, edited by James M. Scott, 329–71. Leiden: Brill, 1997.

Hansen, G. Walter. *Abraham in Galatians: Epistolary and Rhetorical Contexts*. JSNTSup 29. Sheffield: JSOT Press, 1989.

Harmon, Matthew S. *Galatians*. EBTC. Bellingham, WA: Lexham, 2021.

———. *Rebels and Exiles: A Biblical Theology of Sin and Restoration*. ESBT. Downers Grove, IL: InterVarsity Press, 2020.

———. *She Must and Shall Go Free: Paul's Isaianic Gospel in Galatians*. BZNW 168. Berlin: de Gruyter, 2010.

———. *The Servant of the Lord and His Servant People: Tracing a Biblical Theme through the Canon*. NSBT 54. Downers Grove, IL: InterVarsity, 2020.

Johnston, Gordon H. "Messianic Trajectories in Isaiah." In *Jesus the Messiah: Tracing the Promises, Expectations, and Coming of Israel's King*, edited by Herbert

W. Bateman, Darrell L. Bock, and Gordon H. Johnston, 133–67. Grand Rapids: Kregel, 2010.

Keesmaat, Sylvia C. *Paul and His Story: (Re)-Interpreting the Exodus Tradition.* JSNTSup 181. Sheffield: Sheffield Academic Press, 1999.

Kline, Meredith G. *Glory in Our Midst: A Biblical-Theological Reading of Zechariah's Night Visions.* Eugene, OR: Wipf and Stock, 2001.

Longenecker, Bruce W. *The Triumph of Abraham's God: The Transformation of Identity in Galatians.* Nashville: Abingdon Press, 1998.

Moo, Douglas J. *Galatians.* BECNT. Grand Rapids: Baker, 2013.

Schnittjer, Gary Edward. *Old Testament Use of the Old Testament: A Book-by-Book Guide.* Grand Rapids: Zondervan, 2021.

Scott, James M. *Adoption as Sons of God: An Exegetical Investigation into the Background of ΥΙΟΘΕΣΙΑ in the Pauline Corpus.* WUNT 2/48. Tübingen: Mohr, 1993.

Shum, Shiu-Lun. *Paul's Use of Isaiah in Romans: A Comparative Study of Paul's Letter to the Romans and the Sibylline and Qumran Sectarian Texts.* WUNT 2/156. Tübingen: Mohr Siebeck, 2002.

Thompson, J. A. *The Book of Jeremiah.* NICOT. Grand Rapids: Eerdmans, 1980.

Vanhoozer, Kevin J. *The Trinity in a Pluralistic Age: Theological Essays on Culture and Religion.* Grand Rapids: Eerdmans, 1997.

Wagner, J. Ross. *Heralds of the Good News: Isaiah and Paul in Concert in the Letter to the Romans.* Leiden: Brill, 2003.

Wendel, Ute. *Jesaja und Jeremia: Worte, Motive und einsichten Jesajas in der Verkündigung Jeremias.* BThSt 25. Neukirchener-Vluyn: Neukirchener-Verlag, 1995.

Yates, J. W. *The Spirit and Creation in Paul.* WUNT 2/251. Tübingen: Mohr Siebeck, 2008.

## Chapter 2

# Breaking Down, Rebuilding, and Transgressing What in Galatians 2:18?

## *Paul's Use of Scriptural Metaphors and a New Interpretation*

### Nicolai Techow

Galatians 2:18 is a *crux interpretum*.[1] Standard interpretations face persisting challenges to their accounting for the precise flow of Paul's thought. Central explanatory difficulties include Paul's switch to and precise use of the first-person singular as well as the nature of the transgression implied in παραβάτης. Perhaps most challenging, though often overlooked, is the difficulty constituted by the introductory εἰ γὰρ, which, as a default, the reader naturally, but with little success, seeks to understand as a simple, straightforward "for if" directly introducing an explanation of the immediately preceding μὴ γένοιτο in 2:17c. Thus, the very function of 2:18 in relation to the preceding has proven to be difficult for interpreters, and their mutual explicit or implicit differences are legion, which is, indeed, the situation with respect to almost all central interpretive questions in 2:14b–21.[2]

In some contrast to the lack of scholarly agreement on virtually every point of exegesis in 2:14b–21, however, stands an almost universal consensus that the object (ἃ . . . ταῦτα) of the destructive and reconstructive activity of the "I" in 2:18, is the law or some part, aspect, or function of it. In this chapter I challenge this consensus, destructively, as it were, by arguing that its foundations are not as strong as would be expected for such a consensus to stand, and, constructively, by exploring the interpretive potential of seeing Paul's language as use of well-established scriptural metaphors. It is my contention that this hermeneutic allows for a new interpretation of the flow of the argument which meets the challenges mentioned above better than the alternatives.

## THE USUAL REFERENCES

Customarily, commentators appeal to three passages as the intertextual basis for understanding ἅ . . . ταῦτα in Gal 2:18 to be the law: Isa 5:2 and 5; Let. Aris. 139; and Eph 2:14–15.[3] However, these references do not place this interpretation on firm footing.

In Isa 5:2, 5 God has "placed a fence around"[4] his vineyard and "fenced it in"[5] and "built a watchtower"[6] in the middle of it. But having found only wild rather than refined grapes as its fruit, now "I will remove its hedge"[7] and "I will break down its wall."[8] Note that what is said to be "built" here is a watchtower placed in the middle of the vineyard, not a wall placed around it. A wall is indeed said to be "broken down" on the other hand. However, nothing indicates that this wall is a reference to the law, which would mean that God himself would break down and remove his own law to the destruction of his people, a thought finding no evidence in the context. In the context, the scene of destruction points instead to the invasion by the Assyrians.[9] And the destruction of God's vineyard, including the breaking down of its wall is God's response to his people's repeated apostasy.

The Letter of Aristeas 139 states that "the legislator" (ὁ νομοθέτης)—that is, Moses—"surrounded/fenced (περιέφραξεν) us with unbroken/uninterrupted[10] (ἀδιακόποις) palisades (χάραξι) and iron walls (σιδηροῖς τείχεσιν) in order that we not mix/join (ἐπιμισγώμεθα) in anything with any of the other peoples" (my translation). In this passage, "palisades and . . . walls" (both in the plural) are clearly metaphors for the law and/or its commandments. But these "palisades and . . . walls" do not function as objects for verbs meaning "to build" or "to break down/destroy"—which is what is needed for this passage to exert weighty hermeneutical influence over our reading of Gal 2:18. As it is, Let. Aris. 139 and Gal 2:18 are only intertextually connected on the presupposition that ἅ . . . ταῦτα in the latter have the same reference as the "palisades and . . . walls" in the former. Thus, the appeal to Let. Aris. 139 ends up as circular reasoning.

By far the strongest support for interpreting ἅ . . . ταῦτα in Gal 2:18 as referring to the law is found in Eph 2:14–15. In this passage, Christ has "broken down" (λυσας) the "dividing wall, the barrier/of partition" (τὸ μεσότοιχον τοῦ φραγμοῦ), the enmity (τὴν ἔχθραν), abolishing (καταργήσας) the "law of commandments in ordinances" (τὸν νόμον τῶν ἐντολῶν ἐν δόγμασιν). Certainly, this text presents us with the law as a wall which has been broken down and abolished. However, other observations must be considered as well. First, in Eph 2:14–15 the law is not an object of a verb meaning "to build." Indeed, *it is never found in that role in all of Pauline literature*—unless, of course, it is found in Gal 2:18. Secondly, the one doing the breaking down in Eph 2:14–15 is not Paul, but Christ, whereas in Gal 2:18, the "I" hardly includes Christ in its reference. As we shall see, in all other places where Paul says that he himself destroys/breaks down something, the object is very different from the law. Moreover, in Galatians, while people can be "submitted" to the law,[11] they are never said or implied to change or transform the law. People "do," "fulfill," or "transgress" the law when it is the object of their activity (3:10; 5:3, 14; 6:2, 13).[12] Except for this, however, in Galatians it is the law that acts upon people, rather than the other way around (2:19; 3:13, 21, 23, 24).

In addition to the intertextual references, many interpreters think that Paul's use of the word παραβάτης in 2:18b indicates that the law is the entity being broken down and built up again. However, an implied νόμου after παραβάτην is not self-evident,[13] and many scholars think instead the transgression is of God's way of salvation in Christ. Thus, the usual references in support of taking ἅ . . . ταῦτα in Gal 2:18 to be the law are not indisputably convincing.

However, the relative weakness of this standard interpretation becomes even clearer when we examine in more detail the scriptural use of the concepts "breaking down" and "building up."

## "BREAKING DOWN" VS. "BUILDING"
## IN THE MT/LXX AND THE NT

Laying aside Let. Aris. 137 and Eph 2:14–15, when biblical and related texts use walls, deconstruction (as opposed to [re]building), and building as metaphors or in similes, this imagery rarely, if ever, refers to the law, its abrogation, and/or its establishment. Instead, "breaking down" vs. "building up again" most naturally picture judgment and restoration.[14] This is confirmed when we look closer at the details, asking what in each occurrence of "breaking down" and "building up" constitutes the patient, that is, the entity being broken down and/or built.[15]

In the MT/LXX, "breaking down" and "building up" occur approximately[16] twenty-seven times as antithesis within almost the same verse (Judg 6:25–26, 6:28; 2 Kgs 21:3; 2 Chr 26:6; 33:3; Neh 3:35; Isa 5:2, 5; 49:17; Jer 1:10; 12:16–17; 18:7–9; 24:6; 31:28 (38:28 LXX); 36:36; 45:4 (51:34 LXX); Amos 9:11; Mal 1:4; Job 12:14; Ps 28:5 (27:5 LXX); Prov 14:1; Eccl 3:3; Sir 34:23; 49:7; 1 Macc 6:7; 9:62; 2 Macc 2:22; 4 Macc 2:14).[17] In three of these occurrences, no patient of the actions is expressed (Job 12:14; Eccl 3:3; Sir 34:23). In only one of the remaining twenty-four, namely, 2 Macc 2:22, the patient is a law. And the presence of our antithesis here is questionable, since τοὺς μέλλοντας καταλύεσθαι νόμους ἐπανορθῶσαι could mean simply "enforcing/ putting into force again the laws that were about to be abolished."[18] In comparison, at least seven times (Ps 28:5 [27:5 LXX];Jer 1:10; 12:16–17; 18:7–9; 24:6; 31:28 [38:28 LXX]; Sir 49:7),[19] the patients are *human*. In these seven, the breaking down is *always due to sin*, as it is also in twelve out of sixteen where the patients are nonhuman, physical entities (Judg 6:25–26, 28; 2 Kgs 21:3; 2 Chr 26:6 [at least arguably]; 33:3; Isa 5:2–5; 49:17 [if not human]; Jer 45:4 [51:34 LXX]; Ezek 36:36; Amos 9:11 [if not human]; Mal 1:4; 1 Macc 6:7; the remaining four are: Neh 3:35; Prov 14:1; 1 Macc 9:62: 4 Macc 2:14).

Thus, in a noteworthy majority, that is, in nineteen out of twenty-four relevant occurrences of our antithesis, the patients of the destructive events or actions are *sinful people (or constitutes sin), and/or the breaking down is due to sin.*[20] When we include in our survey references where one of the sides of our antithesis is found alone without its counterpart, the same pattern recurs. We find only rare and debatable occurrences with the law as patient and a weighty majority of occurrences where the breaking down is due to sin and/ or the patients are sinful people or even constitute sin.

Turning first to the "breaking down" side,[21] we find approximately 128 references[22] where it occurs. Among these, we find only very few—six that is—where the patients are lawful living, laws, or the law (2 Macc 2:22; 4:11, 4 Macc 4:24; 5:33; 7:9; 17:9). They are all in 2 and 4 Maccabees, and in all of them, a meaning antonymic to "to build" with the law/laws/lawful living as patient is disputable.[23] In contrast, in at least 92[24] of the 128 references, the patients of the destructive events or actions are *sinful people (or constitutes sin), and/or the breaking down is due to sin.*

Turning to the "building" side, we find more than 370[25] occurrences of ἀνοικοδομέω or οἰκοδομέω (as translation of בנה when a MT exists),[26] but *in none of them is the patient a law.* Towers, houses, cities, walls, etc. are the patients in approximately 177 occurrences. With almost the same frequency (167 occurrences), we find religious objects such as temples, altars, etc. in the role as patients. Noticeably, a cluster of 22 references have people, individually or collectively (dynasties, families, "houses"), as patients, and significantly, 8 of these are in Jeremiah (Gen 2:22; Deut 25:9; Ruth 4:11; 1 Sam 2:35; 2 Sam 7:27; 1 Kgs 11:38; 1 Chr 17:10, 25; Pss 28:5 [27:5 LXX]; 89:5 [88:5 LXX]; Prov 24:3; Jer 1:10; 12:16–17; 18:7–9; 24:6; 31:4 [38:4 LXX]; 31:28 [38:28 LXX]; 33:7 [40:7 LXX]; Jer 42:10 [49:10 LXX]; Amos 9:11; Mal 3:15; Sir 49:7).

In sum so far, the use in the LXX and MT of the "breaking down vs. building" antithesis and its two poles provides little if any reason for interpreting ἅ . . . ταῦτα in Gal 2:18 as references to the law. Rather, in a pertinent majority of instances, *the breaking down happens to sinful people (or something constituting sin), and/or the breaking down is due to sin.* When the "building" pole of the antithesis occurs alone, a law is never the patient, but we find a significant cluster of references, especially in Jeremiah, where the semantic patients are people.

Including NT occurrences in our view confirms these tendencies. Outside of Gal 2:18, our antithesis occurs twelve times,[27] with both its sides in (almost) the same verse, but never with the law as patient. Instead, the patients are buildings, particularly the temple (six occurrences: Luke 12:18; Luke 17:28–29;[28] Mark 13:1–2 par.; 14:58 par.; 15:29 par.; John 2:19–20 in one sense), or people (in some cases their consciences) (seven occurrences: John 2:19–20 in another sense; Acts 15:16;[29] Rom 14:19–20; 1 Cor 8:10–11; 2 Cor 5:1; 10:8; 13:10). Notably, in Paul (five occurrences) *it is always the latter*.

Taking all NT occurrences of the "breaking down" side into the count changes little. The patients are distributed as follows: the temple or other constructions or vessels (eight occurrences: Mark 13:2 parr.; 14:58 par.; 15:29 par.; Luke 12:18; John 2:19; Acts 6:14; 27:41; Rom 11:3);[30] the world/heaven and earth (three occurrences: Heb 1:11; 2 Pet 3:6, 10–12); people/their bodies (eleven occurrences: Matt 10:28; Luke 17:29; Acts 5:38–39; 15:16; Rom 14:15, 20; 1 Cor 8:11; 2 Cor 4:9; 5:1; 10:8; 13:10); resistance against God (two occurrences: 2 Cor 10:4; 1 John 3:8); the law (three occurrences: Matt 5:17, 19; Eph 2:14–15).[31] In Matt 5:17, 19, however, note that καταλῦσαι means "to annul as opposed to fulfill," and λύσῃ means "break as opposed to keep and do." Therefore, these are not true occurrences of the destructive pole of our antithesis. Thus, except for Eph 2:14–15 which we have already discussed, we find no true occurrence with the law as patient. We do learn, however, that in Paul and 1 John, *sinful resistance to God* is found as patient. As for the "building" pole,[32] in none of the about fifty-seven occurrences[33] outside of Gal 2:18 is the law the patient. However, in about thirty-six occurrences, the patients are human beings, their consciences or bodies, the church, or God's people (Matt 16:18; Mark 12:10 parr.; John 2:20 in one sense; Acts 4:11; 9:31; 15:16; 20:32; Rom 14:19; 15:2, 20; 1 Cor 3:9–10, 12, 14; 8:1, 10; 10:23; 14:3, 4, 5, 12, 17, 26; 2 Cor 5:1; 10:8; 12:19; 13:10; 1 Thess 5:11; Eph 2:20–21; 4:12, 16, 29; Col 2:7; 1 Pet 2:5; Jude 20). And in the *corpus paulinum* (about twenty-six occurrences), this is *always* the case.

As already mentioned in the notes, my numbers are only approximate and my lists not always exhaustive. Nevertheless, it seems unlikely that qualitative changes in the indications of this evidence would result from even broader searches and more precise counts. Thus, I conclude from the Scriptural and NT usage of "breaking down" vs. "building" language that it does not support taking ἅ . . . ταῦτα in Gal 2:18 as referring to the law. Rather, if we see Paul's language as use of well–established scriptural metaphors, this evidence invites us to take "breaking down" vs. "building up again" as referring to judgment of sinful people and their sin over against restoration of new people who constitute or are part of the church.

## THE JEREMIAH CONNECTION

Paul's use of the metaphors of "breaking down" vs. "building up" in Gal 2:18 especially echoes the use of similar language in Jeremiah[34] who programmatically[35] was called "to pluck up and to pull down, to destroy and to overthrow, to build and to plant" (Jer 1:10, NRSV).[36] In general, Paul seems to see himself, his calling, and ministry as analogous to the prophets in Scripture,[37] a theme also found in Galatians[38] and clearly seen in the allusion to Jer 1:5 in Gal 1:15. Elsewhere, he describes his apostolic activity precisely by using the terminology of "planting" and "building" (1 Cor 3:10–15) and "destroying/breaking down" (2 Cor 10:4–8; 13:10),[39] which again makes us think of Jeremiah.[40] Thus, when Paul here in Gal 2:18 uses metaphors that have programmatic function in Jeremiah's calling (Jer 1:10), it is hardly coincidental but indicates that the implicit "I" refers to the apostle himself as Christ's prophetic representative (cf., e.g., 2 Cor 5:11–21).[41]

Now, consistent with the invitation given by the general evidence of the scriptural use of our metaphors to see them as referring to judgment of sinful people and their sin over against restoration of new people, in Jeremiah, even more clearly, "tearing/breaking down" and "building up" does not happen to the law but to sinful nations in general and sinful Israel/Juda in particular—that is, to *sinful people and their sin*.[42] Moreover, Jeremiah's preaching not only proclaims but *effects* destruction and rebuilding.[43] God, the ultimate agent tearing/breaking down sinful people and their sin and rebuilding new people,[44] does so through Jeremiah proclaiming his word, which *effects* God's destructive and restoring activity.[45]

## A NEW INTERPRETATION OF GALATIANS 2:18

Against this background, the question presenting itself is whether taking the implicit "I" in Gal 2:18 as referring to Paul himself, the prophetic apostle of Christ,[46] called by his preaching to effect God's breaking down sinful people and their sin and building up new people, will yield a satisfactory explanation of the flow of thought through the data of the text. I shall argue that it will by making the following observations and suggestions for interpretation.

## ἅ . . . ταῦτα

I argue extensively elsewhere[47] that Paul in Gal 2:16–17a presents justification, even of "us" Jews, as taking place in and through "our" faith/conversion encounter with God's judgment upon "us" in the cross of Christ, where "even we ourselves" are found as sinners just like the Gentiles,[48] despite "our" typically higher moral-religious starting point (cf. 2:15).[49] This generates the accusation that by this equalizing judgment Christ causes believers to be indifferent toward and thus to commit sin (2:17b), to which μὴ γένοιτο in 2:17c responds.

In Gal 2:18 Paul then speaks of his own effective preaching of the gospel of justification and the judgment which is an integral part of it in terms of "breaking down" and "building up." The relative clause ἅ κατέλυσα is placed in the foreground, and the referent of the relative pronoun is repeated by ταῦτα. This, being otherwise unnecessary, conveys emphasis such that the implied transgression consists neither in the "breaking down" itself, nor in the "building up" itself, but in "building up" again *the same* as that which "I" have broken down. When applied to the line of interpretation I suggest, the result is captured in this paraphrase: "For if I rebuild *the same* sinners (cf. 2:17a) and their sin as I have broken down (in other words, sinful people indifferent to sin), I show myself a transgressor." This paraphrase makes good sense of 2:18 as a straightforward conditional structure explaining 2:17c—provided we can account for the implied transgression and the flow of thought following in 2:19–20.

Before I turn to this challenge, however, let me position my interpretation somewhat within current discussions.

First, there are likely both communal and individual aspects to Paul's statement. Elsewhere, Paul can speak of breaking down and/or building up both individuals (Rom 14:15; 15:2; 1 Cor 8:10, 11; 10:23; 14:4, 17; 1 Thess 5:11), their thoughts (1 Cor 8:1; 2 Cor 10:4–5), their bodies (2 Cor 5:1), "one-another" (Rom 14:19, 20), and communities consisting of people (1 Cor 3:9–10; 14:3–5, 12; 2 Cor 10:8; 12:19; Eph 4:12,16), and in Gal 2:18 he uses neuter plural pronouns with broad fields of denotation. In terms of the argumentative flow in the present context, however, the crucial connection between 2:18 and what immediately precedes is the judgment of God integral to justification in Christ, referred to in 2:17 as "being found sinners," in 2:18 as destruction, and in 2:19 as death. While justification certainly has collective aspects and consequences and Paul even here says that "we" have believed in order to be justified, justification and the judgment integral to it does take place on an individual basis (cf. ἄνθρωπος in 2:16), and in 2:19 Paul speaks in personal terms of his own experience of death (being broken down) and new life (being rebuilt). Indeed, in the present context it can be said that a community across all prior dividing differences among its members, not least those between Jews and Gentiles, is established precisely by virtue of their common experience of justification in Christ (cf. καὶ ἡμεῖς . . . ἐπιστεύσαμεν . . . εὑρέθημεν καὶ αὐτοὶ in the flow of thought from 2:15–17), as in 3:26–29 it is established by faith and baptism. Thus, community and individual aspects should not be pressed into a false either-or but are both present.

Second, while my understanding of justification in Paul is greatly indebted to Mark Seifrid's work, here in Gal 2:18, I differ somewhat from his interpretation. He states: "The significance of 'being found a sinner,' which characterizes justification in v. 17, is clarified in v. 18 by the statement, 'For I have destroyed these things,' . . . The re–creation of life that is integral to this justifying event becomes apparent in vv. 18–20. Those who believe have 'destroyed' sin and the fallen world that it rules."[50] In my interpretation, the "I" in 2:18 (which should be distinguished from the ἐγὼ in 2:19–20) refers to Paul himself personally as apostle, not to believers in general. It is the apostle who breaks down (and rebuilds) by God's effective message; he breaks down not only sin but sinners and their sin; and rather than acting themselves in 2:18, these sinners are acted upon. Finally, the implied transgression would consist of Paul rebuilding *the same* sinners and their sin as he has broken down.

## Παραβάτην

We do not find παραβάτης in the LXX, but sometimes παραβαίνω refers to transgression of or deviance from a mission or task. In Num 22:18; 24:13, Balaam cannot transgress τὸ ῥῆμα κυρίου τοῦ θεοῦ (the mission God sends him on/the oracle God gives him to pronounce). In Num 27:14, Aaron and Moses transgressed God's ῥῆμα (God's sending them to speak to the rock, not strike it). In Josh 11:15, Joshua did not deviate from/transgress οὐδὲν ἀπὸ πάντων Moses commanded him (his being sent to destroy the Canaanites). In 1 Sam 15:24, Saul transgressed τὸν λόγον κυρίου καὶ τὸ ῥῆμα σου (the word sending him on a mission to put the Amalekites under the ban). In Jdt 2:13, Holofernes is commanded not to transgress ἕν τι τῶν ῥημάτων τοῦ κυρίου σου (the destructive orders for the campaign on which the king sends him). In Ps. Sol. 18.12, the stars do not transgress/deviate from the course (ἀπὸ ὁδοῦ) God has commanded.[51] In 1 En. 2.1, they do not transgress/deviate from each their own order (τάξιν), although some of them transgress/deviate from God's ordinance or command (πρόσταγμα: 18.15).

Thus, as the object of the implied transgression in Gal 2:18 Paul could be thinking of *his apostolic calling/authority/mandate* as a divine *command/*

*mission/task* to be obeyed or transgressed. Elsewhere, he seems to imply the thought (Rom 1:14; 1 Cor 9:16; cf. also Jer 20:9, Acts 1:25; 26:19), and the language in Gal 2:18 allows it. Moreover, we are not unprepared for it since it contrasts the apostolic misconduct Paul has referred to in 2:14 by the words οὐκ ὀρθοποδοῦσιν πρὸς τὴν ἀλήθειαν τοῦ εὐαγγελίου. If we paraphrased Paul here, we would have: "For if I rebuild the *same* sinners and their sin as I broke down, I show myself a transgressor of my calling/mission."

## THE FURTHER FLOW OF THOUGHT

This interpretation seems to me to have superior explanatory power with respect to the immediately following flow of thought in 2:19–20 as well. Our reading so far invites us to see the two antitheses in 2:18 and 2:19 as parallels with mutual interpretive significance. But also, 2:19 seems to have explanatory function (cf. γάρ), the "I" undergoes a shift as to its semantic role between the two verses, and the language intensifies from "breaking down" vs. "rebuilding" to "death" vs. "resurrection." See table 2.1.

Now, first, since ἀπέθανον parallels κατέλυσα, it is noteworthy and consistent with our interpretation of 2:18 that in 2:19 the law functions explicitly as *the agent* (cf. διὰ νόμου), not *patient*, of the event.

Second, the parallel and the shift in semantic role we have just observed make it natural to understand the turn in the flow of thought suggested by the emphatic ἐγώ introducing 2:19 to be a turn from (a) the "I" in 2:18 referring to Paul as apostle preaching his effective message to (b) the ἐγώ in 2:19 referring to Paul as paradigm addressee of such preaching. Thus, in 2:19, Paul explains (cf. γάρ) why he will be a transgressor of his own calling/ mission if he rebuilds the same sinful people and their sin as he has broken down. The explanation refers to the paradigm event which is the pattern for the calling/mission given to him by God—namely, his own coming to faith in Christ which was not "only" a being "broken down" and being "rebuilt," but a spiritual *death and resurrection* through union with Christ in his death—under the law's curse (cf. 3:13)—and resurrection. The significance of this is then immediately presented in 2:20 with its distinction between ἐγώ (Paul before his "death" with Christ) and the "I" who "lives" (Paul after his

**Table 2.1. Parallel Antitheses in 2:18–19**

| 2:18 | κατέλυσα | | *as opposed to* | οἰκοδομῶ | *with "I" as semantic agent* |
|------|----------|-----|----------------|----------|------------------------------|
| 2:19 | ἀπέθανον | γάρ | as opposed to | ζήσω | with "I" as semantic patient |

"resurrection"): the "I" now living *is not the same* as the ἐγώ who died. This point corresponds perfectly with the one we saw in 2:18: If Paul rebuilds *the same* sinners and their sin as he destroys, he is a transgressor of his own calling/mission.

## CONCLUSION

Summing up our interpretation: Paul sharply denies (2:17c) that Christ causes believers to be indifferent toward committing sin (2:17b) by the equalizing judgment integral to justification finding "even we" Jewish believers to be sinners just like the Gentiles (2:15–17a). He then explains his denial by an argument we can paraphrase as follows:

Not at all! (2:17c) For if I rebuild the *same* sinners and their sin as I broke down (that is, if I rebuild sinful people who are indifferent toward committing sin), I show myself a transgressor of my God-given calling/mission (2:18). This mission was patterned after my own encounter with Christ, in which I was co–crucified with him under the curse of the law, died under its judgment and was raised to new life (2:19), so that the "I" who now lives is no longer *the same* (2:20). Thus, rebuilding *the same* sinners and their sin would make me a transgressor of my mission.

Thus, taking Paul's language in Gal 2:18 as use of scriptural metaphors allows a new interpretation, not least of ἅ . . . ταῦτα, which, unlike the standard alternatives, can take εἰ γάρ as a simple, straightforward "for if" introducing the explanation for μὴ γένοιτο in 2:17c. This interpretation also better explains Paul's introduction and precise use of the first-person singular in the flow of the argument, and it satisfactorily clarifies the nature of the implied transgression.

## NOTES

1. This chapter summarizes parts of Chapter VII, "Tearing down, building up, dying, living, and not annulling the grace of God," in Nicolai Techow, *Sinners, Works of Law, and Transgression in Gal 2:14b–21: A Study in Paul's Line of Thought*, WUNT 2 (Tübingen: Mohr Siebeck, 2023). For more details and references, see this work. I am grateful to participants in the Scripture and Paul seminar and to Sigurd Grindheim for helpful comments and suggestions.

2. For my detailed discussion of the preceding context (2:11–14a) and its relation to the content and flow of the argument in Paul's speech (2:14b-21), see Techow, *Sinners*, chapters IV–VI.

3. See, for instance, James D. G. Dunn, *A Commentary on the Epistle to the Galatians*, BNTC (London: A. & C. Black, 1993), 142; A. Andrew Das, *Galatians*, Concordia Commentary (Concordia Publishing House, 2014), 265; Craig S. Keener, *Galatians: A Commentary* (Grand Rapids: Baker Academic, 2019), 192.

4. LXX: φραγμὸν περιέθηκα. The MT has: וַיְעַזְּקֵהוּ ("and he dug about it"), which is less relevant for our purposes.

5. LXX: ἐχαράκωσα. The MT has: וַיְסַקְּלֵהוּ ("and he freed it from stones"), which is less relevant for our purposes.

6. MT: וַיִּבֶן מִגְדָּל. LXX: ᾠκοδόμησα πύργον.

7. MT: הָסֵר מְשׂוּכָּתוֹ (qal participle of עָשָׂה preceding). LXX: ἀφελῶ τὸν φραγμὸν αὐτοῦ.

8. MT: פָּרֹץ גְּדֵרוֹ (qal participle of עָשָׂה preceding). LXX: καθελῶ τὸν τοῖχον αὐτοῦ.

9. Cf. Joseph Blenkinsopp, *Isaiah 40–55*, AB 19 (New York: Doubleday, 2000), 208.

10. Rowland J. H. Shutt, "Letter of Aristeas (Third Century B.C.–First Century A.D.) A New Translation and Introduction," in *The Old Testament Pseudepigrapha. Vol 2. Expansions of the "Old Testament" and Legends, Wisdom and Philosophical Literature, Prayers, Psalms and Odes, Fragments of Lost Judeo-Hellenistic Works*, ed. James H. Charlesworth (New York: Doubleday, 1985), 22 note h2, adds the alternative translation "unbreakable."

11. Note the ὑπὸ νόμον expressions in 3:23; 4:4–5, 21; 5:18.

12. This is also implied in 2:16, 21; 3:2, 5; 5:4. Implied human transgression of the law is perhaps seen in 3:19, but cf. below, I do not find it in 2:18.

13. See not least, Michael Bachmann, *Sünder oder Übertreter. Studien Zur Argumentation in Gal 2,15ff*, WUNT 59 (Tübingen: J.C.B. Mohr, 1992), 70–80, who argues that παραβάτης sometimes implies a more basic crossing of God's will and that in Paul the word and its cognates can point to a conflict with the new creation (order). While my interpretation below differs from Bachmann's of παραβάτης as alluding to a "new creation fall," it is not incompatible with it either. Roy E. Ciampa, *The Presence and Function of Scripture in Galatians 1 and 2*, WUNT 2/102 (Tübingen: Mohr Siebeck, 1998), 207–8n174, also argues that an implied νόμου after παραβάτην is dubitable.

14. This is seen from a cursory glance at the relevant entries in Leland Ryken et al., *Dictionary of Biblical Imagery*, electronic ed. (Downers Grove, IL: InterVarsity Press, 2000), 128–29, 844–45, 923–25.

15. More technically, I use the word "patient" to refer to "the entity undergoing the effect of some action, often undergoing some change in state": John Saeed, *Semantics* (Oxford: Blackwell, 1997), 140.

16. My numbers in the following are only approximate. I mostly count references rather than occurrences. Some of the former may contain more than one of the latter. Also, occasionally, my categorization of an occurrence can be debated. Sometimes, a patient must be inferred from the context. However, the general directions in which the numbers point are rather clear.

17. In doubtful cases, I have tended to be inclusive rather than exclusive. Thus, I have included 2 Macc 2:22 and 4 Macc 2:14. On the other hand, I have excluded Odes

7:12 (or 11:2, depending on edition of LXX) (ὁ καταλύων σκηνὴν πήξας) since the contrast in this text is between taking down and pitching a tent (cf. also, e.g., Num 1:51).

18. There is one other instance of ἐπανορθόω in 2 Macc (5:20). In this case, the antithesis is καταλείπω, the contrast being between (in this case) the temple being forsaken and restored, which could fit nicely both vocabulary and context in 2:22 as well.

19. To these could arguably be added Isa 49:17 and Amos 9:11.

20. The fifth exception, to be added to the four just listed, is the arguably less relevant 2 Macc 2:22.

21. For exhaustive lists, we would need to sift all occurrences of all verbs with semantic fields overlapping with the semantic domains "destroy" and "build," respectively. This being hardly manageable, but still aiming to discover indicative patterns, my method has been different. I explain my procedures in the notes. As for the "breaking down" side, I have used the Greek and Hebrew vocabulary of the mentioned twenty-seven occurrences of the full antithesis and of Gal 2:18 as my starting point. The vocabulary used for "breaking down" in these occurrences is relatively varied. For manageability, I have excluded πίπτω (Amos 9:11; 4 Macc 2:14) and its Hebrew *Vorlage* in Amos 9:11, namely, נפל and הרץ from my search. Apart from this exclusion, the following numbers and references cover occurrences of the vocabulary found in the occurrences of the full antitheses well enough. They are based on searches finding in LXX/MT ἀπόλλυμι, καθαιρέω, καταβάλλω, κατασκάπτω, κατασπάω, καταστρέφω, or καταλύω as translation (when a MT exists) of אבד, הרס, ירד, נצה, ערר, ערף, שׁמד, שׁדד, ספה, נסה, or, more rarely, נתץ, נתשׁ, פרץ, or שׁבר, provided a meaning antonymic to "build" appears possible in the context.

22. Gen 18:24, 28, 31, 32; 19:13; Exod 23:24; 34:13; Lev 11:35; 14:45; Deut 7:5; 12:2–3; 28:52; Judg 2:2; 6:25, 28, 30–32; 8:9; 9:45; 2 Sam 11:25; 1 Kgs 18:32; 19:10, 14; 2 Kgs 3:25; 10:27; 11:18; 14:13; 21:3; 23:7, 8, 12, 15; 1 Chr 20:1; 2 Chr 23:17; 25:23; 26:6; 31:1; 32:5; 33:3; 34:4, 7; 36:19; Neh 1:3 (2 Esd 11:3 LXX); 2:3 (12:3 LXX); Job 12:14; Pss 9:7; 11:3 (10:3 LXX); 28:5 (27:5 LXX); 52:7 (51:7 LXX); 60:3 (59:3 LXX); Pss 80:13 (79:13 LXX); 89:41 (88:41 LXX); Prov 11:11; 14:1; 15:25; 21:22; 24:31 (24:46 LXX); 29:4; Eccl 3:3; 10:8; Isa 5:5; 14:17, 25; 15:1, 2 (only LXX); 22:10; 23:1, 11, 14; 24:12; 26:5; 49:17; Jer 1:10; 2:15; 4:7; 24:6; 31:28 (38:28 LXX), 40 (38:40 LXX); 33:4 (40:4 LXX); 42:10 (49:10 LXX); 45:4 (51:34 LXX); 46:8 (26:8 LXX); 50:15 (27:15 LXX); 51:18 (28:18 LXX), 58 (28:58 LXX); 52:14; Lam 2:2, 9; Ezek 13:14; 16:39; 26:4, 9; 26:12; 36:35–36; Dan 7:26; Hos 10:2; Joel 1:17; Amos 9:11; Mic 5:9; 1 Esd 6:15; Tob 13:14 (in the Sinaiticus text family); Jdt 3:8; Sir 10:14, 16–17; 28:14; 34:23; 49:7; 1 Macc 1:31; 2:25, 45; 4:45; 9:54; 11:4; 2 Macc 2:22; 4:11; 10:2; 14:33; 4 Macc 1:6; 1:11; 2:14; 4:24; 5:33; 7:9; 8:15; 11:24; 14:8; 17:2, 9; Odes 10:5; Ps Sol. 2.1. The reader should note that some of these references may contain more than one occurrence.

23. On 2 Macc 2:22, cf. above. In 2 Macc 4:11, τὰς μὲν νομίμους καταλύων πολιτείας stands in contrast to παρανόμους ἐθισμοὺς ἐκαίνιζεν. Thus, καταλύω here means "putting an end to something," not "breaking down as opposed to building up." Also note that, the patients are not the laws but the πολιτείας and ἐθισμοὺς

with the attributes νομίμους and παρανόμους, respectively. 4 Macc 4:24, says of Antiochus that κατὰ μηδένα τρόπον ἴσχυεν καταλῦσαι διὰ τῶν δογμάτων τὴν τοῦ ἔθνους εὐνομίαν, ἀλλὰ πάσας τὰς ἑαυτοῦ ἀπειλὰς καὶ τιμωρίας ἑώρα καταλυομένας. Note the word–playing double occurrence of καταλύω. What Antiochus cannot (i.e., καταλῦσαι . . . τὴν τοῦ ἔθνους εὐνομίαν) resonates with his opposite observation (cf. ἑώρα) that his threats and punishments were being καταλυομένας. Thus, the actualized meaning of καταλύω in context is not "breaking down" or "destroying" as opposed to building, but rather "bringing to an end," or perhaps "disregarding" or "dismissing." In 4 Macc 5:33 Eleazer says, "I do not so pity my old age (τὸ ἐμαυτοῦ γῆρας) as to break (καταλῦσαι) the ancestral law by my own act (δι ἐμαυτοῦ)" (NRSV). He immediately unfolds that he will not "play false to you, O law that trained me, nor will I renounce you, beloved self–control. I will not put you to shame, philosophical reason, nor will I reject you, honored priesthood and knowledge of the law" (4 Macc 5:34–35). Thus, καταλῦσαι in this context means "break," "abandon," or "disregard," not "break/tear down" as opposed to "build." 4 Macc 7:9, praises Eleazar: τὴν ἁγιαστίαν σεμνολογήσας οὐ κατέλυσας. "Speaking highly/in honor of/ praising ritual service/holiness, you did not κατέλυσας [it]." The patient is not the law but ritual service/holiness, and in the context κατέλυσας means "abandon" (rightly, NRSV), not "break/tear down." In 4 Macc 17:9, the martyrs "have been buried here because of the force/violence of the tyrant who wanted to destroy (καταλῦσαι) the way of life/polity (πολιτείαν) of the Hebrews." Admittedly, the meaning "destroy" is likely here, but not necessarily as opposed to "build." And strictly, the law is not the patient, but a "way of life" or "polity."

24. Sinful people or kingdoms/thrones/nations/peoples destroyed due to sin: Pss 28:5 (27:5 LXX); 52:7 (51:7 LXX); 60:3 (59:3 LXX); Isa 14:25; 49:17; Jer 1:10; 24:6; 31:28 (38:28 LXX); 42:10 (49:10 LXX); 45:4 (51:34 LXX); Dan 7:26; Amos 9:11; Sir 10:14, 16–17; 49:7. Morally impure or sinful religious objects: Exod 23:24; 34:13; Deut 7:5; 12:2–3; Judg 2:2; 6:25, 28, 30–32; 2 Kgs 10:27; 11:18; 21:3; 23:7, 8, 12, 15; 2 Chr 23:17; 31:1; 33:3; 34:4, 7; Jer 51:18 (28:18 LXX); Ezek 13:14; 16:39; Hos 10:2; Jdt 3:8; 1 Macc 2:25, 45; 4:45; 2 Macc 10:2. Cities, fortresses, houses, walls, etc. because of sin or offense against God (or another agent): Gen 18:24, 28, 31, 32; 19:13; Deut 28:52; Judg 8:9; 9:45; 2 Sam 11:25; 2 Kgs 3:25; 2 Kgs 14:13; 1 Chr 20:1; 2 Chr 25:23; 26:6; 32:5; 36:19; Neh 1:3 (2 Esd 11:3 LXX); 2:3 (12:3 LXX); Ps 9:7; Prov 11:11; 15:25; Isa 5:5; 23:1, 11, 14; 24:12; 26:5; Jer 2:15; 4:7; Jer 33:4 (40:4 LXX); 50:15 (27:15 LXX); 51:58 (28:58 LXX); 52:14; Lam 2:2, 9; Ezek 26:4, 9; 36:35–36; 26:12; Mic 5:9; Sir 28:14; Odes 10:5. Sinful/negatively seen emotions: 4 Macc 1:6; 14:8. Tyranny: 4 Macc 1:11; 8:15; 11:24; 17:2. To these could arguably be added: Pss 80:13 (79:13 LXX); 89:41 (88:41 LXX).

25. Listing these references would take up too much space. However, the reader can find them by conducting a relatively simple search (cf. the next note). The same is true for the following two quantifications.

26. As for the "build" side of the antithesis, the vocabulary used in the mentioned twenty-seven occurrences of the full antithesis and in Gal 2:18 is relatively narrow. In the Hebrew MT, קום and גדר are used in Amos 9:11 besides בנה, but otherwise the vocabulary is limited to the latter. As for the LXX, in Amos 9:11 we find ἀνίστημι

in addition to ἀνοικοδομέω; in 2 Macc 2:22 (a debatable occurrence) we find ἐπανορθόω; and in 4 Macc 2:14 the verb is συνεγείρω. All the other occurrences employ οἰκοδομέω or ἀνοικοδομέω (LXX) and בנה (MT). Therefore, the following references and numbers are based on a limited search finding ἀνοικοδομέω or οἰκοδομέω (as translation of בנה when a MT exists).

27. In the following, I have sought not to count synoptic parallels.

28. Note that the destruction here clearly involves human beings.

29. This is a quotation from Amos 9:11.

30. This quotes 1 Kgs 19:10, 14.

31. This list represents all occurrences of the following words when a meaning antonymic to "build" is at all possible: ἀπόλλυμι, καθαιρέω, καταβάλλω, κατασκάπτω, κατασπάω, καταστρέφω, καταλύω (cf. the above equivalent LXX/MT search), λύω or καθαίρεσις.

32. The following presents a search of all occurrences of ἀνοικοδομέω, οἰκοδομέω, ἐποικοδομέω, οἰκοδομή, or οἰκοδόμος.

33. Matt 7:24, 26; 16:18; 23:29; Mark 12:1 par., 10 par. (quoting Ps 118:22); Mark 13:1–2 par.; Mark 14:58 par.; 15:29 par.; Luke 4:29; 6:48–49; 7:5; 11:47–48; 12:18; 14:28, 30; 17:28; John 2:20; Acts 4:11 (quoting Ps 118:22); 7:47, 49; 9:31; 15:16 (quoting Amos 9:11); 20:32; Rom 14:19; 15:2, 20; 1 Cor 3:9–10, 12, 14; 8:1, 10; 10:23; 14:3, 4, 5, 12, 17, 26; 2 Cor 5:1; 10:8; 12:19; 13:10; Eph 2:20–21; 4:12, 16, 29; Col 2:7; 1 Thess 5:11; 1 Pet 2:5, 7 (quoting Ps 118:22); Jud 20.

34. Jer 1:10; 12:16–17; 18:7–9; 24:6; 31:4 (38:4 LXX), 28 (38:28 LXX); 33:7 (40:7 LXX); 42:10 (49:10 LXX); 45:4 (51:34 LXX). The similarities being not fully lexical, I point primarily, though not exclusively, to semantic rather than lexical overlap between Paul and Jeremiah. Notably, we also find very clear but not fully lexical allusions to Jer 1:5, 10 in Sir 49:7.

35. Sir 49:7 (alluding to Jer 1:5 and 1:10) says Jeremiah was ἐν μήτρᾳ ἡγιάσθη προφήτης ἐκριζοῦν καὶ κακοῦν καὶ ἀπολλύειν, ὡσαύτως οἰκοδομεῖν καὶ καταφυτεύειν, showing that his commission to "tear down" and "build up" (and to "pluck up" and "plant") was and can be considered as the controlling metaphors for and themes of his calling. Cf. also Karl Olav Sandnes, *Paul, One of the Prophets?: A Contribution to the Apostle's Self-Understanding*, WUNT 2/43 (Tübingen: J.C.B. Mohr, 1991), 32–35; F. B. Huey, *Jeremiah, Lamentations*, NAC (Nashville: Broadman & Holman, 1993), 52. Note also the titles of Walter Brueggemann's two–volume commentary on Jeremiah: Walter Brueggemann, *To Pluck Up, to Tear Down: A Commentary on the Book of Jeremiah 1–25*, ITC (Grand Rapids: Eerdmans, 1988); and Walter Brueggemann, *To Build, to Plant: A Commentary on Jeremiah 26–52*, ITC (Grand Rapids: Eerdmans, 1991).

36. Cf. also Dunn, *A Commentary on the Epistle to the Galatians*, 142; Ciampa, *The Presence and Function of Scripture*, 203. I first presented my understanding of the flow of Paul's argument in my dissertation in 2004, without having read Ciampa's book (to my great embarrassment).

37. Thus, e.g., Rainer Riesner, *Paul's Early Period. Chronology, Mission Strategy, Theology* (Grand Rapids: Eerdmans, 1998), 236; Seyoon Kim, *Paul and the New Perspective: Second Thoughts on the Origin of Paul's Gospel* (Grand Rapids:

Eerdmans, 2002), 101; Sandnes, *Paul, One of the Prophets?*, 53–69; James M. Scott, *Paul and the Nations. The Old Testament and Jewish Background of Paul's Mission to the Nations with Special Reference to the Destination of Galatians*, WUNT 2/84 (Tübingen: Mohr, 1995), 125.

38. See also Sigurd Grindheim, "Apostate Turned Prophet: Paul's Prophetic Self-Understanding and Prophetic Hermeneutic with Special Reference to Galatians 3.10–12," *NTS* 53 (2007): 545–65, who demonstrates the hermeneutical helpfulness as to the *crux* in Gal 3:10–12 of the understanding that Paul draws on Jeremiah and the prophetic tradition.

39. In 2 Cor 10:8 and 13:10, Paul explicitly says his authority is not to break down but to build up. As seen in 2 Cor 10:4–6, however, it is not that Paul has no authority at all to break down but rather that breaking down is not the final "fundamentally constructive objective" of what he has been authorized to do (Victor P. Furnish, *II Corinthians. Translated with Introduction, Notes and Commentary*, AB [New York: Doubleday, 1984], 478).

40. Cf. also B. J. Oropeza, *Exploring Second Corinthians: Death and Life, Hardship and Rivalry*, RRA 3 (Atlanta: SBL, 2016), 566–68, 716. I thank the author for this reference.

41. Cf. similarly Ciampa, *The Presence and Function of Scripture*, 205–6.

42. Note that Jer 12:14–17 and 18:7–9 (and, indeed, 1:10 itself) "universalize" the themes of Jer 1:10. This fact, in addition to features in the context of Gal 2:18 (cf. below), makes it less likely that we should understand the reference of ἅ . . . ταῦτα in that verse as narrowly as "the covenant community" (as does Ciampa, *The Presence and Function of Scripture*, 206–7n173). Indeed, it seems at least questionable if Paul ever speaks of it as part of his apostolic activity to break down or destroy a community as such. Even the ὑμῶν in 2 Cor 10:8 does not necessarily communicate such a thought. This is, of course, not to deny that there are communal aspects to what Paul is talking about, cf. below.

43. On this, see Sandnes, *Paul, One of the Prophets?*, 32–35. See also Sir 49:5–7.

44. See, e.g., Jer 33:7 (40:7 LXX); 42:10 (49:10 LXX).

45. See, e.g., Jer 5:14; 24:6 (with allusion to 1:10); 25:17–18; 31:28 (again with allusion to 1:10); 42:10 (49:10 LXX) (with allusion to 1:10); 45:4 (51:34 LXX) (with allusion to 1:10). Cf. also Ciampa, *The Presence and Function of Scripture*, 205–6. Also, note Hos 6:5, which generalizes this pattern to "the prophets."

46. Notably, if we are right in taking the "I" in 2:18 as referring to Paul as apostle, the breaking down cannot refer to his pre-call/conversion efforts to destroy "God's church" (1:13) or "the faith" (1:23). This activity was the very opposite of his apostolic calling.

47. See Techow, *Sinners*, chapters V and VI.

48. This is in almost precise agreement with Mark A. Seifrid, "Paul, Luther, and Justification in Gal 2:15–21," *WTJ* 65 (2003): 219–20, although I understand "our" being found as sinners in 2:17a in a more objective sense than he seems to do. Seifrid's works on justification in Paul has greatly shaped my understanding.

49. For my detailed argument for understanding ἁμαρτωλοί in 2:15 and 2:17 in a primarily general, moral-religious sense, see Techow, *Sinners*, especially chapters V and VI.

50. Seifrid, "Paul, Luther, and Justification in Gal 2:15–21," 220.

51. Bachmann, *Sünder oder Übertreter*, 79–80, sees that παραβάτην in Gal 2:18 could carry the meaning "Abweichen von einem Weg" and recall οὐκ ὀρθοποδεῖν in 2:14a.

## BIBLIOGRAPHY

Bachmann, Michael. *Sünder oder Übertreter. Studien Zur Argumentation in Gal 2,15ff.* WUNT 59. Tübingen: J.C.B. Mohr, 1992.

Blenkinsopp, Joseph. *Isaiah 40–55.* AB 19. New York: Doubleday, 2000.

Brueggemann, Walter. *To Build, to Plant: A Commentary on Jeremiah 26–52.* ITC. Grand Rapids: Eerdmans, 1991.

———. *To Pluck Up, to Tear Down: A Commentary on the Book of Jeremiah 1–25.* ITC. Grand Rapids: Eerdmans, 1988.

Ciampa, Roy E. *The Presence and Function of Scripture in Galatians 1 and 2.* WUNT 2/102. Tübingen: Mohr Siebeck, 1998.

Das, A. Andrew. *Galatians.* Concordia Commentary. Concordia Publishing House, 2014.

Dunn, James D. G. *A Commentary on the Epistle to the Galatians.* BNTC. London: A. & C. Black, 1993.

Furnish, Victor P. *II Corinthians. Translated with Introduction, Notes and Commentary.* AB. New York: Doubleday, 1984.

Grindheim, Sigurd. "Apostate Turned Prophet: Paul's Prophetic Self-Understanding and Prophetic Hermeneutic with Special Reference to Galatians 3.10–12." *NTS* 53 (2007): 545–65.

Huey, F. B. *Jeremiah, Lamentations.* NAC. Nashville: Broadman & Holman, 1993.

Keener, Craig S. *Galatians: A Commentary.* Grand Rapids: Baker Academic, 2019.

Kim, Seyoon. *Paul and the New Perspective: Second Thoughts on the Origin of Paul's Gospel.* Grand Rapids: Eerdmans, 2002.

Oropeza, B. J. *Exploring Second Corinthians: Death and Life, Hardship and Rivalry.* RRA 3. Atlanta: SBL, 2016.

Riesner, Rainer. *Paul's Early Period. Chronology, Mission Strategy, Theology.* Grand Rapids: Eerdmans, 1998.

Ryken, Leland, Jim Wilhoit, Tremper Longman, Colin Duriez, Douglas Penney, and Daniel G. Reid. *Dictionary of Biblical Imagery.* Electronic ed. Downers Grove, IL: InterVarsity, 2000.

Saeed, John. *Semantics.* Oxford: Blackwell, 1997.

Sandnes, Karl Olav. *Paul, One of the Prophets?: A Contribution to the Apostle's Self-Understanding.* WUNT 2/43. Tübingen: J.C.B. Mohr, 1991.

Scott, James M. *Paul and the Nations. The Old Testament and Jewish Background of Paul's Mission to the Nations with Special Reference to the Destination of Galatians.* WUNT 2/84. Tübingen: Mohr, 1995.

Seifrid, Mark A. "Paul, Luther, and Justification in Gal 2:15–21." *WTJ* 65 (2003): 215–30.

Shutt, Rowland J. H. "Letter of Aristeas (Third Century B.C.–First Century A.D.) A New Translation and Introduction." In *The Old Testament Pseudepigrapha. Vol 2. Expansions of the "Old Testament" and Legends, Wisdom and Philosophical Literature, Prayers, Psalms and Odes, Fragments of Lost Judeo-Hellenistic Works,* edited by James H. Charlesworth. New York: Doubleday, 1985.

Techow, Nicolai. *Sinners, Works of Law, and Transgression in Gal 2:14b–21: A Study in Paul's Line of Thought.* WUNT 2. Tübingen: Mohr Siebeck, forthcoming 2023.

*Chapter 3*

# The "Righteous by Faith Shall Live" ... *in the Spirit*

*Galatians 2:16–3:14 and Salvific Life*

B. J. Oropeza

There has been a blind spot in the various perspectives on Paul championed over the last several decades. Whether traditional perspectives, the new perspective, post-new perspectives, or Paul within Judaism, these various perspectives often lacked intense coverage and foregrounding of the Holy Spirit in relation to Pauline soteriology. We observe this glaring oversight in perhaps the most influential work on Paul in the last generation, E. P. Sanders's *Paul and Palestinian Judaism.* Despite promoting the now famous religious pattern of covenantal nomism, Sanders does not address in any detail the *new* covenant and its association with the Holy Spirit in Paul, and there are no pages for "Spirit" listed from Second Temple sources in the book's index.[1] A number of others who supported or made their point of departure from Sanders's work likewise seemed to follow this trend by either neglecting or not emphasizing the Holy Spirit, whether in Paul or the texts that might inform him. This tendency, however, is now finally showing signs of diminishing as a growing number of recent scholars feature the Spirit's prominence.[2]

The late James Dunn, when writing an update on the new perspective moving forward, underlined the necessity for scholars to address Paul's *entire gospel*, "warts and all," and not just the parts scholars find easy to agree with.[3] He adds that the gospel of Jesus's death and resurrection includes the outworking not only of atonement, justification by faith, and participation in and with Christ, but also equally important is the gift of the Spirit. He suggests that this part of the gospel has been traditionally neglected because technical terms can be "hedged around with rubrics and dogmas more easily monitored and controlled" than the unpredictable and uncomfortable character of the Spirit.[4] But for early followers of Jesus, being "in Christ" and having the Spirit's indwelling presence would be understood as "two sides of the same coin."[5] I wish to add a further analogy that the Spirit, along with participation in Christ and justification/righteousness, are all sides of the same percussion triangle, even though many scholars rarely play the Spirit side.

Paul writes about the Holy Spirit not simply in relation to congregational fellowship and the operation of spiritual gifts but also in relation to justification/righteousness (1 Cor 6:11; 2 Cor 3:8–9; Rom 8:10; 14:17), confessing Jesus as Lord at baptism-initiation (1 Cor 12:3; cf. Rom 10:9–13), initiation in the metaphors of anointing, sealing, and down payment (2 Cor 1:22; cf. Eph 1:13–14), initiation into the corporate body of Christ (1 Cor 12:13; cf. 6:17), being adopted as sons and daughters of God (Gal 4:4–6; Rom 8:14–17), and dwelling in the believers' hearts in contrast with the works of the law and Mosaic covenant (2 Cor 3:3–18; Rom 2:28–29; 6:17; 7:6; cf. 8:9–11). Moreover, without the Spirit, a person does not belong to Jesus Messiah (Rom 8:9b). Paul likewise commands believers to "walk in the Spirit" in contrast with the flesh, a point that cannot simply be relegated to ethics with no soteriological remainder; the converse of such walking has the potential to bring about spiritual "death" (Rom 8:2–13) and failure to inherit God's kingdom (Gal 5:16–21).

It is hardly an understatement, then, to suggest that more attention—perhaps *much* more attention—should be given to the Spirit's activity from a soteriological perspective. In this study I will explore the Spirit's relation to salvific language from an intertextual approach that includes not only allusions to Scripture but also two other informants that are foundational for Paul's gospel convictions: revelations originating from his encounters with the risen Messiah and his knowledge of oral traditions related to the pre-risen Jesus. Galatians 2:16–3:14 will be of special interest here since Paul stresses in this text salvific language and the Spirit. It will turn out that Paul's major informants include his "third heaven" revelation, a saying repeated by Jesus in reference to the promise of the Spirit, and prophetic words from Ezekiel on the Spirit.


## PAUL'S REVELATIONS FROM CHRIST, INSIGHTS FROM SCRIPTURE, AND KNOWLEDGE OF THE JESUS TRADITIONS

Space does not permit thorough investigation of the three authoritative informants that guide Paul's convictions as an apostle of Jesus Messiah.[6] These informants include his personal encounters with the risen Lord and revelations received from those experiences, his post-Damascus interpretation of Scripture, and the Jesus traditions that were passed on to him from those who followed Jesus before him. A brief discussion of each of these will have to suffice for this study.

The first of these informants has to do with the revelatory words Paul received from his encounters with the risen Messiah. Such would seem to be foundational for his convictions pertaining to his calling as an apostle who proclaims the gospel to gentiles.[7] In Galatians he insists that his apostleship did not come from a human source (Gal 1:1). He received the gospel he proclaims not from humans but through revelation from Jesus Messiah (Gal 1:11–12, 15–16). Paul does not reveal specifically what Jesus said to him during this encounter, but this marks for him his turn from a Pharisee to one who proclaims the gospel about Jesus Messiah to the nations (cf. 1 Cor 9:1; 15:8–10; Phil 3:4–10). His commission is prophetic-like, alluding to the prophets—he is called from the "womb" to reach the nations in the new era of salvation and running with the message of righteousness by trust/faith (Isa 49:1–8; Jer 1:1–10; Hab 2:1–4; cf. Gal 1:15–16; 2:2; 2 Cor 6:1–2).

The revelation described in Gal 1 is typically understood as his Damascus experience, which is narrated in Acts 9:1–19 and remembered in 22:6–16 and 26:12–18. Finny Philip encourages the use of Acts for studying Paul's use of the Spirit by first drawing attention to Paul's own repetitive claims of experiencing the Spirit at one's conversion-initiation (1 Cor 2:4–5; 6:11; 12:13; 2 Cor 1:21–22; Gal 3:1–5; 4:4–7; 1 Thess 1:4–6; 2 Thess 2:13–14; Rom 8:15). This should prompt us to re-evaluate assumptions about Paul's own experience of the Spirit related to his transformation, and this should not be evaluated apart from the Damascus event in Acts.[8] Philip focuses on what Paul saw and heard at the event. He argues that Paul refers to his Damascus experience when speaking about turning to the glory of the Lord with unveiled face and experiencing the Spirit that "enabled him to see a superior revelation outside Torah" (2 Cor 3:3–4:6).[9]

For such interpretations we would need to read the Lukan narrative not purely as Lukan invention but perhaps as memory of an actual disciple from Damascus named Ananias who apparently baptized Paul and prayed for him so that he was filled with the Spirit (Acts 9:17–18).[10] This would appear to be the event in which Paul first experienced the Spirit. It did not happen days earlier when seeing the Lord on the way to Damascus, though perhaps the two events should be read together as one prolonged event. Also relevant is the Lukan Paul's own testimony of the experience in Acts 22:6–16. In this version, Ananias directs Paul to be baptized, "calling on the name of the Lord" (Acts 22:16). The phrase recalls the prophet Joel's discourse about the outpouring of the Spirit in the last days, a text that Paul in his letters indeed knows and relates to righteousness by trust (Joel 2:28–32[3:1–5]/Rom 10:9–13; 1 Cor 1:2).

We can only speculate, however, to what extent Ananias actually said something like this to Paul when the Lukan author writes these words and has an invested interest in the same text from Joel (Acts 2:17–22). At best, only the first of the three Damascus narratives explicitly mentions the Spirit, and although probably associated with Paul's baptism, no audible or visible phenomena are mentioned in relation to the Spirit filling Paul.[11] We may be safe to suggest that his reception of the Spirit happened as a result of the Damascus experience, and it seems to be compatible with what Paul writes in his letters regarding a neophyte's first experience with the Spirit. Even so, we can suggest that another revelation *after* his Damascus experience helped shape his view of the Spirit in reference to his gospel message. It is clear that Paul experienced other revelations from the Lord (Gal 2:1–2; 2 Cor 12:1–9, cf. Acts 16:6–10; 18:10; 20:23; 22:17–21; 23:11; 27:23–24). From 2 Cor 12:1–9, in particular, Paul claims to have experienced an ascension to the "third heaven" in the earlier years of his ministry,[12] where he saw and heard amazing things, and at that time he received instruction from the Lord Jesus about his "stake in the flesh" and grace through "power." We will return to this revelation below.

A second major informant on Paul's convictions to proclaim the gospel is his reading of Jewish Scripture. It is clear that a number of his central beliefs are based on his Scripture readings (e.g., Gal 3:11; Rom 1:16–17/Hab 2:4; Isa 51:5–8; Gal 2:16; Rom 3:20/Ps 142[143]:2). It is somewhat disappointing, however, that none of his Scripture quotes in Galatians directly include something about the Spirit of God.[13] Nevertheless, some of his allusions to Scripture are relevant when it comes to referencing God's Spirit as is evident from a number of scholarly studies, though not all of the allusions are equally convincing.[14] Criteria for determining the strength of an allusion or echo remain important; and although Richard Hays's seven tests for echoes helps exclude some readings, ultimately (and regardless of whether all his criteria are met or not), an allusion's presence will often need to be decided on the force of the scholar's interpretation who makes the claim that a given pre-text is present.[15] I will mostly limit my study to explore the Spirit through one of the clearer echoed sources, Ezekiel 36–37.[16]

A third informant is Paul's knowledge of oral traditions about, or attributed to, Jesus (e.g., 1 Cor 7:10–12; 15:1–7). A clear example that combines both narrative and the words of Jesus is from 1 Cor 11:23–26; it speaks of the night Jesus was betrayed and proceeds to cite Jesus's famous words at the Last Supper. Paul claims to have received this information "from the Lord." While it is possible that he received it by revelation or prophecy, more likely it was passed on to him by those who were Jesus's disciples before him, and it originated with Jesus's words recalled at a special event. Perhaps Peter or James first passed this on to Paul when he visited them for a few weeks (Gal 1:18–20; cf. 2:1–10). He almost certainly learned about some of the words and deeds of Jesus when with them. Dodd rightly claims that Paul didn't spend his time with them talking about the weather![17] We also notice how it is only Peter and James whom Paul mentions *by name* as witnesses of the risen Jesus (1 Cor 15:5, 7). Paul may have also learned about Jesus's words and deeds from witnesses whom he heard preach or whom he interrogated as a Pharisee, from other disciples when first becoming a believer in Christ in Damascus, or from Jerusalem refugees who joined the Antioch congregation where he ministered, or traditions handed to him from Barnabas and other disciples with whom he regularly communicated.[18]

The discipline of intertextuality is well-suited for this informant since it extends beyond Old Testament Scripture in seeking to detect the presence of other texts that come from a wider constellation of text presences from the cultural encyclopedia of the communicant, including oral traditions communicated by memories that would later be frozen in written form. As echoes and allusions from Scripture need criteria for determining their presence, so do Jesus traditions. Michael Thompson helpfully raises an eleven-point system in this regard. Most relevant for my purposes are the criteria of conceptual agreement, the Gospel saying's place in the tradition (inclusive of availability, relevance, authenticity, and multiple attestation), presence of dominical indicators (e.g., "Jesus," "Christ," "Lord"), likelihood of the author's knowledge of the tradition, and exegetical value.[19]

This approach to Pauline texts has the potential to multiply insights; Scripture is not Paul's only informant, nor should we think that it is. With this approach intact, we now turn to Galatians.

## RIGHTEOUSING BY TRUST AND THE SPIRIT: SCRIPTURE AND PAUL'S REVELATION (GAL 2:15–3:5)

Paul's famous confrontation with Cephas leads to the central theme of the letter—a person is justified or "righteoused" by trusting the trustworthy Messiah and not by observing works prescribed by Torah's law (Gal 2:16). Psalm 142:2 (143 MT) is likely being echoed here (cf. Rom 3:19–20). The text claims that humans cannot be justified (δικαιωθήσεται) before such a great and holy God in a court trial, and (as the Psalm continues) there must be reliance on the *Spirit* for divine deliverance and protection. The psalmist ("David") appeals to the Lord's faithfulness and mercy (142:1, 11–12), and he trusts that the "Spirit" will guide him (142:10). He also cries out to know the way in which he should "walk" (142:8) and that the Lord in his righteousness would give him "life" delivering him from affliction (142:11). Important touchstones in the pre-text of this verse will come to the surface later on in the letter.

I am of the persuasion that Gal 2:15–16 should be read together as one unit with the verses that follow and pertain to participation in Christ (Gal 2:17–21), along with the Galatians' reception of the Spirit in contrast with the works of the law (3:1–5). The text of 2:15–3:5 should continue to be read in tight-knit fashion with Abraham's trust and being reckoned righteous as the model for gentiles who trust, which comes with the boon of being children and heirs of Abraham (3:6–9). This should be read closely with Paul's catena of Scriptures affirming that the righteous by trust will live, a trust that includes reception of the blessing of Abraham and the promise of the Spirit (3:10–14). The macro-unit of 2:15–3:14 makes righteousness by trust integral not only with participation in Christ and the faith of Abraham but also with the promise of the Spirit.

In Gal 2:19b–20, after claiming that he has died to the law and lives for God, Paul affirms that he has been crucified with Christ; he no longer lives but Christ lives in him (ζῇ δὲ ἐν ἐμοὶ Χριστός) in a trust relationship. This relationship extends Paul's argument from 2:16, which claims that believers are righteoused (justified) by trusting Christ.[20] To be righteoused here not only involves the forgiveness of sins but also God granting new life with Christ living in those who are justified (cf. Rom 3:21–26; 4:3–9; 6:7). The verb ζάω ("I live") appears five times in 2:19–20 stressing its importance. Living appears to be coordinated with righteousing (δικαιόω) in these verses:

righteoused by trust (2:16)/ living by trust (2:20)
righteoused in Christ (2:17)/ Christ living in me (2:20).[21]

Scott Shauf makes lucid the connection of 2:20 with Paul's discussion on justification by positing that in 2:21 Paul rounds up the arguments in 2:15–20 and builds on v. 20 to assert that Paul does not betray the grace of God, "for if righteousness is through the law, then Christ died for nothing." In 2:20, Michael Gorman sums up four features from Scott Shauf about justification related to participation in Christ: (1) Christ's loving action of being crucified is the basis of righteousness; (2) the believer is crucified with Christ, which becomes the righteousing/justifying experience; (3) Christ lives in the believer, which marks reception of the Spirit and divine adoption; and (4) proper existence in Christ centers on a life of trust and not works of the law.[22] The death and life antithesis in these verses intimates a comparison between the death and resurrection of Jesus along with Paul's own dying to his old-creation self and being raised to new life as part of the new creation in Christ (Gal 1:4; 6:15; cf. Rom 6:3–11; 2 Cor 5:17).

Although the Spirit is not explicitly mentioned in 2:15–21, the Spirit appears immediately after this in 3:1–5 (without a chapter and verse break when this letter was read before ancient audiences). It follows from this tightly knit reading that the Spirit is precisely *how* Christ lives in Paul and other believers in 2:20. As Gordon Fee rightly affirms, "Paul's 'but Christ lives in me' most likely is a kind of shorthand for 'Christ by his Spirit lives in me.'"[23] When first believing the gospel, the Galatians received the Spirit, and that is what makes their union with Christ real for them.

Paul carries over the imagery of Christ's death and crucifixion as the gospel message exhibited to the Galatians (3:1), which they now are in danger of replacing with works of the law. He poses a rhetorical question about their own experience of Christ-living-in-them through the Spirit (3:2). The prompted response to the question is that they received the Spirit by the hearing of trust (ἀκοῆς πίστεως), which may be shorthand for "hearing the gospel about Christ that you trusted in." Those who believed and turned to the gospel are identified as those who "receive" the Spirit as a gift (3:2, 14; 1 Cor 2:12; 2 Cor 11:4; cf. Acts 1:8; 2:38; 8:15; John 7:39). The notion of *receiving* sonship in Gal 4:4–6 marks the conversion-initiation experience once again as λαμβάνω did in 3:2 when the Spirit is first received (3:3). Although ἀπολαμβάνω is used in 4:5 to speak of this reception, the meaning is virtually synonymous, and its parallel in Rom 8:15 uses λαμβάνω. Space does not permit further investigation here on why Paul connected the concepts of Spirit, initiation, and adoption as sons and daughters. I argue that this connection originated from Paul's knowledge of an oral tradition about Jesus's own baptism; Jesus was confirmed as son of God and anointed by the Spirit at that event.[24] All the same, the Spirit's reception at the Galatians' conversion-initiation becomes their identity marker.[25] It may be said that, rather than circumcision and other works of the law, the Spirit functions as the token for gentile identity in Christ.[26]

When the Galatians believed and were righteoused, the Spirit became the agent providing their union with Christ and making them aware that Christ now lived in them. This justification was not for them a verbal declaration from God of acquittal but God's *act* of acquittal that they experienced as a subjective realization of being forgiven and reconciled to God. God released them from the prison of S/sin by co-crucifixion of the old self and being co-raised to a new life and relationship with Christ through the Spirit now dwelling in them. The Spirit gives them new life (cf. Gal 3:21; 5:25; 6:8; Rom 1:4; 6:3–10; 8:2–13; 2 Cor 3:6), and this life for them is confirmed not merely through a one-time experience; it is continual and even manifested objectively—Paul speaks of the Lord generously supplying the Galatians' new manner of living with the sustenance of the Spirit and the working of miracles among them, presumably through the Spirit's agency (Gal 3:5, cf. δυνάμεις: 1 Cor 12:10, 28–29).

A relationship between the Galatians' suffering (πάσχω Gal 3:4), the Spirit's presence, and the manifestation of miracles is not by happenstance. Paul expected such things to be normative for those who believe and live out the gospel. I do not find the translation "experience" for πάσχω to be best here, as Fee, who *inter alia* claims that contextually the experiences in the Spirit, not suffering, must be view. For Fee, suffering does not fit with the phrase "many things," given that Paul mentions nothing else about their suffering.[27] However, a good case can be made for the proper meaning here as suffering. First, Paul's rhetorical flurries in this letter (notice in this same context "O foolish Galatians!" 3:1) suggests that "many things" may be hyperbolic, and so we should not hang too much on the phrase. Second, it makes proper sense that both the miracles and suffering the Galatians experienced (3:4–5) would warrant cogently Paul's surprise that this all might turn out to be in vain for the Galatians if they turn aside to the works of the law. Third, the Galatians' suffering is also implied through the one son of the flesh persecuting the other born of the Spirit (4:29). Fourth, that the Galatians suffered social alienation and harassment is clear enough from Acts 13–14 (based on the Southern Galatia hypothesis). Fifth, without legal protection of being an approved religion (*religio licita*), the Galatian Christ-followers would be vulnerable to being persecuted (Gal 5:11; 6:12). Finally and perhaps most importantly, Paul *never* uses πάσχω as "experience" but consistently uses it to mean "suffer" (1 Cor 12:26; 2 Cor 1:6; Phil 1:29; 1 Thess 2:14; 2 Thess 1:5; cf. 2 Tim 1:12), which is also typically how the verb is used both in the LXX and NT (Wis 12:27; 18:1; Sir 38:16; 2 Macc 6:30; 7:32; Heb 2:18; 9:26; 1 Pet 2:20; etc.).[28] The notion of suffering is thus preferable over experiencing.

In these verses, there are neither quotes nor clear allusions to Scripture that ground this combination of suffering + Spirit + miracles. Rather, I suggest for Paul that this conceptual blend comes from a personal revelation he received from the risen Lord. We could surmise that Paul received the Spirit when he turned to Jesus as Messiah, and that his initiation into the corporate body of Christ took place through the Spirit's agency (1 Cor 12:13; cf. Acts 9:17–18). But the conviction that his way of life as a witness for the gospel would entail both suffering and Spirit-enabled miracles was something revealed to him during his third-heaven experience (2 Cor 12:1–10). In this visionary episode, a messenger from Satan attacks Paul, and Paul seeks the Lord three times to help him. The Lord Jesus essentially says "no" to Paul's request to remove his "stake in the flesh."[29] Instead, Jesus responds to Paul with the revelatory words: "My grace is sufficient for you, for in weakness is my power made complete." Having received this revelation, Paul could now "boast" about his weaknesses so that "the power (δύναμις) of Christ may pitch its tent on me"

(2 Cor 12:9).[30] He continues that he approves of the many hardships he undergoes as a minister of the gospel, for when he is weak, he is powerful. Such encounters show that in nothing Paul falls short of his rival "super-apostles," and that the signs of his apostleship among the Corinthians are evident by the miracles (δυνάμεσιν), signs, and wonders he performs despite his afflictions (12:10–12).

It is clear enough through this context that the revelatory δύναμις spoken by Christ to him relates to the manifestation of miracles Paul is empowered to do as an apostolic messenger. We can probe further about this power to identify it as inclusive of the Holy Spirit.[31] First, later on in the same text, Paul again mentions δύναμις, this time as divine power from which the crucified Christ lives (2 Cor 13:3–4), that is, a resurrecting power that elsewhere he identifies as the Holy Spirit (Rom 8:11; cf. 1:4). Second, Paul had previously told the Corinthians that even though he originally visited them in weakness, that visit turned out to be a demonstration of the Spirit and power manifestations (1 Cor 2:3–5; cf. 2 Cor 6:6). Similarly, to the Thessalonians, he claims that his gospel did not come to them in word only but in power and the Spirit (1 Thess 1:5; cf. also Eph 3:16). As signs and wonders go hand in hand, so does the Spirit and power. Third, in a close parallel with 2 Cor 12:12, our apostle speaks of his accomplishment of proclaiming the gospel to the nations "in power of signs and wonders, in power of God's Spirit . . . " (Rom 15:19). Doubtless, these powers overlap with the Spirit as the agent of miracles and also of Paul's empowerment to proclaim gospel messages that make life-changing impacts on the hearers. Fee makes the claim regarding δύναμις in 2 Cor 12:9–10 that:

> Power is designated as 'the power of Christ' that 'dwells in him,' because it is Christ who had spoken to Paul (v. 9a) and whose gospel is in focus, as 13:3–4 finally make clear. The power dwelling in Paul is the power of the gospel at work in the world for the sake of others. But whenever Paul thinks of that power in terms of its actual effectiveness through his ministry, resulting in the conversion of those who hear his preaching of the gospel, then the power is spoken of in terms of the Spirit.[32]

This revelation of power through weakness Paul associates not only with his hardships but also his ability to do signs and wonders before the Corinthians, a power enabled by the Spirit. We thus find a central conviction of Paul's given to him by revelation from Jesus Messiah that focuses on power associated with the Spirit—whenever Paul is afflicted with suffering and hardships, the manifestation of this power becomes evidence of divine favor.

Similar to Paul, though perhaps not quite as much as him, the Galatians have both suffered and yet experienced the Spirit manifested through signs and wonders (Gal 3:5). For Paul, such occurrences are prime examples that the revelation given to him by Christ extends to other believers as well. This Spirit-power-in-weakness does not reflect observance of Mosaic law but trust in the gospel message that is heard. The revelation of power in weakness means that Paul, and the congregations who imitate him, could expect both hardships and the Spirit's power working miracles in the midst of them (1 Thess 1:6–7; Rom 5:3–5; cf. 1 Cor 2:1–5; 2 Cor 1:3–7; Rom 8:34–38; Acts 13:50–52;14:3–6, 22). All who live godly lives could expect persecution (cf. 2 Tim 3:12), but the Spirit supplies them with what they need to continue their new life based on the gospel, so that their righteousness in Christ would not be in vain.


## THE PROMISE OF THE SPIRIT IN JESUS TRADITION AND IN EZEKIEL 36–37 (GALATIANS 3:6–14)

The Galatians' experience in the Spirit is then linked ("just as": καθώς) to Abraham being righteoused by faith;[33] gentiles like the Galatians who trust are blessed sons and daughters of Abraham (Gal 3:6–9/Gen 15:5–6; cf. 12:1–3). The blessing related to being righteoused then finds further explication with γάρ that opens in 3:10, connecting the previous unit with 3:10–14. Andrew Wakefield, Chee-Chiew Lee, and others highlight the connection between these units through a chiasm that has at the A levels faith involving justification/righteousing (Gal 3:6/Gen 15:6) and reception of the Spirit (Gal 3:14b); at the B levels blessing pertaining to Abrahamic promise (Gal 3:7–9/ Gen 12:3) and fulfillment (Gal 3:14a); at the C levels the threat of curse (Gal 3:10/Deut 27:26) and its removal (Gal 3:13/Deut 21:23); and at the D levels, the center of this chiasm, there is the concept that the righteous by faith shall *live* (Gal 3:11/Hab 2:4) and this is set in juxtaposition with those who *live* by the law (Gal 3:12/Lev 18:5).[34] The latter way of living, for Paul, is unable to bring about righteousness (cf. Gal 2:16; 3:21). The important point in this chiasm is that the concept of living is at the center of this structure. The chiasm also poses "trust" antithetically to the "works of the law." The edges (the A levels) connect righteousness by trust and the blessing of the Spirit together as if virtually synonymous. We can infer that trust brings about a type of life characterized by righteousness and the Spirit. The Galatians are primed to understand that being righteoused is by trust, not by works of the law (2:16), and that this new life is activated both by trusting in Christ and by Christ living in them (2:20). This all takes place by reception of the Spirit that happens when they believed (3:2–3, 5), and their belief makes them children of Abraham (3:6–9) so that "the righteous by faith shall live" *in and through* the Spirit (3:10–14). And Spirit-life culminates with eternal life.

In 3:14 the redemption of Christ has as its outcomes: (1) the Abrahamic blessing of righteousness and inheritance as sons and daughters coming to the gentiles; and (2) both Jews like Paul and gentiles like the Galatians receiving the "promise of the Spirit."[35] The two purpose clauses are two expressions of the same reality. Furthermore, the notion of receiving the Spirit in v. 14 "closes the loop" with 3:2 where Paul first mentions Spirit reception.[36] Galatians 3:14a summarizes 3:6–13, and 3:14b summarizes 3:1–5.[37]

Paul seems to have adopted the language of promise connected with the Spirit from earlier disciples of Jesus who spoke of their awaiting and reception of the Spirit's presence, an oral tradition that originates from the time of Jesus. Martyn rightly affirms this promise in 3:14 as "Christian tradition prior to Paul."[38] I suggest further that it comes from sayings reflected in the Gospels and Acts, especially Luke 24:49, Acts 1:4–5, and 11:16 (cf. Acts 2:33, 38–39; Eph 1:13). This promise of anticipating the reception of the Spirit was remembered as spoken by Jesus (Acts 1:4: τὴν ἐπαγγελίαν τοῦ πατρὸς ἣν ἠκούσατέ μου:), probably repetitively (Acts 11:16: ἐμνήσθην δὲ τοῦ ῥήματος τοῦ κυρίου ὡς ἔλεγεν).[39] That promise is more explicitly unpacked in Acts 1:5 and 11:16b: "John indeed baptized in water, but you shall be baptized in the Holy Spirit."[40] These words do not originate with the Lukan author. They appear in variations in all four Gospels as part of the message of John the Baptist about Jesus baptizing with the Spirit. They thus evince multiple attestation (Matt 3:11; Mark 1:8; Luke 3:16; John 1:33). Likewise, Jesus is remembered to have spoken repeatedly of a special endowment by Spirit that the disciples would eventually receive (Matt 10:20; Mark 13:11; Luke 11:11–13; 12:12; 21:14–15; John 3:3–8; 7:37–39; 14:16–17, 25–26; 15:25–26; 16:13–15; cf. 20:22).[41]

What we seem to have here is a saying that originated from John the Baptist, which Jesus then altered and repeated passing it on to his own disciples who experienced baptism and reception of the Spirit at Pentecost (Acts 2:1–4, 33, 38–39; cf. 1:8; 10:47; 11:16). These disciples then eventually passed it on to Paul, who taught it to the Galatians. That our apostle elsewhere ties in conversion-initiation with being baptized in the Spirit (1 Cor 12:13; cf. 12:3 with Rom 10:9–13) makes us less hesitant about connecting this Jesus tradition with Paul.

Doubtless, Jesus and John also associated the Spirit with the in-breaking of God's kingdom because the Scriptures they learned anticipated this (Isa 44:3; 59:20–21; 61:1; Ezek 36–37; Joel 2:28–32[3:1–5]; Zech 12:10). Paul himself knew how God promised beforehand the gospel related to Jesus and "the Spirit of holiness" through Scripture (Rom 1:1–4).[42] We do not need to decide, then, whether Paul's reception of the promised Spirit was informed by Jesus tradition or Jewish Scripture—both are correct.

Fee suggests that the promise in Gal 3:14 points to prophetic Scriptures like Ezekiel and Jeremiah that are presently being fulfilled by the Spirit.[43] Fee doubtless has in mind texts about the Spirit reviving God's people and living in their heart (Ezek 36–37).[44] This is made more explicit by Paul as he continues in Gal 3:21 and 5:25. In the former verse, he writes that if the law could give life, righteousness would be by the law. The law's inability is implicitly juxtaposed with the Spirit's ability to give life and work righteousness. Such life-giving alludes to Ezekiel 36–37.[45] Paul again seems to allude to Ezekiel when speaking of the Spirit in the hearts of believers (Gal 4:6) and when urging the Galatians to live and walk in the Spirit as ways to resist the flesh (5:16, 24–25; cf. 6:8). The apostle claims that in and through the Spirit (πνεύματι) believers eagerly await the hope for final righteousness to be realized at final judgment (5:5); this is eternal life (6:8). Galatians 5:5 points mostly backward, especially to 2:16–3:14, and in 5:6 the working out of faith in love looks forward to 5:11–6:10 wherein believers are to walk in the Spirit, love their neighbors, and bear each other's burdens. The differentiation between walking and loving gets blurred when Paul informs his auditors that the "fruit of the Spirit" is love (5:22).

To be sure, other prophetic voices about the Spirit might be heard in Galatians,[46] and I suspect that Paul linked together and memorized such texts in an unwritten catena. For brevity's sake, however, we will elaborate only on Ezekiel since notions of the Spirit giving life, dwelling in the heart, and helping believers walk in obedience all seem to be derived from it.

Already in Ezek 11:17–20 there is a promise of the Lord gathering Israelites from their exile among the nations, granting them the land of Israel, removing their stony hearts, and giving them a new heart and new spirit so that they may walk in his commandments and do God's righteous requirements. This way, in good covenantal fashion, God will be their God. Allusions to "walking" and keeping the law so that a person may live, based on Lev 18:4–5 (cf. Gal 3:12), repeat themselves in some of the chapters of Ezekiel (e.g., 20:11, 13, 21; 33:19).[47] Significantly, Lev 18:5 (cf. Gal 3:12) is echoed repeatedly in Ezek 18 where it is said, roughly speaking, that if an impious person were to change his ways and do righteousness, his transgressions will not be remembered but he will surely live and not die (Ezek 18:17, 19, 21, 22, 28). Here the Lord commands what he had previously promised—this time Israel is to make themselves a new heart and new spirit (18:31).[48]

Ezekiel 36–37 anticipates that the era of Israel's restoration will be characterized by the Spirit dwelling in the hearts of God's people. The promise of 11:19 (of a new heart) is once again repeated in 36:26, though now the prophecy adds, "and I will grant my Spirit in you" and the people will "walk" in the Lord's righteous requirements and keep his judgments (36:37; 37:24). Ezekiel is to prophesy to the Spirit that it may come and blow on dead bones, representing all the house of Israel, and they shall live (37:9; cf. vv. 3, 6). The Spirit enters the dead and they rise again and live, with the Lord promising that he will give his Spirit to dwell in them and they will live (37:14). What was affirmed earlier for Israel about living, based on the Leviticus command, in these later chapters takes place by the Spirit and implies a new creation. It seems to recall the original creation's breath of life entering into Adam (Gen 2:7),[49] though now the Spirit revives the dead bones of Israel to live again. Reminiscent also of earlier epochs, God establishes a covenant with God's people, though this time it is called an everlasting covenant of peace, and "David" is their king (37:24–26). Significant is that the result of living (or dying) by keeping (or failing to keep) the commands of Mosaic covenant, echoed from Lev 18:5, is now accomplished by God's Spirit working through the people with an everlasting covenant. Paul seems to interpret this covenant elsewhere as the new covenant, linking the words "new," transformation in the "heart," and "everlasting covenant" with Jeremiah's own use of the same words to speak of the new covenant (Jer 39[32]:40; cf. 38[31]:31–34/2 Cor 3:3–4:7).[50] This anticipated restoration, which Paul would seem to interpret as being fulfilled in the new era through Jews and gentiles who are in Christ (notice Ezek 37:28 for the latter) thus includes a number of promises and blessings.

To be sure, there are tensions in the ways Paul might have interpreted these things as being fulfilled. For Paul, these things appear to include "now" and "not yet" elements with the nations now knowing the Lord and inheriting these blessings through their connection with Abraham. And yet, except for the remnant of believing Messianic followers among Israel (e.g., Rom 11:5–7), Paul still awaited the day when God would gather the rest of the Israelites from the nations to live in their own land and serve God (Ezek 36:24; 37:21, 25). That time would include Joseph (the northern tribes) and Israel (Judah and Benjamin) being reunited (37:15–22: "all the house of Israel": 36:10; 37:11, 21/cf. Rom 11:26–27). Among the most relevant points from Ezekiel in Galatians are that the Spirit lives in and transforms the hearts of gentiles and Jews who trust in Christ (Gal 4:6/Ezek 36:26–27; 37:14), the Spirit gives life (Gal 3:21; 5:25/Ezek 37:5, 6, 10, 14), and the Spirit empowers gentiles and Jews to be able to "walk" in a way that pleases God, fulfilling divine requirements. Paul, however, reconfigures these divine requirements to be foremost about keeping the law of love (Gal 5:14–25; 6:2/Ezek 36:27; cf. 37:24).

## CONCLUSION

This chapter has explored texts related to the Holy Spirit in Galatians with the aim of connecting those texts more firmly with soteriological ideas, especially life and justification/righteousness. It has done so through three core informants for Paul, not only Scripture but also revelation and Jesus traditions. First, Paul communicates that the Galatians can be assured that their own experiences in the Spirit are evidence of their being righteoused by trust instead of works of the law. The combination of Spirit manifestations and suffering that has happened to them point to the power-in-weakness revelation Paul received from the Lord Jesus earlier in his ministry and reflected later in 2 Cor 12:1–10. Second, language about the promised Spirit comes from both Jesus tradition and prophetic discourse. The promise begins with John the Baptist, extends to Jesus, is experienced by his disciples, and then handed down to Paul and the Galatians. That promise was also anticipated in Jewish Scripture through texts such as Ezekiel. For Paul, the righteous by trust shall *live,* inclusive of a new life in the Spirit through which union with Christ is maintained and the hope of righteousness, eternal life, is anticipated.

This chapter supports the Spirit's central and ongoing role in relation to salvific righteousness in Paul. In view of the competing perspectives on Paul, perhaps it is time for another perspective to emerge that refuses to relegate the Holy Spirit merely to a section on ethics or ecclesiology, tucked away toward the back of a theological book.

## NOTES

1. E. P. Sanders, *Paul and Palestinian Judaism: A Comparison of Patterns of the Religion* (Minneapolis: Fortress, 1977), 626. The first listed reference to the Spirit is already related to Paul on 439.

2. Pauline perspectives in recent years that feature the Spirit include Preston Sprinkle, *Paul and Judaism Revisited: A Study of Divine and Human Agency in Salvation* (Downers Grove, IL: IVP Academic, 2013); Kyle Wells, *Grace and Agency in Paul and Second Temple Judaism: Interpreting the Transformation of the Heart* (Leiden: Brill, 2014); Matthew Thiessen, *Paul and the Gentile Problem* (Oxford: Oxford University Press, 2016); Ben C. Blackwell, "The Spirit and Justification in the Pauline Corpus," in *The Spirit Says: Inspiration and Interpretation in Israelite, Jewish, and Early Christian Texts,* ed. Ronald Herms, John R. Levison, and Archie T. Wright, Ekstasis 8 (Berlin: de Gruyter, 2021), 251–70; Ben C. Blackwell, *Participating in the Righteousness of God: Justification in Pauline Theology* (Grand Rapids: Eerdmans, forthcoming). Other works without particular "Paul perspective" agendas (as far as I can determine) who have featured the Spirit in Paul include, e.g., Samuel D. Ferguson, *The Spirit and Relational Anthropology in Paul,* WUNT 2/520 (Tübingen:

Mohr-Siebeck, 2020); Nelida Navaros Cordova, *To Live in the Spirit: Paul and the Spirit of God* (Lanham, MD: Lexington/Fortress, 2019); Volker Rabens, *The Holy Spirit and Ethics in Paul,* WUNT 2/283 (Tübingen: Mohr-Siebeck, 2013); John W. Yates, *The Spirit and Creation in Paul,* WUNT 2/251 (Tübingen: Mohr-Siebeck, 2008). Bucking the trend early on was Gordon D. Fee, *God's Empowering Presence: The Holy Spirit in the Letters of Paul* (Peabody, MA: Hendrickson, 1994).

3. James D. G. Dunn, "A New Perspective on the New Perspective on Paul," *Early Christianity* 4 (2013) 157–82.

4. James D. G. Dunn, "The Gospel according to St. Paul," in *The Blackwell Companion to Paul,* ed. Stephen Westerholm (Chichester: Wiley Blackwell, 2014), 139–53 (148).

5. James D. G. Dunn, *The Theology of the Paul the Apostle* (Grand Rapids: Eerdmans, 1998), 414.

6. By convictions, I mean things that are central or core to one's beliefs about reality and nature; things of which Paul is convinced and takes for granted. After the Damascus experience, one such conviction for him would be that God raised Jesus from the dead. Terence L. Donaldson (*Paul and the Gentiles: Remapping the Apostle's Convictional World* [Minneapolis: Fortress, 1997]), who informs my definition, adds that convictions, "serve as the framework within which new perceptions are understood and as axioms for further knowledge" (299).

7. I concur with Donaldson (*Gentiles,* 263) that Paul's gentile convictions are reconfigured by the impact of his Damascus experience.

8. Finny Philip, *The Origins of Pauline Pneumatology,* WUNT 2/194 (Tübingen: Mohr- Siebeck, 2005), 175.

9. Philip, *Origins,* 203.

10. On Acts as historiography, see Craig S. Keener, *Acts: An Exegetical Commentary* (Grand Rapids: Baker Academic, 2012), 1:90–257.

11. Cf. Stanley E. Porter, *Paul in Acts,* LPS (Peabody, MA: Hendrickson, 2001), 67–97, esp. 72.

12. He claims in 2 Cor 12:2 that it took place fourteen years earlier from the time his writing of 2 Corinthians 10–13 (c. 55–56 CE).

13. On the quotes in Galatians, see A. Andrew Das, "Israel's Scriptures in Galatians," in *Israel's Scriptures in Early Christian Writings: The Use of the Old Testament in the New,* ed. Matthias Henze and David Lincicum (Grand Rapids: Eerdmans, 2023), 388–406; Roy E. Ciampa, "Old Testament in Paul," in *DPL²,* 722–39 (729); E. Earle Ellis, *Paul's Use of the Old Testament* (Eugene, OR: Wipf & Stock, 2003), 152.

14. See Scott A. Swanson, "The Instruction of the Spirit: The Wisdom Framework for Pauline Spirit Dependence," *M-AJT* 29 (2018) 81–128; Andrew K. Boayke, *Death and Life: Resurrection, Restoration, and Rectification in Paul's Letter to the Galatians* (Eugene: Pickwick, 2017); Chee-Chiew Lee, *The Blessing of Abraham, the Spirit, and Justification in Galatians: Their Relationship and Significance for Understanding Paul's Theology* (Eugene: Pickwick, 2013), 95–135; Rodrigo J. Morales, *The Spirit and the Restoration of Israel: New Exodus and New Creation Motifs in Galatians,* WUNT 2/282 (Tübingen: Mohr Siebeck, 2010); Matthew S. Harmon, *She Must and Shall Go Free: Paul's Isaianic Gospel in Galatians,* BZNW 168 (Berlin: de

Gruyter, 2010); G. K. Beale, "The Old Testament Background of Paul's Reference to 'the Fruit of the Spirit' in Galatians 5:22," *BBR* 15 (2005): 1–38; Andrew Wakefield, *Where to Live: The Hermeneutical Significance of Paul's Citations from Scripture in Galatians 3:1–14,* AcBib 14 (Atlanta: SBL Press, 2003); William N. Wilder, *Echoes of the Exodus Narrative in the Context and Background of Galatians 5:18,* StBibLit23 (New York: Peter Lang, 2001); Sylvia C. Keesmat, *Paul and His Story: [Re]Interpreting the Exodus Tradition,* JSNTSup 181 (Sheffield: Sheffield Academic Press, 1999). For an evaluation of a number of such sources, see A. Andrew Das, *Paul and the Stories of Israel: Grand Thematic Narratives in Galatians* (Minneapolis: Fortress, 2016).

15. See B. J. Oropeza, "Quotations, Allusions, and Echoes: Their Meaning in Relation to Biblical Interpretation," in *Practicing Intertextuality: Ancient Jewish and Greco-Roman Exegetical Techniques in the New Testament,* ed. Max J. Lee and B. J. Oropeza (Eugene, OR: Cascade, 2021), 17–26 (esp. 23–24). On Richard Hays's criteria, see his *Echoes of Scripture in the Letters of Paul* (New Haven, CT: Yale University Press, 1989), 29–32.

16. As usual, I use echoes and allusions interchangeably.

17. Cf. C. H. Dodd, *The Apostolic Preaching and Its Developments,* 2nd ed. (London: Hodder and Stoughton, 1964), 16. Special thanks to Roy Ciampa for helping me find the source.

18. See further, Ronald D. Witherup, *Scripture and Tradition in the Letters of Paul,* BSCBA 4 (New York: Paulist, 2021), 92–101; Michael B. Thompson, "Paul and Jesus," in *OHPS,* 389–405 (esp. 394–97).

19. See further, Michael B. Thompson, *Clothed with Christ: The Example and Teachings of Jesus in Romans 12.1–15.13,* JSNTSup 59 (Cambridge: Cambridge University Press, 1991), 30–36, 70–76.

20. Rightly, Blackwell, "Spirit and Justification," 259.

21. For more potential juxtapositions in these verses, see Ben C. Blackwell, "The Holy Spirit, Justification, and Participation in the Divine Life in Galatians," in *Cruciform Scripture: Cross, Participation, and Mission,* ed. Christopher W. Skinner, Nijay K. Gupta, Andy Johnson, Drew J. Strait (Grand Rapids: Eerdmans, 2021), 123–43 (130).

22. Cf. Michael J. Gorman, *Inhabiting the Cruciform God: Kenosis, Justification, and Theosis in Paul's Narrative Soteriology* (Grand Rapids: Eerdmans, 2009), 65; Michael J. Gorman, *Participation in Christ: Explorations in Paul's Theology and Spirituality* (Grand Rapids: Baker Academic, 2019), 96–149; Scott Shauf, "Galatians 2:20 in Context," *NTS* 52 (2006): 86–101 (98–101).

23. Cf. Fee, *God's Empowering Presence,* 374.

24. See B. J. Oropeza, *The Gospel according Paul* (Grand Rapids: Eerdmans, forthcoming).

25. So Fee, *God's Empowering Presence,* 383.

26. I am in agreement with the many scholars who claim that the Galatian congregations are mostly if not fully made up of gentiles.

27. Gordon D. Fee, *Galatians,* PCS (Blandford Forum: Deo, 2007), 110.

28. Likewise, in other Hellenistic sources this sense's predominance is evidenced in BrillDAG, *s.v.*

29. On the meaning, see David M. Park, "Paul's ΣΚΟΛΟΨ ΤΗ ΣΑΡΚΙ: Thorn or Stake? (2 Cor. XII 7)," *NovT* 22 (1980): 179–83; B. J. Oropeza, *Exploring Second Corinthians: Death and Life, Hardship and Rivalry,* RRA 3 (Atlanta: SBL Press, 2016), 660–75.

30. The Lord's power, in essence, "tabernacles" (ἐπισκηνόω) over Paul, a metaphor that perhaps alludes to the glory Presence of God (cf. ἐπὶ τῆς σκηνῆς: Num 9:19). If so, that Presence for Paul does not exclude the Spirit: see 1 Cor 10:2; cf. Num 11:16–25; Ps 105[106]:32–33; Isa 63:7–14.

31. In agreement with Margaret E. Thrall, *2 Corinthians,* ICC (London: T. & T. Clark, 2000), 2:825; Scott J. Hafemann, *2 Corinthians,* NIVAppC (Grand Rapids: Zondervan, 2000), 465.

32. Fee, *God's Empowering Presence,* 353.

33. The connection may point immediately to 3:5, as Blackwell, "Holy Spirit," 133: "God supplies them with the Spirit by faith, *just as* Abraham was justified by faith." Or, it can reach back to 3:2 starting with the Galatian's reception of the Spirit by faith (3:2), which is then supplemented with their starting in the Spirit (3:3) and being supplied with the Spirit (3:5).

34. Wakefield, *Where to Live,* 130–45; Lee, *Blessing of Abraham,* 32. For another example, see A. Andrew Das, *Paul and the Jews*, Library of Pauline Studies (Peabody, MA: Hendrickson, 2003), 123.

35. Epexegetical genitive.

36. Rightly, David A. deSilva, *Galatians,* NICNT (Grand Rapids: Eerdmans, 2018), 302.

37. Cf. J. Louis Martyn, *Galatians,* AB (Garden City, NJ: Doubleday, 1997), 323.

38. Martyn, *Galatians,* 323.

39. Keener, *Acts,* 1:679, supports this reading with the imperfect ἔλεγεν, though admitting debate.

40. Acts 1:5 uses a ὅτι *recitativum,* used for quotes and sayings: cf. Luke 2:23; 1 Cor 14:21; BDF §470.1.

41. Keener, *Acts,* 1:678 would add to this list Jesus's own future presence with the disciples that presumably comes through the Spirit: Matt 18:20; 28:20; John 14:16–26.

42. Notice ἐπαγγελία in Gal 3:14 and προεπαγγέλλω in Rom 1:2.

43. Fee, *God's Empowering Presence,* 394–95.

44. Perhaps by extension Paul's interpretation includes the new covenant law of Jer 31[38LXX] living in the heart that he connects via something like *gezerah shawah* with the eternal covenant of Ezek 36–37 so as to link the Spirit with the new covenant (cf. 2 Cor 3:3–18).

45. Fee, *God's Empowering Presence,* 398: the new covenant of Ezek 36–37 giving life "almost certainly stands behind the language of v. 21."

46. E.g., as James Dunn, *Romans,* WBC (Waco: Word, 1988), 1:418, affirms, "The association of Spirit and life is, of course, deeply rooted in Jewish thought of man's dependence for the breath/spirit of life wholly on the Creator (e.g., Gen 6:17; Ps 104:29–30; Ezek 37:5; Tob 3:6; 2 Macc 7:23). The link is equally fundamental to the

earliest Christian theology, particularly of Paul and John (Rom 8:2, 6, 10, 11, 13; 1 Cor 15:45; 2 Cor 3:6; Gal 6:8; John 4:10, 14; 6:63; 7:38–39; 20:22)."

47. See Preston Sprinkle, "Law and Life: Leviticus 18.5 in the Literary Framework of Ezekiel," *JSOT* 31 (2007): 275–293; Preston Sprinkle, *Law and Life: The Interpretation of Leviticus 18:5 in Early Judaism and in Paul*, WUNT 2/241 (Tübingen: Mohr-Siebeck, 2008), 165–90. In relation to the Spirit, that "life" involves both the present (Gal 5:25) and future (eternal life: 6:8): cf. Blackwell, "Holy Spirit," 136.

48. The MT includes in 18:32 the command to "turn and live" (וְהָשִׁיבוּ וִחְיוּ).

49. See Yates, *Spirit and Creation*, esp. 32. For Yates, Ezekiel may be considered "the prophet of the spirit"; the term רוח appears in it fifty-two times. Also see Philip, *Pauline Pneumatology*, 36.

50. On these connections, see further, B. J. Oropeza, "New Covenant Knowledge in an Earthenware Jar: Intertextual Reconfigurations of Jeremiah in 2 Corinthians 1:21–22, 3:2–11, and 4:7," *BBR* 28 (2018): 405–24.

# BIBLIOGRAPHY

Beale, G. K. "The Old Testament Background of Paul's Reference to 'the Fruit of the Spirit' in Galatians 5:22." *BBR* 15 (2005): 1–38.

Blackwell, Ben C. "The Holy Spirit, Justification, and Participation in the Divine Life in Galatians." In *Cruciform Scripture: Cross, Participation, and Mission*, edited by Christopher W. Skinner, Nijay K. Gupta, Andy Johnson, Drew J. Strait, 123–43. Grand Rapids: Eerdmans, 2021.

———. *Participating in the Righteousness of God: Justification in Pauline Theology.* Grand Rapids: Eerdmans, forthcoming.

———. "The Spirit and Justification in the Pauline Corpus." In *The Spirit Says: Inspiration and Interpretation in Israelite, Jewish, and Early Christian Texts*, edited by Ronald Herms, John R. Levison, and Archie T. Wright, 251–70. Ekstasis 8. Berlin: de Gruyter, 2021.

Boayke, Andrew K. *Death and Life: Resurrection, Restoration, and Rectification in Paul's Letter to the Galatians.* Eugene: Pickwick, 2017.

Ciampa, Roy E. "Old Testament in Paul." In *DPL²*, 722–39.

Cordova, Nelida Navaros. *To Live in the Spirit: Paul and the Spirit of God.* Lanham, MD: Lexington/Fortress, 2019.

Das, A. Andrew. "Israel's Scriptures in Galatians." In *Israel's Scriptures in Early Christian Writings: The Use of the Old Testament in the New*, edited by Matthias Henze and David Lincicum, 388–406. Grand Rapids: Eerdmans, 2023.

———. *Paul and the Stories of Israel: Grand Thematic Narratives in Galatians.* Minneapolis: Fortress, 2016.

Donaldson, Terence L. *Paul and the Gentiles: Remapping the Apostle's Convictional World.* Minneapolis: Fortress, 1997.

Dunn, James D. G. "The Gospel according to St. Paul." In *The Blackwell Companion to Paul*, edited by Stephen Westerholm, 139–53. Chichester: Wiley Blackwell, 2014.

———. "A New Perspective on the New Perspective on Paul." *Early Christianity* 4 (2013): 157–82.

Ellis, E. Earle. *Paul's Use of the Old Testament.* Reprint. Eugene, OR: Wipf & Stock, 2003.

Fee, Gordon D. *Galatians,* PCS. Blandford Forum: Deo, 2007.

———. *God's Empowering Presence: The Holy Spirit in the Letters of Paul.* Peabody, MA: Hendrikson, 1994.

Ferguson, Samuel D. *The Spirit and Relational Anthropology in Paul.* WUNT 2/520. Tübingen: Mohr Siebeck, 2020.

Gorman, Michael J. *Inhabiting the Cruciform God: Kenosis, Justification, and Theosis in Paul's Narrative Soteriology.* Grand Rapids: Eerdmans, 2009.

———. *Participation in Christ: Explorations in Paul's Theology and Spirituality.* Grand Rapids: Baker Academic, 2019.

Hafemann, Scott J. *2 Corinthians.* NIVAppC. Grand Rapids: Zondervan, 2000.

Harmon, Matthew S. *She Must and Shall Go Free: Paul's Isaianic Gospel in Galatians.* BZNW 168. Berlin: de Gruyter, 2010.

Hays, Richard B. *Echoes of Scripture in the Letters of Paul.* New Haven, CT: Yale University Press, 1989.

Keener, Craig S. *Acts: An Exegetical Commentary.* Vol. 1. Grand Rapids: Baker Academic, 2012.

Keesmat, Sylvia C. *Paul and His Story: [Re]Interpreting the Exodus Tradition.* JSNTSup 181. Sheffield: Sheffield Academic Press, 1999.

Lee, Chee-Chiew. *The Blessing of Abraham, the Spirit, and Justification in Galatians: Their Relationship and Significance for Understanding Paul's Theology.* Eugene, OR: Pickwick, 2013.

Morales, Rodrigo J. *The Spirit and the Restoration of Israel: New Exodus and New Creation Motifs in Galatians.* WUNT 2/282. Tübingen: Mohr Siebeck, 2010.

Oropeza, B. J. *The Gospel according Paul.* Grand Rapids: Eerdmans, forthcoming.

———. "New Covenant Knowledge in an Earthenware Jar: Intertextual Reconfigurations of Jeremiah in 2 Corinthians 1:21–22, 3:2–11, and 4:7." *BBR* 28 (2018): 405–24.

———. "Quotations, Allusions, and Echoes: Their Meaning in Relation to Biblical Interpretation." In *Practicing Intertextuality: Ancient Jewish and Greco-Roman Exegetical Techniques in the New Testament*, edited by Max J. Lee and B. J. Oropeza, 17–26. Eugene: Cascade, 2021.

Philip, Finny. *The Origins of Pauline Pneumatology.* WUNT 2/194. Tübingen: Mohr Siebeck, 2005.

Porter, Stanley E. *Paul in Acts.* LPS. Peabody: Hendrickson, 2001.

Rabens, Volker. *The Holy Spirit and Ethics in Paul.* WUNT 2/283. Tübingen: Mohr Siebeck, 2013.

Sanders, E. P. *Paul and Palestinian Judaism: A Comparison of Patterns of the Religion.* Minneapolis: Fortress, 1977.

Shauf, Scott. "Galatians 2:20 in Context." *NTS* 52 (2006): 86–101.

Sprinkle, Preston. *Law and Life: The Interpretation of Leviticus 18:5 in Early Judaism and in Paul.* WUNT2/241. Tübingen: Mohr Siebeck, 2008.

———. "Law and Life: Leviticus 18.5 in the Literary Framework of Ezekiel." *JSOT* 31 (2007): 275–93.

———. *Paul and Judaism Revisited: A Study of Divine and Human Agency in Salvation.* Downers Grove, IL: IVP Academic, 2013.

Swanson, Scott A. "The Instruction of the Spirit: The Wisdom Framework for Pauline Spirit Dependence." *M-AJT* 29 (2018): 81–128.

Thiessen, Matthew. *Paul and the Gentile Problem.* Oxford: Oxford University Press, 2016.

Thompson, Michael B. *Clothed with Christ: The Example and Teachings of Jesus in Romans 12.1–15.13,* JSNTSup 59 Cambridge: Cambridge University Press, 1991.

———. "Paul and Jesus." In *OHPS,* 389–405.

Thrall, Margaret E. *2 Corinthians,* ICC. London: T. & T. Clark, 2000.

Wakefield, Andrew. *Where to Live: The Hermeneutical Significance of Paul's Citations from Scripture in Galatians 3:1–14.* AcBib 14. Atlanta: SBL Press, 2003.

Wells, Kyle. *Grace and Agency in Paul and Second Temple Judaism: Interpreting the Transformation of the Heart.* Leiden: Brill, 2014.

Wilder, William N. *Echoes of the Exodus Narrative in the Context and Background of Galatians 5:18.* Studies in Biblical Literature 23. New York: Peter Lang, 2001.

Witherup, Ronald D. *Scripture and Tradition in the Letters of Paul.* BSCBA 4. New York: Paulist, 2021.

Yates, John W. *The Spirit and Creation in Paul.* WUNT 2/251. Tübingen: Mohr Siebeck, 2008.

*Chapter 4*

# Cursed by Law-Breaking, Blessed in Abraham (Galatians 3:8–14)

## Craig S. Keener

In Gal 3:8–14, Paul ingeniously links multiple texts based on shared (or some-times contrasting) key terms. He links Gen 15:6 with 12:3/18:18 and with Hab 2:4, contrasts Gen 12:3/18:18 with Deut 27:26, links Deut 27:26 with Lev 18:5 and Deut 21:23, and contrasts Lev 18:5 with Hab 2:4. Paul begins and ends with blessing in Abraham; he sandwiches between them discussion of the curse. The curse is for lawbreakers, but Jesus experienced his people's curse in their place on the tree. The present experience of the promised bless-ing of Abraham, inheriting the coming world, is experienced through the Spirit (3:5, 14), available to all the families of the earth blessed in Abraham. For the sake of space, I focus especially on Paul's argument in 3:8–13.[1]

### THE STRUCTURE OF PAUL'S ARGUMENT IN 3:6–14

Paul links verses in 3:6–13 based on common key terms or elements.[2] (For simplicity only overt conspicuous quotations are included, see table 4.1.)

Although proposed chiastic structures are typically too asymmetric to con-vince, a basic chiastic structure might dominate here:[3]

A     Blessed are the Gentiles in Abraham (3:8–9)

     B     Cursed are those who disobey the law (3:10)

        C     Shall live by faith (3:11)

        C'     Shall live by works of the law (3:12)

     B'     Cursed is the one hanged on a tree (3:13)

A'     Blessed are the Gentiles in Abraham (3:14)

**Table 4.1. Paul's Intertextual Linking Based on Key Terms/Themes in Gal 3:6–13**

| Set 1: OT Text (Gal Text) | Set 2: OT Text (Gal Text) | Key Term/Theme |
|---|---|---|
| Gen 15:6 (Gal 3:6) | Gen 12:3 (Gal 3:8) | Linking God's promises of blessing for Abraham (reckoned righteousness being the chief blessing) |
| Gen 15:6 (Gal 3:6) | Hab 2:4 (Gal 3:11) | Linking righteousness with faith |
| Gen 12:3 (Gal 3:8) | Deut 27:26 (Gal 3:10) | Linking Abraham's blessing (and, in an unquoted line of Gen 12:3, the curse for his enemies) with the curse of the law |
| Deut 27:26 (Gal 3:10) | Lev 18:5 (Gal 3:12) | Linking those who do not (lit.) "do these things" (works of the law) with those who do "do these things" |
| Deut 27:26 (Gal 3:10) | Deut 21:23 (Gal 3:13) | Linking curses in Deuteronomy (cursed is everybody who) |
| Hab 2:4 (Gal 3:11) | Lev 18:5 (Gal 3:12) | Linking, "that one will live" |

Although it sacrifices some symmetry, a further level of framing is also probable: receiving the Spirit by faith (3:2–5, 14b).[4]

Paul's argument based on Abraham seems to be on exegetical ground first initiated by his rivals, who find the association of the covenant with circumcision (Gen 17:9–14) congenial for their purposes. Indeed, most of Paul's texts in this section, especially Lev 18:5 and Deut 27:26, seem so counterintuitive that most scholars believe that Paul is probably responding to his opponents' use of them.[5]

Five of six quotations Paul offers here are from the Pentateuch, establishing the foundational character of his claim; the other texts, however, are subsidiary to Gen 15:6,[6] the first passage he quotes, which is earlier and more foundational in his canon and in salvation history than most of the others.

## FROM BLESSING TO CURSING

In Gal 3:8 Paul quotes from Gen 12:3/18:18, declaring that "all the nations of the earth shall be blessed in" Abraham.[7] In 3:9, Paul explains that the reason gentiles can be blessed in Abraham (3:8) is because they follow his model of faith. Abraham was reckoned righteous and blessed by faith, so those who are also of faith are the ones who are blessed with him.

Subverting expectations and undoubtedly shocking his audiences, Paul in 3:10 reverses traditional expectations.[8] Whereas Jewish people understood from Scripture that they were blessed and those who walked as gentiles were cursed, Paul argues from Scripture that some gentiles are blessed (Gal 3:8, citing Gen 12:3) and that those under the law (or under the law in the wrong way) are cursed (3:10, citing Deut 27:26). Likewise, whereas "the faith people" (lit., those who were "of faith," in 3:9) are Abraham's children, "the law-works people" (those who are "of works with respect to the law") "stand under a curse" (3:10).

This apparent antithesis between faith and works may be Paul's innovation,[9] needed to address his rivals' insistence on *law-works* already suggested in 3:2, 5, and prefigured in 2:16.[10] "Obeying" or "doing" what the law commands in 3:10 and 12 is equated with *law-works* in the first clause of 3:10.[11] Nevertheless, Paul's antithesis between faith and works makes sense if his point is the antithesis between dependence on God (such as Abraham modeled) and dependence on anything else.

In the other presumed antithesis: Abraham and his allies being blessed, on one hand, and, on the other, his adversaries being cursed, reflects Gen 12:3 (with Israel taking the place of Abraham in Gen 27:29; Num 22:6; 24:9). Paul has already cited part of Gen 12:3 in Gal 3:7. Gen 12:3 promises all the families of the earth blessing in Abraham, suggesting that at least some from all nations will be blessed with him.[12] This passage speaks, however, of curses as well as blessings, inviting Paul to invoke another text to specify to whom such curses apply, which belongs to a larger context contrasting blessings and curses (Deut 28:2–8, 12, 15–20, 45; 30:1).

Paul introduces Deuteronomy 27:26 with a Scripture citation formula familiar in Paul[13] and more generally.[14] Paul can introduce Deut 27:26 precisely because he assumes an implicit *gezerah shevah*, an implicit connection with the not-directly-quoted, yet assumed, remainder of Gen 12:3, a well-enough known text right at the beginning of the Abraham account. This verse is, again, the key text from which Paul has just quoted in Gal 3:8; it addresses curses as well as blessings. Jewish interpretive traditions naturally linked the more developed blessings and curses of Deuteronomy with Abraham's blessing.[15] Whereas Paul's opponents may have linked law-works with Deuteronomy's blessings, Paul appeals to the same context for the curses. These curses apply to those under the law (a hermeneutical principle Paul later invokes in Rom 3:19) who fail to keep it.[16] Paul's introduction of curse in 3:10 in contrast with blessing in 3:8, therefore, is anything but arbitrary.[17]

That those who believe, like Abraham, are blessed with him makes sense; for those who are of law-works to be cursed, however, takes for granted that those who claim to be law-workers are *not* of faith. This assumption in turn sheds light on what Paul means by law-workers (another phrase perhaps borrowed from his opponents): not simply trying to keep the law, but trying to keep it without faith. Surely, one might object, nearly all law-keepers believe in God? But by Paul's apparent definition, they do not depend on God's grace, now revealed in his saving gift in Christ. Works of law cannot justify (2:16), nor were they meant to (2:21; 3:21); what matters for being put right with God is *Christ*-faith (2:16). Paul later clarifies that one can approach the law either with faith (rightly) or (wrongly) on the basis of one's (inadequate) works (Rom 3:27; 9:31–32), rightly from God's Spirit or wrongly from mere flesh (Rom 8:2).

Although few Jews in Paul's day violated any of the specific prescriptions in Deut 27:15–25, Paul's wording borrows from Deuteronomic passages that are more encompassing.[18] Many Jews presumably violated some of Deuteronomy's most fundamental commandments (e.g., the prohibition of coveting in Deut 5:21; cf. Rom 7:7), even in Deuteronomy's day (5:29). More importantly, this entire section of Deuteronomy warns of Israel's apostasy and their being scattered because of the curses (28:63–65, 68), as well as pre-dicting their ultimate turning back to God (Deut 30:1–10; this is a belief that Paul also shares in Rom 11:25–27).[19] Some interpreters contend that Paul's Jewish contemporaries in fact understood themselves as experiencing even the continuing curse of exile.[20] Although this premise is debated, it is difficult to deny that most[21] Jewish thinkers did at least anticipate an eschatological regathering of the scattered tribes,[22] which indicates the belief that *some* tribes remained scattered at this time.[23] (Paul was not of course obligated to understand texts about judgments only the ways that his contemporaries did).

This larger context in Deuteronomy includes another passage or two from which Paul takes the words *written in the book of*, Deut 28:58 and/or 29:20–21 (LXX 29:19–20), both of which refer to curses for disobedience.[24] The former was a familiar passage[25] possibly made all the more familiar to Paul if it was recited during his synagogue beatings (2 Cor 11:24), as some-what later Jewish tradition could suggest.[26] Paul's quotations in Gal 3:10, 12, highlight adherence to the law's many individual stipulations rather than rejecting appreciation for the law as a whole or what we might call the spirit of the law.[27]

Scholars often suggest, probably rightly, that Paul here reframes his oppo-nents' proof-texts. This reframing is likely both because Paul nowhere else uses this terminology for *curse*[28] and because the usual face value reading of Deut 27:26 would support his opponents' emphasis on keeping the law.[29] Paul's rivals may have emphasized "observing" (lit., *doing*) the law in Deut 27:26 (for "doing" the law, see also, e.g., Exod 18:20; Lev 19:37; Deut 29:29), but Paul emphasizes the word "all": one must do all the works of the law (see 5:3).[30] Although "all" is merely implicit in the Hebrew text of this verse, it is explicit in the standard Greek rendering Paul shared with his audi-ence. More importantly, "all" appears in some other passages in this section of Deuteronomy, some of the other wording of which Paul incorporates into his citation.[31] In Deut 28:58 and its context, curses would come on Israel "if you do not diligently observe all the words of this law."

## BREAKING THE LAW

Although many scholars doubt that Paul's argument here presupposes the impossibility of keeping the law,[32] a probably larger number of scholars maintain, I believe correctly, the more traditional view that Paul presupposes here that no one perfectly keeps the law.[33] The question here is not what most Jews believed—though most Jews did believe that virtually everyone sinned—but whether *Paul* believed that no one kept it adequately (or whether any human action could be adequate of itself) to *merit* God's favor. As for keeping all the law, Paul was well aware that not every prescription of the Torah could be or was kept in the Diaspora; certainly, few Diaspora Jews would make a pilgrimage to Jerusalem three times a year (Exod 23:17; 34:23–24; Deut 16:16).

At the very least, those under the law remain under the *threat* of a curse due to nonfulfillment. Whether or not Paul regarded perfect observance as impossible in principle, he at least warns his audience not to place themselves in the position of having to find out (cf. 5:3). Many Jews would have assumed that provisions in the law for atonement resolved the sins they did commit.[34] Paul, however, finds atonement now elsewhere (Gal 1:4; Rom 3:25; 8:3). Moreover, and in the ultimate analysis, the law was never intended for justification anyway (2:21; 3:21).[35]

Critics cannot reasonably object that, because such a premise is not explicit, Paul does not assume it. Paul and other ancient writers often used enthymemes, syllogisms with an obvious minor premise suppressed rather than explicitly stated.[36] Rabbis also often compressed their argumentation by simply assuming premises that their biblically literate peers shared.[37] Today, relevance theory amply illustrates that even in ordinary communication many assumptions are taken for granted and therefore not explicitly stated.

Paul here probably thus assumes a premise that he elsewhere clearly states, namely, that no one keeps all the law[38]—or, relevantly here, at least that the people of the law, Israel, *had* not done so. This premise needed little argument (though Paul dutifully supplies argumentation in Rom 1:18–3:21) precisely because Jewish tradition already understood that everyone sinned.[39] Paul can also take for granted that his fellow Jewish believers, including Peter, recognize that there is no justification apart from Christ (Gal 2:16). Some of Paul's assumed premises may have been evident to the Galatians also from his earlier preaching to them.[40]

Not only so, but Paul may well read even his main specific texts (Deut 27:26 and Lev 18:5) in light of their development in the prophetic tradition, which regularly charged Israel for their failure to keep the law's precepts. The warning in Jer 11:3 recalls Deut 27:26;[41] Ezekiel 20 uses Lev 18:5 to show Israel's historic apostasy.[42] In such passages, Israel's apostasy from the law justifies God's judgment on them.[43] Because Paul reads Lev 18:5 "through the lens of Ezekiel," Sigurd Grindheim notes, it now "has associations, not of life, but of forfeited life, and, consequently, death."[44] More generally, various Second Temple Jewish texts lamented Israel's continuing failure.[45]

Curses were meant to divinely enforce laws that could not be fully enforced humanly. Paul's opponents probably warned the Galatians that whoever broke the laws would experience the covenant curse; they should therefore keep the law. Paul, however, turns the warning back on the Galatians: by accepting circumcision, they would obligate themselves to the entire law (5:3), which they would not perfectly observe, and they would thereby incur the curse. Yet, contrary to what Paul's opponents may have been saying, the law's curse applied only to those under the law,[46] whereas, Paul says, believing gentiles are already blessed in Abraham (3:7–8).

Paul may also here imply that his opponents in particular were, despite their pretense (cf. 2:13), law-breaking apostates who merited the law's curse (cf. 1:7–9). Paul clearly believed that his opponents did not keep all the law (Gal 6:13), and some interpreters contend that his words about lawbreakers in this verse apply especially to his opponents.[47]

## RIGHTED BY FAITH IN GALATIANS 3:11

Paul already affirmed in 2:16 (based on Ps 143) that no one will be righted with God by the (works of) the law; now he argues it based on the alternative in Hab 2:4.[48] Although Paul probably borrowed his citation in Gal 3:10 (Deut 27:26) from his opponents, the case is less clear for his citation of Hab 2:4 in Gal 3:11. If Paul's opponents did employ it, however, they presumably would have expected it to support their position. Non-Christian Judean sources generally applied it to human faithfulness to the Torah.[49] Nevertheless, Paul's application to trusting God in the face of judgment may come closer to Habakkuk's meaning (cf. Hab 3:17–18).[50] Faith rather than the law was the basis for the original covenant.[51]

Arguing against opponents who valued different traditional Jewish inter-pretations, Paul uses to his advantage the Jewish exegetical techniques he had absorbed in his past training (cf. 1:14; Acts 22:3). As already noted, ancient interpreters often linked passages that used shared vocabulary or themes. Paul knew Scripture so well that he readily linked with Gen 15:6 (cited in Gal 3:6) the one other passage that explicitly and relevantly linked righteousness with faith: Hab 2:4.[52] Indeed, some scholars argue plausibly that the lexical connections between the two OT passages may even suggest that Hab 2:4 deliberately echoes Gen 15:6.[53] This passage may supply the template for Paul's language "from faith" (ἐκ πιστεως, as in the Greek text of Gal 2:16; 3:2, 5, 7, 8, 9, 11, 12, 22, 24; 5:5); in Romans, designed with greater forethought, Paul quotes Hab 2:4 before reusing the phrase (Rom 1:17; 3:26, 30; 4:16; 5:1; 9:30, 32; 10:6; 14:23).[54]

## LIFE BY FAITH IN GALATIANS 3:11

As with 3:10 and sometimes 3:11, interpreters often contend that Paul borrowed Lev 18:5 (in Gal 3:12) from his opponents' textual arsenal.[55] This contention is probably correct,[56] but Paul has prepared for it with matching texts that make this citation an obvious choice here. It contains ποιέω (*poieō*) and αὐτα (*auta*; plus ἐν, *en*) like Deut 27:26 (Gal 3:10), and ζησεται (*zēsetai*) like Hab 2:4 (Gal 3:11).[57] Thus Paul can use "Lev 18:5 as the (positive) summary of the latter part of Deut 27:26" as well as the antithesis of Hab 2:4.[58]

Early Jewish sources associate the Torah with life.[59] Although biblical promises of living if one obeyed the Torah (Lev 18:5; Deut 30:6, 19) referred to long life on the land (Deut 4:1, 40; 5:33; 8:1; 30:16, 19–20),[60] it was natural to extrapolate from them (as some later rabbis did), by means of *qal vahomer*,[61] an application to the world to come,[62] as scholars often note.[63] Scripture already promised eschatological resurrection life through the Spirit, a corporate event associated with the restoration of God's people (Ezek 37:6, 14).[64] That is, if life on the promised land depended on obeying the covenant, why should life in the world to come be any different? Qumran's Damascus Document applies Lev 18:5 to eternal life;[65] probably Ps. Sol. 14.1–2, 4 Ezra 7.21, and Luke 10:25, 28 do the same.

Given the failings of human obedience, Paul much prefers—as more practical than this approach to Lev 18:5—the approach of Hab 2:4, already cited in Gal 3:11. For Paul, the life he is discussing here is "eternal life" (cf. Gal 6:8).

Jesus also associated keeping the commandments with eternal life (Mark 10:17, 19, followed by Matthew and Luke), a point probably known to Paul's opponents. Yet even before Jesus's interlocutor professed obedience to all these commandments (10:20), Jesus warned that only God was truly good (10:18)—in Pauline language, all are sinners. Both there (10:21) and for Paul, Jesus himself is the *sine qua non* of eternal life (Gal 2:16; 3:22).

## LEVITICUS 18:5 IN GALATIANS 3:12

In good scribal (and early Christian) fashion, Paul responds to Scripture with Scripture. Despite some significant differences between the contexts of Rom 10:5 and Gal 3:12, they offer similar lines of argument. In one case Paul uses Deut 30 to qualify the possible meaning of Lev 10:5 (Rom 10:5–8), whereas here Paul uses Hab 2:4 to qualify it.[66] Laying texts against each other, using the second to qualify the meaning of the first, was a common midrashic method.

As one received a curse for breaking the law (Deut 27:26 in Gal 3:10), one would receive life for keeping it (Lev 18:5 in Gal 3:12)[67]—assuming that one could. Paul quotes Lev 18:5 only now that he has already made Hab 2:4 a more foundational text that, on his antithetical line of argument, rules it out in practice.[68] He might also respond to his opponents' misapplication of Lev 18:5 rather than to its actual meaning.[69] In any case, Paul's antithesis is surely deliberate.

Paul again links (and in this case contrasts) texts by common key words: one could live by faith (Gal 3:11) or one could live by doing the law (3:12).[70] Paul probably continues to assume as common knowledge that no one perfectly observes the law. Although (as noted) Paul would argue that no one keeps all the law, his main point is that mere adherence to the law in terms of obeying its precepts "is not based on faith."[71]

Although the antithesis between faith and law-works may not seem explicit on the surface, Paul can make use of a well-known principle in contemporary forensic rhetoric, that of *leges contrariae*, typically used for playing one law off against another.[72] That "the law is not based on faith" (3:12a) rules it out as a means of salvation in light of the righteous living by faith (3:11), underlining the reality that justification is not the purpose of the law (2:21; 3:21).[73]

Jewish interpreters often cited one text against another, sometimes citing a third text to break the tie.[74] As some second-century rabbis opined, "Two passages which contradict each other [cannot be reconciled] unless a third passage comes and decides between them."[75] Gentiles also sometimes cited one authoritative text against another proposed by someone else,[76] particularly in (as often with the rabbis) legal argumentation.[77]

The context of Lev 18:5 is avoiding the practices of the gentiles (Lev 18:3, 24), keeping God's practices instead (18:4). Any transgressor would be cut off from the covenant and from God's people (18:29). Paul himself certainly insisted on this minimal standard of morality for God-fearing gentiles (Gal 5:19–20; 1 Cor 5:1; 6:9–20). But Lev 18:5 speaks more generally of "my statutes and ordinances," a phrase that ultimately encompasses all the law (Lev 18:4–5, 26; 19:37; 20:22; 25:18; 26:15, 43, 46). Paul is thus presumably applying it to "everything written in the book of the law" (Gal 3:10), hence, for example, the NRSV's translation of "these things" as "the works of the law" (also NET).

Lev 18:5 continued to have a life in subsequent Scripture and early Judaism;[78] indeed, its very familiarity may be one reason that Paul can cite it without any introductory formula (such as "as it is written" in 3:10).[79] Nehemiah refers to this passage as he confesses Israel's sin (Neh 9:29).[80] Ezekiel recycles it in the context of Israel's disobedience and consequent impending judgment (Ezek 20:11, 13, 21).[81] The Dead Sea Scrolls also place the promise (CD 3.16) in the context of Israel's disobedience (CD 3.11–12, 14)[82] but offer hope for the righteous priestly community (3.18–4.1); Psalms of Solomon 14 similarly condemns violators of Lev 18:5.[83] As David deSilva notes, "Israel's collective experience down to the time of Paul (and all the more in the decades after!) is a testimony to the Sinaitic covenant essentially ensuring a fairly consistent state of 'curse' for Israel."[84] Subjected to other peoples time and again, Israel rarely experienced the promised blessings of the covenant.[85]

Abraham's descendants should be blessed (3:8–9), but the law has introduced for them the possibility (realized repeatedly in Israel's history) of a curse. Yet the law cannot annul the earlier and more foundational promise to and through Abraham (3:17–18). Thus, Christ has endured the curse for those united with him (3:13), and Abraham's spiritual descendants are blessed in Abraham and his seed, especially Christ (3:16, 29).

## CHRIST CURSED FOR US IN GALATIANS 3:13

In Gal 3:13, Paul returns to the thought of 3:10.[86] Again linking texts by shared terminology, Paul offers a second "curse" text from Deuteronomy: if the sufferings ascribed to curses in Deuteronomy 27 represent judgments, then the same could be understood of Jesus's suffering of crucifixion, since it is also a cursed state in Deuteronomy. Paul slightly changes the Greek wording of Deut 21:23 to match the *cursed* in Deut 27:26 (cited in Gal 3:10), to make the connection easier to catch.[87]

In Deuteronomy, what was hanged was the corpse, adding posthumous shame to the execution.[88] Later, however, some peoples would hang a person to death on a stake, a custom adopted widely by Rome. Even one noted Jewish ruler hanged his enemies alive,[89] and some Jewish interpreters viewed this action in light of Deut 21:23.[90] Paul was certainly thus not the first author to apply Deut 21:23 to crucifixion. The Qumran sectarians deemed the biblical punishment appropriate for capital crimes even while the condemned person remained alive.[91] By changing the word sequence in Deut 21, they also clearly applied the text to hanging before rather than after death.[92]

Jews would not think someone necessarily cursed by God simply because he was crucified by Romans.[93] This association may have originated directly from some of Paul's interlocutors in synagogues, or possibly from Paul's own pre-conversion polemic. Paul's rivals probably invoke the curse of the law; Paul's detractors debating him in synagogues may have associated that curse with the cross. But good argumentation turned the perceived advantages of opponents to one's own advantage.[94]

Paul indicates that if they want to view matters purely under the law, then they will have to proclaim Jesus accursed (an ungodly declaration, 1 Cor 12:3)! But even though Jesus was innocent, there was a sense in which, under the law (cf. Gal 4:4), he did embrace the curse, albeit to free others from it (3:13). His Father then vindicated him by raising him.

How could Jesus become a "curse"? This idea was so problematic that Jerome tried to correct Paul on the assumption that Paul misunderstood the Hebrew text.[95] But Christ became a curse presumably the way that he probably became sin in 2 Cor 5:21: as a *representative* of sin, and therefore a sin offering.[96] In a passage that may borrow LXX language for a sin offering,[97] God condemned sin in Christ's flesh (Rom 8:3). Under the law, guilt could be transferred to a lamb or a goat (e.g., Lev 4:24; 5:6; 8:14; 9:15; 16:21; Num 8:12); here it is transferred to Christ.[98] Abraham and surely Christ, his ultimate seed, were blessed; Jesus, who did not merit the curse, experienced it in others' place, to provide others the blessing.[99] Many understand being a curse as figurative for being accursed (as in the Deuteronomy text that Paul cites).[100]

Perhaps in another sense Jesus could become a curse literally—in the same sense that his enemies could count him accursed (1 Cor 12:3). Making someone "a curse" or "for a curse"[101] meant using their accursed condition as an analogy of wretchedness: "May you be cursed like so-and-so" (cf. Jer 29:22; LXX 36:22). (The noun and cognate verb ἐπικαταράομαι are surely connected, appearing together in Mal 2:2.) Thus Jesus, who was accursed (by virtue of hanging on the cross), could be said to be for a curse; people could thus curse others by saying, "Let them be accursed like Jesus," who was hanged on a cross.

## CONCLUSION

In Gal 3:8–14 Paul ingeniously links multiple texts based on shared (or sometimes contrasting) key terms, whether explicit in the texts or implied by their immediate contexts. He begins and ends with blessing in Abraham;

he sandwiches between them discussion of the curse. The curse is for law-breakers, but Jesus experienced his people's curse in their place on the tree. The present experience of the promised blessing of Abraham, inheriting the coming world, is experienced through the Spirit (3:5, 14), available to all the families of the earth blessed in Abraham.

## NOTES

1. I borrow and adapt material here from the relevant sections of my larger Galatians commentary (Craig S. Keener, *Galatians: A Commentary* [Grand Rapids: Baker Academic, 2019]; cf. earlier but in less detail, Craig S. Keener, *Galatians* [Cambridge: Cambridge University Press, 2018]). Thanks to Dwayne Duncombe for his help condensing.

2. For this practice in ancient Jewish hermeneutics, see, e.g., CD 7.15–20; Mekilta Pisha 5.103; Nezikin p. 76.26; p. 77.38; p. 130.17.

3. For the BC level, see also Frank J. Matera, *Galatians*, SP 9 (Collegeville, MN: Liturgical, 1992), 122.

4. With Peter Oakes, *Galatians* (Grand Rapids: Baker Academic, 2015), 99, from whose proposal I differ only slightly.

5. With, e.g., J. Louis Martyn, "A Law-Observant Mission to the Gentiles: The Background of Galatians," *SJT* 38 (3, 1985): 307–24; idem, *Galatians: A New Translation with Introduction and Commentary* (New York: Doubleday, 1997), 306; John M. G. Barclay, *Obeying the Truth: Paul's Ethics in Galatians* (Vancouver: Regent College, 1988), 53, 66–67; Richard N. Longenecker, *Galatians*, WBC 41 (Grand Rapids: Zondervan, 1990), 110; Matera, *Galatians*, 122; A. Andrew Das, *Galatians* Concordia Commentary (St. Louis, MO: Concordia Publishing House, 2014), 8; E. P. Sanders, *Paul: The Apostle's Life, Letters, and Thought* (Minneapolis: Fortress, 2015), 519.

6. Moisés Silva, "Galatians," in *Commentary on the New Testament Use of the Old Testament*, ed. G. K. Beale and D. A. Carson (Grand Rapids: Baker Academic, 2007), 785–812, here 792–93.

7. "Blessed in you" is from Gen 12:3; "nations/gentiles" is from 18:18. Paul's conflation recognizes and highlights the thematic link.

8. Shock served a rhetorical purpose (see R. Dean Anderson Jr., *Glossary of Greek Rhetorical Terms Connected to Methods of Argumentation, Figures, and Tropes from Anaximenes to Quintilian* [Leuven: Peeters, 2000], 88); so did Paul ending the first two clauses of 3:10 with the same word (the device that rhetoricians called *epiphora*; R. Dean Anderson Jr., *Ancient Rhetorical Theory and Paul* [Leuven: Peeters, 1999], 163; on this device, see Anderson, *Glossary*, 54).

9. Sanders, *Paul*, 537, suggests that Paul's underlying belief that the law cannot justify appears in 2:21 and 3:21, whereas 3:10–13 is merely a rhetorical tactic to demonstrate it.

10. On the connection with 2:15–21, cf. also Normand Bonneau, "The Logic of Paul's Argument on the Curse of the Law in Galatians 3:10–14," *NovT* 39 (1997): 60–80, here 65.

11. "Works of law" probably echo the analogous phrase "do the law" in the LXX including, e.g., Exod 18:20; Lev 19:37; 22:31; 26:3, 15; Deut 5:31; 6:1.

12. Or, for Paul, blessed in Jesus the seed of Abraham in 3:16; the gentiles are encountering Abraham and faith in Abraham's God through Christ.

13. See, e.g., 3:13; 4:27; Rom 1:17; 2:24; 3:4, 10; 4:17; 1 Cor 1:19, 31.

14. With this or similar wording, e.g., Mark 1:2; 7:6; 2 Chr 23:18; Neh 10:36; 1 Esd 1:11; Dan 9:11; CD 7.19; 11.18, 20; 1QS 5.15, 17; 8.14; 2Q25 f1.3.

15. Note the verbal reminiscences of Deut 28 in Jub. 20.9–10.

16. Covenants often included curses for those who violated the covenants' stipulations; see, e.g., *ANET* (1955), 199–206.

17. Sanders, *Paul*, 523, reasonably attributes Paul's choice to Deut 27:26 being "the only passage in the LXX that contains 'curse' and 'law' in the same immediate context." For the arguments being ad hoc, see Timothy G. Gombis, "Arguing with Scripture in Galatia: Galatians 3:10–14 as a Series of Ad Hoc Arguments," in *Galatians and Christian Theology: Justification, the Gospel, and Ethics in Paul's Letter*, ed. Mark W. Elliott et al. (Grand Rapids: Baker Academic, 2014), 82–90.

18. Matera, *Galatians*, 119, sees Paul expanding Deut 27:26's statement about twelve curses to the entire law.

19. Reading the entire section or even the entire Deuteronomic cycle, see e.g., James D. G. Dunn, *The Epistle to the Galatians* (London: A&C Black, 1995), 170, 180; Douglas J. Moo, *Galatians,* BECNT (Grand Rapids: Baker Academic, 2013), 28; Das, *Galatians*, 313. Cf. Jub. 1.16.

20. See in detail N. T. Wright, *Paul and the Faithfulness of God* (Minneapolis: Fortress, 2013), 139–62.

21. Some demurred; see m. Sanh. 10:5; t. Sanh. 13:12.

22. See e.g., 2 Macc 2:18; Ps. Sol. 8.28; Pesiq. Rab Kah. Sup. 5.3; Gen. Rab. 73.6; 98.9; cf. (if not an interpolation) T. Benj. 9.2. See especially the many references to the restoration of the twelve tribes in E. P. Sanders, *Jesus and Judaism* (Philadelphia: Fortress, 1985), 96–97, including Bar 4:37; 5:5; Sir 36:11; 48:10; 2 Macc 1:27–28; 2:18; Ps. Sol. 11; 17.28–31, 50; 1QM 2.2–3, 7–8; 5.1; 11Q19 18.14–16; 2 Bar. 78.7; t. Sanh. 13:10; Rev 21:12.

23. See e.g., Josephus *Ant.* 11.133; *Ag. Ap.* 1.33; 4 Ezra 13:40–43.

24. E.g., Longenecker, *Galatians*, 117; Sanders, *Paul*, 73, refer to Deut 28; Das, *Galatians*, 313, refers to Deut 29.

25. Cf. Josephus *Ant.* 4.302, 307–8; 5.70; perhaps CD 1.17; 1QS 2.16; 5.12; 4Q266 f2i.20; 4Q397 f14 21.13; 4Q398 f10.1; f11–13.3; 4Q473 f2.2.

26. Longenecker, *Galatians*, 117, citing m. Mak. 3:10–14. But would this rule be known in the Diaspora in Paul's day?

27. Cf. Michael Bachmann, "Zur Argumentation von Galater 3.10–12," *NTS* 53 (2007): 524–44.

28. Martyn, *Galatians*, 309.

29. E.g., Barclay, *Obeying*, 66–67; Martyn, *Galatians*, 311; Martinus C. de Boer, *Galatians: A Commentary* (Louisville: Westminster John Knox, 2011), 200; Das, *Galatians*, 7, 8, 311, 322.

30. Longenecker, *Galatians*, 117. Rabbinic schools sometimes differed starkly over which term or phrase to emphasize in a verse; see e.g., m. Git. 9:10; Sipre Deut. 269.1.1.

31. Sanders, *Paul*, 73, plausibly attributes this conflation to memory, but Paul might also deliberately evoke the fuller context.

32. E.g., Daniel P. Fuller, *Gospel and Law: Contrast or Continuum?* (Grand Rapids: Eerdmans, 1980), 91; E. P. Sanders, *Paul, the Law, and the Jewish People* (Philadelphia: Fortress, 1983), 28–29; Dunn, *Galatians*, 171; Martyn, *Galatians*, 310; Wolfgang Reinbold, "Gal 3,6–14 und das Problem der Erfüllbarkeit des Gesetzes bei Paulus," *ZNW* 91 (2000): 91–106; Gordon D. Fee, *Galatians: Pentecostal Commentary* (Blandford Forum: Deo, 2007), 119; Sanders, *Paul*, 524–25.

33. See, e.g., citations in Timothy Wengert, "Martin Luther on Galatians 3:6–14: Justification by Curses and Blessings," in *Galatians and Christian Theology*, 91–116, here 109; Franz Mussner, *Der Galaterbrief*, 5th ed. (Freiburg: Herder, 1988), 224–26; Schreiner, *Galatians*, 203–5; Silva, "Galatians," 792; Moo, *Galatians*, 28–29; John M. Barclay, *Paul & the Gift* (Grand Rapids: Eerdmans, 2015), 405–7.

34. Fuller, *Gospel*, 91; Magnus Zetterholm, "Paul within Judaism: The State of the Questions," in *Paul within Judaism: Restoring the First-Century Context to the Apostle*, ed. Mark Nanos and Magnus Zetterholm (Minneapolis: Fortress, 2015), 31–51, here 43. Cf. George Foot Moore, *Judaism in the First Centuries of the Christian Era*, 2 vols. (New York: Schocken, 1971), 1:495.

35. Cf. Reinbold, "Problem der Erfüllbarkeit."

36. Hermogenes *Inv.* 3.8; 3.9.152.

37. Moisés Silva, "Abraham, Faith, and Works: Paul's Use of Scripture in Galatians 3:6–14," *WTJ* 63 (2001): 251–67, here 262; Silva, "Galatians," 798.

38. With, e.g., Mussner, *Galaterbrief*, 224–26; Longenecker, *Galatians*, 118; Silva, "Galatians," 798.

39. 1 Kgs 8:46; Eccl 7:20; 1 Esd 4:37; 1QS 11.9–10; Jub. 21.21; Moore, *Judaism*, 46–68; Fuller, *Gospel*, 91; Karin Hedner Zetterholm, "The Question of Assumptions: Torah Observance in the First Century," in *Paul within Judaism*, 79–103, here 89.

40. Anderson, *Rhetorical Theory*, 160.

41. Sigurd Grindheim, "Apostate Turned Prophet: Paul's Prophetic Self-Understanding and Prophetic Hermeneutic with Special Reference to Galatians 3.10–12," *NTS* 53 (2007): 545–65.

42. Grindheim, "Apostate," 561. Cf. also the use of Lev 18:5 in Ps. Sol. 14.

43. Grindheim, "Apostate," 562.

44. Grindheim, "Apostate," 564.

45. Barclay, *Gift*, 405.

46. Cf. Norman H. Young, "Who's Cursed—and Why? (Galatians 3:10–14)," *JBL* 117 (1998): 79–92.

47. Silva, "Abraham," 263–64; Silva, "Galatians," 799.

48. Due to space constraints, I cannot engage here some capable scholars' argument that Paul applies Hab 2:4 instead to Christ's faithfulness.

49. E.g., 1QpHab 8.1–3; b. Mak. 24a.

50. E. Ray Clendenen, "Salvation by Faith or by Faithfulness in the Book of Habakkuk," *BBR* 24 (2014): 505–13, here 513; Schreiner, *Galatians*, 208 n. 35; Moo, *Galatians*, 220 (cf. also 207); Das, *Galatians*, 320; see esp. Maureen W. Yeung, *Faith in Jesus and Paul* (Tübingen: Mohr Siebeck, 2002), 196–212.

51. Dunn, *Galatians*, 174.

52. Sanders, *Paul*, 72–73.

53. Silva, "Galatians," 802; Bill T. Arnold, *Genesis* (Cambridge: Cambridge University Press, 2009), 157.

54. Richard B. Hays, *The Faith of Jesus Christ: An Investigation of the Narrative Substructure of Galatians 3:1–4:11*, SBLDS 56 (Chico, CA: Scholars, 1983), 150–57; Douglas A. Campbell, "The Meaning of Πίστις and Νόμος in Paul: A Linguistic and Structural Perspective," *JBL* 111 (1992): 91–103 (101–3, esp. 101n30).

55. E.g., Das, *Galatians*, 7–8, 322.

56. Debaters valued turning opponents' own evidence against them; see Galen O. Rowe, "Style," in *Handbook of Classical Rhetoric in the Hellenistic Period, 330 B.C.–A.D. 400*, ed. Stanley E. Porter (Leiden: Brill, 1997), 121–57, here 145–46; cf. Fronto *Ad M. Caes.* 3.15.1.

57. Cf. Barclay, *Gift*, 406.

58. De Boer, *Galatians*, 207.

59. Deut 32:47; Bar. 3:9; 4:1–2; Ps. Sol. 14.1–2; L.A.B. 23.10; 2 Bar. 38.2; m. Ab. 2:7; 6:7, bar.; Sipre Deut. 306.22.1; 336.1.1.

60. So understood in Sir 3:5–6, 12–15; L.A.B. 11.9; cf. long life as a reward for obedience in 1QS 4.7; 11QTemple 65.3–5; Ps.–Phoc. 229–30; b. Ber. 13b, bar.

61. An a fortiori, argument, as in e.g., m. Ab. 1:5; t. Ber. 4:16–17; 6:19; Peah 3:8; Sipre Num. 1.4.1; 1.6.3; 8.1.1; 15.1.1; 78.1.1.

62. Sipra A.M. par. 8.193.1.10 (though cf. pq. 13.194.2.16); Sipre Deut. 336.1.1; cf. m. Mak. 3:15; Peah 1:1.

63. See especially Preston M. Sprinkle, *Law and Life: The Interpretation of Leviticus 18:5 in Early Judaism and in Paul*, WUNT 2/241 (Tübingen: Mohr Siebeck, 2008), 34–130.

64. With Fee, *Galatians*, 132 (on Gal 3:21). For the Spirit and life in Paul, cf. Rom 1:4; 8:10–11, 13; Gal 6:8.

65. CD 3.15–20. See Simon J. Gathercole, *Where Is Boasting? Early Jewish Soteriology and Paul's Response in Romans 1–5* (Grand Rapids: Eerdmans, 2002), 100–102, on CD 3.14–16, esp. 16.

66. Nicole Chibici-Revneanu, "Leben im Gesetz: Die paulinische Interpretation von Lev 18:5 (Gal 3:12; Röm 10:5)," *NovT* 50 (2008): 105–19.

67. Susan Eastman, "Galatians," 825–32 in *The New Interpreter's Bible One Volume Commentary*, ed. Beverly Roberts Gaventa and David Petersen (Nashville: Abingdon, 2010), 828.

68. Barclay, *Obeying*, 67.

69. For a response to legalism here, see Fuller, *Gospel*, 86.

70. On their structural similarity, cf. also Silva, "Galatians," 801; Moo, *Galatians*, 208; David A. deSilva, *Global Readings: A Sri Lankan Commentary on Paul's Letter to the Galatians* (Eugene, OR: Cascade, 2011), 163.

71. Again, e.g., Fee, *Galatians*, 120–21.

72. Here, Johan S. Vos, "Die hermeneutische Antinomie bei Paulus (Galater 3.11–12; Römer 10.5–10)," *NTS* 38 (1992): 254–70 (258–60).

73. See Eastman, "Galatians," 828.

74. Sanders, *Law and People*, 161 (not on this passage), citing, e.g., CD 4.20–21 and rabbis.

75. Beraita de Rabbi Ishmael Pereq 1.7 (trans. Neusner, in Sipra 1:63). When this happened, the opponent had to find an additional text (Gen. Rab. 15.2).

76. See, e.g., Lucian, *Dead Come to Life/Fishermen*, 3.

77. For posing apparently or actually conflicting laws, e.g., Pliny *Ep.* 2.19.8; Hermogenes *Issues* 40.20; 41.1–13; 83.19–88.2 (esp. 87.2–9).

78. Cf. e.g., Joel Willitts, "Context Matters: Paul's Use of Leviticus 18:5 in Galatians 3:12," *TynBul* 54 (2003): 105–22; especially Sprinkle, *Law and Life*.

79. Moo, *Galatians*, 208.

80. Gombis, "Arguing," 89.

81. Grindheim, "Apostate," 561–62; Gombis, "Arguing," 88–89.

82. Cf. Gombis, "Arguing," 89.

83. Grindheim, "Apostate," 563.

84. deSilva, *Readings*, 175–76.

85. deSilva, *Readings*, 176.

86. With e.g., Moo, *Galatians*, 210.

87. With e.g., Martyn, *Galatians*, 321; Moo, *Galatians*, 222. Such changes are stylistic and do not affect meaning (Silva, "Galatians," 796).

88. Also in Josephus *Ant.* 4.202; cf. Gen 40:19; Polybius 8.21.3; Pliny E. Nat. 36.24.107.

89. Josephus *Ant.* 13.380; *War* 1.97.

90. 4Q169 f3-4i.7–8. For discussions of Deut 21:23 in early Judaism, see, e.g., Max Wilcox, "'Upon the Tree'—Deut 21:22–23 in the New Testament," *JBL* 96 (1977): 85–99; Mark T. Finney, "Servile Supplicium: Shame and the Deuteronomic Curse-Crucifixion in Its Cultural Context," *BTB* 43 (2013): 124–34 (128–32).

91. 11Q19 64.8–11.

92. Silva, "Galatians," 798.

93. Agreeing here with Terence L. Donaldson, *Paul and the Gentiles: Remapping the Apostle's Convictional World* (Minneapolis: Fortress, 1997), 171; Das, *Galatians*, 326; Schreiner, *Galatians*, 217. This association was not pervasive; see Kelli S. O'Brien, "The Curse of the Law (Galatians 3.13): Crucifixion, Persecution, and Deuteronomy 21.22–23," *JSNT* 29 (2006): 55–76.

94. See e.g., Malcolm Heath, "Invention," pages 89–119 in *Handbook of Classical Rhetoric*, 97; Rowe, "Style," 145–46.

95. A point on which Luther, preferring to let Deuteronomy and Paul speak separately, criticizes Jerome; Wengert, "Luther," 112. Karla Pollmann and Mark W. Elliott, "Galatians in the Early Church: Five Case Studies," 40–61 in *Galatians and*

*Christian Theology*, ed. Mark W. Elliott et al. (Grand Rapids: Baker Academic, 2014), 52, cite Jerome as implying that Jews changed the Hebrew text.

96. Cf. Ambrosiaster *Ep. Gal.* 3.13.1–2; Thomas Aquinas (Lecture 1) on Rom 8:3; see also James D. G. Dunn, *The Theology of Paul the Apostle* (Grand Rapids: Eerdmans, 1998), 217, 219.

97. So most commentators, e.g., N. T. Wright, *The Climax of the Covenant* (Edinburgh: T & T Clark, 1991), 220–25; Moo, *Romans,* 480; Dunn, *Romans* 1:422; Dunn, *Theology of Paul*, 216; Richard B. Hays, *The Conversion of the Imagination: Paul as Interpreter of Israel's Scripture* (Grand Rapids: Eerdmans, 2005), 182.

98. Hans Joachim Schoeps, *Paul: The Theology of the Apostle in the Light of Jewish Religious History* (Philadelphia: Westminster, 1961), 132; here, substituting one death for another, Sanders, *Paul*, 527.

99. Cf. Haimo of Auxerre (ninth century) on Gal 3:13; Luther on Gal 3:13. Robert of Melun (mid-twelfth century) on Gal 3:13 explains that this means that Christ for others bore death, the punishment of sin. In the cross, Jesus embraced the divine punishment due humanity in the cross; see, e.g., Arland J. Hultgren, *Paul's Letter to the Romans: A Commentary* (Grand Rapids: Eerdmans, 2011), 214.

100. E.g., Mussner, *Galaterbrief,* 233; de Boer, *Galatians,* 211; cf. Gregory of Nazianzus *Letter* 101.61.

101. Isa 64:10 (LXX 64:9); Jer 24:9; 26:6; 44:8 (51:8); 44:12 (51:12); Zech 8:13; cf. Jer 42:18 (49:18).

# BIBLIOGRAPHY

Anderson, R. Dean, Jr. *Ancient Rhetorical Theory and Paul*. Leuven: Peeters, 1999.
———. *Glossary of Greek Rhetorical Terms Connected to Methods of Argumentation, Figures, and Tropes from Anaximenes to Quintilian*. Leuven: Peeters, 2000.
Arnold, Bill T. *Genesis*. Cambridge: Cambridge University Press, 2009.
Bachmann, Michael. "Zur Argumentation von Galater 3.10–12." *NTS* 53 (2007): 524–44.
Barclay, John M. *Obeying the Truth: Paul's Ethics in Galatians*. Vancouver: Regent College, 1988.
———. *Paul & the Gift. Grand Rapids: Eerdmans, 2015.*
Boer, Martinus C. de. *Galatians: A Commentary*. Louisville: Westminster John Knox, 2011.
Bonneau, Normand. "The Logic of Paul's Argument on the Curse of the Law in Galatians 3:10–14." *NovT* 39 (1997): 60–80.
Campbell, Douglas A. "The Meaning of Πίστις and Νόμος in Paul: A Linguistic and Structural Perspective." *JBL* 111 (1992): 91–103.
Chibici-Revneanu, Nicole. "Leben im Gesetz: Die paulinische Interpretation von Lev 18:5 (Gal 3:12; Röm 10:5)." *NovT* 50 (2008): 105–19.
Clendenen, E. Ray. "Salvation by Faith or by Faithfulness in the Book of Habakkuk." *BBR* 24 (2014): 505–13.

Das, A. Andrew. *Galatians*. Concordia Commentary. Saint Louis: Concordia Publishing House, 2014.

deSilva, David A. *Global Readings: A Sri Lankan Commentary on Paul's Letter to the Galatians*. Eugene, OR: Cascade, 2011.

Donaldson, Terence L. *Paul and the Gentiles: Remapping the Apostle's Convictional World*. Minneapolis: Fortress, 1997.

Dunn, James D. G. *The Epistle to the Galatians*. London: A & C Black, 1995.

———. *The Theology of Paul the Apostle*. Grand Rapids: Eerdmans, 1998.

Eastman, Susan. "Galatians." Pages 825–32 in *The New Interpreter's Bible One Volume Commentary*, edited by Beverly Roberts Gaventa and David Petersen. Nashville: Abingdon, 2010.

Elliott, Mark W., Scott J. Hafemann, N. T. Wright, and John Frederick, eds. *Galatians and Christian Theology: Justification, the Gospel, and Ethics in Paul's Letter.* Grand Rapids: Baker Academic, 2014.

Fee, Gordon D. *Galatians: Pentecostal Commentary*. Blandford Forum: Deo Publishing, 2007.

Finney, Mark T. "Servile Supplicium: Shame and the Deuteronomic Curse-Crucifixion in Its Cultural Context." *BTB* 43 (2013): 124–34.

Fuller, Daniel P. *Gospel and Law: Contrast or Continuum?* Grand Rapids: Eerdmans, 1980.

Gathercole, Simon J. *Where Is Boasting? Early Jewish Soteriology and Paul's Response in Romans 1–5*. Grand Rapids: Eerdmans, 2002.

Grindheim, Sigurd. "Apostate Turned Prophet: Paul's Prophetic Self-Understanding and Prophetic Hermeneutic with Special Reference to Galatians 3.10–12." *NTS* 53 (2007): 545–65.

Hays, Richard B. *The Conversion of the Imagination: Paul as Interpreter of Israel's Scripture*. Grand Rapids: Eerdmans, 2005.

———. *The Faith of Jesus Christ: An Investigation of the Narrative Substructure of Galatians 3:1–4:11*, SBLDS 56. Chico, CA: Scholars, 1983.

Hultgren, Arland J. *Paul's Letter to the Romans: A Commentary*. Grand Rapids: Eerdmans, 2011.

Keener, Craig S. *Galatians*. Cambridge: Cambridge University Press, 2018.

———. *Galatians: A Commentary*. Grand Rapids: Baker Academic, 2019.

Longenecker, Richard N. *Galatians*, WBC 41. Grand Rapids: Zondervan, 1990.

Martyn, J. Louis. *Galatians: A New Translation with Introduction and Commentary*. New York: Doubleday, 1997.

———. "A Law-Observant Mission to the Gentiles: The Background of Galatians." *SJT* 38 (1985): 307–24.

Matera, Frank J. *Galatians*. SP 9. Collegeville, MN: Liturgical, 1992.

Moo, Douglas J. *Galatians*. BECNT. Grand Rapids: Baker Academic, 2013.

Moore, George Foot. *Judaism in the First Centuries of the Christian Era*. 2 vols. New York: Schocken, 1971.

Mussner, Franz. *Der Galaterbrief*. 5th ed. Freiburg: Herder, 1988.

Nanos, Mark, and Magnus Zetterholm, eds. *Paul within Judaism: Restoring the First-Century Context to the Apostle*. Minneapolis: Fortress, 2015.

Oakes, Peter. *Galatians*. Grand Rapids: Baker Academic, 2015.

O'Brien, Kelli S. "The Curse of the Law (Galatians 3.13): Crucifixion, Persecution, and Deuteronomy 21.22–23." *JSNT* 29 (2006): 55–76.

Porter, Stanley E., ed. *Handbook of Classical Rhetoric in the Hellenistic Period, 330 B.C.–A.D. 400*. Leiden: Brill, 1997.

Reinbold, Wolfgang. "Gal 3,6–14 und das Problem der Erfüllbarkeit des Gesetzes bei Paulus." *ZNW* 91 (2000): 91–106.

Sanders, E. P. *Jesus and Judaism*. Philadelphia: Fortress, 1985.

———. *Paul: The Apostle's Life, Letters, and Thought*. Minneapolis: Fortress, 2015.

———. *Paul, the Law, and the Jewish People*. Philadelphia: Fortress, 1983.

Schoeps, Hans Joachim. *Paul: The Theology of the Apostle in the Light of Jewish Religious History*. Philadelphia: Westminster, 1961.

Schreiner, Thomas R. *Galatians*. Grand Rapids: Zondervan, 2010.

Silva, Moisés. "Abraham, Faith, and Works: Paul's Use of Scripture in Galatians 3:6–14." *WTJ* 63 (2001): 251–67.

———. "Galatians." Pages 785–812 in *Commentary on the New Testament Use of the Old Testament*, edited by G. K. Beale and D. A. Carson. Grand Rapids: Baker Academic, 2007.

Sprinkle, Preston M. *Law and Life: The Interpretation of Leviticus 18:5 in Early Judaism and in Paul*. WUNT 2.241. Tübingen: Mohr Siebeck, 2008.

Vos, Joharl S. "Die hermeneutische Antinomie bei Paulus (Galater 3.11–12; Römer 10.5–10)." *NTS* 38 (1992): 254–70.

Wilcox, Max. "'Upon the Tree'—Deut 21:22–23 in the New Testament." *JBL* 96 (1977): 85–99.

Willitts, Joel. "Context Matters: Paul's Use of Leviticus 18:5 in Galatians 3:12." *TynBul* 54 (2003): 105–22.

Wright, N. T. *The Climax of the Covenant*. Edinburgh: T & T Clark, 1991.

———. *Paul and the Faithfulness of God*. Minneapolis: Fortress, 2013.

Yeung, Maureen W. *Faith in Jesus and Paul: A Comparison with Special Reference to "Faith That Can Remove Mountains" and "Your Faith Has Healed/Saved You."* WUNT 2.147. Tübingen: Mohr Siebeck, 2002.

Young, Norman H. "Who's Cursed—and Why? (Galatians 3:10–14)." *JBL* 117 (1998): 79–92.

Zetterholm, Magnus, and Mark D. Nanos, ed., *Paul within Judaism: Restoring the First-Century Context to the Apostle*. Fortress, 2015.

## Chapter 5

# Habakkuk 2:4 in Galatians

## *Rewritings and Snippet Quotations*

### Roy E. Ciampa

The Scripture indices of most commentaries on Galatians confirm that their authors do not tend to mention Hab 2:4 other than discussing its appearance in Gal 3:11 (or 3:11–12). In his commentary on Galatians, Longenecker mentions Hab 2:4 only in his comments on 3:10–11.[1] That means there is no mention whatsoever in his discussion of Gal 2:16; 3:7–9, 12, 22, 24; 5:5, all of which include reference to ἐκ πίστεως. In Betz's commentary on Galatians, he only mentions Hab 2:4 in his discussion of 3:11.[2] Dunn only mentions Hab 2:4 in his comments in Gal 3:11–12 in his commentary and does not mention the presence of the key phrase in the other texts in Galatians.

This is not just a modern tendency. In his preface to Habakkuk, Martin Luther emphasizes the importance of Hab 2:4 for Paul:

> St. Paul honors Habakkuk greatly, quoting his statement "The righteous shall live by faith" (Hab. 2:4) more than once (Gal. 3:11; Rom. 1:17; Heb. 10:38). He immediately makes this the theme of his finest letter, the Epistle to the Romans. Furthermore, Luke cites him twice in the Book of Acts. This reflects the high regard Habakkuk must have enjoyed among the apostles.[3]

Despite his appreciation of the place of Habakkuk in Paul's theology, in his lectures on Galatians the only place Luther references Hab 2:4 apart from where Paul very explicitly quotes the verse in Gal 3:11, is in a comment on 3:8 regarding an objection Jews might make to Paul's forthcoming citation of Hab 2:4 in Gal 3:11.[4] In Calvin's commentary on Galatians, the only place he cites Hab 2:4 other than where Paul very explicitly quotes it in Gal 3:11 is in a comment on Gal 3:6 (as a kind of cross-reference).[5]

This chapter will argue that Habakkuk 2:4 is in play in numerous other places in Galatians,[6] including 2:16, 20; 3:7; 3:8; 3:9; 3:12; 3:14; 3:22; 3:24; 3:26; 5:5 (and possibly in 3:2, 5). It argues that Paul's letter to the Galatians has a number of rewritings and snippet quotations from Hab 2:4, that are more likely to be recognized once one recognizes the pattern of interpretation by glossing, and that the distinctive expression from the Old Greek of Hab 2:4, ἐκ πίστεως, was found to be awkward and tended to be rewritten in less opaque terms for the sake of clarity.

The implications of recognizing that Paul alludes to and rewrites parts of Hab 2:4 both before and after the citation of the text in Gal 3:11 will also be explored for the way it may inform arguments about Paul's understanding of Hab 2:4 in Gal 3:11 and elsewhere in the letter, his understanding of righteousness by faith as expressed in various texts, and the meaning of πίστις Χριστοῦ in Galatians.

## THE ANCIENT TEXT, TRANSLATION, AND CITATION OF HABAKKUK 2:4

The basic data regarding the Hebrew text of the relevant part of the verse, its rendering in the Old Greek, and the differences between them and Paul's own abbreviated form of the LXX are all well-known and can be merely summarized, while the questions of interpretation are less clear-cut.[7] The Hebrew text of the relevant part of Hab 2:4 as found in the MT reads: וצדיק באמונתו יחיה, while the Old Greek MSS read ὁ δὲ δίκαιος ἐκ πίστεώς μου ζήσεται (MSS S B Q V and W*) or ὁ δὲ δίκαιος μου ἐκ πίστεως ζήσεται (MSS A and C). The first person possessive pronoun found in the Greek texts (in two different places) where one might have expected αὐτοῦ, based on the third person masculine singular suffix in the Hebrew, constitute the primary difference between the OG and MT.[8] Paul's rendering of the text is distinctive in that he omits any pronoun at all, so that his rendering of the relevant part of Hab 2:4 reads, ὁ δὲ δίκαιος ἐκ πίστεως ζήσεται.

## THE EARLY HISTORY OF REWRITING HABAKKUK 2:4B (LXX)

As a preposition, ἐκ is one of the most common words in Greek, and yet the expression ἐκ πίστεως has yet to be found in in any extant Greek text prior to the OG translation of Hab 2:4 (including Greek literature, papyri, and inscriptions). However, the expression became ubiquitous in early Christian literature that was influenced by Hab 2:4—or the use of its expression—in the New Testament.⁹

Not only is the expression ἐκ πίστεως unknown elsewhere in ancient Greek before the OG translation of Hab 2:4, but it seems that ancient scribes and interpreters found that expression so opaque that they frequently rewrote it, using other words they considered more transparent ways of expressing its thought. The expression ἐκ πίστεως was rewritten (or retranslated from Hebrew) as ἐν πίστει in the Greek Minor Prophets Scroll from Nahal Hever (8HevXIIgr) and in (the early Greek version) Aquila. It was rendered by Symmachus simply as πίστει.¹⁰

In Heb 10:38, Hab 2:4 LXX is quoted with its distinctive use of ἐκ πίστεως but then the author rewords the expression as πίστει eighteen times in Hebrews 11 (11:3, 4, 5, 7, 8, 9, 11, 17, 20, 21, 22, 23, 24, 27, 28, 29, 30, 31) and then once as διὰ πίστεως (Heb 11:33) and another time as διὰ τῆς πίστεως (Heb 11:39). Evidently, these were all considered to be more natural or transparent ways of saying "by/through faith."¹¹

Unless they were familiar with the expression from Hab 2:4, Paul's readers would not have been familiar with the expression ἐκ πίστεως. Paul, however, uses the expression repeatedly in Galatians and Romans, more often than not keeping to that precise wording. But often enough he also rewords it, and in doing so he provides some clarification regarding the way he thinks his readers should interpret it (using διὰ πίστεως in Rom 3:22; Gal 2:16; Phil 3:9, etc., ἐν πίστει in Gal 2:20, and εἰς πάντας τοὺς πιστεύοντας, also in Rom 3:22, probably disambiguating his use of εἰς πίστιν in Rom 1:17 as another gloss on ἐκ πίστεως).¹²

It may seem harder for modern Christians to recognize ἐκ πίστεως as a snippet quotation from Hab 2:4 in part because it is used so frequently by Paul (nineteen times besides the explicit citations of Hab 2:4 for a total of twenty-one times: Rom 1:17 [x2]; 3:26, 30; 4:16; 5:1; 9:30, 32; 10:6; 14:23; Gal 2:16; 3:7–9, 11–12, 22, 24; 5:5) that the expression "by faith" became such a common feature of Christian speech through history that its roots in Hab 2:4 are easily missed.¹³

As was argued in the chapter on Hab 2:4 in Romans, this essay will also argue that each occurrence of ἐκ πίστεως should be understood as a snippet quotation from Hab 2:4.¹⁴ Where Paul writes ἐκ πίστεως in conjunction with any term with the δικαι-root I suggest we are dealing with a rewriting of Hab 2:4b that includes a snippet quotation of the LXX version of that text. That is, the snippet consists of ἐκ πίστεως and the combination of that snippet quotation with any term with the δικαι-root (but something other than ὁ δίκαιος) constitutes a rewriting of ὁ δίκαιος ἐκ πίστεώς. In other cases, Paul's understanding of what ἐκ πίστεως signifies is represented by rewriting that expression, with some rewritings differing only slightly from ἐκ πίστεως (e.g., διὰ πίστεως)¹⁵ and others differing quite significantly (e.g., ἐν πίστει τῇ τοῦ υἱοῦ τοῦ θεοῦ in Gal 2:20 and δοθῇ τοῖς πιστεύουσιν in Gal 3:22). Proving that all of these are rewritings or snippet citations of Hab 2:4 is not feasible, and some of the proposals will undoubtedly prove to be more persuasive than others. Hopefully the cumulative argument to the effect that the influence of Hab 2:4 on Paul's letter to the Galatians is much greater than is normally recognized will be persuasive.

Paul's rendering (or rewriting) of Hab 2:4 and the statements he constructs out of the parts of Hab 2:4 touch on a number of issues that have occupied Pauline scholars in recent debates. Among the interpretive questions that need to be informed by this issue are the following. Does Paul take ἐκ πίστεως to modify ζήσεται or ὁ δίκαιος? Does Paul take ὁ δίκαιος to refer to "the righteous person" as a general category (i.e., any righteous member of God's people), or does he take it to be a messianic text, referring explicitly to Christ? If Paul takes ἐκ πίστεως to modify ζήσεται, does he take the life to refer to future resurrection life, or does he take it to mean the righteous will live their daily lives ἐκ πίστεως? Since Paul indicates the ἐκ πίστεως is to be understood in relationship to Christ Jesus, does he take the πίστις to refer to faith in Christ (or faithfulness to Christ), or to Christ's own faithfulness?

These and other questions about Paul's meaning of these texts and how they might be informed by understanding many of these texts as rewritten versions and interpretations of Hab 2:4 will be considered as we work our way through examples in Galatians.

## REWRITING AND SNIPPET QUOTATIONS
## OF HABAKKUK 2:4 IN GALATIANS

A critical problem in Gal 2:16 has to do with the debate about πίστις Χριστοῦ, which certainly cannot be fully considered here. In this case, should διὰ πίστεως Ἰησοῦ Χριστοῦ be taken to mean "through faith in Jesus Christ" or "through the faithfulness of Jesus Christ"? Teresa Morgan has argued (fairly persuasively, in my view) that "Greek speakers understand the operation of *pistis* (and Latin speakers that of *fides*) in general as always double-ended, and as incorporating both trust and trustworthiness, faithfulness and good faith, and so on."¹⁶ When πίστις refers to people, it should not be thought of in terms of simple intellectual assent (as with ideas) but in terms of the semantic domain of interpersonal relationships (often or typically asymmetrical interpersonal relationships), where it refers to "a nexus of faithfulness, trustworthiness, and trust which runs in all directions."¹⁷ She argues that while the term refers to a kind of reciprocal (though not equal) relationship, in Greek and Latin literature, usually only the πίστις of one of the parties is explicitly mentioned in any particular text:

> The inescapable reciprocity of *pistis/fides* means that within relationships of *pistis/fides*, power (encompassing all kinds of status and authority) never runs all one way. . . . That being so, it is worth noting that Greek and Latin texts tend to avoid referring to the *pistis/fides* of both parties to a relationship in the same text or passage. Where the social status of the participants is unequal, in particular, our sources seem to shy away from marking the reciprocal nature of their relationship.[18]

In light of her observations, it is interesting to note that a quick survey within just biblical Greek reminds us how often love and faith[fulness] are mentioned together in ways that may point to their being overlapping ways of referring to interpersonal commitments (between God and his people or within the people of God).[19] A subset of those texts suggests that the nature of the reciprocal relationship is sometimes marked by the use of the language of faith/fulness on one side (usually the subordinate side) and the language of love (ἀγαπ- or φίλ-) on the other, with a common enough pattern being to describe a person as "faithful and beloved" marking the reciprocal relationship not in terms of πίστις on both sides (although, as Morgan argues, that is probably understood), but in terms of love coming from the superior to the subordinate and faith or faithfulness from the subordinate to the superior.[20] Similar, perhaps is the expression, "faithful friend" where, as Louw and Nida put it, a φίλος is a "person with whom one associates and for whom there is affection or personal regard"[21] (so they are beloved and are faithful in return). Thus, in John 3:16 the relationship between God's love for people and their act of putting their faith in him fits with this broader pattern.

Coming back to the question of πίστις Χριστοῦ in Paul (and the role of Hab 2:4), we may see this pattern in Gal 2:20, where Paul says he now lives by faith in the Son of God (ἐν πίστει ζῶ τῇ τοῦ υἱοῦ τοῦ θεοῦ), who loved him and gave himself up for him (τοῦ ἀγαπήσαντός με καὶ παραδόντος ἑαυτὸν ὑπὲρ ἐμοῦ).[22] The traditional reading here would reflect a reciprocal relationship, with the believer's faith in Christ being a response to Christ's act of love toward the believer. It would point to the reciprocal relationship while naming πίστις only on the part of the subordinate, while referring to the part emanating from the superior in terms of love.

Morgan's study suggests that references to πίστις between people (human and/or divine) suppose a reciprocal relationship of trust and trustworthiness and that suggests that we do not need to find explicit references to Christ's faithfulness to understand that it is assumed as part of the conceptual background. Morgan's study also suggests that Paul may be avoiding explicit

references to faith/fulness on the part of the superior (Christ) and leaving it to
be understood or referring to it in terms of love or other terms (as is consistent
with the traditional interpretation of the final clause of Gal 2:20). By all (or
most) accounts, Paul is ambiguous in the πίστις Χριστοῦ passages, and that
makes it more difficult to decide whether an ambiguous reference to Christ's
faithfulness would count as conforming to or pushing beyond the normal linguistic practice in Greek and Latin literature. It seems to me (in light of the
variety of rewritings in both Romans and Galatians) that Paul normally (or
most often) understands Hab 2:4 in terms of the faith of believers (though I
would argue that in some cases—especially in the first half of Gal 2:20—he
seems to have felt free to interpret it as potentially referring to Christ's own
faith/fulness).[23] I do not hold the view that Paul must have only one meaning
in mind when he references πίστις Χριστοῦ. Morgan may also be right that
"it is rarely possible to confine the interpretation of *pistis* to a single meaning; moreover, some of the most convincing interpretations of New Testament
passages are those which decline to segregate, for instance, faith and faithfulness in their interpretations, but hear Paul invoking both."[24]

While rewritings of the ζήσεται of Hab 2:4 are rarer than rewritings of ὁ
[δὲ] δίκαιος, Gal 2:19–20 may be a case where ζήσεται has been rewritten
as ζῇ [ἐν ἐμοὶ Χριστός] in v. 19 and ζῶ in Gal 2:20 (with θεῷ ζήσω in 2:19
anticipating Paul's references to his living by faith in 2:20) and the references
to being crucified and living by the Spirit in 5:24–25 echo the similar themes
of 2:19b–20.

With all that being said, the combined force of Paul's multiple rewritings
and snippet quotations of Hab 2:4 in Galatians (and Romans) suggests that
while in some cases he is somewhat ambiguous and understands the relationship to be one of mutual faith/faithfulness,[25] he puts somewhat heavier (and
certainly less ambiguous) emphasis on the faith/loyalty that believers have
toward Christ (their believing in him).[26] That is repeatedly reflected in those
rewritings that are unambiguous, and neither we nor the ancient readers can
or could be sure whether they are intended to supplement the ambiguous ones
or to disambiguate them.

At this point we will begin to move (rather quickly) through the various
places in Galatians where it is proposed that Paul is rewriting and/or including a snippet quotation of Hab 2:4, with brief comments in each case that
address some of the questions raised above. What might a sensitive Greek
reader of Galatians detect?

## Galatians 2:16

In this one verse we have three references to being justified by faith. One of
them entails the snippet quotation ἐκ πίστεως in conjunction with the verb

δικαιόω, which is arguably standing in for the ὁ δίκαιος of Hab 2:4 LXX (so that to be justified ἐκ πίστεως is the same as to be δίκαιος ἐκ πίστεως). But before getting to the case just mentioned, and at the beginning of the verse, we have an example of διὰ πίστεως standing in for ἐκ πίστεως, as the means by which a person is justified (δικαιοῦται ἄνθρωπος). Here one can also see δικαιοῦται standing in for Hab 2:4's δίκαιος. We do not have space here to go into the arguments about the meaning of the πίστις Χριστοῦ texts.[27] But by considering all of the proposed rewritings of Hab 2:4 in Romans and Galatians, and looking at the argument in Gal 3:1–14 as a whole, my judgment is that Paul repeatedly reinforces the idea that it is on the basis of believers' faith that they receive the Spirit (Gal 3:1–6), are justified, become sons of Abraham and receive that which was promised to Abraham (Gal 3:6–9), including the Spirit (Gal 3:14). A similar pattern is found in Romans.

In the middle of Gal 2:16 we find the less ambiguous statement about "believing in Christ Jesus" (εἰς Χριστὸν Ἰησοῦν ἐπιστεύσαμεν), which I take to provide a clear statement by which the more ambiguous expressions are expected to be disambiguated. Schliesser takes Paul's unusual usage in Gal 3:23–26 as his starting point and reads aspects of the meaning he finds there back into the rest of Paul's references, including 2:16. Among other things, for him, πίστις "emblematizes an eschatological divine act, as becomes apparent on account of Gal. 3.23 and 25. . . . Secondly, at the same time, πίστις includes a 'local-ontological' or 'relational-ontological' element."[28] I think this is too much to be attributing to one word (and wonder if some of James Barr's critiques have been forgotten). I also think this approach fails to take into account the way in which an author constructs a "discourse concept" over the course of an argument, with later material building on earlier parts of the argument but not creating meaning that should be read back into the earlier parts of the argument.[29] In this case, the reference to faith in Gal 3:23 comes between two verses that each includes a rewriting of Hab 2:4 (in v. 22 ἐκ πίστεως Ἰησοῦ Χριστοῦ is arguably disambiguated in the following phrase, δοθῇ τοῖς πιστεύουσιν, and in v. 24 we have the reference to being justified, δικαιωθῶμεν ἐκ πίστεως; see the comments on 3:22 and 3:24). The legal adage, "hard cases make bad law," like the principle that clearer texts should inform our reading of more ambiguous texts, can be invoked here. It makes better sense for the broader evidence in Galatians about what faith Paul's numerous references to justification by faith and Hab 2:4 have in mind and to let that inform the more ambiguous case of v. 23, than to work in the opposite direction.[30] A paraphrase of this verse could possibly read, "Yet we know that a person is justified not by the works of the law but through faith [διὰ πίστεως] in Jesus Christ. And we have come to believe [ἐπιστεύσαμεν] in Christ Jesus, so that we might be justified 'from faith' (per Hab 2:4 [ἐκ πίστεως]), in/of Christ, and not by doing the works of the law, because no one will be justified by the works of the law."

## Galatians 3:7

Given the arguments above regarding authors' and scribes' tendency to reword ἐκ πίστεως with expressions that seems clearer or more natural, even when they do cite Hab 2:4 with those words, it seems plausible to take each occurrence of ἐκ πίστεως as a snippet quotation of that part of Hab 2:4. So in Gal 3:7, Paul's line may be understood to say, "You see, those who are (per Hab 2:4) 'from faith' (ἐκ πίστεως) are the descendants of Abraham" or "Those who have that Hab 2:4 faith (or that Hab 2:4 righteousness by faith) are the descendants of Abraham" or "Those who have experienced justification in the Hab 2:4 ἐκ πίστεως way, are sons/children of Abraham."[31]

## Galatians 3:8

In this verse we have not only the "snippet quotation" ἐκ πίστεως, but that prepositional phrase also modifies δικαιοῖ ("would justify"), leaving us with a variation of δίκαιος ἐκ πίστεως where the verb of the same root as the adjective stands in for the latter: "And the scripture, foreseeing that God would justify the Gentiles ἐκ πίστεως [per Hab 2:4], declared the gospel beforehand to Abraham, saying, 'All the Gentiles shall be blessed in you' (or "would justify the Gentiles 'from faith,' declared the gospel beforehand to Abraham . . . ")."

## Galatians 3:9

The situation here is the same as in v. 7 both in terms of the use of the snippet quotation and in terms of the local context making it clear that justification as the blessing of Abraham is in mind: "For this reason, those who are [per Hab 2:4] 'from faith' (ἐκ πίστεως) are blessed with Abraham who believed."

## Galatians 3:12

The snippet quotation ἐκ πίστεως shows up here again immediately following the explicit citation of Hab 2:4, which should leave little doubt that it is a snippet quotation alluding back to the text just cited: "But the law does not operate 'from faith' (ἐκ πίστεως), per Hab 2:4; on the contrary, 'Whoever does the works of the law will live by them.'" That is, the law operates on a different principle than the "from faith" principle of Hab 2:4.

## Galatians 3:22

In this text we have the snippet quotation ἐκ πίστεως again, with the assertion that this is how "what was promised" is found and is "given to those who believe." The theme of "the promise" runs through vv. 14–22, and along the way Paul makes it clear that it has to do with justification and the Spirit as fulfillments of God's promise to bless the nations/Gentiles through Abraham. So here it seems plausible that ἡ ἐπαγγελία "stands in" for the Spirit and justification and so also to be δίκαιος. The last three words of the verse, "given to those who believe" (δοθῇ τοῖς πιστεύουσιν) find parallels in texts like Rom 1:16 (σωτηρίαν παντὶ τῷ πιστεύοντι), Rom 3:22 (εἰς πάντας τοὺς πιστεύοντας), and Rom 10:4 (δικαιοσύνην παντὶ τῷ πιστεύοντι), and may suggest that the same verb ("given") is to be understood in those texts as well.[32] The parallel language here, and its colocation with a concept closely tied in Paul's argument to justification (as just argued) suggests that this verse (partly paralleled in Rom 1:17 and 3:22) may include both the snippet quotation of Hab 2:4 in the words ἐκ πίστεως and a redundant explicative rewriting/paraphrase of those words in the expression δοθῇ τοῖς πιστεύουσιν, clarifying that Paul understands δίκαιος ἐκ πίστεως to refer to righteousness (and the promise of the Spirit) which is given to those who believe (δοθῇ τοῖς πιστεύουσιν). It also seems that δοθῇ τοῖς πιστεύουσιν might be another interpretive explication of the meaning Paul attributes to ἐκ πίστεως. "But the scripture has imprisoned all things under the power of sin, so that what was promised [per Hab 2:4] 'from faith' [ἐκ πίστεως] in/of Jesus Christ might be given to those who believe."

## Galatians 3:24

The situation here is very similar to that found in v. 8. We have not only the "snippet quotation" ἐκ πίστεως, but that prepositional phrase modifies δικαιωθῶμεν ("we would be justified"), leaving us with another variation of δίκαιος ἐκ πίστεως where the verb of the same root as the adjective stands in for the latter: "Therefore the law was our disciplinarian until Christ came, so that we might be justified 'from faith' [ἐκ πίστεως] [per Hab 2:4]."

## Galatians 5:5

In this text we have the snippet quotation, ἐκ πίστεως, which has just the single word ἐλπίδα separating that prepositional phrase from the noun of the same root as δίκαιος, namely, δικαιοσύνης. So instead of reading about being "righteous from faith" (δίκαιος ἐκ πίστεως) we read about how, "through the

Spirit, 'from faith' [ἐκ πίστεως] [per Hab 2:4], we eagerly wait for the hope of righteousness [ἐλπίδα δικαιοσύνης]."

These traces of Hab 2:4 still do not account for all the ways and places where Paul has rewritten ἐκ πίστεως as διὰ πίστεως (as in Rom 3:22; 2 Cor 5:7; Gal 2:16; Eph 2:8; Phil 3:9; 2 Tim 3:15), as ἐν πίστει (as in Gal 2:20), as παντὶ τῷ πιστεύοντι (as in Rom 1:16; 10:4), as εἰς πάντας τοὺς πιστεύοντας (as in Rom 3:22) of which εἰς πίστιν seems to be an abbreviated form in Rom 1:17, as ἐπὶ τῇ πίστει (as in Phil 3:9), or simply as πίστει (as in Rom 3:28 and, possibly, 2 Thess 2:13), as δοθῇ τοῖς πιστεύουσιν (as in Gal 3:22, where Paul seems to be intentionally redundant: ἵνα ἡ ἐπαγγελία ἐκ πίστεως Ἰησοῦ Χριστοῦ δοθῇ τοῖς πιστεύουσιν), or possibly as τῆς πίστεως (Rom 4:11) or simply πίστεως (Rom 4:13; Gal 3:8). These cases may already be translated in ways that sound close enough to traditional translations of citations of Hab 2:4 that attentive readers may recognize the echo. In Galatians, it seems that Paul usually leaves ἐκ πίστεως intact (Gal 2:16; 3:7–9, 12, 22, 24; 5:5), but as mentioned above, he sometimes rewrites it as διὰ πίστεως (Gal 2:16; διὰ τῆς πίστεως in 3:14, 26), ἐν πίστει (Gal 2:20), or, more indirectly, as δοθῇ τοῖς πιστεύουσιν (as in Gal 3:22) and possibly as ἐξ ἀκοῆς πίστεως (Gal 3:2, 5). These cases deserve some closer attention.

## Galatians 3:14

In this text we find an expression that would be a natural rewriting or paraphrase of ἐκ πίστεως in the case of διὰ τῆς πίστεως, at the end of the verse. That also raises the question whether the thing that is obtained through faith (διὰ τῆς πίστεως) might also be understood as substituting for either ὁ δίκαιος or ζήσεται. In this verse it is "the promise of the Spirit" (τὴν ἐπαγγελίαν τοῦ πνεύματος) that is received through faith. The relationship between the first and second parts of the verse suggests that the promise of the Spirit is related to "the blessing of Abraham" (ἡ εὐλογία τοῦ Ἀβραάμ). And just a few verses earlier, in v. 8, Paul had said that God's intention to justify the Gentiles would bring about the fulfillment of his promise that all the Gentiles/nations "would be blessed" (ἐνευλογηθήσονται) in him. So, the close relationship had already been asserted between being justified and receiving the Spirit. Thus, it seems plausible that "receiving the Spirit through faith" (τὴν ἐπαγγελίαν τοῦ πνεύματος λάβωμεν διὰ τῆς πίστεως) in this verse could be understood as an interpretive paraphrase Hab 2:4 (quoted just three verses earlier) understood as a promise about people becoming "righteous from faith" (δίκαιος ἐκ πίστεως).

## Galatians 3:26

In 4:6 Paul will argue that it is because the Galatians are "sons of God" that God sent the Spirit of his son into their hearts. So there, sonship is associated with possession of God's Spirit, which we just saw is associated, for Paul (in 3:8, 14) with the blessing of Abraham/justification. In this verse we find a potential rewriting of ἐκ πίστεως in the form of διὰ τῆς πίστεως (ἐν Χριστῷ Ἰησοῦ), and when we stop to see what it is that is acquired through faith here, it is divine sonship (υἱοὶ θεοῦ ἐστε). It seems plausible, then, that "being sons of God through faith" (υἱοὶ θεοῦ ἐστε διὰ τῆς πίστεως) in this verse could be understood as an interpretive paraphrase Hab 2:4 with the inference that to be one of God's sons/children (υἱοὶ θεοῦ ἐστε) is to be δίκαιος and that διὰ τῆς πίστεως = ἐκ πίστεως.

## Galatians 3:2, 5

It seems more difficult to discern whether or not these verses reflect Paul's thinking about Hab 2:4. Rom 10:16–17 suggests Paul's references to "hearing with/of faith" may be indebted to the expression τίς ἐπίστευσεν τῇ ἀκοῇ ἡμῶν in Isa 53:1 LXX. However, the relationship between faith and the Spirit implied in these verses may be more fully understood in light of what has been argued above concerning potential rewritings of Hab 2:4 where the reception or experience of the Spirit stands in for references to being δίκαιος, with ἐξ ἀκοῆς πίστεως being another, less common, rewording or paraphrase of ἐκ πίστεως.

## CONCLUSION

The key to recognizing a rewriting of Hab 2:24 is in noting places where the δικαι- root (a form of δικαιοσύνη or δικαιόω) is used in direct relationship with the πίστ- root (a form of πίστις or πιστεύω), where faith (in noun or verb form) is understood to be the cause or condition of having righteousness or being justified, in a context where he has already cited Hab 2:4 earlier in his argument (or in the case of Gal 2:16, where he is leading up to his citation of Hab 2:4). We also have the unusual case of Gal 2:20 where Paul connects the πίστ- root with a form of ζάω (ἐν πίστει ζῶ).

My analysis of Galatians and the role of Hab 2:4 within it has suggested that more often than not, Paul takes ἐκ πίστεως to modify ὁ δίκαιος[33] and that in those cases that are clear (and probably most cases where it is not) Paul seems to have in mind the πίστις of "the righteous person" as a general category rather than as a reference to Christ in particular. It seems he usually, if not always, takes the πίστις to refer to faith in Christ (or faithfulness/allegiance to Christ) rather than as a statement of Christ's own faithfulness, although numerous texts are ambiguous and may in fact be intentionally so. Also, even where the texts are referring to believers' faith in or faithfulness to Christ, I think Morgan is right that the background suggests it is understood to be part of a reciprocal relationship of faith/faithfulness/trust/trustworthiness/ allegiance,[34] and although it was unusual for the two-sided aspect of the faith-relationship to be explicit in the same text, Paul sometimes hints at it, at the very least. Studies of the πίστις Χριστοῦ debate that do not take into consideration the cumulative evidence of Paul's use and interpretation of Hab 2:4 across much of his letter to Galatians (as well as Romans)—which includes virtually all such contributions—are leaving relevant evidence out of the discussion, as becomes clear once it is recognized that the πίστις Χριστοῦ passages are a subset of a wider range of texts that reflect Paul's understanding of Hab 2:4.

In those cases where he does refer to the life that comes to those who are righteous ἐκ πίστεως, it seems he may have either future resurrection life, or the daily and current experience of the newness of (eternal) life, in mind. The πίστις, which is essential to the establishment of the believer's salvation in Christ, is also the same faith by which they are to live out every aspect of their existence thereafter (Gal 5:6).

Paul repeatedly reiterates the importance and the message of Hab 2:4, sometimes using the distinctive language of the verse and sometimes rewriting it, expressing it in forms he thinks provide greater clarity in communicating the verse's main theological contribution—helping us understand the role of faith in our salvation.

The central point of this chapter, which I hope will stand even if some of the particular interpretations offered above are rejected, is that Hab 2:4 has left its imprint on a much larger portion of Paul's letter to the Galatians than has been previously or usually recognized. Luther was right to affirm that "St. Paul honors Habakkuk greatly, quoting his statement 'The righteous shall live by faith' (Hab. 2:4) more than once."[35] We can go even further than Luther and the history of interpretation in recognizing the extent to which Paul "honored Habakkuk" by paying even closer attention to the extent to which rewritings and snippet quotations of Hab 2:4 are found within his letters, not least in his letter to the Galatians.

## NOTES

1. Richard N. Longenecker, *Galatians*, WBC 41 (Dallas: Word, 1998), 116, 118–19, 124.

2. Hans Dieter Betz, *Galatians: A Commentary on Paul's Letter to the Churches in Galatia*, Hermeneia (Philadelphia: Fortress, 1979), 146.

3. Martin Luther, "Lectures on Habakkuk, 1525," in *Luther's Works,* American Edition, ed. Jaroslav Pelikan and Helmut T. Lehman (Philadelphia: Muehlenberg and Fortress, and St. Louis: Concordia, 1955–86), 19:151–152.

4. See Martin Luther, "Lectures on Galatians, 1535, Chapters 1–4," in *Luther's Works,* American Edition, ed. Jaroslav Pelikan and Helmut T. Lehman (Philadelphia: Muehlenberg and Fortress; St. Louis: Concordia, 1955–86), 26:238, 268.

5. John Calvin, *Commentaries on the Epistles of Paul to the Galatians and Ephesians*, trans. and ed. William Pringle (Edinburgh: Thomas Clark, 1841; Bellingham, WA: Logos Bible Software, 2010), 85. Cf. John Calvin, *Commentary on the Epistle of Paul the Apostle to the Romans,* trans. John Owen (Edinburgh: Calvin Translation Society, 1849), 65.

6. For my treatment of Romans, see Roy E. Ciampa, "Habakkuk 2:4 in Romans: Echoes, Allusions, and Rewriting" in *Scripture, Texts, and Tracings in Romans*, ed. A. Andrew Das and Linda Belleville (Lanham, MD: Lexington/Fortress Academic, 2021), 11–29.

7. Inasmuch as the issues to be covered to lay the foundation for understanding the preliminary background for his use of Hab 2:4 in Galatians are precisely the same as for understanding the preliminary background for his use of the same text in Romans, the material in the next few pages is only slightly adapted from the introduction to these issues presented in my essay on Hab 2:4 in Romans: "Habakkuk 2:4 in Romans: Echoes, Allusions, and Rewriting," 12–14.

8. It is not clear whether the translators had before them a Hebrew text with a different reading than is found in the MT or a damaged MS that left the reading ambiguous (although if the latter case is to hold one might need to assume a lack of prior familiarity with the text on the part of the translators). We also lack space to address debates about the referent of the pronominal suffix in the MT and the question whether the μου in the OG could be taken as an objective genitive ("by faith in me/faithfulness to me"), which would result in an interpretation closer to the Hebrew. Our focus will remain strictly on Paul's rendering, which omits any pronoun (first or third person), since he makes his understanding known (to a greater or lesser degree) through his own comments on and interpretations of the text.

9. Following Hab 2:4 LXX and the twenty-one occurrences in Galatians and Romans, the expression shows up once each in Hebrews and James, and then (once each except where otherwise indicated [all numbers are from *TLG,* accessed 3/7/2022]) in Clement of Rome, Ignatius, Justin Martyr, Sextus Empiricus (twice), Clement of Alexandria (twenty-eight times), Origen (eighty-seven times), Gregory of Nyssa (four times), Eusebius (seven times), etc. The earliest occurrence found of ἐκ πίστεώς in ancient Greek papyri comes in the third century A.D. in PSI 10.1162 (according to the papyrological materials aggregated and searchable at Papyri.info; accessed 3/7/2022). The earliest occurrence found of ἐκ πίστεώς in ancient Greek inscriptions comes in the fourth century A.D. in SEG 6:442 (according to the Searchable Greek Inscriptions of The Packard Humanities Institute found at http://epigraphy .packhum.org; accessed 3/7/2022).

10. Cf. Douglas Moo, *Galatians*, BECNT (Grand Rapids, MI: Baker Academic, 2013), 219 (citing Fitzmyer's "Habakkuk 2:3–4 and the New Testament" in his *To Advance the Gospel: New Testament Studies* [Grand Rapids: Eerdmans, 1998], 236–46); Benjamin Schliesser, "'Christ-Faith' as an Eschatological Event (Galatians 3.23–26): A 'Third View' on Πίστις Χριστοῦ," *JSNT* 38 (2016): 277–300, here 288.

11. Of course, these "rewritings" or glosses provide subtle interpretations of the text. A similar approach to interpretation by glossing or rewriting may be found in the interpretation of Hab 2:4 provided in 1QPesher to Habakkuk vii 17–8.3.

12. Cf. Francis Watson, *Paul and the Hermeneutics of Faith* (London: T & T Clark International, 2004), 54–75.

13. Cf. Ciampa, "Approaching Paul's Use of Scripture in Light of Translation Studies," in *Paul and Scripture: Extending the Conversation*, ed. Christopher D. Stanley; Early Christianity and Its Literature, 9 (Atlanta: Society of Biblical Literature, 2012), 315.

14. Cf. D. A. Campbell, "The Meaning Of Πίστις and Νόμος in Paul: A Linguistic and Structural Perspective," *JBL* 111 (1992): 103, and my comments on his essay (and Hays's messianic interpretation of Hab 2:4) in Ciampa, "Habakkuk 2:4 in Romans: Echoes, Allusions, and Rewriting" (13, and 126nn10–13).

15. Heinrich Schlier, *Der Römerbrief: Kommentar*, HThKNT, Band VI (Freiburg: Herder, 1977), 118, points out that "[ἐ]κ πίστεως und διὰ τῆς πίστεως ist nur rhetorisch-stilistischer Wechsel (vgl. 3,22.25:24; Gal. 2:6, ähnlich wie 4, 11f; 5, 10; 1 Kor 12, 8; 2 Kor 3,11)."

16. Theresa Morgan, *Roman Faith and Christian Faith Pistis and Fides in the Early Roman Empire and Early Churches* (Oxford: Oxford University Press, 2017), 290.

17. Morgan, *Roman Faith and Christian Faith*, 281. Here she refers to the nexus between God, Christ, and humans, but the point applies more broadly as well, it would seem.

18. Morgan, *Roman Faith and Christian Faith*, 53.

19. See, e.g., Deut 7:9; Ps. Sol. 14.1; John 3:16; 1 Cor 4:17; Gal 2:20; 5:6; Eph 1:15; 3:17; 6:21; Col 1:4, 7; 4:7, 9; 1 Thess 3:6; 2 Thess 1:3; 1 Tim 1:14; 6:2; 2 Tim 1:13; 2:22; Titus 2:2; Phlm 5; Jas 2:5; 1 Pet 1:8; 1 John 3:23; 4:16; 5:1; 3 John 5; Jude 20; Rev 1:5; 2:19. Cf. 1 Macc 7:8; 3 Macc 3:10; 5:44; Sir 6:14–16; 27:16–17; John 16:27; Titus 3:15; Jas 2:23.

20. See, e.g., Deut 7:9 (where that pattern is reversed); Ps. Sol. 14.1; John 3:16; 1 Cor 4:17; Gal 2:20; Eph 6:21; Col 1:7; 4:7, 9; 1 Tim 6:2; Jas 2:5; 1 John 4:16; Jude 20.

21. Johannes P. Louw and Eugene A. Nida, *Greek-English Lexicon of the New Testament: Based on Semantic Domains* (New York: United Bible Societies, 1996), 446.

22. See the discussion of Gal 2:20 in Roy E. Ciampa, *The Presence and Function of Scripture in Galatians 1 and 2*, WUNT 2/102 (Tübingen: Mohr Siebeck, 1998), 210–12, where it is argued that there Paul may be playing with the possibilities of both a messianic and an ecclesiocentric interpretation of Hab 2:4. B. Schliesser suggests ἐν πίστει should be understood locatively: I live "in the Son of God-faith" ("'Christ-Faith' as an Eschatological Event [Galatians 3.23–26]: A 'Third View' on Πίστις Χριστοῦ," *JSNT* 38 (2016): 286–88). But this goes against the grain of the

various ways in which Paul rewords Hab 2:4 to express instrumentality in both Galatians (including in 2:16 and 3:2, in the near context of 2:20) and Romans.

23. See again, Ciampa, *The Presence and Function of Scripture in Galatians 1 and 2*, 210–12, where it is suggested that the reference in the first part of Gal 2:20 to Christ "living" rather than Paul, just before Paul says, "I live by faith," may hint that Paul recognizes the possibility that Hab 2:4 may refer to Christ as the righteous one who "lives" by his faith or faithfulness, even as he goes on to state (reflecting an alternative reading of Hab 2:4) that Paul himself "lives by faith" in Christ (taking the reference to faith as Paul's own, and the mention of Christ's love and self-giving at the end of v. 20 as a way of referencing Christ's faithfulness to which Paul's faith is the appropriate response).

24. Morgan, *Roman Faith and Christian Faith*, 289. For further discussion of some of these issues, see my chapter, "'By faith'? Ongoing Translation Issues (500 Years after the Reformation)," in *Reformation Celebration: The Significance of Scripture, Grace, Faith, and Christ*, ed. Eckhard Schnabel and Gordon Isaac (Peabody, MA: Hendrickson, 2018), 143–56.

25. Or, as Matthew W. Bates has argued, one of (mutual and hierarchical) allegiance. See his *Salvation by Allegiance Alone: Rethinking Faith, Works, and the Gospel of Jesus the King* (Grand Rapids: Baker Academic, 2017).

26. Which, as BDAG reminds us often includes the "implication of total commitment to the one who is trusted" (817).

27. See the chapter in *The Faith of Jesus Christ: Exegetical, Biblical, and Theological Studies*, ed. Michael F. Bird and Preston M. Sprinkle (Peabody, MA: Hendrickson, 2010). See also the brief overview of the history of the debate, and James D. G. Dunn's argument for the traditional interpretation and translation ("faith in Christ") in James D. G. Dunn, "Once More, ΠΙΣΤΙΣ ΧΡΙΣΤΟΥ," Appendix 1 in Richard B. Hays, *The Faith of Jesus Christ: The Narrative Substructure of Galatians 3:1–4:11* (Grand Rapids: Eerdmans, 2002), 249–71 and, more recently, B. J. Oropeza, "Justification by Faith in Christ or Faithfulness of Christ? Updating the ΠΙΣΤΙΣ ΧΡΙΣΤΟΥ Debate in Light of Paul's Use of Scripture," *JTS* 72 (2021) 102–24. For a brief defense of the traditional (objective genitive) view, see also Moisés Silva, "πιστεύω, πίστις," in the *New International Dictionary of New Testament Theology and Exegesis* (5 vols., Grand Rapids: Zondervan, 2014), 3:768–69.

28. Schliesser, "'Christ-Faith' as an Eschatological Event," 286.

29. See Peter Cotterell and Max Turner, *Linguistics & Biblical Interpretation* (Downers Grove, IL: InterVarsity, 1989), 152–53. The semantic principle of maximal redundancy is also important to consider in this argument (cf. Moisés Silva, *Biblical Words and Their Meaning: An Introduction to Lexical Semantics* [Grand Rapids: Zondervan, 1994], 153–56, for a discussion of the principle; for his application of the principle to the question of πίστις Χριστοῦ, see his *Philippians*, BECNT [Grand Rapids: Baker Academic, 2005], 161–62).

30. For a helpful updated discussion of the "Eschatological Christ-Event" view, see Johnathan Harris, "A Tale of Two Siblings: Re-Reading Abraham in Galatians in the Light of Eschatological Christ-Faith" (Ph.D. diss., Wheaton College, 2020) 41–55. Even the position that the πίστις in view is that of believers' faith in Christ recognizes

that such faith was realized upon the eschatological arrival of Christ and is thus tied up in the arrival of the eschatological Christ-event and is no less a Christocentric πίστις than the objective genitive view of πίστις Χριστοῦ.

31. Note how 3:8 makes it even clearer that the ἐκ πίστεως of this verse is about being justified ἐκ πίστεως, which is what Paul takes the verse to be about.

32. See Ciampa, "Habakkuk 2:4 in Romans: Echoes, Allusions, and Rewriting," 14–15.

33. That ἐκ πίστεως should be understood to modify ὁ δίκαιος rather than ζήσεται is supported by a number of scholars besides Cranfield. See, e.g., M. Wolter, *Der Brief an die Römer, Teilband 1: Röm 1–8*, EKKNT VI/1 (Neukirchen-Vluyn: Neukirchener Theologie, 2014), 127; See also Ulrich Wilckens, *Der Brief an die Römer (Röm 1–5)*, EKKNT VI/1 (Neukirchen-Vluyn: Neukirchener, 1978), 90, 199, 209. Pace H. Schlier, *Der Römerbrief*, 46.

34. See Bates, *Salvation by Allegiance Alone.*

35. Luther, "Lectures on Habakkuk, 1525," 19:151–152.


# BIBLIOGRAPHY

Arndt, William, Frederick W. Danker, Walter Bauer, and F. Wilbur Gingrich. *A Greek-English Lexicon of the New Testament and Other Early Christian Literature.* Chicago: University of Chicago Press, 2000.

Bates, Matthew W. *Salvation by Allegiance Alone: Rethinking Faith, Works, and the Gospel of Jesus the King.* Grand Rapids: Baker Academic, 2017.

Betz, Hans Dieter. *Galatians: A Commentary on Paul's Letter to the Churches in Galatia.* Hermeneia series. Philadelphia: Fortress, 1979.

Bird, Michael F., and Preston M. Sprinkle, eds. *The Faith of Jesus Christ: Exegetical, Biblical, and Theological Studies.* Peabody, MA: Hendrickson, 2010.

Calvin, John. *Commentaries on the Epistles of Paul to the Galatians and Ephesians.* Translated and edited by William Pringle. Edinburgh: Thomas Clark, 1841.

Campbell, D. A. *The Deliverance of God: An Apocalyptic Rereading of Justification in Paul.* Grand Rapids: Eerdmans, 2009.

———. "The Meaning Of Πίστις and Νόμος in Paul: A Linguistic and Structural Perspective." *JBL* 111 (1992): 91–103.

Ciampa, Roy E. "'By Faith'? Ongoing Translation Issues. 500 Years after the Reformation." In *Reformation Celebration: The Significance of Scripture, Grace, Faith, and Christ*, edited by Eckhard Schnabel and Gordon Isaac, 143–56. Peabody, MA: Hendrickson, 2018.

———. "Habakkuk 2:4 in Romans: Echoes, Allusions, and Rewriting." In *Scripture, Texts, and Tracings in Romans*, edited by A. Andrew Das and Linda Belleville, 11–29. Lanham, MD: Lexington/Fortress Academic, 2021.

———. *The Presence and Function of Scripture in Galatians 1 and 2.* WUNT 2/102. Tübingen: Mohr Siebeck, 1998.

Cotterell, Peter, and Max Turner. *Linguistics & Biblical Interpretation.* Downers Grove, IL: InterVarsity Press, 1989.

Cranfield, C. E. B. *A Critical and Exegetical Commentary on the Epistle to the Romans*. ICC. London; New York: T&T Clark International, 2004.

Dunn, James D. G. "Once More, ΠΙΣΤΙΣ ΧΡΙΣΤΟΥ." Appendix 1 in Richard B. Hays, *The Faith of Jesus Christ*, 249–71.

———. *Romans 1–8*. WBC 38A. Dallas: Word, 1998.

Fitzmyer, Joseph A. "Habakkuk 2:3–4 and the New Testament." In *To Advance the Gospel: New Testament Studies*, 236–46. Grand Rapids: Eerdmans, 1998.

———. *Romans: A New Translation with Introduction and Commentary*. Anchor Yale Bible 33. New Haven; London: Yale University Press, 2008.

Harris, Johnathan. "A Tale of Two Siblings: Re-Reading Abraham in Galatians in the Light of Eschatological Christ-Faith." PhD diss., Wheaton College, 2020.

Hays, Richard B. *The Faith of Jesus Christ: The Narrative Substructure of Galatians 3:1–4:11*. Grand Rapids: Eerdmans, 2002.

Longenecker, Richard N. *Galatians*. WBC 41. Dallas: Word, 1998.

Louw, Johannes P., and Eugene A. Nida, *Greek-English Lexicon of the New Testament: Based on Semantic Domains*. New York: United Bible Societies, 1996.

Luther, Martin. "Lectures on Habakkuk, 1525." In *Luther's Works,* American Edition. 55 vols. Vol. 19, edited by Jaroslav Pelikan and Helmut T. Lehman, 149–237. Philadelphia: Muehlenberg and Fortress, and St. Louis: Concordia, 1955–86.

———. "Lectures on Galatians, 1535, Chapters 1–4." In *Luther's Works,* American Edition. 55 vols. Vol. 26, edited by Jaroslav Pelikan and Helmut T. Lehman, 1–461. Philadelphia: Muehlenberg and Fortress, and St. Louis: Concordia, 1955–86.

Moo, Douglas J. *Galatians*. BECNT. Grand Rapids: Baker Academic, 2013.

Morgan, Theresa. *Roman Faith and Christian Faith Pistis and Fides in the Early Roman Empire and Early Churches*. Oxford: Oxford University Press, 2017.

Nygren, Anders. *Commentary on Romans*. Philadelphia: Fortress, 1967.

Oropeza, B. J. "Justification by Faith in Christ or Faithfulness of Christ? Updating the *ΠΙΣΤΙΣ ΧΡΙΣΤΟΥ* Debate in Light of Paul's Use of Scripture." *JTS* 72 (2021): 102–24.

Schlier, Heinrich. *Der Römerbrief: Kommentar*. HThKNT, Band VI. Freiburg: Herder, 1977.

Schliesser, Benjamin. "'Christ-Faith' as an Eschatological Event (Galatians 3.23–26): A 'Third View' on Πίστις Χριστοῦ." *JSNT* 38 (2016): 277–300.

Silva, Moisés. *Biblical Words and Their Meaning: An Introduction to Lexical Semantics*. Grand Rapids: Zondervan, 1994.

———. *New International Dictionary of New Testament Theology and Exegesis.* 5 vols. Grand Rapids: Zondervan, 2014.

———. "Old Testament in Paul." In *Dictionary of Paul and His Letters*. Downers Grove, IL: InterVarsity, 1993; 630–42.

Thesaurus Linguae Graecae® Digital Library. Ed. Maria C. Pantelia. University of California, Irvine. http://www.tlg.uci.edu (accessed 3/7/2022).

Watson, Francis. *Paul and the Hermeneutics of Faith*. London: T & T Clark International, 2004.

Wilckens, Ulrich. *Der Brief an die Römer (Röm 1–5)*. EKKNT VI/1. Neukirchen-Vluyn: Neukirchener, 1978.

Wolter, Michael. *Der Brief an die Römer (Teilband 1: Röm 1–8)*. EKKNT VI/1. Neukirchen-Vluyn: Neukirchener Theologie, 2014.

*Chapter 6*

# "These Things Are Spoken Allegorically"

## Paul and Christian Interpretation of Scripture

Mark A. Seifrid

Near the close of his argument in Galatians, Paul resumes its opening, taking up the Genesis narrative of Abraham with which he began (Gal 3:6–14). He now interjects an interpretive comment to his reading of the text that has long been problematic for interpreters. The things concerning Abraham's sons, the story of their births through Hagar and Sarah, "are spoken allegorically" (Gal 4:24). The figural interpretation of the text that follows is no less remarkable; the two women turn out to be two covenants, two mountains of encounter with God where two differing peoples are born, and thus two differing "Jerusalems." Paul's interpretive comment is no *obiter dictum*; even if Abraham now recedes into the background, the argument revolves around him. It is with Abraham that Paul's argument began (Gal 3:6–14). It is with Abraham that it closes (Gal 4:21–31). Correspondingly, although Paul does not comment on his use of Scripture in his first appeal to Abraham, his reading of it there is no less provocative than it is here.[1] The Abrahamic *inclusio* makes clear that Paul's interpretive comment provides indication of a hermeneutic that guides his reading of Scripture. In this chapter I will briefly explore this hermeneutic and offer reflections on its significance.

Current interpretation of Paul's interpretive comment in Gal 4:24, ἅτινά ἐστιν ἀλληγορούμενα, is divided and somewhat confused, just as it has been historically. The lexica are properly ambivalent, allowing that ἀλληγορεῖν may signify either "speaking allegorically" or "interpreting allegorically."[2]

The English versions are divided, some attributing the allegorizing to Paul, others ascribing it to the Genesis narrative.[3] Recent commentaries univocally ascribe the allegorization of the Genesis text to Paul.[4] And here lies the confusion. Paul's opening address to the Galatians provides an unmistakable indication of the meaning of his provocative gloss: "Tell me, you who want to be under the Law, do you not listen to the Law?" (Gal 4:21).[5] Paul does not ask whether the Galatians are listening to him. He asks whether they are listening to "the Law." It is not his allegorizing to which they are to give heed, but the allegory found in the Law itself. He is not putting his rhetorical skills on display. He is providing a lesson in biblical hermeneutics.

This interpretive confusion almost certainly arises from the predilections of interpreters, to which I will turn later. It is materially based on the sense of Paul's usage, a *hapax* in the biblical literature. The evaluation of Paul's declaration ἅτινά ἐστιν ἀλληγορούμενα (Gal 4:24) consequently requires a lexical judgment based on a broader body of literature,[6] of which the most relevant source is Philo of Alexandria. Paul's contemporary is connected with him in regard to this usage in at least two ways: (1) Philo and Paul are apparently the first to offer commentary on Scripture (as opposed to contemporizing it, as, for example, at Qumran or the book of Jubilees); (2) not coincidentally, they are also the first with whom the hermeneutical language of allegory appears in a Hellenistic-Jewish context.[7]

In relation to Philo's usage, three observations are in order. First, he writes in a period in which the meaning of "allegory" (ἀλληγορία)—originally a rhetorical term for speaking of something indirectly through figures—had become a technical term for the interpretation of religious speech.[8] This shift in the usage of "allegory" is reflected in a cluster of terms appearing with Philo,[9] which make clear that Philo understands "allegory" as arising from Moses and from the structure of reality itself.[10] Especially the terms ὑπονοία ("hidden meaning") and αἰνίττεσθαι ("to riddle"), which Philo uses in reference to Moses as well as the text, make it clear that he understands the Scripture itself as the source of allegory.[11]

Secondly, and more narrowly related to our concern, in half of Philo's usage of the verb ἀλληγορέω, he refers to Moses as having spoken allegorically.[12] Where he speaks of his own allegorizing (or, in one instance, that of the Essenes), it is clear that he regards the divine mode of speaking and the structure of reality as calling for allegorical interpretation.[13] Philo does not regard himself as creating allegories but as discovering them.[14]

Thirdly, Philo's allegorizing is an attempt to trace the intent of Moses.[15] His insistence on this matter derives not merely from his Platonism, but from his concern to guard the Scriptures from a literal reading that would lead to the charge that they are filled with "myths," as contemporary Alexandrian interpreters had done with the Homeric writings.[16]

Interpreters of Paul often legitimate their ascription of allegorizing to Paul by appealing to Philo's occasional use of the verb ἀλληγορέω in the sense "to allegorize." Viewed through Philo's interpretive lens, however, the distinction between discovering allegory in the text and allegorizing the text is a distinction without a difference.[17]

Philo's reading of Scripture furthermore seems fanciful to most modern interpreters because they do not share his Platonic conception of reality. Origen did. His reception of Philonic allegory served the church as a means of problem-solving difficult texts and thus retaining the Old Testament, in much the same way that allegory served Philo. Within the church, Christian doctrine and the clear passages of Scripture came to replace Platonism in an Augustinian hermeneutic of "letter" and "Spirit" that shaped Christian interpretation of Scripture into the medieval period and beyond. These differing approaches to Scripture share a common understanding: within their many human words, the Scriptures bear a hidden, unified message that is disclosed by the recognition of their divine subject matter. Admittedly, the development of "method," as is evidenced, for example, by the *quadriga*, came to encroach upon a proper reading of the text and required a historical corrective. The allegorical interpretation of Scripture, nevertheless, was thought to arise from the Spirit and the Scripture itself, even if it often arose from the imagination of the interpreter.

Before we turn to Paul, a brief note on "the letter" is in order. When Philo speaks of his own allegorizing, he uses the active voice of the verb. When he employs the passive voice—as does Paul—it almost always refers to Moses's having spoken allegorically in Scripture. A single exception appears in Philo's reference to the Essenes, who "possessed books of ancients who left many memorials of the form in which things (namely, of Scripture) were allegorized" (Philo, *Contempl.* 28–29). Philo in no instance refers to his own acts of allegorizing with the passive voice. It is unlikely that Paul does.

Finally, although it is not entirely clear whether the compound verb ἀλληγορέω (ἄλλος-ἀγορεύω) retains the sense of "public speaking" within Philo's usage, as its early rhetorical sense and etymology might suggest, it is certainly possible, perhaps even likely, since Philo generally introduces citations of Scripture with "it says," or "Moses said" (or "says"). It is similarly likely with Paul that in Gal 4:24 the idea of public speaking is present. That the Galatians are to "listen" to the Law, which speaks of "other things," implies that the Law speaks in an open and public way. In the interpretation of "Abraham" it is the reading of Scripture itself that is under contention. Paul is teaching the Galatians how the Scriptures are to be read.

Summa: although interpreters often appeal to Philo's usage as a basis for claiming that Paul speaks of his own allegorizing in Gal 4:24, that usage offers no support for such an interpretation of Paul. In a way that clearly differs from that of Philo, Paul hears the Scripture, or more precisely, the Law speaking allegorically and wants the Galatians to do so as well.

For Paul, then, the Law speaks within the Genesis narrative of Abraham, in the two-part story of Hagar and Sarah (Gen 16:1–16; 21:1–21). Why, however, does he return to the figure of Abraham so late in his argument? In the first instance, this return to Abraham reflects the hermeneutic that guides his earlier argument. The apostle understands himself as doing nothing other than echoing the prophetic voice of Scripture in his proclamation of Christ. The Scripture thus anticipates the voice of the apostle, proclaiming the Gospel to Abraham in advance (Gal 3:8). Paul's appeal to the Law at the closing of his argument (Gal 4:21–31) corresponds to his appeal to Scripture at its opening (Gal 3:6–14).

The closing of Paul's argument also displays a thematic shift over against its opening that provides a significant indication of his hermeneutic. In both instances, Paul appeals to Abraham in order to instruct the confused Galatians on the question of believing identity. In the opening, before he even speaks of God's promise to Abraham, he points to Abraham's response to that promise: Abraham believed God. This response of faith brought to Abraham the divine reckoning of righteousness (Gal 3:6; Gen 15:6). Paul then admonishes the Galatians, "Know that 'those of faith' are the sons of Abraham" (Gal 3:7). The faith of the patriarch provides the pattern that all those who are to share in the promised blessing must follow. They, too, must believe God (Gal 3:9). The "sons of Abraham" are those who imitate their father, as in Rom 4:9–12. Contrastingly, in Paul's second appeal to Abraham at the close of his argument, the patriarch makes only a cameo appearance: "It is written that Abraham had two sons" (Gal 4:22). This brief summary opens the way to the recollection of Hagar and Sarah, who bear two sons to Abraham. If the earlier Abraham narrative centers on faith as the human response to divine promise, the latter focuses on "birth." The "sons" (υἱοί) who imitate their father are replaced by the "children" (τέκνα) who are born to Hagar and Sarah.[18] If in the earlier text identity is conceived in a constructivist manner, here it is conceived in essentialist terms.[19]

This new perspective bears hermeneutical implications. The two opposing mothers correspond to the two opposing words of God, promise and Law, which Paul already has presented as the basis for understanding Scripture (Gal 3:15–29). Paul might simply have pointed to Sarah and the story of Isaac's birth in order to underscore the work of the promise. Instead, he appeals to Hagar, bringing into view the other woman, the other son, the other "covenant," the other, earthly "mountain," and "the present Jerusalem."[20] Each of the two covenants thus has its own location. Each gives birth to a people, one born "according to the flesh" (Gal 4:23, 29), the other born "through promise" and thus "according to the Spirit" (Gal 4:23, 28–29). One is born into slavery (Gal 4:24). The other is born into freedom (Gal 4:23, 26, 31).[21] Paul's appeal to the story of Hagar and Sarah is a reminder to the Galatians of their birth identity, given in the face of the temptation to construct an identity by joining "the present Jerusalem" through circumcision and commitment to the Law. *The Law itself speaks of promise.*

The contrast and conflict between the two peoples born of the two women come to expression in three oppositional pairings, each of which reflects Paul's larger argument in the letter. In fact, within his closing they appear *prior* to his appeal to the Law and its allegory. His opening address to the Galatians, "Do you not listen to the Law?" presupposes the opposition between promise and Law which he already has presented: the promise to Abraham has priority over the Law. The Law serves the promise by effecting slavery under sin. This takes place in order that the promise might be given to those who are of Christ and of faith (Gal 3:15–22; 3:23–29). It is evident that Paul's description of the Galatians as those "who want to be under the Law" presupposes this ordering of the relation between promise and Law, especially in light of his announcement that the advent of Christ and of faith brings deliverance from this subjugation (Gal 3:23).[22]

In a similar way, the appeal to the figures of Hagar and Sarah, "the slave-girl" and "the free woman" takes up the second, existential opposition between "slavery and freedom" that appears in metaphorical, theological form earlier in the letter, now making it the leitmotif of the argument. Paul already has indicated pointedly that freedom is present in Christ alone. The false brothers have spied out this freedom in order to enslave "us" (Gal 2:4). Outside of Christ, the promised seed, Scripture has imprisoned "all things under sin" including Jews themselves (Gal 3:22).[23] Freedom is a liberation from "the present evil age" through Christ's redeeming act (Gal 1:4). This apocalyptic note resounds loudly in Paul's reading of the story of Hagar and Sarah. It is "the Jerusalem above" who is free. She "is our mother." Paul does not conceive of this "Jerusalem above" as descending into the present world and merely transforming it.[24] It is opposed to the "present Jerusalem" and shall supplant it.[25] As is well-known, the prophetic literature and the psalms bear a productive ambiguity, in which earthly promises take on transcendent dimensions, as is the case with Isa 54:1, to which Paul appeals. The apostle offers an apocalyptic resolution of this prophetic ambiguity. For Paul, this "apocalyptic" is born of the risen Christ, who has set "us" free and in whom nothing matters but a new creation.[26] Paul thus finds the final, eschatological reality of "freedom" in the story of Hagar and Sarah in the metaphor of earthly enslavement and freedom.

The two births are defined ontologically by the third opposition between "the flesh" and "the Spirit." As is apparent from Paul's usage and its biblical antecedents, when used in reference to the human being, "flesh" signifies material existence in estrangement from God, which for Paul means existence under the power of sin and death.[27] "The Spirit" in contrast is never used in reference to the human being as such, but only in reference to the human being indwelt by God, an indwelling in which God remains distinct from the human person, even if the Spirit constitutes human identity. Correspondingly, "the Spirit" appears with Paul as a divine agent and power acting upon the human being, creating life and faith, bringing the birth of a new person.[28] This language of "flesh" and "Spirit" is implicitly universal, provocatively so in the Antioch speech, when, echoing the Scriptures, Paul instructs Cephas (and the Galatians) that "no flesh" shall be justified before God by means of "works of the Law" (Gal 2:16; Gen 6:3; Ps 143:2). The birth of Isaac "according to the Spirit" (Gal 4:28) corresponds to the new birth of the Galatians "according to promise." They are thus born of "the Jerusalem above" (Gal 4:26, 31). Just as for Paul "freedom" takes on eschatological and apocalyptic dimensions, so does "the birth according to the Spirit" (Gal 4:29).

Paul's appeal to the story of Hagar and Sarah corresponds fundamentally to these three opposing pairings of Law and promise, slavery and freedom, and flesh and Spirit, which constitute the essence of his argument in Galatians. The opposition between Law and promise lies behind his appeal to the text, as is clear from his introductory query. The opposition between enslavement and freedom is embodied in Hagar and Sarah, who serve as the basis of the metaphor that Paul finds in the text. The distinction between the birth of the two sons, one "according to the flesh" and one "through promise" comes to expression prior to Paul's appeal to the allegorical voice of the Law in Gal 4:24. All three pairings finally entail an opposition between earthly and temporal existence in alienation from God, and the life and existence of the eschaton. They have a common source, which correspondingly may be seen to lie behind his reading of the Law. Paul's hermeneutic is material. It arises from the crucified and risen Christ and God's revelation of him "in" Paul for proclamation among the pagans (Gal 1:16).

The content of the allegory that Paul presents bears out this thought. The women do not appear in Paul's retelling of the story as the dramatic characters of the Genesis narratives, but as textual figures embodying the oppositions that Paul already has introduced. Hagar is named merely as a "slave-girl" (παιδίσκη)[29] who gives birth to a son of Abraham, a son who must be expelled from Abraham's house and inheritance (Gal 4:22–23, 30). Her identity is transferred to the covenant from Mount Sinai that "gives birth for slavery," and, further, to "the present Jerusalem," who, Paul asserts "is enslaved along with her children" (Gal 4:24–25).[30] Sarah does not appear by name at all.[31] She disappears into the figure of the barren, desolate, and abandoned "Jerusalem" who in an Isaianic oracle is promised children (Gal 4:27; Isa 54:1).

Correspondingly, even before Paul cites the Isaianic oracle, he transposes it to a pre-existent, eschatological reality in which the promise already is fulfilled. Sarah, "the free woman" yields her identity to "the Jerusalem above" (Gal 4:26–27).[32] The metaphor of motherhood serves a series of metalepses and brings Paul's allegorical leaps—from covenant to mountain-city, to heavenly, eschatological reality—to their apocalyptic conclusion: "The Jerusalem above is free, she is our mother" (Gal 4:26). The conclusion significantly recalls Paul's immediately preceding description of his apostolic travail with the Galatians: "My children, with whom I again suffer birth-pangs until Christ is formed in you." (Gal 4:19). Paul's retelling of the story of Hagar and Sarah is directed to the identity and existence of "the children" who are determined by their birth—an "apocalyptic birth" that takes place by the proclamation of Christ.

Paul subsumes an Isaianic citation within his allegorical reading of the story of Hagar and Sarah as an explication of his naming "the Jerusalem above" as "our mother" (Gal 4:26). While the citation does not determine Paul's reading of Genesis, it reveals the scope of his hermeneutic and introduces a dramatic element into what otherwise would be a mere series of metaphorical leaps. The appeal to the founding narrative of Genesis, including the prior recollection of the promise to Abraham, makes clear that Paul hears the Law in the context of God's primal dealings with humanity. The Isaianic reference shows that he hears its voice also in harmony with the voice of the prophets. "Listening" to the Law is to listen to one of the many concordant witnesses to God's dealings in Christ. As Paul puts it in Romans, the whole of Scripture, "the Law and the prophets," bear witness to "the righteousness of God" that is revealed in the Gospel (Rom 3:21).

The Isaianic citation is a divine promise addressed to the desolated and barren Jerusalem, assuring her that it is she who will have numerous children, rather than her opponent, who has a husband (Isa 54:1). The text reflects a rivalry between Jerusalem and Babylon (cf. Isa 47:1–15), which Paul translates into one between "the Jerusalem above" and "the present Jerusalem," contemporizing the Scriptural figures.[33] He thereby illumines the present situation of believers in Christ as one entailing persecution from "the one born according to the flesh" (Gal 4:29). While the larger context of Galatians suggests Jewish (and not Roman) persecution of believers in Jesus, Paul's language allows broader implications for the life of believers in the world. The contrastive "shall have many children rather than the one having a husband" (Gal 4:27) finds its fulfillment only in the word of Sarah, which Paul transposes to the prophetic voice of Scripture: "The son of the slave girl shall not inherit with the son of the free woman" (Gal 4:30).[34] Correspondingly, the opposition between "the present Jerusalem" and "the Jerusalem above" signals that the "freedom" that Paul announces is the freedom of the eschaton, which already is present in Christ and in faith (Gal 4:25–26).[35] Paul does not conceive of "the Jerusalem above" as a reality that merely descends into the present world, as in Jewish tradition.[36] It shall supplant the "present Jerusalem."[37] Here again is Paul's apocalyptic resolution of the ambiguity of the Isaianic text (cf. Isa 54:1–10). As with the story of Hagar and Sarah, Paul reads the book of Isaiah in the light of the crucified and risen Christ.

We may now return to Paul's declaration that the story of Hagar and Sarah "is spoken allegorically," the only instance of this language in the Septuagint and the entire New Testament. What calls it forth? The answer may be deceptively simple. Within the Genesis narrative of the promise given to Abraham and Sarah, with all their human weaknesses and moral failures—not least Sarah's desperate attempt to obtain a child through Hagar—Paul hears a radically different story of enslavement and freedom, the weakness of the flesh and the work of the Spirit, the curse of the Law and the blessing of the promise, in which God in Christ has overcome sin and death, and has established the freedom of the new creation. Paul finds in the figures of the enslaved woman and the free woman, to whom the divine promise was given, a coincidence of opposites that finds its resolution and fulfillment in Christ.[38] The polarities that govern the Genesis narrative are transcended by the reality of the Jerusalem above that has intersected the world in Christ: in Christ there is neither Jew nor Greek, neither slave nor free, not even male and female. The apostle is thus giving birth to the Galatians (4:19). Sarah has the last word to Abraham (4:30). The mundane, if dramatic, story of Hagar and Sarah speaks of a radically other hidden reality, the reality of the new creation, the eschaton that has entered the world in Christ. Even Jerusalem serves as a figure, both in promise and in its imprisonment, of the transcendent that now has been revealed. When heard in its narrative context, the Law that imprisoned all things under sin speaks of the promise, and thus of Christ and the Gospel that proclaims him.[39] To "speak of something *other*" is the very sense of ἀλληγορέω in its original, rhetorical usage. And just as this verb had come to signify "speaking of something hidden," the Law speaks of the promise to Abraham and its fulfillment in Christ. It therewith speaks of its own giving birth for slavery, its alien work that in the end serves the birth for freedom by Another. The apostolic proclamation has made the secret of the Genesis narrative an open secret, one which the Galatians themselves ought to be able to hear, and one to which Paul calls them to respond.[40] In other contexts, Paul readily appeals to τύποι from the past, in which God's dealings with humanity are made visible for instruction and warning. The present context is one of sheer opposition, the opposition between the Law and the promise that finds its coincidence in the crucified and risen Christ. Precisely for this reason, Paul indicates that the Law, which serves the promise, speaks of something other and beyond itself: "These things are spoken allegorically."

The confusion of contemporary interpreters on the question of the allegory of Scripture itself, which I have noted above, is understandable. Doesn't Paul's daring hermeneutic open itself to arbitrary interpretation, a reading of meaning into the text rather than out of it? Unless we are prepared to accept the *quadriga* that became characteristic of interpretation in the medieval period or throw open the door to a radical reader-response criticism, the question is legitimate. It is especially pressing for Protestant interpreters, who have insisted on the primacy of the *sensus literalis*. In the wake of the development of historical-criticism in the nineteenth century, this *sensus literalis*, also understood as the *sensus historicus*, has become the criterion for the interpretation of Scripture. For many conservative interpreters of the nineteenth century—and in the present as well—the concept of a "salvation-history" internal to the Scriptures, in which the progressive course of God's dealings with Israel could be traced, came to serve as an alternative "histori-cal method" by which to understand the unity of Scripture as it is fulfilled in Christ.[41] In varying ways and measures "salvation-history" thus plays a significant role within conservative interpretation today, not least in its con-nection with "typology" and the question of Paul's hermeneutic. Three obser-vations about contemporary typological interpretation are relevant here. First, in its salvation-historical form "typology" no less than historical-criticism implies a method of interpretation, one that is bound to a reconstruction of a "storyline" or progress in revelation.[42] Just as historical criticism does, this method seeks an interpretive key to the Old Testament behind the text. Paul, in contrast, calls his readers to stand before the text of the Law to "hear" (ἀκούω) its witness to the promise fulfilled in Christ, its "message of faith" (ἀκοὴ πίστεως; Gal 4:21; 3:3, 5). Historical method is by all means to be embraced and employed. Whether it can serve as the final and decisive cri-terion for interpretation is another question. One need only trace the history of the interpretation of Scripture—whether critical or conservative—to see that its course largely has been determined by the questions and judgments of the times.

Secondly, the commonly accepted salvation-historical paradigm for under-standing "types" has been challenged. We may understand τύπος (and for that matter, ἀντίτυπος, which bears the same sense) as "that which makes something visible," without embedding it within one form of "salvation his-tory" or another.[43] The (implicit) historical referentiality of a "type" is not thereby necessarily eliminated. It is, however, set within a wider range of possibilities. The text, its figures, and its narratives come into prominence. Understood in this way, a "τύπος" does not differ appreciably from "alle-gory." It signals the revelatory nature of the text, while "allegory" points to the paradoxical hiddenness of the divine revelation.

From Philo of Alexandria, through the medieval period, and with new vigor in our own time, interpreters have appealed to allegory in order to solve problems and to understand the Scriptures. Paul, in his own way, too, appeals to allegory, in order to solve the problem of the relationship between Law and promise and to bring understanding to his Galatian readers. For most modern readers, in contrast, Paul does not solve problems, he creates them. Despite postmodern challenges, for most of us the "meaning" of the text remains bound up with historical method, whether that entails historical-critical investigation, or one form or another of salvation-history. Philo had no need of method in order to secure a reliable reading of the text; his Platonic conception of the text and the world already did that for him. *Mutatis mutandis*, this applies to the history of Christian allegorical interpretation, in which commonly accepted doctrine, morals, and hope were supposed to guide interpretation. Paul, in contrast, offers neither a philosophical or theological construct nor a historical method by which the Scriptures might be rightly understood. His reading of the figures of Hagar and Sarah provides us with an indication of his radically different, material hermeneutic, grounded in the risen Christ. It is a hermeneutic that is intended to "give birth to children," to remake persons, just as the apostle presents himself to the Galatians as sharing in the role of Sarah and the heavenly Jerusalem: "My children . . . with whom I have birth-pangs until Christ is formed in you" (Gal 4:19). His rehearsal of the stories of the women is directed to the question of believing identity which at that moment was at stake in Galatia: "We are children . . . of the free woman!" (Gal 4:31). This identity, according to Paul, is not constructed. It is given by birth. The apostle is not calling the Galatians to figure out the Scriptures. He is announcing to them that they have been figured out in the Scriptures by the promise fulfilled in Christ.[44] The difference between the application of historical method—which, once more, undeniably has its place—and the apostolic call to faith becomes apparent here. There is no method that takes us out of our time and place, lifting us above the earthly plain. According to the apostle, however, that is precisely what the proclamation of Christ does. The allegory of slavery and freedom is a call to find ourselves in the Genesis narratives of Hagar and Sarah: *Mutatio nomine, de te fabula narratur* (Horace, *Satires* 1.1.69).[45] Naturally, Paul's reading of Genesis invites scrutiny and reflection, and critical, historical analysis. I trust that this chapter, by its very nature, has shown that method is not to be excluded. Historical method, like the Law itself, nevertheless has its limit and end.[46]

## NOTES

1. I am recalling the Scripture's proclamation of the Gospel to Abraham (Gal 3:8) and Paul's identification of Christ as the sole seed of Abraham (Gal 3:16).

2. BDAG, "ἀλληγορέω," 46, has "to speak allegorically": BrillDAG, "ἀλληγορέω," 92, which allows the sense "to interpret allegorically," has the indeterminate passive "to be expressed by way of allegory" for Gal 4:24; LSJM "ἀλληγορέω," 69, glosses Gal 4:24 as "to be spoken allegorically." A. Kretzer ("ἀλληγορέω," *EDNT* 1:62) goes both ways, rendering Gal 4:24 as "all of which is spoken allegorically," while attributing a "typological allegorizing" to Paul. F. Büchsel ("ἀλληγορέω," *TDNT*, 1:263) attributes the allegorizing to Paul.

3. The ESV, for example, has "Now this may be interpreted allegorically." The NIV seems to attribute the allegorizing to Paul, while avoiding the term: "These things are being taken figuratively." The CSB renders the text similarly. The NRSV in contrast has Paul attribute allegory to the biblical narrative, as does the RSV: "Now this is allegory."

4. Frank Matera is one of the few who treat the passage consistently: Paul refers to his own words in 4:22–23 when he says that "these things are spoken allegorically," *Galatians*, SP (Collegeville, MN: Liturgical Press, 1992), 169n24. Richard B. Hays, who attributes the allegorical "misreading" of the text to Paul, at the same time regards Paul as finding this meaning in the Genesis narrative, *Echoes of Scripture in the Letters of Paul* (New Haven, CT: Yale University Press, 1989), 111–21, esp. 116; Richard B. Hays "The Letter to the Galatians," *NIDB* 11:299–310, esp. 302, 307. David DeSilva, *The Letter to the Galatians*, NICNT (Grand Rapids: Eerdmans, 2018), 392–96, acknowledges that the usage of the verb suggests that Paul finds the meaning in the text, but goes on to speak of Paul's own allegorical interpretation of the text. Martin Meiser, despite acknowledging that the wording of Gal 4:24 might signal that Paul regards the biblical text as speaking allegorically, likewise regards Paul as providing his own allegorical interpretation of the Genesis narrative, *Der Brief des Paulus an die Galater*, THKNT 9 (Leipzig: Evangelische Verlagsanstalt, 2022), 214–18. Martinus de Boer argues that Paul provides his own allegorical interpretation of the passage, even though it is unclear as to whether Paul regarded the Genesis story as an allegory. At the same time, he underscores Paul's insistence that the Galatians "really listen to the law," *Galatians: A Commentary*, NTL (Louisville: Westminster/John Knox, 2011), 286–95. A. Andrew Das similarly argues that Paul himself is interpreting the text allegorically and yet characterizes Paul's address to the Galatians as an insistence that they must understand "these Scriptures," *Galatians*, Concordia Commentary (St. Louis: Concordia Publishing House, 2014), 491–94. Douglas J. Moo attributes the allegory to Paul's conviction about the direction of salvation history; the allegory is controlled by "Paul's hermeneutical axioms." Nevertheless, Paul wants the Galatians to "learn" what the Law is saying, *Galatians*, BECNT (Grand Rapids: Baker, 2013), 294–300. Schreiner falls into the same difficulty, *Galatians*, Zondervan Exegetical Commentary (Grand Rapids: Zondervan, 2010), 298–300; as does Craig S. Keener, *Galatians: A Commentary* (Grand Rapids: Baker, 2019), 399–410, and

Ben Witherington III, *Grace in Galatia: A Commentary on St. Paul's Letter to the Galatians* (Grand Rapids: Eerdmans, 1998), 321–28.

5. The usage of ἀκούω with the accusative signals not the mere hearing of a source of a sound, but the reception of its message and content, e.g., Acts 2:22; 4:4; 10:44; Gal 1:13; Phlm 5.

6. The vocabulary of "allegory" is lacking not only elsewhere in the New Testament, but also in the Septuagint.

7. On this topic, see the rich and nuanced work of Maren R. Niehoff, *Philo of Alexandria: An Intellectual Biography* (New Haven, CT: Yale University Press, 2018), 173–91, especially p. 177, from which I draw her remarks on Scriptural commentary. Cf. Daniel Lanzinger, *Ein "unerträgliches Possenspiel"? Paulinische Schriftverwendung im Kontext antiker Allegorese*, NTOA 112 (Göttingen: Vandenhoeck & Ruprecht, 2016), 194–236, argues that Paul's allegorical reading is to be understood as fundamentally argumentative and discursive, i.e., rhetorical, rather than interpretive, in accord with its background in the Hellenistic world.

8. Cf. Hans-Josef Klauck, *Allegorie und Allegorese in Synoptischen Gleichnistexten* (2nd rev. ed., NTAbh.NF 13 (Münster: Aschendorff, 1986), 43–45.

9. They include ὑπονοία ("hidden meaning"), σύμβολον and the related adjective, τύπος and related terms, and αἰνίττεσθαι ("to riddle"). Cf. Klauck, *Allegorie*, 99–102.

10. This is especially clear in Philo's naming Moses a hierophant and crediting him with the revelation of mysteries (ἱεροφαντέω). Cf. Philo, *Leg.* 3.151; 3.173; the same is true of Jeremiah, Philo, *Cher.* 49.

11. E.g., Philo's discussion of sacrifices: "Which things he (Moses, the lawgiver) has set in riddles, through such things as through symbols, we have, allegorizing, interpretively investigated in other places" (Philo, *Spec.* 1, 269).

12. Philo, *Leg.* 2.5; 2.10; 3.4; *Cher.* 25; *Ebr.* 99; *Migr.* 131; *Somn.* 67.1; *Ios.* 28; *Decal.* 101; *Spec.* 1.269; *Praem.* 125; 159.

13. Philo, *Leg.* 3.60; 3.238; *Post.* 51; *Agr.* 27; 157; *Migr.* 205; *Mut.* 67; *Somn.* 2.31; 2.207; *Abr.* 99; *Spec.* 1.269; 2.29. Here I am in basic agreement with Steven Di Mattei, "Paul's Allegory of the Two Covenants (Gal 4.21–31) in Light of First-Century Hellenistic Rhetoric and Jewish Hermeneutics," *NTS* 52 (2006): 104–7, with the slight caveat that Philo's interpretive approach significantly qualifies his usage of ἀλληγορέω in reference to his allegorizing.

14. Cf. Klauck, *Allegorie*, 96–98. A clear expression of Philo's hermeneutic appears in reference to the temptation of humanity by the serpent (Gen 3:1–13) in Philo, *Opif.* 157: "These things are not fashioned from myth, which are delightful to the poetical and rhetorical class of persons, but are examples of figures (τύποι), which summon to allegory (ἀλληγορία) according to interpretations that come through a deeper sense." Note that Philo speaks of "types" as invitations to allegory: they make visible what is hidden and invite the interpreter to discover a deeper meaning in the text. Cf. Philo, *Conf.* 190.

15. Niehoff, *Philo of Alexandria*, 176: "Philo wishes to show that Moses himself 'has provided starting points' for allegory, implying that the latter is not a whimsical reading of the text but expresses the author's intention. In Philo's view, 'the sacred oracles most clearly provide clues for the allegorical interpretation." She points to

*Conf.* 190–91, *Plant.* 36, and *Det.* 167, where, in her words, "Philo stresses that Moses 'wishes to convey' the allegorical meaning." See further her comments on Philo's anchoring of allegory within the literal text and authorial intention, which sharply separates him from the Stoics (*Philo of Alexandria*, 181).

16. Niehoff, *Philo of Alexandria*, 173–77.

17. The two references to allegorizing that we find with Josephus correspond to Philo's understanding of the allegorizing language of Scripture that reflects the structure of reality: "Everything (in the Law) has an arrangement that is harmonious with the nature of all things. On the one hand, the Lawgiver deftly make some things riddles, and sets forth other things with dignified allegories," Josephus, *Ant.* 1.24. Like Philo, Josephus thus rejects the allegories of Greek mythology, appealing to Plato's critique of Homer, *C. Ap.* 2.255.

18. Although Paul uses the gender-neutral verb γεννάω to describe Hagar's giving birth, in the references to children which—aside from the citation of LXX Gen 21:10—Paul consistently employs τέκνα, in which "birth" resonates.

19. On this distinction, see Fredrik Barth: "Introduction," in *Ethnic Groups and Boundaries: The Social Organization of Culture Difference* (ed. F. Barth; Bergen: Scandinavian University Books 1969), 9–38.

20. Paul's move from the figure of mountains to that of two "Jerusalems," rather than Zion traditions, enables the twofold "Jerusalem" motif by leaving aside the imagery of a transcendent Zion.

21. Paul's appeal to the traditional image of Jerusalem as "mother" therewith transposes the language and hope of Ps 87:1–7 from the earthly plain and the hegemony of Zion to eschatological hope.

22. Cf. Gal 3:10, 22 and Gal 4:4–5, as well as Gal 4:1–3.

23. This imprisonment is a bondage under "the elements of the world," which through the Law has been subjected to "sin" (4:1–7, 8–9).

24. Cf. 4 Ezra 10:25–59; 2 Bar 4.1–7; 32.1–9; 68.1–74.4. In this respect, Paul differs from early Jewish tradition. Cf. Mark A. Seifrid, "The Voice of the Law and the Children of Promise (Gal 4,21–31)," in *Bestimmte Freiheit: Festschrift für Christof Landmesser zum 60. Geburtstag*, ed. J. U. Beck, M. Bauspieß, and F. Portenhauser, ABG 64 (Leipzig: Evangelische Verlagsanstalt, 2020), 68–75.

25. Although we cannot pursue this matter further here, this opposition does not mean that for Paul the Jewish people have been cut off from salvation (cf. Rom 11:1–36).

26. Thus, for example, the Isaianic transposition of Sarah's identity to the desolate Jerusalem, brings with it an alteration of Sarah as a figure: she did have a husband, while Jerusalem is left without its God (cf. the judgment on Babylon, Isa 47:5–11). Or does the citation presuppose the time when Sarah gave Hagar to Abraham? With Paul, "Jerusalem" is elevated to an eschatological reality. No husband is necessary, because its children are born of the promise and the Spirit.

27. Gal 2:16; cf. Gen 6:3,12; LXX Ps 55:5; Jer 17:5.

28. Cf. Gal 3:15; 4:4–6; 5:16–26; 6:8–10.

29. The Greek diminutive παιδίσκη, which also appears in the Septuagint (LXX Gen 16:1) goes beyond the Hebrew שִׁפְחָה ("female slave") in implying inferiority or

inferior status. This shift in meaning fits the narrative of the contention between the two women well (cf. Gen 16:4; 21:1–14). Both the Hebrew text and the Septuagint refer to Hagar's Egyptian ethnicity. Paul makes no use of it in his recounting of the Genesis narrative. At this juncture, his argument has shifted from the distinction between Jew and Gentile to that between Law and promise, and thus the new creation in Christ and the present, evil age.

30. Cf. Gal 4:25, τὸ . . . Ἀγὰρ. The neuter article signals a reference to the text, rather than to the person or character.

31. Likewise, in a mirror-image of the naming of Hagar and not Sarah, it is not Ishmael, but only Isaac who is named. He is given only a figural role, as one born of promise and the Spirit (Gal 4:28).

32. It is consequently clear, that although the prophetic text serves Paul's reading of the Genesis narrative, it does not determine it, contrary to the thesis of Matthew S. Harmon, *She Must and Shall Go Free: Paul's Isaianic Gospel in Galatians*, BZNW 168 (Berlin/New York: de Gruyter 2010), 183. Cf. Seifrid, "The Voice of the Law," 72–75.

33. He already has associated "the present Jerusalem" with Sinai and implicitly transferred the Zion traditions to "the Jerusalem above" (Gal 4:25).

34. Here, again, Paul first has in view the attraction that Judaism held for the Galatian churches, but he does not directly identify "the son of the slave girl" with Jews. His earlier reference to the enslavement of "the present Jerusalem" is not to be understood as limited to unbelieving Israel, but as applying to it: *even* "the present Jerusalem" is enslaved under sin—and not Roman occupation—along with the rest of creation.

35. On this theme, see S. Vollenweider, *Freiheit als neue Schöpfung: Eine Untersuchung zur Eleutheria bei Paulus und in seiner Umwelt*, FRLANT 147 (Göttingen: Vandenhoeck & Ruprecht, 1989).

36. See note 24 of this chapter.

37. Once again, although we cannot pursue this matter further here, this opposition does not mean that for Paul the Jewish people permanently have been cut off from salvation (cf. Rom 11:1–36).

38. My language is a christologically modulated and limited borrowing from Nicholas of Cusa. I am aware of the language of J. Louis Martyn, "Apocalyptic Antinomies in Paul's Letter to the Galatians," *NTS* 31 (1985): 410–24, who overlooks the crucified and risen Christ as the basis of Paul's "apocalyptic" and thus the "place" where these oppositions are resolved. I am also aware that the "resolution" of opposites in Christ takes a twofold form, one in the cross and resurrection and another in the coming of the kingdom to all the earth.

39. As far as I can see, this phenomenon appears only in one other place in Paul's letters where Paul, as he "listens" to the words of the Lord at the regifting of the Law to Israel, hears them speak of the final gift of the apostolic proclamation of Christ incarnate, crucified and risen (Rom 10:6–8; Deut 30:11–14). Paul hears this whisper at the conclusion of Deuteronomy, a reminder to Israel that the Law comes to it as a gift—albeit one that will bring a curse upon rebellious Israel—and hears within it the promise of the transcendent and final gift of Christ. The Law announces Christ

as its own τέλος (Rom 10:4). In this case, Paul focuses on the constancy of a giving God, and perhaps for this reason does not suggest that the Law speaks allegorically. He simply interprets the words of Deuteronomy "as" apostolic proclamation. See also the christological interpretation of the creational mandate of marriage in Eph 5:29–32.

40. The same hermeneutic appears in Paul's earlier appeal to Abraham (Gal 3:6–14, 15–18), who here, too, appears as a textual figure, to whom the Scripture "preaches the Gospel" of the blessing of the nations in advance (Gal 3:8). Isaac, who might have appeared in this passage, is displaced by Christ, the *one* seed to whom the promises belong (Gal 3:16).

41. Cf. F. Mildenberger, "Heilsgeschichte," *RGG⁴* 3:1584–1586. The hermeneutical use of the concept of development in the divine work in history goes back at least to Irenaeus in the second century. The appeal to "types"—which are part of Paul's vocabulary—goes back to the Antiochian response to Origen's allegorical interpretation of Scripture. The joining of these two hermeneutical approaches came into fruition with the "discovery" of the explanatory power of "history" as a constructive intellectual endeavor in the nineteenth century. On typology as a polemical response to Origen's allegorical interpretation, see Di Mattei, "Paul's Allegory," 102–4.

42. The same may be said of the questionable attempt to reconstruct "grand thematic narratives" on the basis of Scriptural echoes and allusions, which by its very nature is largely dependent on the imagination of the interpreter. On this question, cf. A. Andrew Das, *Paul and the Stories of Israel: Grand Thematic Narratives in Galatians* (Minneapolis, MN: Fortress, 2016), 217–38.

43. Karl-Heinrich Ostmeyer, *Taufe und Typos Elemente und Theologie der Tauftypologien in 1. Korinther 10 und 1. Petrus 3*, WUNT 118 (Tübingen: Mohr Siebeck, 2000).

44. Cf. Simon Butticaz, *La crise Galate ou l'anthropologie en question*, BZNW 229 (Berlin/New York: de Gruyter, 2018), 218–24.

45. I borrow from Oswald Bayer, *Autorität und Kritik: Zur Hermeneutik und Wissenschaftstheorie* (Tübingen: Mohr Siebeck, 1991), 28–29, who has borrowed from Johann Georg Hamann.

46. I have offered further reflections on this topic in Mark A. Seifrid, "Noch eine Kritik der historischen Kritik: Erwägungen zur neueren anglo-amerikanischen Hermeutik," in *Heiligen Schriften in der Kritik: XVII. Europäischen Kongress für Theologie (5.-8. September 2021 in Zürich)*, ed. K. Schmid, VWGTh 68 (Leipzig: Evangelische Verlagsanstalt, 2022), 321–30.

## BIBLIOGRAPHY

Barth, Fredrik, ed. *Ethnic Groups and Boundaries.* Bergen; Boston: Universitetsforlaget/Little, Brown and Company, 1969.

Bayer, Oswald. *Autorität und Kritik: Zu Hermeneutik und Wissenschaftstheorie.* Tübingen: Mohr Siebeck, 1991.

Butticaz, Simon. *La crise Galate ou l'anthropologie en question.* BZNW 229. Berlin/New York: de Gruyter, 2018.

Das, A. Andrew. *Galatians*. Concordia Commentary. St. Louis, MO: Concordia Publishing House, 2014.

———. *Paul and the Stories of Israel: Grand Thematic Narratives in Galatians.* Minneapolis: Fortress, 2016.

De Boer, Martinus C. *Galatians: A Commentary.* NTL. Louisville, KY: Westminster John Knox Press, 2011.

DeSilva, David A. *The Letter to the Galatians.* NICNT. Grand Rapids: Eerdmans, 2018.

Di Mattei, Steven. "Paul's Allegory of the Two Covenants (Gal 4.21–31) in Light of First-Century Hellenistic Rhetoric and Jewish Hermeneutics." *NTS* 52 (2006): 102–22.

Harmon, Matthew S. *She Must and Shall Go Free: Paul's Isaianic Gospel in Galatians.* BZNW 168. Berlin/New York: de Gruyter 2010.

Hays, Richard B. *Echoes of Scripture in the Letters of Paul.* New Haven, CT: Yale University Press, 1989.

———. "The Letter to the Galatians." In vol. 11 of *The New Interpreter's Bible*, edited by Leander Keck et al., 181–348. Nashville: Abingdon, 2000.

Hollmann, Joshua. "Nicholas of Cusa and Martin Luther on Christ and the Coincidence of Opposites." In *Nicholas of Cusa and the Making of the Early Modern World*, edited by S. J. G. Burton, J. Hollmann, and E. M. Parker, 153–72. Studies in the History of the Christian Tradition 190. Leiden: Brill, 2019.

Keener, Craig S. *Galatians: A Commentary.* Grand Rapids: Baker, 2019.

Klauck, Hans-Josef. *Allegorie und Allegorese in Synoptischen Gleichnistexten.* 2nd rev. ed. F 13; Münster: Aschendorff, 1986.

Lanzinger, Daniel. *Ein "Unerträgliches Possenspiel"? Paulinische Schriftverwendung im Kontext Antiker Allegorese.* NTOA 112. Göttingen: Vandenhoeck & Ruprecht, 2016.

Martyn, J. Louis. "Apocalyptic Antinomies in Paul's Letter to the Galatians." *NTS* 31 (1985): 410–24.

Matera, Frank J. *Galatians.* SP 9. Collegeville, MN: Liturgical Press, 1992.

Meiser, Martin. *Der Brief des Paulus an die Galater.* THKNT 9. Leipzig: Evangelische Verlagsanstalt, 2022.

Moo, Douglas J. *Galatians.* BECNT. Grand Rapids: Baker, 2013.

Niehoff, Maren R. *Philo of Alexandria: An Intellectual Biography.* New Haven, CT: Yale University Press, 2018.

Oepke, Albrecht. *Der Brief des Paulus an die Galater.* THKNT. Berlin: Evangelische Verlagsanstalt, 1957.

Ostmeyer, Karl-Heinrich. *Taufe und Typos Elemente und Theologie der Tauftypologien in 1. Korinther 10 und 1. Petrus 3.* WUNT 118. Tübingen: Mohr Siebeck, 2000.

Schreiner, Thomas R. *Galatians.* Zondervan Exegetical Commentary. Grand Rapids: Zondervan, 2010.

Seifrid, Mark A. "Noch eine Kritik der historischen Kritik: Erwägungen zur neueren anglo-amerikanischen Hermeutik." In *Heiligen Schriften in der Kritik: XVII. Europäischen Kongress für Theologie (5.–8. September 2021 in Zürich)*, edited by K. Schmid, 321–30. VWGTh 68. Leipzig: Evangelische Verlagsanstalt, 2022.

————. "The Voice of the Law and the Children of Promise (Gal 4,21–31)." In *Bestimmte Freiheit: Festschrift für Christof Landmesser zum 60. Geburtstag*, edited by J. U. Beck, M. Bauspieß, and F. Portenhauser, 57–80. ABG 64. Leipzig: Evangelische Verlagsanstalt, 2020.

Vollenweider, Samuel. *Freiheit als neue Schöpfung: Eine Untersuchung zur Eleutheria bei Paulus und in Seiner Umwelt*. FRLANT 147. Göttingen: Vandenhoeck & Ruprecht, 1989.

Witherington, Ben III. *Grace in Galatia. A Commentary on St. Paul's Letter to the Galatians*. Grand Rapids/Edinburgh: Eerdmans/T & T Clark, 1998.

## Chapter 7

# Listening with Philo to Our Mother Sarah

## *Assessing the Validity and Value of Allegoresis Implicit in Paul's Use of It*

### Ernest P. Clark

In his letter to the assemblies in Galatia, Paul develops his argument in frequent interaction with Israel's Scriptures. He quotes the Scriptures—Genesis, Leviticus, Deuteronomy, Isaiah, and Habakkuk—as evidence for his arguments (Gal 3:6, 8, 10, 11, 12, 13, 16; 4:27, 30; 5:14). He summarizes some ancient Jewish narratives: the promises to Abraham (3:6–18) and the giving of the law (3:17–24). He alludes to others: Israel's exodus from Egypt and Abraham's migration from Ur (4:1–9).[1] And he introduces a novel analogy to show Scripture's purpose for the law and Israel's experience of it (3:23–4:2).[2] Throughout, Paul explicates or interacts with the literal meaning of each text.

However, in Gal 4:24, Paul switches suddenly to allegoresis. This change is strange. In other letters, Paul reads Adam the human as a τύπος of Christ, and the events of the exodus and wanderings are τύποι "for us," "written down to instruct us" (Rom 5:14; 1 Cor 10:6, 11). But Paul's allegoresis in Gal 4:24–31 is the only explicit allegoresis of Scripture in the works collected in the New Testament, the Septuagint, and the Dead Sea Scrolls.[3]

Why, in this one place, does Paul employ allegoresis? To what end does he apply it? And does his use of it imply that he considers allegoresis hermeneutically valid or just rhetorically valuable?

This study compares Paul's allegorical method and rationale with those of his Jewish contemporary Philo. It demonstrates the singular relevance of Philo, both for understanding methods of early Jewish allegoresis and for appreciating the significance of Paul's allegory here. It analyzes Paul's argument: both his distribution of the argument's weight across allegoresis and exegesis (suggesting Paul's distrust of allegoresis) and also his use of hearing the law to dismiss hearing the law. Finally, it concludes that Paul impugns the hermeneutical validity of scriptural allegoresis but exploits it here for its rhetorical value.

## ALLEGORESIS IN EARLY JUDAISM

As Craig Keener's review shows, centuries of scholarly dispute on Gal 4:21–5:1 begin with the form itself: Is this indeed allegoresis, or is it typological or simply figural?[4] Steven di Mattei argues that Paul's interpretation in Gal 4:21–31 conforms to both Tryphon's and Heraclitus's definitions of ἀλληγορία: "Paul speaks of one thing, παιδίσκη and ἐλευθέρα, but intends something other than what is said, two covenants."[5]

Early Jews also allegorized. Menahem Kister follows Richard Hanson in citing the Damascus Document's "allegorical interpretation" of Num 21:16–20.[6] "And [God] raised from Aaron men of knowledge and from Israel wise men, and made them listen. And they dug the well: 'A well which the princes dug, which the nobles of the people delved with the staff.' The well is the law" (CD 6.2–4).[7]

However, Philo's vast *Allegory of the Law* is more relevant for comparison. While some scholars question the relevance of Philo's allegoreses for understanding Paul's, others argue just the opposite.[8] Jason Zurawski, following Peder Borgen, asserts that "Paul's interpretation has at its foundation a tradition akin to Philo's."[9] Keener focuses his comparative analysis on Philo's allegoreses of Hagar and Sarah.[10] And, reading the letter as a whole, Maren Niehoff compares the views of Abraham's faith in these two contemporary, diaspora interpreters of the Septuagint.[11]

## PHILO'S ALLEGORIES

Disputes about Philo's relevance to Paul's allegoresis may relate to the two interpreters' allegorical method or their allegorical rationale. About their method, Di Mattei contends, "Paul's allegory is no different" from Philo's: Both allegorize by using a pesher-like "this is that" formula.[12] On the other hand, writing about their rationales, N. T. Wright asserts, "Paul is not setting up an 'allegory' after the manner of Philo."[13] This section summarizes Philo's allegorical method and rationale and then describes his allegoreses of Abraham's family. The following section will then compare these with Paul's similar allegorical method, his distinct rationale, and his opposite allegoresis of the same family.

## Philo's Allegorical Method

Philo combines earlier Alexandrian modes of exegesis to frame his own approach: spiritual allegoresis.[14] While Philo can use his approach to dislodge a literal reading of the text (*Leg.* 2.19; *Plant.* 32–36; *Agr.* 96–97), he uses it normally to develop the text's didactic intent.[15] Philo's approach leads him to a "conservative" method that arises from the text itself. "Indeed the sacred oracles most evidently afford us the clues for the use of this method" (*Plant.* 36). So, as Niehoff describes, "Philo proceeds verse by verse in the *Allegory of the Law*, quoting a biblical passage, identifying a particular problem or question raised by it, and then discussing and ultimately resolving it on the allegorical level."[16]

## Philo's Allegorical Rationale

For Philo, the law's own words demand to have their spiritual significance revealed, for Moses himself intended it (*Her.* 197). As Adam Kamesar explains, the narrative "part of the Pentateuch constitutes an allegorical portrayal of the ethical and spiritual progress of the individual" which "Philo sees . . . represented allegorically in the various personae of the Pentateuchal narrative."[17] As Charles Anderson argues, Philo used allegory, more than exposition, to help "advanced readers, adept in philosophy and familiar with allegorical exegesis of Scripture, . . . progress further."[18] Mikołaj Domaradzki labels this "function of allegory," which helps "one pass from flesh (the literal) to spirit (the figurative)," "salvific."[19]

The chief impediment to the progress of the soul or mind is the body, whose sensory experiences (πάθη) and desires (ἐπιθυμίαι), mediated by the material elements of the cosmos, enslave the soul (*Abr.* 164; *Spec.* 3.9–10; 4.91, 113; *Praem.* 119–121; *Leg.* 2.49–50). Philo promotes the law, as Yedidya Etzion asserts, as "the best tool to address the weakness of human-nature."[20] For example, observing the sabbath and the various festivals inculcates self-control, reason, and other virtues (*Spec.* 2.56–175; *Migr.* 91).[21] Similarly, both the symbol and the practice of circumcision are effective for cutting off excessive desires (*Spec.* 1.9; *QG* 3.47–48; *Migr.* 92–93).[22] Thus, as Philo concludes in his exposition of the law's blessings in Deut 28, when a mind which lay recently "under the yoke of many pleasures and many ἐπιθυμίαι" follows these and the other "holy laws," it will be "redeemed into freedom by God, who broke asunder the miseries of its slavery" (*Praem.* 119, 124).[23]

Having received bodily health and life, the soul is now free to practice the righteousness that "the ten pronouncements . . . exhort" (*Spec.* 4.134; see *Leg.* 72). And as the soul migrates from bodily senses, it becomes an "heir of divine things," the "intellectual" blessings God promised for the nations in Isaac and his offspring (*Her.* 8, quoting Gen 26:3–5; *Her.* 64–70, 98). This system of studying and practicing the law in order to receive its redemptive benefits I have called Philo's "redemptive nomism."[24]

## Philo's Allegories of Abraham's Family

Among the characters in the Pentateuchal narratives, Philo attends most to Abraham, presenting him as a pattern of the soul's migration, its ascent to God.[25] Philo previews his allegoresis of Abraham, his women, and their children in *Leg.* 3.244–245; *Cher.* 3–10; *Sobr.* 8–9; and *Migr.* 28–30. He then develops it at length in his running allegorical commentary on Gen 16:1–6 (*Congr.*), 6–12 (*Fug.*), and 17:1–5, 15–22 (*Mut.*).

Philo presents Abraham's two wives in a sequential scheme, with Abraham maturing from one stage to the next. Abraham's relationship with each woman produces a son that corresponds to his mother.

For Philo, Sarah's handmaid Hagar stands for "preliminary learning," the course of study taught in schools (*Leg.* 3.244). As "preliminary studies," "the school subjects" are necessary, but inferior (*Congr.* 13, 18, 19; *Leg.* 3.245). They serve wisdom as Hagar serves Sarah (*Congr.* 9–10). After all, Hagar is from Egypt, which stands for the "earthly . . . body" and its senses, and the sensible phenomena which the school subjects study are "the staple," but not the fullness, of philosophy (*Congr.* 20–21, 85–86, quoting Lev 18:1–5).

The mind's intercourse with "lower instruction" and then with "virtue" bears children, and the sons correspond to their mothers. Ishmael inherits sophistry, but "wisdom is Isaac's inheritance," for he is self-taught (*Sobr.* 8–9; *Mut.* 255).

Since the school subjects are "preliminary learning," when the soul matures, they are no longer necessary. As Abraham progresses, he becomes "the wise, the lover of God," and Sarah the general virtue "sovereignty" (*Cher.* 7). Indeed, Sarah has "ceased from the manner of women"; that is, she has "died to the πάθη" (*Cher.* 8, alluding to Gen 18.11). Then, at that time, it is right for the handmaiden Hagar (preliminary studies) and her son Ishmael (the sophist) to be "cast forth" (*Cher.* 8–9). Isaac will not inherit alongside Ishmael, for the self whom God has blessed to be its own teacher cannot "still live in concubinage with the slavish (δούλαι) arts" (*Congr.* 36).

When Abraham hesitates to reject Hagar—"the education by means of which he was brought into union with virtue"—God prompts his obedience with the words, "In all that Sarah saith to thee listen to her voice" (*Leg.* 3.245, quoting Gen 21:12). Philo charges his readers, too, to "listen" as to a "law" to whatever seems good to virtue (*Leg.* 3.245).

Though scattered through several works, Philo's presentation of the allegory of Abraham's wives is fairly consistent. Unable to beget a child with Sarai (virtue), Abram (mind) mates with Sarai's Egyptian (bodily) handmaiden Hagar (preliminary studies) and begets Ishmael (sophistry). This relationship makes Abraham wise and prepares him to beget Isaac (happiness and joy) with Sarah (sovereignty). No longer needed, Hagar is cast forth with her son. Finally, Isaac (self-taught virtue), like his post-menopausal (passionless) mother, lives free from the passions of the flesh and the slavery of bastard thoughts. Philo's allegoresis is strikingly similar to and markedly different from Paul's allegoresis in Gal 4.

## PAUL'S ALLEGORY

Paul presents his allegoresis of Abraham, Sarah, Hagar, and their sons at the climax of his argument against submitting to the law in order to gain the blessings of life, righteousness, and the inheritance God promised Abraham. Like Philo, Paul focuses his interpretation of scripture on the narrative of Abraham. Unlike Philo, Paul tracks God's promises and their fulfillment in the unfolding of human history on earth, not in the soul's progress toward incorporeal intelligence. Similarities and differences persist in Paul's allegorical method, his allegorical rationale, and the particulars of his allegoresis.

### Paul's Allegorical Method

Paul's allegory is similar to Philo's in its characters, plot, and form. First, Paul works with Philo's favorite allegorical character: Abraham. Second, Paul uses two of Philo's schematic pairs—Hagar and Sarah, and Ishmael and Isaac—and both writers use Hagar to represent "elementary learning."[26] Third, Paul situates the allegory within an argument that addresses Philo's central aim: the freedom of the person from slavery to the flesh.

Paul and Philo are also similar in their form. Paul follows the allegorical method that Philo uses: he cites a scripture, raises an issue, indicates explicitly that he is moving to allegory, and then solves the issue on the level of allegory.[27] As di Mattei asserts, the operation of allegory as a rhetorical trope "in Philo . . . is exactly the same as allegory for Paul."[28] "Paul's allegory is no different" from Philo's.[29] Paul's allegory is what he says it is, an allegory.[30]

## Paul's Allegorical Rationale

While Paul's allegorical method is similar to Philo's, his rationale is different. As Domaradzki states, "Philo wants his reader not only to understand the law of Moses but also to live by it." Paul, on the other hand, wants his readers to understand the scripture and live by faith and the Spirit.[31] Paul is especially concerned about people following the law, all the more if they look to the law for redemption.

As Douglas Moo argues, "any . . . contemporizing reading of the OT . . . is inevitably the product of some set of extratextual hermeneutical axioms."[32] For Philo, those axioms are the soul's migration from enslavement to the body toward incorporeal intelligence. For Paul, the axioms are "eschatological."[33] From Wright's perspective, Paul "is talking about *the covenant history of Israel*, and the ways in which the long and winding Abrahamic story had done what Deuteronomy said it would."[34]

Paul has constructed and worked within this redemptive-historical metanarrative since his first mention of Abraham (Gal 3:6). The reckoning of Abraham's faith as righteousness, the promise of the blessing of the Spirit to the nations, the addition of the law until the offspring should come, the sending of the Son and of the Spirit (3:6–4:9)—alongside all these, faith persists as promise leads eventually to fulfillment, when it breaks forth into joy (4:26–28). This metanarrative is the structure within which and these scriptures are the beams upon which Paul builds his exegetical logic and his allegorical rhetoric.

Paul's logic builds out his apostolic concerns about his brothers and sisters from non-Jewish nations adopting the law: first, that God's promised blessing to the nations would not reach non-Jewish nations if the "foreskins" among those nations first become Jews by circumcising themselves (Gal 3:6–14; see 2:7–9, 14–16); second, that they would come to see doing the law, rather than believing God, as the way to receive life, righteousness, or the inheritance, ends for which the law was never given (2:21; 3:18, 21); and third, that they would accept the law as guard and guide though they had received the Spirit of God's Son, who fulfills those roles better (3:19–4:11).

These concerns Paul expounds by exegesis, analogy (Gal 3:24–4:7), and allusion (4:1–9). Now he switches unexpectedly to allegoresis. Paul's decision to allegorize suggests its rhetorical value for the particular case he is making, yet his scriptural allegory itself will undermine the hermeneutical validity of scriptural allegory.

**Table 7.1: Philo's and Paul's Allegories**

| Feature | Philo | Paul |
|---|---|---|
| Abraham (Abram) | Wise mind (Mind studying nature) | [No equivalent] |
| Hagar | Preliminary learning | Enslavement<br>Covenant from Mt Sinai<br>Gives birth εἰς δουλείαν<br>Present Jerusalem |
| | *To be cast out*<br>*Will not inherit* | *To be cast out*<br>*Will not inherit* |
| Sarah (Sarai) | Sovereignty (Virtue) | Freedom<br>A second covenant<br>Jerusalem above |
| Postmenopausal | Without πάθη | [No equivalent] |
| Isaac | Happiness and joy, self-taught virtue | Born δι' ἐπαγγελίας<br>Born κατὰ πνεῦμα<br>Free<br>Children of Jerusalem above |
| | *Will inherit* | *Will inherit* |

Note: From Clark, "Enslaved Under the Elements," 186.

## Paul's Allegory of Abraham's Family

Paul picks up the basic plot of Philo's allegories. For Paul, as for Philo, Hagar is a provisional character that serves Sarah; Hagar and her son are cast out; and Isaac becomes Abraham's sole heir. But, in stunning contrast with Philo, Paul aligns the Sinai covenant not with Sarah, but with Hagar (see *Congr.* 81–88).[35] "Lined up this way, the adherents of the law find themselves not freed, as Philo promises, but enslaved, indeed cast out of Abraham's family and cut off from the inheritance."[36]

Paul takes three steps to reach that conclusion. First, he connects the enslaved woman Hagar with the law of Moses. Second, he affirms that his brothers and sisters are Abraham's and Sarah's children, free heirs according to promise. Third, he connects Hagar's enslaved child with those who agitate the Galatian believers. And then, finally, he states clearly that the law and its children will be dismissed from the household of faith.

### The Covenant from Mount Sinai Is Hagar

First, within the realm of the allegory, Paul asserts: the enslaved woman is a covenant, the one from Mount Sinai, which gives birth into slavery; this is Hagar; Sinai is a mountain in Arabia, but it corresponds to the present Jerusalem, which is enslaved together with its children.[37] Paul establishes the Hagar–Sinai connection by geography and analogy.

Paul uses the geographic region of Arabia to connect Hagar with Sinai. As Wright summarizes, "Hagar was the mother of the Arabian peoples, Ishmael and his wide family," and "Mount Sinai itself is located in Arabia, Hagar's land, the land of the slave people."[38] Samuel Tedder notes that Israel's scriptures identify the Hagrites "as an Arab group" (1 Chr. 5:10, 19–20; 27:31; Ps 83:6).[39]

Tedder discerns two "distinct and yet related" covenants in Gen 17: (1) the promise that Abraham will be the father of many nations (17:1–6) and (2) the covenant of circumcision (17:10–14).[40] Ishmael receives the latter but not the former and is later banished (17:16–21; 21:10). Hence, Paul recognizes that both Hagar and Sinai bear children of Abraham who are nevertheless enslaved and disinherited.[41] Further, Paul sees also that both Hagar and the law, as παιδαγωγός, are slaves themselves.[42]

Matthew Emerson argues that Paul finds a connection between Hagar and the Sinai covenant in the Pentateuch itself. He follows Phyllis Trible and Franz Greifenhagen in identifying "a number of linguistic and thematic connections between Hagar/Ishmael and Israel in the Exodus and at Sinai."[43] Both Hagar and Israel are oppressed by masters (Gen 15:13; 16:9), who cast them out (גרש, Gen 21:10; Exod 10:11), and both flee (ברח) toward Shur (Gen 16:6–8; Exod 14:5; 15:22). Thus, "the Hagar narrative foreshadows the Exodus narrative."[44] However, with this evidence, Emerson has connected Hagar not with the Sinai covenant, as Paul does, but with those who receive the Sinai covenant, whom Paul aligns with the enslaved son.

Rather, the point of contact in the allegory is that both Hagar and the Sinai covenant bear offspring εἰς δουλείαν (Gal 5:24). The law's children are not free but enslaved under the cosmic elements (4:1, 3, 8). Those adopt the law's practices accept again a yoke of slavery (4:9; 5:1). And it is under this law that the false siblings in Jerusalem sought to reduce Paul, Barnabas, Titus— and the believers among the nations—to slavery (2:4). Thus, by analogy and geography, Paul makes "the connection between Hagar and Sinai . . . on the allegorical level."[45]

### *"You, Brothers and Sisters, Like Isaac, Are Children of Promise"*

Second, Paul correlates the free woman with God's covenant with Abraham: the blessing of the nations and the promise of the Spirit (Gal 4:22–24; see 3:6–9, 14–18). As Philo quotes Hannah's song to affirm that barren Sarah can indeed bear offspring (*Mut.* 143, quoting 1 Sam 2:5), so Paul uses two scriptures from later in the redemptive metanarrative to reinforce his connection (Gal 4:26–27). First, as Wright demonstrates, "Paul alludes . . . to Psalm 87:5 (86:5 LXX). . . . Just as God promised Abraham a family of a multitude

of nations, so God promised Sion . . . a family of a multitude of nations."[46]
The reference to εὐφραίνω in the Greek translation of the psalm's closing line
resonates with the first word in the following quotation and second reference:
Isaiah's encouragement to the childless woman that she will have more children than the married woman.[47] In the later Jewish three-year cycle, Isa 54:1
is the *haftarah* reading set to accompany Gen 16:1.[48]

"Now you, brothers and sisters," Paul concludes, "like Isaac are children
of promise" (Gal 4:28). Paul may have any or all of four promises in mind:
(1) God's covenant with Abraham, whose name he changes, for he will be
the father of many nations (Gen 17:4–6); (2) God's promise that Sarah would
become nations (17:16); (3) the Lord's promise to record as born in Zion
people from other nations who know him (Ps 86:4–6); or (4) the prophet's
promise that the desolate woman will have many children (Isa 54:1).

These promises extend from the redemptive metanarrative to brace Paul's
allegory. They reinforce his contention that his brothers and sisters in Galatia
are among the multinational multitude God promised Abraham, Sarah, and
Zion. So doing, Paul distributes the weight of his argument between allegoresis—in which he aligns Jerusalem above with the free woman—and
redemptive-historical exegesis.

## Children Born According to the Flesh

Third, Paul uses analogy to connect the enslaved woman's son with those
who are agitating the brothers and sisters in Galatia: both are κατὰ σάρκα.
The fleshiness of the enslaved woman's son is seen in his birth κατὰ σάρκα,
his fleshy behavior (persecuting the child born according to the Spirit), and
his eventual expulsion (Gal 4:23–25, 29–30). The agitators' behavior is also
fleshy. They disturb and confuse, they ostracize and manipulate, they twist the
gospel of Christ, and they boast (1:7; 4:17; 5:7–12; 6:12–13). Their behavior
corresponds with the actions of the flesh—enmities, strife, jealousy, anger,
quarrels, dissensions, factions, and envy (5:20–21). And, as Paul will write,
"those who practice such things will not inherit God's kingdom" (5:21).

The analogy works as Paul applies his exegesis to social analysis. (Allegory
may also have some small role in freeing him to read Ishmael's ambiguous
"play" [צחק, παίζω] as "persecute" [διώκω]; Gen 21:9; Gal 4:29).[49] Paul will
extend this connection to contend that getting circumcised does not empower
law-keeping (Gal 5:6; 6:13), for, as he has argued already, law-keeping does
not set people free from enslavement to sin's infection of their weak flesh
(3:21; 4:9–10).

*Expel the Law and Its Children!*

With these three connections in place—the enslaved woman with the Sinai covenant, the free woman and her son with the Abrahamic covenant and believers, and the enslaved woman's son with the agitators—Paul is ready to amplify the voice he wanted those who desire to be under the law to hear from the law (4:21). "But what does the scripture say? 'Expel the enslaved woman and her son, for the enslaved woman's son will certainly not inherit with the son'" of the free woman (Gal 4:30, quoting Gen 21:10)!

Paul is not the first to call people to hear this statement. This is Sarah's voice which God told Abraham to heed (Gen 21:12). And this is the voice of Sarah, that is virtue, which Philo repeatedly commends "wise Abraham" for "complying" with (*Leg.* 3.244–245; *Cher.* 9; *Congr.* 63–69). Philo notes, too, that Abraham "is represented not as hearing (ἀκούων), but as hearkening (ὑπακούων), a word which exactly expresses assent and obedience" (*Congr.* 68). And Philo calls his readers to follow Abraham's example, "to hearken to all that virtue recommends" as to a "law" (*Leg.* 3.245).

Paul has reached his goal, and it is "ironic," if not startling.[50] Opening with "You who want to be under the law, are you hearing the law?," Paul aligns the enslaved woman with the Sinai covenant and then has his readers hear, "Expel the enslaved woman, that is the law!"

Read in the context of the churches in Galatia, the allegory and its application say, "You, believers from other nations—slave and free, male and female—are Abraham and Sarah's free 'sons,' the multitude God promised them, heirs of the blessing, recipients of the promised Spirit. Those who agitate for the law, circumcised though they be, are still powerless to oppose the flesh, as their behavior shows. They will be dismissed from the Messiah and will not inherit God's kingdom. But you are children of promise, members of the household of faith, and God's peace is upon you. So stand firm and free, and do not go back to a law that leads only to slavery and eventual dismissal."

## ASSESSING THE IMPLICIT VALIDITY AND VALUE OF ALLEGORESIS

Paul could have grounded this apostolic charge in exegesis and the metanarrative of redemptive history. Why does he deviate suddenly from his normal practice and resort to allegory? Does his use of allegoresis imply that he considers it hermeneutically valid? If not, what is the allegoresis's rhetorical value? And why choose this story to interpret?

## Paul's Use of Allegoresis Does Not Imply Its Hermeneutical Validity

Scholars dispute whether Paul is indeed allegorizing in Gal 4:24–31 and whether he regards allegoresis as a valid hermeneutical approach to scripture. Paul's allegoresis was not unusual among the Greek traditions of allegoresis.[51] Ilaria Ramelli contends that "Paul was likely using the Stoic allegorical tradition, applying a philosophical hermeneutical tool (perhaps already present in his formation within Judaism)."[52] Philo considered allegoresis true to the nature of the scriptures and, thus, necessary. Clement and Origen continued this Alexandrian tradition, Origen citing "Paul's words here to support his own approach to texts" (*Cels.* 4.44).[53] Jerome and Augustine promoted allegorical interpretation over literal (Jerome, *Comm. Gal.* 2.4.24; Augustine, *Letter to Pulinus* 186; *Easter Sermon* 251.7).[54] More recently, Ardel Caneday argues that Paul's allegoresis is legitimate because "the Abraham narrative itself is *written allegorically*." Characters and "experiences, . . . all symbolically representative of things greater than themselves," are "embedded into the text."[55] Other scholars deny that Paul is actually allegorizing. He is using typology, analogy, or figural reading, they say.[56]

Each perspective sees some of the picture. Paul himself says he is allegorizing, but his approach implies—and his conclusion all but states—that he disapproves of allegorical interpretation of the law. First, neither Paul nor any other first-century Jewish Christian writer allegorizes scripture anywhere else. If allegoresis were hermeneutically valid, we should expect to encounter it elsewhere, especially when it would seem useful. Second, Paul uses allegoresis of the law to undo hearing the law and, thus too, allegoresis of the law. He introduces an allegoresis of the law with the question, "Are you hearing the law?" and shortly concludes, "Expel the law!" Paul's scriptural allegory invalidates scriptural allegory.

If allegoresis is indeed invalid for expounding the meaning of scripture, why would Paul use it at all? And why would Paul choose a narrative whose plotline runs directly against his apostolic vocation to ensure the privileges of the good news to the disenfranchised? This story showcases the unfaithful, unloving, unjust mistreatment of an enslaved non-Jewish girl (the epitome of intersectional exclusion; see 3:28) by the mother of Israel with the approval of the father of faith.

## The Rhetorical Value of This Allegoresis in This Letter

The most probable explanation is that Paul allegorizes this scriptural narrative in this letter because he is opposing, in mode and message, an allegorical application of this particular narrative to promote the observance of the law in the quest for redemption.[57] The outlines of such an allegoresis do not require hypothetical reconstruction. Historical evidence for contemporary, complete allegoreses, within a paradigm of redemptive nomism, is concrete, clear, and extensive.

Some scholars hesitate to assert that Paul is opposing an expression of early Jewish interpretation and application of the law like Philo's. On the other hand, scholars readily cite Isa 54:1 as the *haftarah* reading set for Gen 16:1 to show that Paul is reading Israel's scriptures in customary Jewish ways. Yet concrete evidence for *haftarah* readings in the first century is still missing.[58] However, no one disputes that Philo was a Jewish scholar, contemporary with Paul, devoted to the study and exposition of Israel's scriptures, conversant with Greek thought, with an extensive body of writing (still extant), known within decades in other parts of the Mediterranean world.[59] Nor is it disputed that Philo and Paul interpret the same passage of scripture, read the same characters as figures of other concepts, and quote the same verse to the effect that one concept (or way of thought and life) should be dismissed in favor of another. Yet rarely do we read of Philo's writings as at least illustrative of a compelling and, from Paul's perspective, concerning teaching that Paul is opposing.[60]

What then is the rhetorical value of Paul's scriptural allegory? The evidence suggests that Paul is opposing teaching like Philo's: allegorical readings of this and other scriptural narratives to promote practicing the law in order to gain life, righteousness, and the inheritance. Paul writes exegetically to confront this teaching, arguing that it is by faith, through the Spirit, that he and his brothers and sisters wait for righteousness in hope, not as a goal achieved by action according to the law (Gal 5:6).[61] Then, to this exegesis, Paul adds allegoresis, demonstrating the futility of scriptural allegoresis. And, finally, Paul may also be retuning the ears of non-Jewish, enslaved, and female believers so that, when they hear this ancient narrative, they picture themselves not as Hagar or Ishmael (the abused foreigner or rejected child) but as Isaac, the promised child and certain heir.

## NOTES

1. James M. Scott, *Adoption as Sons of God: An Exegetical Investigation into the Background of Yiothesia in the Pauline Corpus*, WUNT 2/48 (Tübingen: Mohr Siebeck, 1992), 149–51, 186; Scott J. Hafemann, "Paul and the Exile of Israel in Galatians 3–4," in *Exile: Old Testament, Jewish, and Christian Conceptions*, ed. James M. Scott, JSJSup 56 (Leiden: Brill, 1997), 327–71, here 331–49; Nancy Calvert-Koyzis, *Paul, Monotheism and the People of God: The Significance of Abraham Traditions for Early Judaism and Christianity*, JSNTSup 273 (London: T&T Clark,

2004), 109–10; Sylvia C. Keesmaat, *Paul and His Story: (Re)Interpreting the Exodus Tradition*, LNTS 181 (Sheffield: Sheffield Academic, 1999), 155–214. For a critical response, see A. Andrew Das, *Paul and the Stories of Israel: Grand Thematic Narratives in Galatians* (Minneapolis: Fortress, 2016).

2. On the παιδαγωγός metaphor, see Ernest P. Clark, "Enslaved Under the Elements of the Cosmos" (University of St Andrews, PhD thesis, 2018), 146–56.

3. See ἀλληγορέω in Josephus, *Ant.* 1.24 and 45 instances of αλληγορέω in Philo. As examples of allegory and allegoresis more broadly understood, Ramelli includes both Jesus's parables and Revelation's apocalyptic symbolism; Ilaria L. E. Ramelli, "The Role of Allegory, Allegoresis and Metaphor in Paul and Origen," *JGRChJ* 14 (2018): 130–57.

4. Craig S. Keener, *Galatians: A Commentary* (Grand Rapids: Baker Academic, 2019), 402–7.

5. Steven Di Mattei, "Paul's Allegory of the Two Covenants (Gal 4.21–31) in Light of First-Century Hellenistic Rhetoric and Jewish Hermeneutics," *NTS* 52 (2006): 102–22, here 105–6, See Tryphon, *De tropis* 1.1; Heraclitus, *Homeric Allegories* 5.2.

6. Menahem Kister, "Allegorical Interpretations of Biblical Narratives in Rabbinic Literature, Philo, and Origen: Some Case Studies," in *New Approaches to the Study of Biblical Interpretation in Judaism of the Second Temple Period and in Early Christianity: Proceedings of the Eleventh International Symposium of the Orion Center for the Study of the Dead Sea Scrolls and Associated Literature, Jointly Sponsored by the Hebrew University Center for the Study of Christianity, 9–11 January, 2007*, ed. Gary A. Anderson, Ruth A. Clements, and David Satran (Leiden: Brill, 2013), 133–83, here 145–48. See Richard P. C. Hanson, *Allegory and Event: A Study of the Sources and Significance of Origen's Interpretation of Scripture* (London: SCM, 1959), 22.

7. DSS quotations from Florentino García Martínez and Eibert J. C. Tigchelaar, eds., *The Dead Sea Scrolls Study Edition* (Leiden: Brill, 1997).

8. C. K. Barrett, "The Allegory of Abraham, Sarah, and Hagar in the Argument of Galatians," in *Rechtfertigung: Festschrift für Ernst Käsemann zum 70. Geburtstag*, ed. Johannes Friedrich, Wolfgang Pöhlmann, and Peter Stuhlmacher (Tübingen: Mohr Siebeck, 1976), 1–16, here 11n24.

9. Jason M. Zurawski, "Mosaic Torah as Encyclical Paideia: Reading Paul's Allegory of Hagar and Sarah in Light of Philo of Alexandria's," in *Pedagogy in Early Judaism and Christianity*, eds. K. M. Hogan, M. Goff, and Emma Wasserman, EJL 41 (Atlanta: SBL, 2017), 283–307, here 293; see Peder Borgen, "Some Hebrew and Pagan Features in Philo's and Paul's Interpretations of Hagar and Ishmael," in *The New Testament and Hellenistic Judaism*, ed. Peder Borgen and Søren Giversen (Peabody, MA: Aarhus University Press, 1997), 151–64.

10. Keener, *Galatians*, 408–9; see Ben Witherington III, *Grace in Galatia: A Commentary on St. Paul's Letter to the Galatians* (Grand Rapids: Eerdmans, 1998), 324–28.

11. Maren R. Niehoff, "Abraham in the Greek East: Faith, Circumcision, and Covenant in Philo's Allegorical Commentary and Paul's Letter to the Galatians," *SPhiloA* 32 (2020): 227–48, here 227–28.

12. Di Mattei, "Paul's Allegory," 109, citing Richard Longenecker, *Biblical Exegesis in the Apostolic Period* (Grand Rapids: Eerdmans, 1974), 28, 39, 54.

13. N. T. Wright, *Galatians*, CCF (Grand Rapids: Eerdmans, 2021), 295, 303–4.

14. Borgen, "Philo's and Paul's Interpretations," 38; Maren R. Niehoff, "Philo, Allegorical Commentary," *The Eerdmans Dictionary of Early Judaism*, 1070. This section follows closely the analysis in Clark, "Enslaved Under the Elements," 115–17.

15. Borgen, "Philo's and Paul's Interpretations," 11, quoting Thomas H. Tobin, *The Creation of Man: Philo and the History of Interpretation*, CBQMS 14 (Washington, DC: Catholic Biblical Association of America, 1983), 177–78. See Adam Kamesar, "Biblical Interpretation in Philo," in *The Cambridge Companion to Philo*, ed. Adam Kamesar (Cambridge: Cambridge University Press, 2009), 65–92, here 77; Niehoff, "Philo, Allegorical Commentary," 1070–71.

16. Niehoff, "Philo, Allegorical Commentary," 1071.

17. Kamesar, "Biblical Interpretation in Philo," 85.

18. Charles A. Anderson, *Philo of Alexandria's Views of the Physical World*, WUNT 2/309 (Tübingen: Mohr Siebeck, 2011), 10.

19. Mikołaj Domaradzki, "The Value and Variety of Allegory: A Glance at Philo's *De Gigantibus*," SPhiloA 31 (2019): 13–28, here 27.

20. Yedidya Etzion, "Philo's Jewish Law: Uncovering the Foundations of a Second-Temple System of Jewish Law" (University of California, Berkeley, PhD diss., 2015), 116, https://escholarship.org/uc/item/3qk4420v. See James W. Thompson, *Moral Formation According to Paul: The Context and Coherence of Pauline Ethics* (Grand Rapids: Baker Academic, 2011), 141.

21. Maren R. Niehoff, *Philo on Jewish Identity and Culture*, TSAJ 86, eds. Martin Hengel and Peter Schäfer (Tübingen: Mohr Siebeck, 2001), 259–66.

22. A. Andrew Das, *Galatians*, Concordia Commentary (St Louis: Concordia, 2014), 483; Domaradzki, "Allegory," 27.

23. See also *Leg.* 1.69; *Prob.* 159.

24. Clark, "Enslaved Under the Elements," 93–122.

25. Jerome Moreau, "A Noocentric Exegesis: The Function of Allegory in Philo of Alexandria and Its Hermeneutical Implications," *SPhiloA* 29 (2017): 61–80, here 78–80. See Valentin Nikiprowetzky, *Le commentaire de l'Écriture chez Philon d'Alexandrie: son caractère et sa portée, observations philologiques*, ALGHJ 11, ed. Karl Heinrich Rengstorf (Leiden: Brill, 1977), 239. This section develops my observations in "Enslaved Under the Elements," 120–21.

26. Keener, *Galatians*, 409, citing Witherington, *Grace in Galatia*, 324–25; Zurawski, "Paul's Allegory in Light of Philo," 304–5.

27. Niehoff, "Philo, Allegorical Commentary," 1071.

28. Di Mattei, "Paul's Allegory," 108.

29. Di Mattei, "Paul's Allegory," 109, citing Longenecker, *Biblical Exegesis*, 28, 39, 54.

30. Witherington, *Grace in Galatia*, 326; Di Mattei, "Paul's Allegory," 102–9; Martinus C. de Boer, *Galatians: A Commentary*, NTL (Louisville, KY: Westminster John Knox, 2011), 296.

31. Domaradzki, "Allegory," 27.

32. Douglas J. Moo, *Galatians*, BECNT (Grand Rapids: Baker, 2013), 296.

33. Richard Longenecker, *Galatians*, WBC 41 (Dallas: Word, 1990), 209–10; James D. G. Dunn, *The Epistle to the Galatians*, BNTC (London: A & C Black, 1993), 248; Witherington, *Grace in Galatia*, 334–36; Di Mattei, "Paul's Allegory," 119; de Boer, *Galatians*, 296; Moo, *Galatians*, 294.

34. Wright, *Galatians*, 295.

35. Das, *Galatians*, 485, citing Richard B. Hays, "The Letter to the Galatians: Introduction, Commentary, and Reflections," in *NIB* 11:301.

36. Clark, "Enslaved Under the Elements," 179–80.

37. Here I follow the short reading in א, C, F, G—το γαρ σινα ορος εστιν—over against longer readings in 𝔓⁴⁶; A, B, D; and K, L, P, Ψ. See Wright, *Galatians*, 296–98.

38. Wright, *Galatians*, 298.

39. Samuel John Tedder, "Children of Laughter and the Re-Creation of Humanity: The Theological Vision and Logic of Paul's Letter to the Galatians from the Vantage Point of 4:21–5:1" (Durham University, PhD thesis, 2017), 208n791, http://etheses .dur.ac.uk/12219/, citing F. F. Bruce, *The Epistle to the Galatians*, NIGTC (Grand Rapids: Eerdmans, 1982), 220.

40. Tedder, "Children of Laughter," 208. See de Boer, *Galatians*, 298.

41. Tedder, "Children of Laughter," 210.

42. Tedder, "Children of Laughter," 210–11.

43. Matthew Y. Emerson, "Arbitrary Allegory, Typical Typology, or Intertextual Interpretation? Paul's Use of the Pentateuch in Galatians 4:21–31," *BTB* 43 (2013): 14–22, here 19, citing Phyllis Trible, *Texts of Terror: Literary-Feminist Readings of Biblical Narratives*, OBT 13 (Philadelphia: Fortress, 1984), 9–35; Franz V. Greifenhagen, *Egypt on the Pentateuch's Ideological Map: Constructing Biblical Israel's Identity*, JSOTSup 361 (London: Sheffield Academic, 2002), 32.

44. Emerson, "Arbitrary Allegory," 19–20, citing Gordon J. Wenham, *Genesis 16–50*, WBC 2 (Waco, TX: Word, 1994), 10; Alison Schofield, "The Wilderness Motif in the Dead Sea Scrolls," in *Israel in the Wilderness: Interpretations of the Biblical Narratives in Jewish and Christian Traditions*, ed. Kenneth E. Pomykala (Leiden: Brill, 2008), 37–54, here 43.

45. Tedder, "Children of Laughter," 208.

46. Wright, *Galatians*, 299–300. See Christl M. Maier, "Psalm 87 as a Reappraisal of the Zion Tradition and Its Reception in Galatians 4:26," *CBQ* 69.3 (2007): 473–86; Das, *Galatians*, 500; N. T. Wright, "Mother Zion Rejoices: Psalm 87 as a Missing Link in Galatians 4," in *Cruciform Scripture: Cross, Participation, and Mission* (Grand Rapids: Eerdmans, 2020), 225–39.

47. Wright, *Galatians*, 301.

48. Di Mattei, "Paul's Allegory," 114–19; Keener, *Galatians*, 408.

49. See Keener, *Galatians*, 431.

50. Wright 293.

51. Keener, *Galatians*, 402; see Di Mattei, "Paul's Allegory," 105–8.

52. Ramelli, "Paul and Origen," 150–51.

53. Keener, *Galatians*, 402.

54. Keener, *Galatians*, 403.

55. Ardel B. Caneday, "Covenant Lineage Allegorically Prefigured: 'Which Things Are Written Allegorically' (Galatians 4:21–31)," *SBJT* 14 (2010): 50–77, here 66.

56. For typology and analogy, Keener, *Galatians*, 404–5 cites E. P. Sanders, *Paul and Palestinian Judaism* (Philadelphia: Fortress, 1977), 545; Richard B. Hays, *Echoes of Scripture in the Letters of Paul* (New Haven, CT: Yale University Press, 1989), 57, 116; Scott W. Hahn, *Romans*, CCSS (Grand Rapids: Baker Academic, 2017), 85, et al. For figural, see David I. Starling, "Justifying Allegory: Scripture, Rhetoric, and Reason in Galatians 4:21–5:1," *JTI* 9 (2015): 227–45; Wright, *Galatians*, 294.

57. See Das, *Galatians*, 483–85.

58. Di Mattei, "Paul's Allegory," 114 n. 44; Das, *Galatians*, 503 n. 134.

59. See "Longinus's" quotation of *Drunkenness* 198 in *On the Sublime* 44.1–5 and Josephus's reference to Philo in *Ant.* 18.259. See Gregory E. Sterling, "'Philo Has Not Been Used Half Enough': The Significance of Philo of Alexandria for the Study of the New Testament," *PRS* 30 (2003): 251–69, here 261–68; Niehoff, "Abraham in the Greek East," 227–28.

60. Keener, *Galatians*, 408–10 is a notable recent exception.

61. Tedder, "Children of Laughter," 62; Keener, *Galatians*, 409.


# BIBLIOGRAPHY

Anderson, Charles A. *Philo of Alexandria's Views of the Physical World.* WUNT 2/309. Tübingen: Mohr Siebeck, 2011.

Barrett, C. K. "The Allegory of Abraham, Sarah, and Hagar in the Argument of Galatians." In *Rechtfertigung: Festschrift für Ernst Käsemann zum 70. Geburtstag*, edited by Johannes Friedrich, Wolfgang Pöhlmann, and Peter Stuhlmacher, 1–16. Tübingen: Mohr Siebeck, 1976.

de Boer, Martinus C. *Galatians: A Commentary.* NTL. Louisville, KY: Westminster John Knox, 2011.

Borgen, Peder. "Some Hebrew and Pagan Features in Philo's and Paul's Interpretations of Hagar and Ishmael." In *The New Testament and Hellenistic Judaism*. Edited by Peder Borgen and Søren Giversen, 151–64. Peabody, MA: Aarhus University Press, 1997.

Bruce, F. F. *The Epistle to the Galatians.* NIGTC. Grand Rapids: Eerdmans, 1982.

Calvert-Koyzis, Nancy. *Paul, Monotheism and the People of God: The Significance of Abraham Traditions for Early Judaism and Christianity.* JSNTSup 273. London: T&T Clark, 2004.

Caneday, Ardel B. "Covenant Lineage Allegorically Prefigured: 'Which Things Are Written Allegorically' (Galatians 4:21–31)." *SBJT* 14 (2010): 50–77.

Clark, Ernest P. "Enslaved Under the Elements of the Cosmos." PhD thesis, University of St Andrews, 2018.

Das, A. Andrew. *Galatians.* Concordia Commentary. St Louis: Concordia, 2014.

———. *Paul and the Stories of Israel: Grand Thematic Narratives in Galatians.* Minneapolis: Fortress, 2016.

Di Mattei, Steven. "Paul's Allegory of the Two Covenants (Gal 4.21–31) in Light of First-Century Hellenistic Rhetoric and Jewish Hermeneutics." *NTS* 52 (2006): 102–22.

Domaradzki, Mikołaj. "The Value and Variety of Allegory: A Glance at Philo's *De Gigantibus*." SPhiloA 31 (2019): 13–28.

Dunn, James D. G. *The Epistle to the Galatians*. BNTC. London: A & C Black, 1993.

Emerson, Matthew Y. "Arbitrary Allegory, Typical Typology, or Intertextual Interpretation? Paul's Use of the Pentateuch in Galatians 4:21–31." *BTB* 43 (2013): 14–22.

Etzion, Yedidya. "Philo's Jewish Law: Uncovering the Foundations of a Second-Temple System of Jewish Law." PhD diss., University of California, Berkeley, 2015. https://escholarship.org/uc/item/3qk4420v.

García Martínez, Florentino, and Eibert J. C. Tigchelaar, eds. *The Dead Sea Scrolls Study Edition*. Leiden: Brill, 1997.

Greifenhagen, Franz V. *Egypt on the Pentateuch's Ideological Map: Constructing Biblical Israel's Identity*. JSOTSup 361. London: Sheffield Academic, 2002.

Hafemann, Scott J. "Paul and the Exile of Israel in Galatians 3–4." In *Exile: Old Testament, Jewish, and Christian Conceptions*, edited by James M. Scott, 329–71. JSJSup 56. Leiden: Brill, 1997.

Hahn, Scott W. *Romans*. CCSS. Grand Rapids: Baker Academic, 2017.

Hanson, Richard P. C. *Allegory and Event: A Study of the Sources and Significance of Origen's Interpretation of Scripture*. London: SCM, 1959.

Hays, Richard B. *Echoes of Scripture in the Letters of Paul*. New Haven, CT: Yale University Press, 1989.

———. "The Letter to the Galatians: Introduction, Commentary, and Reflections." In "The Letter to the Galatians." In vol. 11 of *The New Interpreter's Bible,* 181–348. Nashville: Abingdon, 2000.

Kamesar, Adam. "Biblical Interpretation in Philo." In *The Cambridge Companion to Philo*, edited by Adam Kamesar, 65–92. Cambridge: Cambridge University Press, 2009.

Keener, Craig S. *Galatians: A Commentary*. Grand Rapids: Baker Academic, 2019.

Keesmaat, Sylvia C. *Paul and His Story: (Re)Interpreting the Exodus Tradition*. LNTS 181. Sheffield: Sheffield Academic, 1999.

Kister, Menahem. "Allegorical Interpretations of Biblical Narratives in Rabbinic Literature, Philo, and Origen: Some Case Studies." In *New Approaches to the Study of Biblical Interpretation in Judaism of the Second Temple Period and in Early Christianity: Proceedings of the Eleventh International Symposium of the Orion Center for the Study of the Dead Sea Scrolls and Associated Literature, Jointly Sponsored by the Hebrew University Center for the Study of Christianity, 9–11 January, 2007*, edited by Gary A. Anderson, Ruth A. Clements, and David Satran, 133–83. Leiden: Brill, 2013.

Longenecker, Richard. *Biblical Exegesis in the Apostolic Period*. Grand Rapids: Eerdmans, 1974.

———. *Galatians*. WBC 41. Dallas: Word, 1990.

Maier, Christl M. "Psalm 87 as a Reappraisal of the Zion Tradition and Its Reception in Galatians 4:26." *CBQ* 69 (2007): 473–86.

Moo, Douglas J. *Galatians*. BECNT. Grand Rapids: Baker, 2013.

Moreau, Jerome. "A Noocentric Exegesis: The Function of Allegory in Philo of Alexandria and Its Hermeneutical Implications." SPhiloA 29 (2017): 61–80.

Niehoff, Maren R. "Abraham in the Greek East: Faith, Circumcision, and Covenant in Philo's Allegorical Commentary and Paul's Letter to the Galatians." SPhiloA 32 (2020): 227–48.

———. "Philo, Allegorical Commentary." *The Eerdmans Dictionary of Early Judaism*, 1070–72.

———. *Philo on Jewish Identity and Culture*. TSAJ 86, edited by Martin Hengel and Peter Schäfer. Tübingen: Mohr Siebeck, 2001.

Nikiprowetzky, Valentin. *Le commentaire de l'Écriture chez Philon d'Alexandrie: son caractère et sa portée, observations philologiques*. ALGHJ 11, edited by Karl Heinrich Rengstorf. Leiden: Brill, 1977.

Ramelli, Ilaria L. E. "The Role of Allegory, Allegoresis and Metaphor in Paul and Origen." *JGRChJ* 14 (2018): 130–57.

Sanders, E. P. *Paul and Palestinian Judaism*. Philadelphia: Fortress, 1977.

Schofield, Alison. "The Wilderness Motif in the Dead Sea Scrolls." In *Israel in the Wilderness: Interpretations of the Biblical Narratives in Jewish and Christian Traditions*, edited by Kenneth E. Pomykala, 37–54. Leiden: Brill, 2008.

Scott, James M. *Adoption as Sons of God: An Exegetical Investigation into the Background of Yiothesia in the Pauline Corpus*. WUNT 2/48. Tübingen: Mohr Siebeck, 1992.

Starling, David I. "Justifying Allegory: Scripture, Rhetoric, and Reason in Galatians 4:21–5:1." *JTI* 9 (2015): 227–45.

Sterling, Gregory E. "'Philo Has Not Been Used Half Enough': The Significance of Philo of Alexandria for the Study of the New Testament." *PRSt* 30 (2003): 251–69.

Tedder, Samuel John. "Children of Laughter and the Re-Creation of Humanity: The Theological Vision and Logic of Paul's Letter to the Galatians from the Vantage Point of 4:21–5:1." PhD thesis, Durham University, 2017. http://etheses.dur.ac.uk /12219/.

Thompson, James W. *Moral Formation According to Paul: The Context and Coherence of Pauline Ethics*. Grand Rapids: Baker Academic, 2011.

Tobin, Thomas H. *The Creation of Man: Philo and the History of Interpretation*. CBQMS 14. Washington, DC: Catholic Biblical Association of America, 1983.

Trible, Phyllis. *Texts of Terror: Literary-Feminist Readings of Biblical Narratives*. OBT 13. Philadelphia: Fortress, 1984.

Wenham, Gordon J. *Genesis 16–50*. WBC 2. Waco, TX: Word, 1994.

Witherington, Ben, III. *Grace in Galatia: A Commentary on St. Paul's Letter to the Galatians*. Grand Rapids: Eerdmans, 1998.

Wright, N. T. *Galatians*. CCF. Grand Rapids: Eerdmans, 2021.

———. "Mother Zion Rejoices: Psalm 87 as a Missing Link in Galatians 4." In *Cruciform Scripture: Cross, Participation, and Mission*, edited by Christopher W.

Skinner, Nijay K. Gupta, Andy Johnson, and Drew J. Strait, 225–39. Grand Rapids: Eerdmans, 2020.

Zurawski, Jason M. "Mosaic Torah as Encyclical Paideia: Reading Paul's Allegory of Hagar and Sarah in Light of Philo of Alexandria's." In *Pedagogy in Early Judaism and Christianity*, edited by K. M. Hogan, M. Goff, and Emma Wasserman, 283–307. EJL 41. Atlanta: SBL, 2017.

## Chapter 8

# Galatians 6:16's Riddles and Isaiah 54:10's Contribution

## Gentiles Joining the Israel of God?

### A. Andrew Das

In Galatians 6:16 Paul pronounces peace upon those who adhere to his rule about circumcision and uncircumcision, and then mercy upon the Israel of God. "Mercy" (ἔλεος) and "peace" (εἰρήνη) occur together in only a few instances in the Jewish Scriptures and literature of Paul's day and, of those, some are in very different contexts.[1] Philo (*Somn.* 2.149) describes a fervent plea for God to offer mercy and a taste of peace. In Tob 7:12 Symmachus translates using the two words together for one person's blessing another. The Hebrew text of Jer 16:5 is a judgment oracle as God *withdraws* "peace" (שָׁלוֹם/ εἰρήνη) and "mercy" (חֶסֶד) at the time of the exile, but the Hebrew חֶסֶד is not translated by the Septuagint. The Jeremianic context of judgment does not parallel Paul's pronouncement of blessing.

More promising parallels are Ps 85:7–11 (MT 85:8–11; LXX 84:8–12) and Isa 54:10. In Ps 85:10 (LXX 84:11) mercy and peace are restored after the exile as the "fruits" of God's new creative work (cf. Gal 5:22; 6:15). Isaiah 54:10 (LXX) uses the two words in the context of God's eschatological restoration of Jerusalem. G. K. Beale noted the parallels in Isa 54:10 and Ps 85:11 and initially conceded the possibility of a collective allusion to both. He then provided his rationale for an allusion *exclusively* to Isa 54:10. First, Paul has been drawing on this section of Isaiah throughout Galatians, including Isa 54:1 in Gal 4:27.[2] Second, the verb συστοιχέω ("is aligned with") in Gal 4:26 conspicuously precedes the citation of Isa 54:1 in Gal 4:27, even as the related verb στοιχέω ("will follow") appears in Gal 6:16 immediately before the Isaianic allusion. Third, peace and mercy are linked with God's new creation activity in Isa 54:10–12 as also in Gal 6:15–16 (cf. 1QH 13.5–12; Jub. 22.9; Rev 21). Fourth, Isaiah refers to the Abrahamic covenant (cf. Isa 54:10: "covenant of your peace"), the seed, the inheritance, the return of sinful people to God, and the new creation, as does Paul.[3] Whether or not the Galatians themselves recognized the allusion, Paul likely has in view Isa 54:10's promises.

A more useful question would be if an Isa 54:10 allusion provides leverage on the perennial question of whether Paul is *identifying* or *distinguishing* Gal 6:16b's "them" and the "Israel of God." For Beale, the Isa 54:10 allusion indicates that Paul is *including* gentiles (as "them") *within* the Israel of God.[4] Many interpreters have pointed to the inclusive thrust of Galatians: The gentiles are joining God's people in Christ, much as Isaiah 40–55 had presumably offered an inclusive, eschatological hope for the gentiles' inclusion. Beale pointed to how gentiles are joining and becoming part of Israel in LXX Isa 54:15, barely a few verses after Isa 54:10(!). Paul's inclusion of his gentile readers within the Israel of God therefore draws directly from Isaiah's thought.

What follows will test whether an Isa 54:10 allusion does, in fact, provide support for identifying Jews and gentiles together as the Israel of God in Gal 6:16. First, although many Galatian interpreters are convinced that the letter allows for no other interpretation, the letter is nowhere near as decisive as these interpreters assume. Paul may even be arguing *against* such an inclusion. Second, the rightful place and role of the gentiles in Isa 40–55 has been debated. How "inclusive" *are* these chapters? Third, how helpful is LXX Isa 54:15? Finally, as context for the interpretation of Isaiah, the Second Temple trajectory of discussions about the *future* place and role of the gentiles does not envision gentiles converting to Judaism or joining Israel. An allusion to Isa 54:10 would therefore support the gentiles joining God's people *as gentiles* even as a *distinct* Israel retains priority among that people.

## THE CONTEXT OF GALATIANS 6:16

Galatians 6:16 is a difficult verse, syntactically. A prepositional phrase "upon them" (ἐπ᾽ αὐτούς) is strangely located *between* "peace" and "mercy." This phrase is followed by a pronouncement "upon the Israel of God" (ἐπὶ τὸν Ἰσραὴλ τοῦ θεοῦ): Peace be upon them and mercy (καί / even?) upon the Israel of God. One possibility is that both "them" and the "Israel of God" are the *same* group. This has been the most popular understanding. A second possibility: "peace" is to be "upon them," but mercy "upon the Israel of God" as a *separate* group. Still a third possibility is that *both* peace and mercy are upon *both* them and the Israel of God, again as separate groups. To restate the interpretive options:

Option 1—Peace and mercy be upon them, namely, the Israel of God (both blessings to the same group).
Option 2—Peace be upon them and mercy upon the Israel of God (separate blessings to separate groups).
Option 3—Peace and mercy be upon them and upon the Israel of God (both blessings to the separate groups).

Most interpreters begin in 6:16 with the presence of the Greek καί immediately before "upon the Israel of God" (ἐπὶ τὸν Ἰσραὴλ τοῦ θεοῦ) and translate it as "namely" (an epexegetical καί): "Peace be upon them and mercy, *that is*, upon the Israel of God" (option 1).[5] The "they" group would be identical to "the Israel of God." In favor of this understanding, Paul has spent the bulk of the letter blasting circumcision and Moses's Law as entry requirements for the people of God. The stark contrast between circumcision and the cross of Christ in 6:11–16 would be his parting shot. Galatians 6:16b would be a rhetorically powerful redefinition that includes both Jews and gentiles within the same Israel of God. Surely the Galatians would recall how Paul had described them as members of "the Jerusalem above," "*our* mother" (4:26, 28–29). They were brought together as gentiles with Jews in Christ (Gal 3:29) as the true children of Abraham (3:6) and Sarah, "the free woman" (4:30–31). The "Israel *of God*" at the end of the letter would be inclusive of Jews and gentiles, paralleling the "assembly *of God*" or church of 1:13.[6] The rivals had been laboring to incorporate the gentile Galatians into Israel as Jewish converts. No, writes Paul, the gentile Galatians are *already* part of Israel, the Israel of God, the *true* Israel! Beale dismissed the syntactical evidence of 6:16 as ambiguous and considered the contextual support of the letter for this first option the decisive consideration. Taking both "them" (αὐτούς) and "the Israel of God" as a church composed of Jews and gentiles is "far better than a sudden distinction between Jew and Gentile."[7] Recent commentators have concurred, based almost solely on the inclusion of the gentiles in God's people throughout Galatians.[8]

Option 1, however, is problematic. The syntax of the verse favors a *distinction*. First, more natural expressions for apposition are absent here—e.g., οἵτινές εἰσιν or τουτέστιν.[9] Second, the repeated preposition "upon" (ἐπί) normally distinguishes a *second* group from those serving as the object of the first instance of the preposition. In Matt 27:25, for instance, the Jews call upon themselves and upon their children the blood of Christ. Separate groups are in view: the adults on the one hand and their children on the other. In Acts

5:11 fear came not only upon the whole church but also upon "*all* who heard of these things," i.e., people outside of the church. In Acts 11:15 the Holy Spirit came upon the gentiles as upon the Jews at the very beginning. In Heb 8:8 a new covenant "upon" the house of Israel stands juxtaposed with "upon" the house of Judah. Revelation 20:8 refers to the mark upon the foreheads or upon the hands.[10] The repeated ἐπί /"upon" in Gal 6:16 likely designates a second, separate group.[11] Third, the awkward syntax with the second καί draws attention to the last four words of the verse as a separate group from those who follow the rule.[12] Had Paul intended to convey that "the Israel of God" is the same group as "those who follow this rule," he would have omitted the unnecessary second καί ("also"/"even"). For option 1, the identity of "them" (αὐτούς) is the same as its logical antecedent, "as many who will follow this rule" (ὅσοι τῷ κανόνι τούτῳ στοιχήσουσιν), *and* the postcedent, "the Israel of God" (τὸν Ἰσραὴλ τοῦ θεοῦ), which is separated from "them" by the words καὶ ἔλεος καὶ ἐπί. Such a syntactical structure is not only unexpected and unlikely but also unprecedented.[13] Finally, the epexegetical καί ("namely") is rather infrequent in Paul.[14] As Moo candidly conceded: "The syntactical evidence favors interpreting 'the Israel of God' as an entity separate from 'those who follow this rule.'"[15] Options 2 and 3 have been too casually dismissed by the majority of interpreters: the καί immediately preceding "upon the Israel of God" distinguishes two separate groups of people and should be translated "also" or "as well as."[16]

Moo and Beale are representative in overruling the syntactical evidence on the basis of the letter's content to affirm the inclusion of gentiles in the Israel of God. Advocates for option 1 lose sight of the fact that Paul consistently *distinguishes* Jews and gentiles in the letter. Paul stresses the oneness of Jew and gentile in Christ in 3:28, but the category of "oneness" and unity is "*in Christ*." Even as oneness in Christ in 3:28 does not dissolve the distinction between male and female, the gentiles do not become Jewish nor do Jews cease to be Jews in God's salvation. While Paul included Christ-believing gentiles among Abraham's "seed" in Christ (3:29), he has conspicuously avoided including the gentiles in *Israel* elsewhere in the letter, a consistency that is clear throughout the undisputed Pauline corpus.[17] Peter must preach the one gospel in a *distinct* mission to Jews as Jews (the circumcised) even as Paul must preach that same gospel message to the gentiles as gentiles (the uncircumcised; 2:7–8). Paul never dissolves "we who are Jews by birth" who recognize the exclusive, saving value of faith in/of Christ (2:15–16). He patiently explains that the Galatians enjoy all the rights of Abraham's heirs *without* becoming members of ethnic Israel by circumcision.

Again, interpreters overlook how the letter provides excellent contextual warrant for a *distinction* between "them" and the "Israel of God" in 6:16. Paul has been opposing the Jewish rivals' insistence that circumcision is somehow necessary, contrary to the "rule" of 6:15. Paul therefore contrasts the cross of Christ with the message of the Jewish rivals. Galatians 6:11–16 closes on as fiercely polemical a note as the letter opens (1:6–9). Galatians 6:16 serves as one last warning against the false brothers at Galatia (cf. 1:8–9; 2:4–5).[18] Jews preaching "another gospel" of gentile Law observance are excluded from "the Israel of God" and God's blessings (1:8–9; 2:4–5). Paul may have begun his letter by invoking a curse upon the Jewish rivals (1:8–9); now his hope is that these rivals would experience God's mercy at the judgment, but only if they abide by this "rule" regarding circumcision.[19] The closing section of the letter, in recapping its content, stresses *repeatedly* the difference between the cross that Paul has preached and the circumcision preached by the Jewish Christ-believing rivals—precisely the distinction in 6:16 between the Israel *of God* and the *rival Jewish* teachers and their circumcision message, an Israel *not* of God.

Thus, for Paul, the "Israel of God" language keeps the focus on the Jewish rivals, and not on the gentile Galatians. The Israel of God is a *redefined* Israel consisting of those *ethnic Jews* who adhere to his gospel of Jesus Christ and who recognize the irrelevance of circumcision in the new creation. This "Israel" understands that gentiles remain gentiles in God's salvation. Paul is simultaneously commending the Jewish Christians who affirm his gospel message and at the same time denigrating the Jewish Christian rivals who demand gentile circumcision as necessary.[20] Lest anyone mistakenly draw a conclusion from the letter that Paul is abandoning any place for Israel in God's plan, he offers a blessing for the ethnic Israel that is *of God*.[21]

Context militates equally as well, then, for options 2 and 3 with a Jewish "Israel of God." While the letter's language of Abraham's seed and heirs, Sarah's children (4:22–24, 30–31), and the Jerusalem above (4:26) apply to believing gentiles and Jews, only ethnic Jews would be members of the "present" Jerusalem (non-Christ-believers; 4:25), Hagar's children (non-Christ-believers; 4:22–25, 30), "Jews" (believers and non-Christ-believers), and the "Israel of God' (Christ-believers). In short, while the syntax favors a distinction between gentiles and the Israel of God, the context of the letter could go either way. Perhaps Beale's appeal to Isa 54:10 may offer further leverage.

## WHAT FUTURE FOR THE GENTILES IN ISAIAH?

Isaianic scholarship remains divided over the future place of gentiles and the surrounding nations, with three interpretive options:

1. The gentiles/nations will eventually enjoy God's salvation as circumcised proselytes.[22]
2. The gentiles/nations will eventually enjoy God's salvation but *as gentiles*.[23]
3. The gentiles/nations will not enjoy salvation but be subject to Israel. Diaspora *Israelites* are the ones streaming to Zion.[24]

Of the three possibilities, with respect to what is commonly labeled "Second Isaiah" (Isa 40–55), most scholars subscribe to either the second or third option and would eliminate the first. As for Isa 40–55, the Servant of Yahweh in 42:4 brings the Torah to the coastlands, as does Yahweh in 51:4. Some of these passages identify the Torah in connection with gentiles. Nevertheless, if Isa 40–55 envisions a positive future for the gentiles, then it is for the gentiles *as gentiles*. The gentiles do not become incorporated *into* Israel. (A few passages in *Isa 56–66,* esp. 56:1–8, *could* be understood as anticipating the conversion of the nations to the Israelite faith, but the consensus even here is that the foreigners remain foreigners.[25])

For instance, D. W. Van Winkle labored to show the problems in the third view (no salvation for the gentiles) and advocated himself for the second position (a future salvation for gentiles *as gentiles*).[26] In a separate essay, Van Winkle offered a point-by-point critique of the case on the basis of Isa 44:1–4 for the first view: gentiles saved by conversion; the passage "reveals nothing about proselytism nor does it disclose anything about whether Deutero-Isaiah thought circumcision was important."[27] The nations may be saved, confessing Yahweh as God and their own gods as nonexistent (Isa 45:14, 22–23), and they may worship Yahweh (Isa 42:4; 51:5), but the prophet does not envision them becoming members of Israel. Ultimately: "Although the prophet foresees the nations' salvation, he does not envision their incorporation into Israel. . . . The prophet does not envisage the co-equality of Jews and gentiles."[28] Or with Roy Melugin, "Even when the nations are saved, it seems, they are not relieved of their burden as Israel's servants."[29] In agreement with A. Gelston's nuanced defense of a universalistic strand in Second Isaiah: "Such a universal offer of salvation . . . by no means precludes the continued subordination of the nations to Israel, nor does it detract from the unique place of Israel in the divine purpose"[30] As Michael Grisanti put it, Israel remains "God's servant nation before the world."[31]

To sketch the progress of this debate, many Isaianic scholars in the early- to mid-twentieth century (some even claim a majority at the time) interpreted the nations enjoying salvation as proselytes in Isa 40–55.[32] Then in the latter half of the twentieth century arose dissenting voices that saw *no* promise of future salvation for gentiles those chapters. A mediating position between the "nationalists" and the "universalists" emerged since the 1990s allowing for strands of both positions, but most of these scholars view Isaiah 40–55 as maintaining a distinction between Israel and the nations in that future salvation. In other words, the prophet does not envision the nations proselytizing or becoming part of Israel.

To state this in terms of the situation at Galatia, Isaianic interpreters previously favored a position with which Paul's Galatian rivals would have agreed: the gentiles need to be converted to the religion of Israel. Isaianic specialists have now settled on an understanding of Isaiah that matches *Paul's own*: Gentiles enjoy God's salvation as gentiles.[33] Given Paul's allusion to Isa 54:10, and the influence of Isaiah on Paul, this more likely reading of the prophet provides evidence for Paul's maintaining a *distinction* between the gentile "them" and the Jewish "Israel of God"; both groups in Gal 6:16 would recognize that neither circumcision nor uncircumcision is salvific.

## LXX ISAIAH 54:15

Although the Hebrew text of Isaiah 40–55 does not likely anticipate gentile converts or their incorporation into the people of Israel, a Septuagintal passage has suggested a *later* interpretation of Isaiah as supportive of proselytism. God promises to restore Israel (Isa 54:1). In Isa 54:5: "The one redeeming you [the Lord of hosts], he himself is the God of Israel, and he will be called so by the whole earth." The Septuagintal translators may have understood the fulfillment of this promise to protect and restore Israel in the gentiles streaming to Zion as *proselytes*. In LXX Isa 54:15, a few verses later: "Behold *proselytes* will come to you through me, and they will sojourn with you, and they will run to you for refuge." According to Beale: "From the Septuagintal translator's perspective, the Gentiles cannot enjoy these blessings separately from Israel but only by becoming a part of national, theocratic Israel."[34] They must convert and become "proselytes" (προσήλυτοι).

The Septuagint's Isa 54:15 also drew the attention of Terence Donaldson as the *only* Second Temple text he could find that anticipated the gentiles at the end of time joining Israel as converts. Such a positive attitude toward gentiles in Isa 54:15 is at odds with a context emphasizing the futility of *attacking* Zion on the day of Yahweh. In view of that context, the Septuagintal translators' use of the Greek προσήλυτοι to render גּוּר ("to sojourn") may be motivated by *other* considerations. BDB renders the Hebrew word in Isa 54:15 "to stir up strife," an unusual meaning for the word but more fitting for the immediate context. The Greek translator, on the other hand, ignored the context and woodenly employed the usual meaning of the Hebrew word. As Donaldson explained: "While the translator evidently did not consider such a rendering impossible, it results from the need to make sense of a difficult

Hebrew text rather than from any desire to clarify the status of Gentiles in the eschatological future."[35] Isaiah 54:15 would not, then, provide evidence for a pro-circumcision/conversion understanding of gentiles at the time of God's future restoration.

Alex Douglas has recently drawn attention to Septuagintal patterns of translation in Isaiah 8 that emphasize the need for *gentiles* to observe the Mosaic Law.[36] Whereas passages such as Isa 2:3 are teasingly vague in the Hebrew about how gentiles will walk in Yahweh's ways, the second-century BCE translator of the Hebrew text of Isa 8 interpreted what was unstated in the original in terms of gentile observance of Moses's Law. The translation did not answer exactly *how much* gentiles were to observe that Law—e.g., whether they were to observe dietary restrictions or to adopt a fully Jewish identity with circumcision—but the gentiles are, in principle, to observe the Law, even its "hard" parts; cf. also LXX Isa 24:16; 26:9; 41:1; 45:16.[37] If Douglas is correct, the Septuagintal translation of Isaiah provides evidence that *some* Second Temple Jews understood the nations one day converting and joining Israel and observing Israel's Law. One may also point to the later Hebrew text of Isa 56:1–8 where foreigners are included in Israel's worship.

Paul has been responding to several of the rival teachers' pro-proselyte prooftexts from the Scripture, whether it be the promise of a curse on any who do not observe the entirety of Moses's Law (Deut 27:26 in Gal 3:10), its promise of life for its adherents (Lev 18:5 in Gal 3:12), or even living by faithfulness (to Moses's Law—Hab 2:4 in Gal 3:11). The most recent instance of the pattern was in Gal 4:27, which is a quotation of a verse (Isa 54:1) not long before Isa 54:15: "For it is written: 'Rejoice, O barren woman who does not bear [children]; break forth and cry aloud, you who have no labor pains, because the children of the desolate woman [will be] more numerous than [the children] of her who has a husband.'" In later centuries the Jews associated the barren woman of Isa 54:1 with Jerusalem—an association that may have been current already in Paul's day.[38] 4Q164 cites Isa 54:11–12 as foreseeing the Qumran community as the foundation of an eschatologically restored Jerusalem. Jerusalem had been left desolate in Isa 54:1 because her inhabitants *had abandoned Moses's Law!*[39] Adherence to the Torah would reverse Jerusalem's fortunes and result in a multitude of children for the barren woman. Isaiah 54:1 would therefore conform neatly to Paul's rivals' emphasis on Law observance. Paul understands Isa 54:1 in very different terms: a zealous adherence to the Law is precisely what has *led* to the present Jerusalem's predicament.[40]

Similarly, the allusion to LXX Isa 54:10 in Gal 6:16 may reflect the use of this very verse in the rivals' body of teaching: the Galatians are to be circumcised and *join* the Israel of God. An Isa 54:10 allusion, if originating from the rivals' body of teaching, would conform to the pattern in which the apostle interprets differently textual support for their position.[41] In other words, those who stress the incorporation of gentiles into God's Israel may well be inadvertently promoting the view of Paul's rivals and not Paul himself. For Paul, the gentiles are saved as and remain gentiles *without* circumcision or proselytizing. He is appealing to a *different* trajectory of Isaianic interpretation!

## ESCHATOLOGICAL GENTILES IN
## SECOND TEMPLE LITERATURE

The Hebrew text of Isaiah 40–55 provides little or no support for gentile proselytism since gentiles in the future will *maintain* their identity, whether their fate is positive or negative. Some evidence suggests that during the Second Temple period the Greek translators of Isaiah stressed the need for gentiles to convert and obey the Mosaic Law, a perspective that would have been agreeable to Paul's rivals at Galatia. What other Second Temple perspectives on the gentiles may have been brought to bear on the interpretation of Isaiah?

Terence Donaldson has documented four patterns of "universalism," in which Second Temple authors anticipate a positive outcome for gentiles.[42] First, many Second Temple Jews demanded that gentiles become circumcised converts to enjoy the benefits of God's people.[43] Inscriptions celebrated proselytes.[44] Greek and Roman authors frequently mention (or lament) them.[45] Metilius promises to Judaize to the point of circumcision (Josephus, *J.W.* 2.454). Josephus describes the uncircumcised Izates as not "genuinely (βεβαίως) a Jew" (trans. Feldman, LCL; Josephus, *Ant.* 20.38). Reception of circumcision was the defining mark of a convert; Donaldson therefore concluded that "it is highly unlikely that there were 'uncircumcised proselytes.'"[46]

As a second category, as opposed to the circumcised convert, Second Temple Jews distinguished various levels of gentile sympathizing.[47] For Izates and Metilius, conversion required circumcision; anything less was sympathizing (Josephus, *Ant.* 20.34–53; *J.W.* 2.454). Sympathizers were only "in some measure incorporated" (trans. Thackeray, LCL; Josephus, *J.W.* 7.45). There are "casual visitors" and those "who should be admitted to the intimacies of our daily life" (trans. Thackeray, LCL; Josephus, *Ag. Ap.* 2.209–10). The gentile nations are identified as such, often with modification—e.g., "all" or "other" or "whole world." Terms such as "alien," "foreigner," "stranger," or "mortal" would explicitly identify the sympathizer as maintaining gentile identity—much like the resident alien of the Hebrew Bible.[48]

Donaldson's third category is that of the ethical monotheist: gentiles could come to know of the one true God and relate to this God without knowledge of Judaism or association with the Jewish community. They typically came to a monotheistic conclusion by means of God's testimony in the natural world or through a Stoic-like natural law. Moses's Law was not a factor, and the gentile remained a gentile.[49]

Donaldson's final category is that of participation in eschatological salvation. Many Jews affirmed a future for the gentiles after God's promises to Israel had been fulfilled.[50] Gentiles would abandon their sinful ways and turn to the God of Israel. Second Temple texts discussing this pattern are not always entirely clear whether the eschatological gentiles would proselytize or continue as gentiles. "Or are these basic identities somehow to be transformed in a more fundamental way, along with other categories of the created order?"[51]

Sometimes texts exemplifying this pattern refer to gentile observance of the "law" (conversion?), but these are most likely references to a natural law independently accessible to gentiles. For instance, T. Levi 18.9's mention of the law should be understood in light of 14.4's law given for the enlightenment of *every* person! Similarly, Sib. Or. 3.719 has gentiles pondering the law of God, which initially suggests conversion, but 3.757–58 then mentions that this is a law for people throughout the whole earth. Even the Law of Moses at Mt. Sinai (3.254–58) is presented in Sib. Or. 3 not in terms of circumcision or the other boundary markers separating Jews from gentiles but rather as a *moral* code available to all people. It entails abandoning idolatry, worshipping at the Temple, and adhering to that moral code.[52] The proselytes of Sib. Or. 3, on closer inspection, look more like righteous gentiles. Philo (*Mos.* 2.43–44) writes of gentiles at the end of time turning to "our law."[53] He nevertheless offers no indication elsewhere that gentile observance would include circumcision. In fact, where Philo explicitly discusses circumcision in relation to proselytism (*Q.E.* 2.2), he *denies* that proselytism requires circumcision. The proselyte is to abandon idols and live virtuously.[54] Philo defines observance of the "laws and customs" as gentile abandonment of idols to worship the one God (*Virt.* 219).[55] Even for the Jews, virtue is what is essential (*Praem.* §164). In other words, to insist on gentile *circumcision* is to go beyond the evidence.

Other Second Temple texts exemplifying this pattern explicitly state that the gentiles will remain gentiles. For instance, in Ps. Sol. 17, esp. 17.28, 30–31, the gentile nations serve under the Lord's yoke and are not identified with the children. Instead, they bring the children, who had been driven out, back to Jerusalem. The Lord will be compassionate to all the nations in 17.35; they do not join Israel but rather, in 17.31, 44, *witness* the good fortune of Israel.[56] In Sib. Or. 5.484–99, Egyptians will abandon idols and construct a temple to the true God *in Egypt*, where they will bring their sacrifices.

Although most texts are ambiguous on the matter, gentile identity is most likely maintained even in these instances. As T. Levi 18.9 *contrasts* Israel and the nations that have been illumined, nothing indicates that the distinction between Israel and the nations is collapsed.[57] The two most promising Second Temple texts for an identification of the gentiles with Israel are Tob 14:5–7 and 1 En. 90–105, especially 90.30, 37–38. As for Tob 14:5–7, "all the nations," in abandoning their idols, will "turn" (ἐπιστρέψουσιν) to worship (φοβεῖσθαι) God—and yet the Israelites are still identified in 14:7 as a *distinct* entity.[58] The passage says nothing of the gentiles being circumcised, taking on the Law and its commandments, or joining in Israel's covenant.[59] First Enoch 90.30 *distinguishes* the animals on the earth and the birds of the air that worship (as gentiles) from the sheep (Israel). First Enoch 90.37–38, however, then envisions the animals being transformed into white bulls, like the Jewish patriarchs. Is this a unique departure from the consistent distinction of Jew and gentile in Second Temple literature?[60] First, 90.38 *continues* to refer to "the Lord of the sheep" (trans. *OTP*). Second, the "they" transformed in 90.37 are limited to the beasts of the field and the birds of the sky and does *not* include the sheep/Israel. In fact, "all their species" is similar to 89.10's "all classes," also in reference to the beasts of the fields and the birds. In other words, the focus in 90.37–38 is on the change to take place among the gentiles, and not that they become part of Israel (the sheep). The gentiles will gather peaceably in the house/Jerusalem, having abandoned the worship of their gods. Circumcision is never mentioned.[61]

As Paula Fredriksen rightly concluded, "Saved Gentiles are *not* Jews. They are Gentiles; they just do not worship idols any more."[62] In *no* Second Temple text of this pattern are gentiles identified as "Israel" in the coming age, an important point in relation to Gal 6:16.

To summarize the four patterns of universalism with respect to their implications for gentile identity:

1. Conversion—gentile identifies as and becomes a Jew.
2. Gentile sympathizer—the gentile remains a gentile.
3. Ethical monotheist—the gentile remains a gentile.
4. Eschatological Participation—in the majority of texts, if not all, the gentiles explicitly remain gentiles at the end of the ages; gentiles are never labeled "Israel."

Paul's rivals at Galatia favored gentile conversion, the first approach. Paul disagreed, but his gospel was not an ethical monotheism based on natural law (the third approach). That leaves the other two possibilities. Whether Paul's thought approaches gentile sympathizing or eschatological participation in salvation of the Jewish people, the gentile sympathizer remains a gentile as most likely does the gentile participating in the salvation of the Jews. To state it differently, Second Temple literature does not envision gentiles identifying with "Israel," that is, apart from conversion.[63] In terms of Isaiah, Second

Temple authors would interpret Isaiah from a conversionist standpoint (as in the LXX translation) or as maintaining the distinction between Jew and gentile (with the Hebrew text). If so, the weight of the Second Temple parallels would suggest that Paul, in opposing a conversionist approach, would likewise read Isaiah as maintaining a distinction between the gentiles and Israel.

## CONCLUSION: THE CONTRIBUTION OF AN ISAIANIC ALLUSION TO THE DEBATE

If Paul is alluding to Isa 54:10, then the allusion increases the likelihood that "them" and the "Israel of God" should be *distinguished*. The Hebrew text of Isaiah 40–55 most likely did not envision gentiles converting to Judaism but being included as gentiles. The Septuagintal translational approach to Isaiah may agree with the perspective of the rival teachers at Galatia that circumcision and Law observance are necessary, but Paul would have disagreed. Second Temple understandings of the gentiles' eschatological salvation maintain the distinction between Israel and the nations, paralleling the distinction in the Hebrew text of Isaiah 40–55. Paul likely did as well.

## NOTES

1. "Peace" and "mercy" feature in ancient *Jewish* letters, *not* in non-Jewish epistolography, suggesting that the "Israel of God" consists of ethnic Jews—thus the question of this chapter; Lutz Doering, *Ancient Jewish Letters and the Beginnings of Christian Epistolography*, WUNT 298 (Tübingen: Mohr Siebeck, 2012), 207, 409–13, 427, 451–52, 489–90.

I am indebted to the discussion with members of the 2021 SBL Scripture and Paul Seminar, especially B. J. Oropeza, Jeffrey A. D. Weima, Ernest Clark, G. K. Beale, and J. David Stark.

2. G. K. Beale, "Peace and Mercy upon the Israel of God: The Old Testament Background of Galatians 6,26b," *Bib* 80 (1999): 204–23, here 208–11. Paul alludes to Isa 43:19 and 65:17 in the "new creation" of 2 Cor 5:17 (cf. Rev 3:14's use of the same Isaianic texts); G. K. Beale, "The Old Testament Background of Reconciliation in 2 Corinthians 5–7 and Its Bearing on the Literary Problem of 2 Corinthians 6:14–7:1," *NTS* 35 (1989): 550–81; idem, "Old Testament Background of Rev 3,14," *NTS* 42 (1996): 133–152. For a catalog of Paul's possible use of Isaiah, see Matthew S. Harmon, *She Must and Shall Go Free: Paul's Isaianic Gospel in Galatians*, BZNW 168 (Göttingen: De Gruyter, 2010).

3. See earlier in Gal 4:24, 27 for the two Abrahamic covenants.

4. Beale, "Peace and Mercy," 216–18.

5. E.g., J. Louis Martyn, *Galatians*, AB 33A (New York: Doubleday, 1997), 574–77.

6. On the other hand, this argument may better support an identification of "Israel" with ethnic Jewish Christians since, technically, in 1:13 Paul is referring to assemblies of *Jewish* believers. For potentially clearer references to gentile churches of God, see 1 Cor 1:2; 10:32; 11:22; 15:9; 2 Cor 1:1.

7. Beale, "Peace and Mercy," 236n197.

8. Douglas J. Moo, *Galatians*, BECNT (Grand Rapids: Baker, 2013), 403; David A. deSilva, *The Letter to the Galatians*, NICNT (Grand Rapids: Eerdmans, 2018), 513; Craig S. Keener, *Galatians: A Commentary* (Grand Rapids: Baker, 2019), 580.

9. Theodor Zahn, *Der Brief des Paulus an die Galater*, 2nd ed. (Leipzig: A. Deichert [Georg Böhme], 1907), 283, 283n45.

10. For a similar linking of two ἐπί prepositional phrases with an "and" (καί), see Rom 4:9 (cf. 4:7–8, 11–12); Michael Bachmann, *Anti-Judaism in Galatians? Exegetical Studies on a Polemical Letter and on Paul's Theology*, trans. Robert L. Brawley (Grand Rapids: Eerdmans, 2008), 109.

11. Gottlob Schrenk lists Matt 27:25; Luke 23:38; Acts 5:11; cf. 11:15; Heb 8:8; Rev 20:4 and also notes Matt 5:45; Acts 8:10; 19:16; 20:4; Heb 10:16; "Was bedeutet 'Israel Gottes'?" *Judaica: Beiträge zum Verständnis des jüdischen Schicksals in Vergangenheit und Gegenwart* 5 (1949): 81–94, here 86n10.

12. Peter Richardson, *Israel in the Apostolic Church*, SNTSMS 10 (Cambridge: Cambridge University, 1969), 82–83.

13. Richardson, *Israel*, 81.

14. An epexegetical or explanatory καί is not likely in the "grace and apostleship" of Rom 1:5 in view of the first-person plural verb (in contrast to 1:1, 8). Paul is likely ascribing grace but not apostleship to the Romans; so also Bachmann, *Anti-Judaism*, 199n49. Schrenk ("'Israel Gottes,'" 85n9) helpfully lists as possible uses of an epexegetical καί 1 Cor 8:12; 12:27–28; 14:27; 15:38; 2 Cor 5:15; and καὶ τοῦτο in Rom 13:11; 1 Cor 2:2; 5:1; 6:6, 8, 10–11; Eph 2:8.

15. Moo, *Galatians*, 402.

16. E.g., Richardson, *Israel*, 74–84, esp. 82–83; cf. Hans Dieter Betz, *Galatians: A Commentary on Paul's Letter to the Churches in Galatia*, Hermeneia (Philadelphia: Fortress, 1979), 322–23.

17. For a discussion of Paul's consistent avoidance of including gentiles within "Israel," see A. Andrew Das, "Israel," in *The Pauline Mind*, Routledge Philosophical Minds, ed. Stanley E. Porter and David I. Yoon (New York: Routledge, forthcoming). First Corinthians 10:18 is the closest parallel to Gal 6:16 with its ethnic "Israel according to the flesh," suggesting an "Israel according to the Spirit" as the church inclusive of the gentile Corinthians. What is not always appreciated in the commentary literature is that Paul scrupulously *avoids* identifying that corresponding "Israel according to the Spirit." He never applies the name "Israel" in 1 Cor 10 to gentile believers.

18. Thus also Gottlob Schrenk, "Der Segenswunsch nach der Kampfepistel," *Judaica: Beiträge zum Verständnis des jüdischen Schicksals in Vergangenheit und Gegenwart* 6 (1950): 170–90, here 177–86; cf. also Schrenk, "'Israel Gottes,'" 81–94.

On this point and the OT background to the phrase, see D. W. B. Robinson, "The Distinction between Jewish and Gentile Believers in Galatians," *ABR* 13 (1965): 29–48, here 45–48.

19. Ben Witherington, III, *Grace in Galatia: A Commentary on Paul's Letter to the Galatians* (Grand Rapids: Eerdmans, 1998), 452.

20. If this reading of 6:16 is correct, the possibility cannot be excluded that the beginning of 6:17 should be translated "let no one of the rest (*of Israel*, i.e. the rivals)" cause Paul trouble (so Marcion).

21. James D. G. Dunn, *The Epistle to the Galatians*, BNTC (Peabody, MA: Hendrickson, 1993), 344–45. Some think Paul distinguishes the Mosaic Law from the Law of God and from the Law of Christ (6:2). More likely, "the Law of Christ" is a reference to Moses's Law understood through the lens of Christ's saving work; see the discussion in A. Andrew Das, *Galatians*, Concordia Commentary (St. Louis: Concordia, 2014), 607–11. Even as the Law may be viewed through an eschatological lens, so also would ethnic Israel in 6:16. The "Israel of God" would be the ethnic Israel that adheres to the gospel message of God.

22. Carroll Stuhlmueller helpfully lists the exegetical evidence cited for this position, *Creative Redemption in Deutero-Isaiah*, AnBib 43 (Rome: Biblical Institute, 1970), 129–31, esp. in Isa 44:5—although Stuhlmueller disagrees with the position.

23. Thus Charles Cutler Torrey, *The Second Isaiah: A New Interpretation* (Edinburgh: T & T Clark, 1928), 118: "side by side with Israel," but remaining distinct while part of the "the family of the One God"; on p. 130: "Least of all was the distinction between Jew and Gentile to be lost"; so also Claus Westermann, *Das Buch Jesaja, Kapitel 40–66*, 4th ed., ATD (Göttingen: Vandenhoeck & Ruprecht, 1981), 84.

24. Thus Antoon Schoors, *I Am God Your Saviour: A Form-Critical Study of the Main Genres in Is. XL-LV*, VTSup 24 (Leiden: Brill, 1973), 302–3; D. E. Hollenberg, "Nationalism and 'the Nations; in Isaiah XL-LV," *VT* 19 (1969): 23–36, esp. 25–27; R. N. Whybray, *Isaiah 40–66*, NCB (London: Oliphants, 1975), 31–32, 111–12, 139. Norman H. Snaith describes a "nationalist, even anti-Gentile, attitude" across the pages of Isaiah (p. 159) were it not for the mistranslation of Isa 49:6 as "a light to the *Gentiles*," where "nations" should be preferred; "Isaiah 40–66: A Study of the Teaching of the Second Isaiah and Its Consequences," in Harry M. Orlinsky and Norman H. Snaith, *Studies on the Second Part of the Book of Isaiah*, VTSup 14 (Leiden: Brill, 1967), 135–264, here 154–65; idem., "The Servant of the Lord in Deutero-Isaiah," in *Studies in Old Testament Prophecy*, ed. H. H. Rowley (Edinburgh: T & T Clark, 1950), 187–200, here 191; see also pp. 192–200). J. Severino Croatto argues vigorously that the nations simply serve as transportation for the *Israelite* "nations" to return home: "The 'Nations' in the Salvific Oracles of Isaiah," *VT* 55 (2005): 143–61.

25. The third part of Isaiah, Isaiah 56–66, or "Trito-Isaiah," is sandwiched by two passages that are *distinctive* in the Isaianic corpus with gentiles holding fast to God's covenant and offering sacrifice (Isa 56:6–8) and worshiping at Yahweh's holy mountain (Isa 66:21). Terence L. Donaldson notes that none of these passages explicitly claims that the gentiles will convert or receive circumcision, however later readers may have construed them; "Proselytes or 'Righteous Gentiles'? The Status of ̵ntiles in Eschatological Pilgrimage Patterns of Thought," *JSP* 7 (1990): 3–27, here

11–12. Paula Fredriksen likewise grants that gentiles may abandon idolatry, observe sabbath, and offer sacrifices, but unless they receive circumcision they are not proselytes; "Judaism, the Circumcision of Gentiles, and Apocalyptic Hope: Another Look at Galatians 1–2," *JTS* 42 (1991): 532–64, here 545–47. Raymond De Hoop reports how readers envision gentiles characterized by positive ethical behavior but not by circumcision; "The Interpretation of Isaiah 56:1–9: Comfort or Criticism?" *JBL* 127 (2008): 671–95, here 680–81. Ulrich Berges comments: "Daß die ethische Forderung zusammen mit der Sabbatobservanz als die einzigen Bedingungen für die Heilsteilhabe gelten, ist in der hebräischen Bibel einmalig. Besonders auffällig is dabei die bewußte Umgehung der Beschneidung als Bundeszeichen (Gen 17; P[riestly material])"; *Das Buch Jesaja: Komposition und Endgestalt,* Herder's Biblische Studien 16 (Freiburg: Herder, 1998), 511; cf. similar comments on 419. Jan L. Koole finds the key in v. 7's inclusion of the *uncircumcised* in Israel's worship; otherwise: "The promise made in v. 7 would contain nothing new because circumcised proselytes could probably always take part in the cult"; *Isaiah Chapters 56–66*, Volume 3 of Part III of *Isaiah*, HCOT (Leuven: Peeters, 2001), 15, cf. 24, who adds (p. 27): "The common exegesis today rightly believes that both Israelites and non-Israelites are meant here, who will share in the coming salvation. This view fits the immediate context and its elaboration in chap. 66." Thus Sabbath-observance characterizes this new community and *not* circumcision; Bernard Gosse, "Sabbath, Identity and Universalism Go Together after the Return from Exile," *JSOT* 29 (2005): 359–70, here 369, 369n15. Others consider the minority position possible that gentiles join Israel (by proselytism) in Isa 56:1–8; e.g., D. W. Van Winkle, "Isaiah 56:1–8," in *SBL Seminar Papers* 36 (1997): 234–52, esp. 242–49, who believes that this specific text represents a *departure* from the perspective on the gentiles in Isa 40–55. Joseph Blenkinsopp, nevertheless, remarks on the absence of circumcision in this account (cf., e.g., Exod 12:43–49), and yet the foreigners are participating in cultic functions and the Sabbath; *Isaiah 56–66*, AB 19B (New York: Doubleday, 2003), 135–37.

26. D. W. Van Winkle, "The Relationship of the Nations to Yahweh and to Israel in Isaiah XL–LV," *VT* 35 (1985): 446–58.

27. D. W. Van Winkle, "Proselytes in Isaiah XL–LV?: A Study of Isaiah XLIV 1–5," *VT* 47 (1997): 341–59, here 358; contra Stuhlmueller, *Creative Redemption.*

28. Van Winkle, "Relationship of the Nations," 457. Agreeing with Van Winkle that the nations' salvation does not eliminate their identity as gentiles, see also, e.g., Rikk E. Watts, "Echoes from the Past: Israel's Ancient Traditions and the Destiny of the Nations in Isaiah 40–55," *JSOT* 28 (2004): 481–508, here 505–7. Note also the positions on the nationalist-universalist debate in Isaiah of Schultz and Hays, neither of whom sees the saved gentile nations being circumcised or taking on an Israelite ethnic identity; Richard L. Schultz, "Nationalism and Universalism in Isaiah," in *Interpreting Isaiah: Issues and Approaches*, ed. David G. Firth and H. G. M. Williamson (Downers Grove, IL: InterVarsity, 2009), 122–44; Richard B. Hays, *The Conversion of the Imagination: Paul as Interpreter of Israel's Scripture* (Grand Rapids: Eerdmans, 2005), 45–47.

29. Roy F. Melugin, "Israel and the Nations in Isaiah 40–55," in *Problems in Biblical Theology: Essays in Honor of Rolf Knierim*, ed. Henry T. C. Sun and Keith L.

Eades with James M. Eades and Garth I. Moller (Grand Rapids: Eerdmans, 1997), 249–64, here 261.

30. A. Gelston, "Universalism in Second Isaiah," *JTS* ns 43 (1992): 377–98, here 396.

31. Michael A. Grisanti, "Israel's Mission to the Nations in Isaiah 40–55: An Update," *The Master's Seminary Journal* 9 (1998): 39–61, here 61.

32. This position has some later advocates—e.g., J. Blenkinsopp, "Second Isaiah— Prophet of Universalism," *JSOT* 41 (1988): 83–103, but Blenkinsopp predates the flurry of discussion of this issue in the 1990s and beyond.

33. No major modern approach to Isaiah has the prophet's anticipating the nations enjoying God's salvation and becoming coterminous with Israel *without having been converted.*

34. Beale, "Peace and Mercy," 216.

35. Donaldson, "Proselytes," 12–13.

36. Alex P. Douglas, "A Call to Law: The Septuagint of Isaiah 8 and Gentile Law Observance," *JBL* 137 (2018): 87–104. He plans to extend his published case to the rest of LXX Isaiah.

37. Douglas, "A Call to Law," 102–4.

38. The Targum on Isa. 54:1 (Jerusalem); Song Rab. 1.5; 4.4 (Israel); Hermann L. Strack and Paul Billerbeck, *Kommentar zum Neuen Testament aus Talmud und Midrash*, 3d ed. (München: C.H. Beck, 1926), 3.574–75; Richard N. Longenecker, *Galatians*, WBC 51 (Dallas: Word, 1990), 215; Betz, *Galatians*, 248n102.

39. Cf. 4Q164 (Isa 54:11–12); Bar 4:12 ("desolate"); Dunn, *Galatians*, 255.

40. Dunn, *Galatians*, 255.

41. For a fuller description of this pattern, see A. Andrew Das, *Paul and the Stories of Israel: Grand Thematic Narratives in Galatians* (Minneapolis: Fortress, 2016), 23–28.

42. Terence L. Donaldson, *Judaism and the Gentiles: Jewish Patterns of Universalism (to 135 CE)* (Waco, TX: Baylor University Press, 2007). On Second Temple attitudes toward gentiles, see also Wolfgang Kraus, *Das Volk Gottes: Zur Grundlegung der Ekklesiologie bei Paulus*, WUNT 85 (Tübingen: Mohr Siebeck, 1996), 45–110.

43. Donaldson, *Judaism*, 483–92.

44. Donaldson, *Judaism*, 438–43.

45. Donaldson, *Judaism*, 386–95, 406–9; e.g., Juvenal *Sat.* 14.96–106.

46. Donaldson, *Judaism*, 490. See especially John Nolland's convincing case against the existence of a category of uncircumcised proselytes in the Second Temple period; "Uncircumcised Proselytes?" *JSJ* 12 (1981): 173–94.

47. Donaldson, *Judaism*, 473.

48. Donaldson, *Judaism*, 473–74, 485–86, who stresses that conversion did not emerge as a category until the Hellenistic era.

49. Donaldson, *Judaism*, 493–98.

50. Donaldson, *Judaism*, 499–505.

51. Donaldson, *Judaism*, 503; e.g., an emphasis on a new humanity, with less focus on Israel as a distinct identity in 1 En. 10.21–11.2; 48.4–5; 50.2–5.

52. John J. Collins, *Between Athens and Jerusalem: Jewish Identity in the Hellenistic Diaspora*, 2nd ed. (Grand Rapids: Eerdmans, 2000), 161–63, esp. 162: this is more along the lines of adhering to the natural law.

53. On T. Levi 18.9 in the context of the universal law of 14.4, see Donaldson, *Judaism*, 130; cf. Kraus, *Volk Gottes*, 87–88.

54. Donaldson, "Proselytes," 15.

55. Donaldson, "Proselytes," 16.

56. See the discussion of this text in Kraus, *Volk Gottes*, 50–52.

57. Kraus, *Volk Gottes*, 73.

58. Kraus, *Volk Gottes*, 78–79 writes (p. 78): "Von einer Eingliederung der Heiden ins Gottesvolk oder einer Gleichstellung mit Israel ist jedoch auch hier kaum die Rede." The verb (ἐπιστρέψουσιν) does not, of itself, mean to "convert."

59. Donaldson, *Judaism*, 45.

60. Kraus, *Volk Gottes*, 53–55, and esp. 55–57.

61. Donaldson, *Judaism*, 89.

62. Fredriksen, "Judaism," 547–48.

63. Paul may draw in Galatians on an eschatological participation strand of thought; see the critical review of this thesis in Das, *Paul and the Stories of Israel*, 33–63. Nevertheless, Second Temple understandings of gentiles enjoying salvation as gentiles—apart from conversionist approaches—place a burden of proof on interpreters to show that a Christ-believing passage is departing from that pattern.

## BIBLIOGRAPHY

Bachmann, Michael. *Anti-Judaism in Galatians? Exegetical Studies on a Polemical Letter and on Paul's Theology*. Translated by Robert L. Brawley. Grand Rapids: Eerdmans, 2008.

Beale, G. K. "The Old Testament Background of Reconciliation in 2 Corinthians 5–7 and Its Bearing on the Literary Problem of 2 Corinthians 6:14–7:1." *NTS* 35 (1989): 550–81.

———. "Old Testament Background of Rev 3,14." *NTS* 42 (1996): 133–152.

———. "Peace and Mercy upon the Israel of God: The Old Testament Background of Galatians 6,26b." *Bib* 80 (1999): 204–23.

Berges, Ulrich. *Das Buch Jesaja: Komposition und Endgestalt*. Herder's Biblische Studien 16. Freiburg: Herder, 1998.

Betz, Hans Dieter. *Galatians: A Commentary on Paul's Letter to the Churches in Galatia*. Hermeneia. Philadelphia: Fortress, 1979.

Blenkinsopp, J. "Second Isaiah—Prophet of Universalism." *JSOT* 41 (1988): 83–103.

Blenkinsopp, Joseph. *Isaiah 56–66*. AB 19B. New York: Doubleday, 2003.

Collins, John J. *Between Athens and Jerusalem: Jewish Identity in the Hellenistic Diaspora*, 2nd ed. Biblical Resource Series. Grand Rapids: Eerdmans, 2000.

Croatto, J. Severino. "The 'Nations' in the Salvific Oracles of Isaiah." *VT* 55 (2005): 143–61.

Das, A. Andrew. *Galatians*. Concordia Commentary. St. Louis: Concordia, 2014.

————. "Israel." In *The Pauline Mind*. Routledge Philosophical Minds, edited by Stanley E. Porter and David I. Yoon. New York: Routledge, forthcoming.

————. *Paul and the Stories of Israel: Grand Thematic Narratives in Galatians.* Minneapolis: Fortress, 2016.

De Hoop, Raymond. "The Interpretation of Isaiah 56:1–9: Comfort or Criticism?" *JBL* 127 (2008): 671–95.

DeSilva, David A. *The Letter to the Galatians*. NICNT Grand Rapids: Eerdmans, 2018.

Doering, Lutz. *Ancient Jewish Letters and the Beginnings of Christian Epistolography*. WUNT 298. Tübingen: Mohr Siebeck, 2012.

Donaldson, Terence L. *Judaism and the Gentiles: Jewish Patterns of Universalism (to 135 CE)* Waco, TX: Baylor University Press, 2007.

————. "Proselytes or 'Righteous Gentiles'? The Status of Gentiles in Eschatological Pilgrimage Patterns of Thought." *JSP* 7 (1990): 3–27.

Douglas, Alex P. "A Call to Law: The Septuagint of Isaiah 8 and Gentile Law Observance." *JBL* 137 (2018): 87–104.

Dunn, James D. G. *The Epistle to the Galatians*. BNTC. Peabody, MA: Hendrickson, 1993.

Fredriksen, Paula. "Judaism, the Circumcision of Gentiles, and Apocalyptic Hope: Another Look at Galatians 1 and 2." *JTS* 42 (1991): 532–64.

Gelston, A. "Universalism in Second Isaiah." *JTS* 43 (1992): 377–98.

Gosse, Bernard. "Sabbath, Identity and Universalism Go Together after the Return from Exile." *JSOT* 29 (2005): 359–70.

Grisanti, Michael A. "Israel's Mission to the Nations in Isaiah 40–55: An Update." *The Master's Seminary Journal* 9 (1998): 39–61.

Harmon, Matthew S. *She Must and Shall Go Free: Paul's Isaianic Gospel in Galatians*. BZNW 168. Berlin: De Gruyter, 2010.

Hays, Richard B. *The Conversion of the Imagination: Paul as Interpreter of Israel's Scripture*. Grand Rapids: Eerdmans, 2005.

Hollenberg, D. E. "Nationalism and 'the Nations; in Isaiah XL–LV." *VT* 19 (1969): 23–36.

Keener, Craig S. *Galatians: A Commentary*. Grand Rapids: Baker, 2019.

Koole, Jan L. *Isaiah Chapters 56–66*. Volume 3 of Part III of *Isaiah*. HCOT. Leuven: Peeters, 2001.

Kraus, Wolfgang. *Das Volk Gottes: Zur Grundlegung der Ekklesiologie bei Paulus*. WUNT 85. Tübingen: Mohr Siebeck, 1996.

Longenecker, Richard N. *Galatians*. WBC 51. Dallas: Word, 1990.

Martyn, J. Louis. *Galatians*. AB 33A. New York: Doubleday, 1997.

Melugin, Roy F. "Israel and the Nations in Isaiah 40–55." In *Problems in Biblical Theology: Essays in Honor of Rolf Knierim*, edited by Henry T. C. Sun and Keith L. Eades with James M. Eades and Garth I. Moller, 249–64. Grand Rapids: Eerdmans, 1997.

Moo, Douglas J. *Galatians*. BECNT. Grand Rapids: Baker, 2013.

Nolland, John. "Uncircumcised Proselytes?" *JSJ* 12 (1981): 173–94.

Richardson, Peter. *Israel in the Apostolic Church.* SNTSMS 10. Cambridge: Cambridge University, 1969.

Robinson, D. W. B. "The Distinction between Jewish and Gentile Believers in Galatians." *ABR* 13 (1965): 29–48.

Schoors, Antoon. *I Am God Your Saviour: A Form-Critical Study of the Main Genres in Is. XL–LV.* VTSup 24. Leiden: Brill, 1973.

Schrenk, Gottlob. "Der Segenswunsch nach der Kampfepistel." *Judaica: Beiträge zum Verständnis des jüdischen Schicksals in Vergangenheit und Gegenwart* 6 (1950): 170–90.

———. "Was bedeutet 'Israel Gottes'?" *Judaica: Beiträge zum Verständnis des jüdischen Schicksals in Vergangenheit und Gegenwart* 5 (1949): 81–94.

Schultz, Richard L. "Nationalism and Universalism in Isaiah." In *Interpreting Isaiah: Issues and Approaches,* edited by David G. Firth and H. G. M. Williamson, 122–44. Downers Grove, IL: InterVarsity, 2009.

Snaith, Norman H. "The Servant of the Lord in Deutero-Isaiah." In *Studies in Old Testament Prophecy,* edited by H. H. Rowley, 187–200. Edinburgh: T & T Clark, 1950.

———. "Isaiah 40–66: A Study of the Teaching of the Second Isaiah and Its Consequences." In *Studies on the Second Part of the Book of Isaiah,* Harry M. Orlinsky and Norman H. Snaith, 135–264. VTSup 14. Leiden: Brill, 1967.

Strack, Hermann L., and Paul Billerbeck. Vol. 3 of *Kommentar zum Neuen Testament aus Talmud und Midrash.* 3rd ed. München: C.H. Beck, 1926.

Stuhlmueller, Carroll. *Creative Redemption in Deutero-Isaiah.* AnBib 43. Rome: Biblical Institute, 1970.

Torrey, Charles Cutler. *The Second Isaiah: A New Interpretation.* Edinburgh: T & T Clark, 1928.

Van Winkle, D. W. "Isaiah 56:1–8." *SBL Seminar Papers* 36 (1997): 234–52.

———. "Proselytes in Isaiah XL–LV?: A Study of Isaiah XLIV 1–5." *VT* 47 (1997): 341–59.

———. "The Relationship of the Nations to Yahweh and to Israel in Isaiah XL–LV." *VT* 35 (1985): 446–58.

Watts, Rikk E. "Echoes from the Past: Israel's Ancient Traditions and the Destiny of the Nations in Isaiah 40–55." *JSOT* 28 (2004): 481–508.

Westermann, Claus. *Das Buch Jesaja, Kapitel 40–66.* 4th ed. ATD. Göttingen: Vandenhoeck & Ruprecht, 1981.

Whybray, R. N. *Isaiah 40–66.* NCB. London: Oliphants, 1975.

Witherington, Ben III. *Grace in Galatia: A Commentary on Paul's Letter to the Galatians.* Grand Rapids: Eerdmans, 1998.

Zahn, Theodor. *Der Brief des Paulus an die Galater.* 2nd ed. Leipzig: A. Deichert (Georg Böhme), 1907.

*Chapter 9*

# Justification by Suffering

## *The Register of Old Testament Lament in Galatians*

### Channing L. Crisler

At the close of his letter to the Galatians, an exasperated Paul makes one final request: "From now on, let no one cause trouble for me; for I bear the marks of Jesus (τὰ στίγματα τοῦ Ἰησοῦ) in my body" (Gal 6:17). The enigmatic phrase τὰ στίγματα τοῦ Ἰησοῦ is a final dramatic reminder that suffering "marks" the lives of the righteous, especially the apostle to the Galatians.[1] Suffering also marks the letter in exegetically significant ways as some interpreters have recently noted. For example, John Anthony Dunne argues that in Galatians "suffering for the sake of the cross" is an "alternative" mark to circumcision which "demarcates the true people of God, and sets them apart for future blessing."[2] Similarly, Jeff Hubing observes that the tension between "suffering and power" experienced by both Paul and his recipients "serve as marks of the authenticity of the message and the status of the Galatians as righteous."[3] If then suffering plays a significant role in the letter as these interpreters suggest, more consideration should be given to the linguistic register that Paul engages to describe the afflictions of the righteous.[4] The suggestion here is that Paul engages the register of lament in ways that shape his rhetoric and thereby the theological inferences to be drawn from it.[5]

Lament is the classic language of suffering in Israel's Scriptures long assessed by OT scholars.[6] It is a form of prayer scattered across various genres and too frequently only associated with jarring cries such as "How long, O Lord," or "My God, my God, why have you forsaken me."[7] However, such cries represent only one aspect of a larger idiom, pattern, and theology that collectively constitute lament across various OT genres. Lament, in fact, provides a conceptual structure for communal and individual experiences of pain within Israel's history. The late Claus Westermann went as far as to suggest, "The cry to God out of deep anguish accompanies Israel through every stage of her history."[8] These frequent cries are in tension within prior promises and lead to various experiences of deliverance which result in an impermanent shift to praise. In short, lament provides both language for the afflicted to utter and a theological structure to understand those very afflictions.

Against this intertextual backdrop, the overarching argument in what follows is that through the combination of his engagement with the register of lament in Israel's Scriptures, his own affliction, and the truth of his gospel, Paul teaches the Galatians that justification in Christ is a painful experience. Just as OT lamenters struggled to maintain their grip on YHWH's promise that they are righteous before him, Paul places himself and the Galatians in the same predicament, even if his recipients do not fully realize it.[9] It is no coincidence that in warning the Galatians about this predicament Paul draws from and or reconfigures four aspects of the lament register which we will consider: (1) imprecatory lament; (2) answered laments; (3) messianic lament; and (4) human–divine participation in lament.

## PAUL'S IMPRECATORY LAMENT IN GAL 1:6–9

Since John Barclay's seminal essay on "mirror reading" in Galatians, which he finds "essential and extremely problematic," it has been fashionable to find in the letter a reflection of "the people and the arguments under attack."[10] The mirror reading here has a slightly different aim, which is to understand better the nature of Paul's anger toward his opponents by assessing the lament language he uses to describe them. Gal 1:6–9 provides a helpful example because Paul's "scripturalized" uses of ἀνάθεμα ἔστω encapsulate his imprecation against the Galatian opponents, which he crafted by merging the OT's "*locus classicus* on false prophecy" with the ethos of speakers from the Psalms of Lament (PssLm).[11] The interplay between OT pre-texts and Paul's imprecation emphatically launches his warnings to the Galatians about the painful experience of justification in Christ. The pain in question is a sense of righteous indignation aroused by those who challenge the gospel which Paul asserts he received δι' ἀποκαλύψεως Ἰησοῦ Χριστοῦ (Gal 1:12). As the late E. P. Sanders imagines, "I think that Paul was angry when he wrote the letter, and I picture him as pacing while he dictated, sometimes shouting, occasionally pleading."[12] To this I would add that I picture Paul uttering imprecatory laments such as the one captured in Gal 1:6–9.

Deuteronomy 13 is the *locus classicus* that Paul reconfigures. It prescribes death for false prophets, family members, and entire cities whose teachings promote idolatry and lure the community away from Israel's God (Deut 13:1–18). The final prescription includes, "You shall certainly kill all those who dwell in that city by slaughter through a sword, and you shall certainly anathematize it (ἀναθέματι ἀναθεματιεῖτε) and all the things in it" (Deut 13:16).[13] The ultimate objective of ἀναθέματι ἀναθεματιεῖτε is to remove divine wrath from the community (Deut 13:18). Pauline interpreters have noted the semantic, structural, and contextual overlap between this prophetic anathematization and Gal 1:6–9.[14] Paul reconfigures it in three ways: (1) he does not encourage physical violence against the opponents but encourages the Galatians to regard them as false prophets deserving of rejection; (2) he asks God to eschatologically anathematize the opponents; and (3) he seeks the opponents' anathematization to keep the Galatians from present and eschatological wrath. We will return to these reconfigurations below.

Paul merges the Deuteronomic anathematization with the ethos of the PssLm. He does not evoke a specific psalm; however, the use of ἀνάθεμα ἔστω with its emotionally charged introduction (ἀλλὰ καὶ ἐὰν ἡμεῖς ἢ ἄγγελος ἐξ οὐρανοῦ εὐαγγελίζηται) reflects the ethos of lamenters whose affliction caused by enemies compels them to make violent requests. For example, in Psalm 68 LXX, the speaker cries out, "Let their table become a trap before them and a retribution and a stumbling block; let their eyes be darkened so as not to see and bend their backs continually" (Ps 68:23–24 LXX). This is of course an imprecation familiar to Paul. He includes it in a catena of citations aimed at bolstering his claim that God had not rejected Israel. Instead, God distinguished the remnant from the "rest" of Israel whose hearts were hardened and whose backs he "bent" (Ps 68:23–24 LXX; Rom 11:9).[15] Paul's citation of this imprecatory lament suggests that he is not hesitant to take up such language. He certainly does not hesitate in Gal 1:6–9; however, he does not cite a specific imprecation, and his focus is upon false teachers rather than upon hardened Israel. Overall, Paul's ethos mimics that of lamenters in the PssLm, but he culls the content of his prayer utterance from Deuteronomy, which results in an unprecedented imprecatory lament, namely the cry for someone's eschatological anathematization.

It follows that the nature of Paul's anger outpaces his lamenting predecessors. Within Paul's "emotional regime" righteous indignation against enemies of the gospel is both acceptable and authorized when the truth of the gospel is at stake.[16] Loss of that truth in exchange for the opponents' gospel would result in an experience of divine wrath even beyond what Deuteronomy 13 forecasts. Consequently, Paul advises the Galatians to consider the opponents as false prophets worthy of excommunication and cries out for God to anathematize them.[17] The twice repeated ἀνάθεμα ἔστω is no mere "ritual

curse," or "emotive declaration," as some have labeled it.[18] It is an imprecatory lament that suggests Paul's concern for the eschatological fate of the
Galatians justifies and necessitates the kind of linguistic register he engages,
namely imprecatory lament.

Rhetorically and theologically, this intertextually charged imprecation
indicates to the Galatians that justification in Christ is fraught with present
and eschatological dangers. As in ancient Israel, false prophets enter the community to lead God's people away from the one who delivered them from
the present evil age (Deut 13; Gal 1:4). The Galatians need to expel the false
teachers, which Paul knows ultimately requires God's present and eschatological anathematization of them. Therefore, Paul utters an imprecatory
lament against the opponents because without it the Galatians run the risk of
facing divine wrath themselves. Nevertheless, in keeping with the theology
of lament, the imprecation implies that Paul knows the "final responsibility"
for the opponents and Galatians "must remain in God's hands."[19]

## ANSWERED LAMENT IN GAL 2:11–14

Paul's public rebuke of Peter at Antioch has often captured the interpretive
imagination and even contributed to misguided historical reconstructions
of early Christianity.[20] Paul recalls the incident to bolster his claim to the
Galatians that both his apostleship, and thereby his gospel, originated from
the risen Jesus. The rebuke of Peter, or Κηφᾶς, whom he refers to in Gal 2:9
as an apostolic στῦλος, illustrates to the Galatians that Paul countenanced no
denial of his gospel, not even by "pillar" apostles. Although most interpretive energy gets directed to issues surrounding the identity of the James party
(τινας ἀπὸ Ἰακώβου), my interest lies with an oft-overlooked echo embedded
in Paul's description of Peter's hypocritical actions. The interplay between
this echo and Gal 2:11–14 further informs Paul's warning to the Galatians
that justification in Christ is a painful experience. Specifically, it requires
resistance to any authoritative agent whose teachings or actions depart from
truth of the gospel which he preached to them.

The echo in question appears in Gal 2:12, "For before some from James
came, he was eating with the Gentiles; but when they came, he was shrinking
back (ὑπέστελλεν) and separating himself because he was fearing those from
the circumcision." The use of ὑποστέλλω in this context evokes Hab 2:4, "If
he should shrink back (ἐὰν ὑποστείληται), my soul does not delight in him;
but the righteous one will live by my faith" (Hab 2:4). Originally, this verse
functioned as the divine answer to Habakkuk's two interrelated laments:
(1) a lament that the righteous are afflicted by the ungodly in Judea and not
even the Mosaic Law curtails their actions (Hab 1:1–4); and (2) a lament that

divinely appointed judgment at the hands of the Chaldeans is unbecoming of YHWH's character (Hab 1:12–17). In response to these laments, Habakkuk receives a vision of the Chaldean's destruction via YHWH as a divine warrior who saves his people through the judgment of their enemies (Hab 2:5–3:19). However, until the realization of that vision, Israel's God answers Habakkuk's lament by laying out a binary choice crystallized in the verbs πιστεύω and ὑποστέλλω. The righteous will either wait for and believe in the saving vision or shrink back from it.

This binary serves as the intertextual lens through which Paul viewed and then described Peter's actions at Antioch. For Paul, Peter's withdrawal from eating with Gentiles is not merely a form of ethnic bias or an attempt to placate a faction of Christians still wrestling with Jewish–Gentile relations. It is nothing less than choosing the displeasing (οὐκ εὐδοκεῖ ἡ ψυχή μου ἐν αὐτῷ) disposition toward the saving "vision" which YHWH warned about in his answer to Habakkuk's lament. Paul saw Peter's withdrawal as "shrinking back" (ὑποστέλλω) from the revelation of God's work in Christ. Moreover, as Paul expresses it in Gal 2:13–14, this "shrinking back" from faith in the gospel had a deleterious effect on Barnabas and potentially other members of the community in Antioch whom Peter was forcing to live like Jews ('Ιουδαΐειν) even though he lived like a Gentile (ἐθνικῶς). As with the false teachers in Galatia, Paul could sense the eschatological danger of Peter's actions for the apostle and those around him.

This suggested echo is not often discussed among interpreters. Therefore, it is necessary briefly to defend the suggestion before drawing broader exegetical and theological inferences from it. When intertextual tests are deployed, this echo fairs surprisingly well.[21] To begin, although the semantic and syntactical overlap between Gal 2:12 and Hab 2:4 relies solely upon the shared use of ὑποστέλλω, it is noteworthy that the verb is a *hapax legomenon* in the Pauline corpus, which implies Paul may draw from a specific source rather than a personal or common idiom. Many interpreters locate that source in Greco-Roman military and/or political terminology.[22] However, Hab 2:4 is an equally close, if not closer, source to Paul. He even cites it in Gal 3:11, which I will discuss below. Moreover, among those who establish criteria for vetting proposed intertexts, Lange and Weigold allow that "a linguistic parallel of one word as evidence for an allusion to an anterior texts (*sic*)" is sometimes permissible.[23] Next, with respect to Hays's tests of *availability* and *historical plausibility*, besides the citations of Hab 2:4 in Rom 1:17 and Gal 3:11, we should also consider the broader use of the pre-text in early Christian tradition.[24] Most notably, the writer of Hebrews cites the entirety of Hab 2:3–4 which clearly establishes the binary of πιστεύω and ὑποστέλλω. In this way, we find an early Christian writer who shows an awareness of Habakkuk's binary which may have been available to others including Paul. Finally, within the *history of interpretation*, some interpreters have noted a possible connection between Hab 2:4 and Gal 2:12 based on the lexeme ὑποστέλλω.[25] However, discussions are generally not as protracted as what I offer here.

With these tests in tow, it is possible to draw a few inferences from the interplay between Hab 2:4 and Gal 2:12. First, Paul's illustration from Antioch clarifies how one should and should not respond to the apocalyptic vision of the gospel which is the divine answer to the cries and suffering of the righteous. The Galatians can either "shrink back" from their faith in the gospel that Paul preached and face divine wrath, or they can believe in it and live beyond the judgment. If Peter was not excluded from this binary, neither are the Galatians. Second, just as Peter's withdrawal from table fellowship had larger soteriological and eschatological implications in Paul's view, the Galatians' participation in circumcision does as well. It is a kind of "shrinking back" from the saving vision that answers the cry of the afflicted, the very response for which Paul excoriated Peter. Paul does not exempt the Galatians from the same treatment. After all, if Peter is not invulnerable to "shrinking back," neither are they.

## ANSWERED LAMENT IN GAL 2:15–21

Interpreters have often noted the close tie between Gal 2:11–14 and 2:15–21 by suggesting that the latter represents a summation of what Paul said to Peter at Antioch. Although these verses represent the *propositio* of the letter, and are thereby teeming with several key points, the focus here is largely limited to an echo of lament in Gal 2:16: "Knowing that a man is not justified by works of the law except through faith *from* Jesus Christ and not by works of the law, even we believed in Christ Jesus, in order that we might be justified by faith *from* Jesus Christ and not from works of the law, because from the works of the law no flesh will be justified (ὅτι ἐξ ἔργων νόμου οὐ δικαιωθήσεται πᾶσα σάρξ)" (Gal 2:16).[26] As interpreters have noted, the causal clause ὅτι ἐξ ἔργων νόμου οὐ δικαιωθήσεται πᾶσα σάρξ resembles a clause from Ps 142:2 LXX, an individual lament, "And do not enter into judgment with your servant, because no living thing will be justified before you (ὅτι οὐ δικαιωθήσεται ἐνώπιόν σου πᾶς ζῶν)."[27] Paul alters the lament by removing ἐνώπιόν σου and shifting πᾶς ζῶν to πᾶσα σάρξ. The latter alteration may reflect Paul's penchant for employing σάρξ as synecdoche for the human's vulnerability, culpability, and slavery to an age ruled by sin and death. It may also reflect the opponents push for circumcision in the flesh (Gal 6:12).[28]

Even with an altered line from Psalm 142 LXX, the larger context and theological underpinning of this lament inform Paul's summation of his speech to Peter. To briefly summarize the psalm, the speaker frames the prayer with opening and closing appeals to God's δικαιοσύνη, "Hear me in your righteousness (ἐν τῇ δικαιοσύνῃ σου)" and "In your righteousness (ἐν τῇ δικαιοσύνῃ σου) you will bring my soul out of distress" (Ps 142:1, 11 LXX). What it means for God to answer the lamenter ἐν τῇ δικαιοσύνῃ becomes clearer within the movement of the psalm. While the lamenter ultimately needs and requests deliverance from his enemies, it is significant that he first seeks divine mercy in his own judgment before God "And do not enter into judgment with your servant, because no living thing will be justified before you" (Ps 142:2 LXX). Only after God passes merciful judgment upon the lamenter can he receive the guidance (Ps 142:8 LXX) and the deliverance he asks for, "Deliver me from my enemies, O Lord" (Ps 142:9 LXX). The prerequisite of a right standing is in keeping with the theology of the PssLm. God only answers cries for deliverance that are uttered by the righteous.[29] However, that is a problematic requisite for everyone since no living thing can be justified before God as the lamenter notes. It follows that God answer the lamenter ἐν τῇ δικαιοσύνῃ through two interrelated righteous actions: (1) mercy in judgment to the lamenter; and (2) deliverance of the lamenter through judgment of his enemies.

By including an altered form of the psalmist's cry for mercy, Paul frames Gal 2:15–21 within a theological pattern of lament. Like the lamenter, all people, including Peter, Paul, and the Galatians, need Israel's God to be "for them" if they are to be delivered from the "present evil age" with its requisite consequences, namely inclusion in the eschatological judgment for which the age is slated. The prerequisite of a right standing can only be a gift because no flesh will be justified otherwise. Paul locates that gift in Christ's death and in his union by faith with the crucified (Χριστῷ συνεσταύρωμαι) and living Christ (Gal 2:19–20). If the lamenter asked God to act in his righteousness with two interrelated actions, that is, mercy in judgment toward him and salvation through the judgment of enemies, Paul finds both in Christ. Paul reconfigures these two actions by identifying himself and Peter not only as "living things/flesh" that cannot be justified before God but also the enemies, or sinners (αὐτοὶ ἁμαρτωλοί, Gal 2:17), from whom the lamenter sought deliverance. In short, Paul is both lamenter in need of mercy and the enemy slated to be judged. Consequently, the crucified Christ lovingly "handed himself over" (παραδόντος ἑαυτὸν ὑπὲρ ἐμοῦ) so that his death provides both the judgment of an enemy, who is Paul, and the mercy for a lamenter, who is also Paul. Circumcision, then, like withdrawal from table fellowship, is tantamount to rejecting this divine answer to lament which requested that God act in his righteousness. Paul finds that God provides that answer uniquely and only in Christ (Gal 2:20–21).

To summarize, within Paul's overarching concern to show the Galatians that justification in Christ is a painful experience, the interplay between Psalm 142 LXX and Gal 2:15–21 reassures them that Christ graciously supplies the need of "all flesh." That need is for God to act in his righteousness wherein he is merciful in judgment and delivers through judgment.

## ANSWERED LAMENT IN GAL 3:1–14

As Paul turns his attention more directly to the recipients in Gal 3:1, his engagement with Israel's Scriptures surges.[30] This includes two citations that in their original contexts functioned as answers to lament, namely Gen 15:6 and Hab 2:4. Their inclusion at this point in the argument implies that pain characterized Abraham's justification, as it does the Galatians', and emphasizes that God's answer to Habakkuk's lament is all that stands between the Galatians and an eschatological curse. Of course, Paul has suffering in his purview before these citations. For example, as part of his criticism that the Galatians risk finishing their justification in Christ in a way incongruent with how they started, Paul asks, "Did you suffer (ἐπάθετε) so many things in vain? If indeed it was in vain?" (Gal 3:4).[31] Interpreters struggle to identify the historical referent of ἐπάθετε, which is likely historically irrecoverable.[32] However, if Paul's juxtaposition of flesh and Spirit in Gal 5:16–24 is any indication, the Galatians' suffering includes a constant internal struggle. Whatever the Galatians have suffered within their own persons and at the hands of external agents within the community, they risk rendering it meaningless by a turn to another gospel. Even more, they now face a kind of defining and justifying suffering that aligns them with their scriptural predecessors.

Καθώς in Gal 3:6, not the typical introductory formula καθὼς γέγραπται, both introduces the citation of Gen 15:6 and links it to the preceding line of thought. While interpreters debate the full scope of what the link entails, the comparison is at least that "both Abraham and the Galatians exercised faith."[33] More precisely, given the wider context of Gen 15:6, both Abraham and the Galatians suffered in the faith that they exercised. Before the Genesis narrator concludes that Abraham's faith was reckoned as righteousness, the reader hears his cries of distress elicited by the tension between YHWH's promise of reward on the one hand and the absence of an heir on the other. Abraham's cries include "Master, what will you give me? But I am departing childless" and "You have not given a descendant to me" (Gen 15:2–3).[34] YHWH answers Abraham's cries in typical lament fashion, namely by reiterating the promise, this time with a cosmic metaphor (ἀρίθμησον τοὺς ἀστέρας, Gen 15:5). Only then does the narrator note, "And Abraham believed God and it was reckoned to him as righteousness" (Gen 15:6). In the subsequent narrative, pain marks Abraham's experience of righteousness, even if the patriarch's subsequent laments are assumed rather than explicitly stated.[35] It follows, then, that the Galatians' share in the blessings of believing Abraham includes lamenting and suffering as he did (Gal 3:9). If suffering marks the justification of Abraham, it must mark those who follow in his steps.

With respect to the citation in Gal 3:11, it matters that Hab 2:4 originally functioned as God's answer to the prophet's lament as described above. It is not necessary to rehash that description here; however, Paul now employs Hab 2:4 for a different rhetorical purpose. Rather than warn about the danger of "shrinking back" from the gospel in the vein of YHWH's warning to Habakkuk, Paul incorporates Hab 2:4 as part of his warning about the eschatological curse awaiting those who seek justification ἐξ ἔργων νόμου. The latter threatens to place the Galatians "under a curse" given the Deuteronomic warning, "Cursed (ἐπικατάρατος) is everyone who does not abide in all the things written in the book of the law so as to do them" (Deut 27:26; Gal 3:10). The wider context of this pre-text does not prescribe ceremonial acts such as circumcision but a slew of ethical warnings related to dishonoring parents, idolatry, social injustices, and the like.[36] While the push on the ground in Galatia revolved around participation in circumcision, Paul recognized the larger soteriological implications of such actions as indicated in his subsequent warnings.[37]

Given these soteriological implications, Paul evokes and reconfigures the divine answer to Habakkuk's laments which, to reiterate, arose because (1) the righteous were afflicted by the ungodly in Judea so that not even the Mosaic Law curtailed their action and (2) because of YHWH's response to the first cry which seemed unbecoming of his character. Paul reconfigures the answered lament to make clear that, in stark contrast to the opponents' teaching, God's answer to his afflicted people remains that their standing with him hinges upon whether they believe the vision of redemption now fulfilled in the crucified Christ. As in Habakkuk's lament (Hab 1:4), the law does avail them of the standing they graciously receive before God but the curse they should seek to avoid. Paul explains the redemption provided in Christ noting that he redeemed (ἐξαγοράζω) the Galatians by "having become a curse" for them, which implies that he suffered the divine curse of death actualized against those who fail to do all that the law prescribes.[38] Consequently, while the Galatians suffer in their justification with Christ, their suffering need not and should not include the very divine curse which Christ suffered for them.

## MESSIANIC LAMENT IN GAL 3:16

In her analysis of lament in Galatians, Sylvia Keesmaat detects an allusion to lament language from Psalm 89 (88 LXX) in Gal 3:16 based on the phrase καὶ τῷ σπέρματι σου, ὅς ἐστιν Χριστός. Paul cites a portion of Gen 17:18 in which YHWH promises land to Abraham and his seed, whom Paul identifies as Christ.[39] Keesmaat, however, suggests that Paul is "moving within a story line where the promises made to the seed of Abraham are continued with the seed of David."[40] Psalm 88 LXX shares some modest semantic links with Gal 3:15–18 such as the use of σπέρμα and Χριστός.[41] However, the more compelling link is the conceptual overlap between the psalm and Paul's argument.

Lament dominates the second and third strophes of the psalm in which the speaker cries out against divine rejection of God's Χριστός beginning with, "But you have rejected and despised, you have thrown over your Christ (τὸν χριστόν σου)" (Ps 88:39 LXX).[42] The full lament features complaints about God's rejection of his messianic servant, the defilement of the sanctuary, and the endangerment of prior promises to David. The latter is reflected in one of the closing cries, "Where are your ancient mercies, O Lord, which you swore to David in your truth?" (Ps 88:50 LXX). In short, the speaker laments God's seeming rejection of what he promised to his Χριστός and thereby the mercy the nation hoped to experience through him. God had promised such an experience as the speaker notes, "Forever I will establish your seed (τὸ σπέρμα σου) and I will build your throne forever and ever" (Ps 88:5 LXX).

If one traces the promissory (ἐπαγγελία) trajectory from Abraham to David in Paul's identification of the σπέρμα as Χριστός, one arrives at the rejected and lamentable Χριστός in Ps 88:39–53 LXX. Messianic rejection is in Paul's purview as indicated by his description of Jesus as ἐπικατάρτος in his crucifixion upon the tree (Gal 3:13). The Abrahamic σπέρμα who is Christ is at the same time the accursed and crucified Christ. Therefore, the promises (αἱ ἐπαγγελία) spoken to Abraham are ultimately fulfilled in Abraham's seed who is also the rejected Davidic Χριστός. Through this rejected and resurrected Christ, God has answered the psalmist's lament and thereby the cries of those who wished to share in Davidic mercies.[43] Therefore, Paul once again accentuates for the Galatians the painful nature of justification. Specifically, sharing in the promises of Abraham depends upon faith in a rejected and resurrected Χριστός who alone possesses the Abrahamic-Davidic inheritance and only allows others to share in it based on their faith in him rather than any work of the law.

## HUMAN–DIVINE PARTICIPATION
## IN LAMENT IN GAL 4:1–20

As a final example of Paul's engagement with the register of lament, we turn to the Spirit's participation in the laments of adopted children and Christ's participation in a lamenting apostle. These examples do not contain echoes of specific pre-texts; however, they reflect once again Paul's use of the lament register, specifically the way that Israel's God participates in the cries of his people.

In Gal 4:1–7, as part of his explanation as to how Abrahamic descendants move from slaves to heirs, Paul notes, "And because you are sons, God sent out the Spirit of his son into our hearts crying out, 'Abba Father'" (Gal 4:6). As is well-known, the only other NT instances of αββα ὁ πατήρ occur in Mark 14:36 and Rom 8:15. The former serves as Jesus's divine address at Gethsemane where he asks for removal of the divine cup of wrath which awaits him at the cross while simultaneously submitting himself to his father's will. The address signals both the depth of pain to be experienced and the depth of commitment to enduring such pain. Paul describes Jesus as crying to his father in this moment (τὸ πνεῦμα τοῦ υἱοῦ αὐτοῦ as κρᾶζον). Paul also locates the crying πνεῦμα of Jesus "in the hearts" of adopted children. Therefore, just as an adoptive status depends upon Christ's redemptive work which he accomplished while being "under the law," the cries of the adopted to God are the result of his presence in their hearts. Therefore, crucifixion with Christ (Χριστῷ συνεσταύρωμαι) produces life before God and elicits laments before him.

These laments differ from the one uttered at Gethsemane in the sense that Jesus experienced the divine cup of wrath on behalf of the Galatians, or, as Paul puts it, he became a "curse." However, the adoptees' laments are similar in the sense that the Spirit of Jesus cries out within them, which implies that they share in the pain of Gethsemane. The adoptees share in the tension between the prospect of divine wrath and submission to the divine will. It is in the tension represented by the Galatians' shared cry with Jesus to the Father that they must trust in the redemption (ἐξαγοράζω) secured by Christ rather than in the misguided attempt to do God's will through works of the law. Specifically, they must not submit to circumcision as if they were submitting to the divine will because it will only place them back under the elemental forces from which Christ redeemed them (Gal 4:8–10).

Gal 4:12–20 also reflects divine-human participation in lament as doubts (ἀπορούμια ἐν ὑμῖν) about the status of the Galatians prompt him to cry out like an expectant mother. Paul juxtaposes their initial acceptance of him in his weakness with their potential/present rejection of him. The latter stems from his proclamation of truth, which the opponents have changed so that the Galatians might be devoted to them (Gal 4:12–17). Paul closes out his exhortation for the Galatians to be like him (γίνεσθε ὡς ἐγώ) by express-ing his doubt in the form of a lament metaphor. He addresses the Galatians as children "for whom I am again suffering birth pains (ὠδίνω) until Christ should be formed in you." The lexeme ὠδίνω sometimes appears in prophetic laments such as, "And like one who suffers birth pains (ἡ ὠδίνουσα) comes near to give birth and cries out in her birth pains (τῇ ὠδῖνι αὐτῆς), in this way we have been to your beloved because of fear of you, O Lord" (Isa 26:17).[44] The wider context wrestles with the tension between judgment and the hope of deliverance which has resurrection as its ultimate outcome (Isa 26:18–19). An expectant mother who suffers until the birth of a child provides a fitting metaphor for this tension.

Not surprisingly, Paul reworks this lament metaphor around Christ. The expression μέχρις οὗ μορφωθῇ Χριστὸς ἐν ὑμῖν (Gal 4:19) indicates that Paul does not suffer alone in this "rebirth" (πάλιν ὠδίνω) of the Galatians. The hope through and beyond Paul's suffering is that Christ would be formed in the Galatians.[45] Christ is both the one who carries out the birth through Paul's maternal-like pain and the goal toward which he painfully moves. To put it another way, justification is by suffering.

## CONCLUSION

The register of OT lament provides Paul the language and theological framework he needs to express to the Galatians how painful justification in Christ can be. Enemies of Paul's gospel drew his apostolic ire, which can be quantified by his use of an imprecatory lament that goes beyond his OT predecessors given its eschatological objective. In his effort to stem the influ-ence of these false teachers, Paul recalls his rebuke of Peter that powerfully illustrates the binary of "faith" or "shrinking back" just as Israel's God pre-sented it to a lamenting Habakkuk. No one is impervious to "shrinking back" from faith in the gospel nor excluded from its eschatological consequences. Therefore, what the Galatians must do is hold to the answered laments heard by Abraham, psalmists, and Habakkuk. God has acted righteously in Christ as needed and as requested. The Galatians are both the lamenter in need of mercy before God's judgment and the sinners from whom the lamenter hoped to be delivered through God's judgment of his enemies. Christ, the proprietor of the Abrahamic and Davidic blessings, has provided such righteousness in his work and person as one cursed by God in his crucifixion upon the tree. Even more, through the Spirit whom God sent, Christ participates in the pain and laments of Paul and the Galatians. By taking up the register of lament, Paul teaches "his children" that the faith which justifies is the faith which suffers.

## NOTES

1. For a list of possible referents related to τὰ στίγματα τοῦ Ἰησοῦ, see Peter von der Osten-Sacken, *Der Brief an die Gemienden in Galatien* (Stuttgart: Kohlhammern, 2019), 316–17.

2. John Anthony Dunne, *Persecution and Participation in Galatians*, WUNT 2/454 (Tübingen: Mohr Siebeck, 2017), 4.

3. Jeff Hubing, *Crucifixion and Creation: The Strategic Purpose of Galatians 6.11–17*, LNTS 508 (London: T&T Clark, 2015), 8–9.

4. James Scott also notes some parallels between the "ongoing persecution" of "the eschatological community" in Galatians and 1 Enoch. See James A. Scott "A Comparison of Paul's Letter to the Galatians with the Epistle Galatians and 1 Enoch," in *The Jewish Apocalyptic Tradition and the Shaping of New Testament Thought*, ed. Benjamin E. Reynolds and Loren T. Stuckenbruck (Minneapolis: Fortress, 2017), 215–16.

5. "Register" refers to a "specialized code or variety of language associated with a specific social practice and designed to serve a specific social goal. It consists of distinctive linguistic patterns (vocabulary, grammar, phonology, etc.) which have become conventionalized and are relatively durable" (Paul Barker and Sibonile Ellece, *Key Terms in Discourse Analysis* [London: Continuum, 2011], 113). With respect to the link between rhetoric and theology, as James Thompson has recently concluded, "Starting with his (i.e., Paul's) basic convictions, he both makes theological arguments and speaks for rhetorical effect with the larger aim of ensuring the transformation of his churches into the image of Christ" (James W. Thompson, *Apostle of Persuasion: Theology and Rhetoric in the Pauline Letters* [Grand Rapids: Baker, 2020], 271). Regarding other interpreters who have noticed the use of lament in Galatians, though she comes to different conclusions than what I offer here, see Sylvia C. Keesmaat, "The Psalms in Romans and Galatians," in *The Psalms in the New Testament*, ed. Steve Moyise and Maarten J. J. Menken (London: T&T Clark, 2004), 157–161.

6. For an overview of OT lament, see Mark J. Boda, "Lament," in *Dictionary of the Old Testament Prophets*, ed. Mark J. Boda and J. Gordon McConville (Downers Grove: IVP, 2012), 473–77.

7. See, e.g., MT Pss 13:2–3; 22:2–3; 62:4.

8. Claus Westermann, "The Role of Lament in the Theology of the Old Testament," *Int* 28 (1974): 20–38, here 23.

9. That the Galatians are in a kind of theological malaise is evident in Paul's rhetorical questions such as, "Tell me, you who want to be under the law, do you not read the law?" (Gal 4:21).

10. John M. G. Barclay, "Mirror-Reading a Polemical Letter: Galatians as a Test Case." *JSNT* 31 (1987): 73–93, here 73–74.

11. Judith Newman defines "scripturalization" as the "reuse of biblical texts or interpretive traditions to shape the composition of new literature" (Judith H. Newman, *Praying by the Book: The Scripturalization of Prayer in Second Temple Judaism* [Atlanta: SBL, 1999], 12–13). Additionally, Todd Wilson refers to Deuteronomy 13 "*locus classicus* on false prophets" while assessing its role in Gal 1:6–9. See Todd A. Wilson, *The Curse of the Law and the Crisis in Galatia: Reassessing the Purpose of Galatians*, WUNT 2/225 (Tübingen: Mohr Siebeck, 2007), 25.

12. E. P. Sanders, *Paul: The Apostle's Life, Letters, and Thought* (Minneapolis: Fortress, 2015), 475.

13. The phrase ἀναθέματι ἀναθεματιεῖτε is the LXX translator's rendering of החרם in Deut 13:16. LXX translators often use ἀνάθεμα and ἀναθεματίζω to render the nominal and verbal forms of חרם ("devote to the ban"). See, e.g., Num 18:14; 21:2, 3; Deut 20:17.

14. See, e.g., Roy E. Ciampa, *The Presence and Function of Scripture in Galatians 1 and 2*, WUNT 2/102 (Tübingen: Mohr Siebeck, 1998), 83–88; Karl Olav Sandnes, *Paul—One of the Prophets? A Contribution to the Apostles's Self-Understanding*, WUNT 2/43 (Tübingen: Mohr Siebeck, 1991), 71–72.

15. For a recent discussion of the citation of Ps 68:23–24 LXX in Rom 11:9–10, see Channing L. Crisler, *An Intertextual Commentary on Romans: Volume 3 (Rom 9:1–11:36)* (Eugene, OR: Pickwick, 2022), 236–39.

16. On the identity shaping influence of emotions in the Pauline corpus and his "emotional regime," which is a heuristic device that refers to the emotions Paul "authorized" detected through the interplay between symbolic, ritual, and social elements in his letters, see Ian Y. S. Jew, *Paul's Emotional Regime: The Social Function of Emotion in Philippians and 1 Thessalonians*, LNTS 629 (London: T&T Clark, 2021), 18–19.

17. As Gordon Wiles notes in his analysis of Gal 1:8–9, Paul "intends at least excommunication from the church" for these opponents. See Gordon P. Wiles, *Paul's Intercessory Prayers: The Significance of the Intercessory Prayer Passages in the Letters of Paul*, SNTSMS 24 (Cambridge: Cambridge: University Press, 1974), 128.

18. David Aune labels Gal 1:8–9 along with 1 Cor 16:22 and Rev 22:18–19 as a "ritual curse." See David E. Aune, "Prayer in the Graeco-Roman World," in *Into God's Presence: Prayer in the New Testament,* ed. Richard N. Longenecker (Grand Rapids: Eerdmans, 2002), 41. Additionally, in his examination of Paul as an intercessor, David Crump omits Gal 1:8–9 from consideration noting that such curses "seem to function as emotive declarations, not prayers" (David Crump, *Knocking on Heaven's Door: A New Testament Theology of Petitionary Prayer* [Grand Rapids: Baker, 2006], 231).

19. Wiles, *Paul's Intercessory Prayers*, 129. Regarding righteous lamenters' expectations that their cries will be heard, see, e.g., Ps 33:16–18 LXX.

20. See, e.g., F. C. Baur, *Paul the Apostle: His Life and Works, His Epistles and Teachings* (Grand Rapids: Baker, 2011), 1:134–35.

21. While more current versions of testing echoes are available, scholars have not progressed much further than Richard Hays's tests enumerated in his seminal work.

Such tests in a modified form are taken up here. See Richard B. Hays, *Echoes of Scripture in the Letters of Paul* (New Haven, CT: Yale University Press, 1989), 29–33.

22. For typical lexical analysis of ὑποστέλλω, see Hans Dieter Betz, *Galatians* (Philadelphia: Fortress, 1979), 108; J. Louis Martyn, *Galatians*, AB 33A (New York: Doubleday, 1997), 233.

23. Armin Lange and Matthias Weigold, *Biblical Quotations and Allusions in Second Temple Jewish Literature* (Göttingen: Vandenhoeck & Ruprecht, 2011), 30.

24. See also the use of ὑποστέλλω in Acts 20:20, 27, and Heb 10:38.

25. See, e.g., Gregory J. Lockwood, *1 Corinthians* (St. Louis: Concordia, 2000), 138.

26. Within the well-worn *pistis Christou* discussion, I have treated the syntactical link between πίστεως and Χριστοῦ in a way that the latter functions as a genitive of source, or *genetivus auctoris*. For a defense of this reading, see Mark A. Seifrid, "The Faith of Christ," in *The Faith of Jesus Christ: Exegetical, Biblical, and Theological Studies*, ed. Michael F. Bird and Preston M. Sprinkle (Peabody: Hendrickson, 2009), 129–46.

27. See, e.g., von der Osten-Sacken, *Der Brief an die Gemeinden*, 114–15.

28. On this point, see Keesmaat, "The Psalms in Romans and Galatians," 158.

29. See, e.g., Pss LXX 11:6; 33:16–18. Cf. John 10:31.

30. See, e.g., the citations in Gal 3:6, 10, 11, 12, 13, 16.

31. Dunne notes that since the work of Justus Christoph Schomer (1648–1693) some have treated ἐπάθετε as a reference to what the Galatians experienced rather than what they suffered. Nevertheless, lexical and contextual factors favor a reference to suffering. See the discussion in John Anthony Dunne, "Suffering in Vain: A Study of the Interpretation of ΠΑΣΧΩ in Galatians 3.4," *JSNT* 36 (2013): 3–16.

32. For a discussion on the historical referent of suffering in Gal 3:4 and the rest of the letter, see Dunne, *Persecution and Participation*, 29–40.

33. Thomas R. Schreiner, *Galatians* (Grand Rapids: Zondervan, 2010), 191.

34. In assessing the way Abraham responds to YHWH's promise of protection and reward in Genesis 15, J. Richard Middleton notes, "Abraham responds with questions in both cases, honestly expressing his doubts (15:2–4, 8), and in both cases God takes his questions seriously and responds appropriately in order to bolster Abraham's faith" (J. Richard Middleton, *Abraham's Silence: The Binding of Isaac, the Suffering of Job, and How to Talk Back to God* [Grand Rapids: Baker, 2021], 198).

35. In his analysis of Genesis 22, Middleton suggests, "The Aqedah testifies to the patriarch's missed opportunity for lament" (Middleton, *Abraham's Silence*, 240).

36. See Deut 27:15–25.

37. See Gal 4:21–31; 5:1–6.

38. See Gal 3:10; 5:1–6.

39. The phrase καὶ τῷ σπέρματί σου occurs in Gen 13:15; 17:8; 24:7.

40. Keesmaat, "The Psalms in Romans and Galatians," 159.

41. See, e.g., Ps LXX 88:5, 10, 30, 37, 39, 52.

42. In trying to locate the historical background of Psalm 89 (88 LXX), Samuel Terrien suggests "A national calamity has killed the king of Judah, a son of David. No charge of iniquity is made against him. Is this King Josiah, who died after the

defeat of Meggido in 609?" (Samuel Terrien, *The Psalms: A Strophic Structure and Theological Commentary* [Grand Rapids: Eerdmans, 2003], 639).

43. See Ps 88:51–52 LXX.

44. See also the use of ὠδίνω in Isa 28:19.

45. Cf. the paternal metaphor in 1 Cor 4:15; Phlm 10.

# BIBLIOGRAPHY

Aune, David E. "Prayer in the Graeco-Roman World." In *Into God's Presence: Prayer in the New Testament*, edited by Richard N. Longenecker, 23–42. Grand Rapids: Eerdmans, 2002.

Barclay, John M. G. "Mirror-Reading A Polemical Letter: Galatians as a Test Case." *JSNT* 31 (1987): 73–93.

Barker, Paul and Sibonile Ellece. *Key Terms in Discourse Analysis*. London: Continuum, 2011.

Baur, F. C. *Paul the Apostle: His Life and Works, His Epistles and Teachings*. Grand Rapids: Baker, 2011.

Betz, Hans Dieter. *Galatians*. Hermeneia. Philadelphia: Fortress, 1979.

Boda, Mark J. "Lament." In *Dictionary of the Old Testament Prophets*, edited by Mark J. Boda and J. Gordon McConville, 473–77. Downers Grove: IVP, 2012.

Ciampa, Roy E. *The Presence and Function of Scripture in Galatians 1 and 2*. WUNT 2/102. Tübingen: Mohr Siebeck, 1998.

Crisler, Channing L. *An Intertextual Commentary on Romans: Volume 3 (Rom 9:1– 11:36)*. Eugene, OR: Pickwick, 2022.

Crump, David. *Knocking on Heaven's Door: A New Testament Theology of Petitionary Prayer*. Grand Rapids: Baker, 2006.

Dunne, John Anthony. *Persecution and Participation in Galatians*. WUNT 2/454. Tübingen: Mohr Siebeck, 2017.

———. "Suffering in Vain: A Study of the Interpretation of ΠΑΣΧΩ in Galatians 3.4." *JSNT* 36 (2013): 3–16.

Hays, Richard B. *Echoes of Scripture in the Letters of Paul*. New Haven: Yale University Press, 1989.

Hubing, Jeff. *Crucifixion and Creation: The Strategic Purpose of Galatians 6.11–17*, LNTS 508. London: T&T Clark, 2015.

Jew, Ian Y. S. *Paul's Emotional Regime: The Social Function of Emotion in Philippians and 1 Thessalonians*. LNTS 629. London: T&T Clark, 2021.

Keesmaat, Sylvia C. "The Psalms in Romans and Galatians." In *The Psalms in the New Testament*, edited by Steve Moyise and Maarten J. J. Menken, 139–61. London: T&T Clark, 2004.

Lange, Armin and Matthias Weigold. *Biblical Quotations and Allusions in Second Temple Jewish Literature*. Göttingen: Vandenhoeck & Ruprecht, 2011.

Lockwood, Gregory J. *1 Corinthians*. St. Louis: Concordia, 2000.

Martyn, J. Louis. *Galatians*. AB 33A. New York: Doubleday, 1997.

Middleton, J. Richard. *Abraham's Silence: The Binding of Isaac, the Suffering of Job, and How to Talk Back to God.* Grand Rapids: Baker, 2021.

Newman, Judith H. *Praying by the Book: The Scripturalization of Prayer in Second Temple Judaism.* Atlanta: SBL, 1999.

Sanders, E. P. *Paul: The Apostle's Life, Letters, and Thought.* Minneapolis: Fortress, 2015.

Sandnes, Karl Olav. *Paul—One of the Prophets? A Contribution to the Apostle's Self-Understanding.* WUNT 2/43. Tübingen: Mohr Siebeck, 1991.

Schreiner, Thomas R. *Galatians.* Grand Rapids: Zondervan, 2010.

Scott, James A. "A Comparison of Paul's Letter to the Galatians with the Epistle Galatians and 1 Enoch." In *The Jewish Apocalyptic Tradition and the Shaping of New Testament Thought*, edited by Benjamin E. Reynolds and Loren T. Stuckenbruck, 193–218. Minneapolis: Fortress, 2017.

Seifrid, Mark A. "The Faith of Christ." In *The Faith of Jesus Christ: Exegetical, Biblical, and Theological Studies*, edited by Michael F. Bird and Preston M. Sprinkle, 129–46. Peabody: Hendrickson, 2009.

Terrien, Samuel. *The Psalms: A Strophic Structure and Theological Commentary.* Grand Rapids: Eerdmans, 2003.

Thompson, James W. *Apostle of Persuasion: Theology and Rhetoric in the Pauline Letters.* Grand Rapids: Baker, 2020.

von der Osten-Sacken, Peter. *Der Brief an die Gemienden in Galatien.* Stuttgart: Kohlhammern, 2019.

Westermann, Claus. "The Role of Lament in the Theology of the Old Testament." *Int* 28 (1974): 20–38.

Wiles, Gordon P. *Paul's Intercessory Prayers: The Significance of the Intercessory Prayer Passages in the Letters of Paul.* SNTSMS 24. Cambridge: Cambridge: University Press, 1974.

Wilson, Todd A. *The Curse of the Law and the Crisis in Galatia: Reassessing the Purpose of Galatians.* WUNT 2/225. Tübingen: Mohr Siebeck, 2007.

# Chapter 10

# Counternarratives in Galatians

## Christoph Heilig

While the issue of Empire in Galatians has received some monograph-length treatments,[1] it plays a negligible role in edited volumes that are meant to give an overview of anti-imperial perspectives in different writings of the New Testament.[2] In what follows, we will re-evaluate the apparently meager results of a quest for anti-imperial allusions to Roman ideology in Galatians. However, before doing so, we first need to address the question of the appropriate methodology for such an endeavor.

## METHODOLOGY

### Criteria for Echoes

One methodological tool that was introduced quite early into the "Paul and Empire" debate and that has been a dominating idea ever since is the differentiation between public and hidden transcript by the sociologist James C. Scott.[3] Neil Elliott has argued that in Paul's letters, the hidden transcript of the suppressed becomes visible in "veiled" form.[4] What has made the approach by Elliott ultimately so successful is arguably that he and N. T. Wright combined this notion of a somehow coded critique of Roman ideology with the criteria that Richard B. Hays had suggested for identifying subtle scriptural references in the letters of Paul, "echoes," as he calls them.[5]

These criteria still enjoy great popularity in intertextual studies in general and continue to be applied with respect to the specific issue of intertextuality to Roman texts in particular.[6] However, as I have tried to demonstrate elsewhere[7] they ultimately do not seem helpful for establishing intertextuality—be it Scriptural or Roman.

Behind my skepticism stands the fundamental insight from confirmation theory that whenever we make the claim that certain evidence makes a hypothesis more "probable" we enter a realm in which our argumentation needs to follow "Bayes's theorem" for it to be coherent.[8] The implications of the theorem can be summarized in nontechnical language and should be intuitively cogent.[9] The most basic implication is that if we are comparing two hypotheses and want to find out which one is more probable, we need to take into account two parameters and consider them with equal weight:

1. Assuming that the hypotheses were true, how well would they each explain the evidence in question? (Their "likelihoods" or simply "explanatory potentials")
2. How plausible are the hypotheses against the backdrop of the rest of our knowledge, regardless of the new evidence that is to be integrated? (The "prior-probabilities" of the hypotheses, or, in less technical language, their "background plausibilities")

If scrutinized along these lines, Hays's set of criteria seems problematic. For example, the criteria are of very different significance. Most notably, the criterion of "satisfaction" carries *half* the weight of the entire argument because it is basically equivalent to the explanatory potential. In other words, when working with these criteria it can happen very easily that a practitioner might overemphasize one of the two above mentioned "metacriteria" (even though they must be considered equally for the inference to be correct).

## Necessary Conditions

These Bayesian metacriteria also explain why the critique of the Wright/ Elliott-paradigm by Barclay[10] is seen by many as having obliterated the entire anti-imperial approach. While Barclay does not object to Hays's criteria in general, he does not think they can be applied successfully to the realm of Roman propaganda. The following list summarizes the critical questions toward the Wright/Elliott-hypothesis that can be deduced from Barclay's article and other contributions that follow his general line of critique:[11]

1. Are the Pauline letters affected by the rules of public discourse at all?
2. Do these rules forbid open criticism of aspects of the Roman Empire?
3. Did Paul have an exposure to these elements and perceive them as specifically Roman?
4. Can we expect him to have a critical stance toward those elements?
5. Can we even identify a plausible occasion that might have compelled Paul to express these opinions in a specific situation?

6. Is it reasonable in light of Paul's personality to assume that he expressed this critical stance in the subtext of his letters?

If only one of these questions can be answered with certainty as "no," then we do not even have to consider the subsequent questions, let alone check whether the hypothesis would explain the Pauline texts well. After all, the prior-probability would immediately be reduced to zero and the whole hypothesis falsified entirely. In other words, each of these questions introduces a necessary condition that needs to be fulfilled for the subtext-hypothesis to remain a valid option.

The second of the six questions concerning the dangers of open criticism of Rome seems to be of special significance with respect to Galatians. After all, the suggestion by Winter and then, in modified form, Hardin that the "persecution" in Gal 6:12 is connected with the danger of refusing to participate in (certain aspects of) imperial cults seems to be pertinent in that regard.[12] In general, the idea that early Christians might have stressed their continuity with Judaism in order to avoid uncomfortable consequences of their rejection of imperial (and other pagan) cults seems very likely to me. To be sure, Judaism did not constitute a safe haven in the sense of a *religio licita,* as Das rightly points out.[13] However, I would go even further and argue that the situation of the early Christians was precarious from the beginning, regardless of Roman religious policies altogether.

Recent historical research has demonstrated that there was no law banning Christianity before Trajan's rescript to Pliny (*Ep.* 10.97)—but neither did the rescript establish such a legal precedent.[14] Being a Christian did not automatically result in condemnation after that alleged watershed moment—nor was it safe to be a follower of Christ before that date. Rather, what the incident documents is an overworked governor who adopts a quite usual shoot-first policy with respect to a minority that then later turns out to be substantial enough to have the potential of hurting his further career. This is why he writes to Trajan to get confirmation that he has acted appropriately. For these Christians to be executed, it did not take more than a couple of rumors about their asocial behavior, some tangible effects of their changed behavior on the local economy, and a governor who in one of way too many court cases made the quick decision to play it safe—eliminate these people for the sake of securing societal peace.

Das argues that the earliest Christians "were of no importance to the governing authorities."[15] I would maintain that they were indeed of interest to them if and when fellow citizens brought them to their attention and accused them of asocial behavior. And it was precisely if and when they were recognized as a small group of troublesome individuals, and not as part of a larger movement, that they were in danger of being executed simply to quell trouble at an early stage. In such a precarious situation, any perceived distance between the Jesus followers and Jews would have increased their social isolation—and thus their immediate risk of being dealt with in a radical manner whenever accusations would arise.

It thus seems very likely that this aspect of social belonging and connected risk-reduction will have played an important role in the formation of early Christian identity.[16] In contrast, the emphases by some scholars on the supposed safety of Christian believers at the time of Paul[17] and the alleged religious freedom granted by Rome[18] are misplaced. They are based on a category mistake and do not follow from the recognition that there was no central "persecution of Christianity" in the first century.[19] We can thus reaffirm the conclusion that the necessary condition no. 2—the requirement that open criticism of Roman ideology would have been dangerous—does not constitute an obstacle for the idea that we might find coded criticism of the Roman Empire in Galatians. Even if Hardin and Winter are wrong about their specific interpretation of Gal 6:12, the general dynamics were most certainly active at the time of Paul. So far, Wright's hypothesis seems to hold up against the critique of Barclay, and it is reasonable to further consider whether "coded criticism" of the Roman Empire might be a good explanation for some features of Galatians.

## CODED CRITICISM IN GALATIANS?

In my view, the greatest obstacle for identifying cases of coded criticism of Roman ideology in Galatians comes with necessary condition no. 5 above, i.e., the requirement that there must be a specific occasion that would have necessitated a critique of Rome (despite the associated risks). To be sure, *if* the Winter/Hardin-hypothesis were true, this criterion would indeed be met perfectly. After all, what would be a better reason to indeed address the issue of imperial cults than the (from Paul's view commendable) attempt to avoid participation in such practices by the (from Paul's view inadvisable) solution of stressing continuity with Judaism? However, Galatians does not look the way we would expect it to look if the hypothesis were right. The literature has little to say beyond Wright's pointing to εὐαγγέλιον as an alternative kind of "good news."[20] Would we not expect more instances of critical interaction with the Roman Empire than just this emphasis on the gospel? Moreover, it does not even seem clear to me whether we need that Roman backdrop to explain the said emphasis. After all, the proclamation of a competing—non-Roman—gospel in Galatia already seems to offer a sufficient reason for Paul's focus.[21]

To be sure, this is an argument from silence—but an argument from silence where a lot of noise is to be expected. After all, in the alleged scenario, necessary condition no. 5 would be fulfilled not just barely but rather *so well* that we would expect the issue of imperial cults to feature, if only implicitly, throughout the letter. Paul is not particularly calm when it comes to insinuations concerning the motives of his opponents in Galatia. Why would he think them worthy of such scorn because of their disloyalty to Christ but not also sprinkle in some insults about the Emperor, who, after all, is ultimately the driving force behind their efforts?

To be sure, an imperial herald is certainly much less than an angel and would, thus, undoubtedly fall under the curse of Gal 1:8–9, if he should attempt to seduce the Galatians with his imperial good news; but according to Gal 1:6 this is not, of course, the direction to which the Galatians are turning. In fact, if it is indeed the *potential* turn to imperial cults that motivates the *imminent* turn to Jewish cults, it is at least striking that Paul seems not at all concerned with the first option. Nowhere in Galatians does he speak about the danger of the believers being seduced by the imperial cult. In fact, Gal 4:6–10 works rhetorically only if the former religious tendencies are once and for all a phenomenon of the distant past.[22] Does Paul really assume that *actually* going back to the imperatorial "non-gods" might not also be a real risk, especially if he succeeds combatting the more immediate move, which, after all, is a move away from pressure to participate in such cults? "Strong" believers could simply, just as in Corinth, make a case for at least a superficial participation in imperial cults. And in 1 Corinthians Paul indeed addresses the issue of idol worship head-on.

Thus, I am not convinced by the idea that pressure to participate in imperial cults is the determining factor behind the push to circumcision in the Galatian churches. This hypothesis has a strong prior-probability (cf. last section). But it shares this feature with alternative hypotheses (we must not forget to assess this parameter *comparatively!*).[23] Moreover—and, given this deadlock—it decisively displays insufficient explanatory potential. We would expect a different letter if the reconstructed background were correct.

One could save the hypothesis only by drastically increasing the explanatory potential. Most notably the auxiliary assumption that *only the opponents* are trying to avoid persecution (Gal 6:12) would make the evidence more explicable, as Hardin argues: "This understanding not only *explains* why Paul felt it necessary to show through complex theological arguments why his readers must not be circumcised. . . ."[24] However, such an artificial increase in predictive power is purchased at great cost—because any additional assumption that is added automatically lowers the prior probability as a side-effect. This problem is increased even further in this particular case because it emphasizes the purity of motivations in an unrealistic manner; i.e., it is an especially unlikely auxiliary assumption. Does it not assume a striking degree of naivety among the "normal" Galatians for only the agitators to be aware of the social pressures that cause them to act?

Moreover, even with this additional assumption the explanatory potential of the hypothesis still remains unsatisfactory. Note how Hardin continues the above quote: " . . . but also reveals the sheer magnitude of Paul's statements in the postscript. With Paul's finale to this letter, they heard for the first time that the agitators' real intentions in wanting them to be circumcised included a 'social' dimension. We could easily imagine the shock on the faces of Paul's readers as they watched the curtain fall and the agitators' motives lay bare for all to see."[25] If they were in fact that clueless, Paul's hint at the end of the letter would have left them entirely confused. And even if we accept the idea that Paul deemed this formulation sufficient to blow their cover—and the Galatians for this reason are no longer in the dark but can now see through the conspiracy—we just run again into the problem that the letter does not offer them any resources to deal with this new challenge of imperial cults that they are now suddenly faced with once the curtain has been removed.

What does all that imply for the search for counter-imperial echoes in Galatians? If one assumes that the Winter/Hardin-hypothesis concerning the occasion of Galatians is basically correct, the Wright/Elliott-hypothesis seems to offer a very promising paradigm for interpretation but turns out to be heuristically quite unfruitful. However, if we do *not* presuppose the imperial cult to be so central to the letter, our expectations concerning anti-imperial statements do not need to be so high that they are disappointed in the end. Perhaps, what Wright finds in Galatians then is pretty close to what one might predict on the basis of his hypothesis.

Still, necessary condition no. 5 seems to pose a *lasting* challenge to the Wright/Elliott-hypothesis. The greater we assume the contribution of the Roman Empire to have been for the occasion of the letter, the more Paul would have been forced to make not only implicit but also *explicit* comments, to make sure his important points are understood. As Robinson rightly remarks, if "Paul's coded subversion of the Roman government was so subtle that Romans would not hear it," this seems to imply that "it would be useless as a code for Roman Christians."[26] Thus, at one end of the spectrum Paul's comments could hardly be labeled "coded" criticism anymore. Conversely, if at the other end of the spectrum conflict with the Roman Empire is not an issue at all, there is also no reason for Paul comment on it in the first place. This is a dilemma that in my view is *inherent* to the Wright/Elliott-hypothesis.

Perhaps both factors can be balanced in some situations so that the hypothesis is a plausible explanation for the text in question. But in any case, this observation diminishes the heuristic value of the paradigm because it limits the contexts in which the explanation is applicable. Against this backdrop, it seems reasonable to me to think about alternative conceptions, which take the Roman Empire seriously as a contextual factor and do not downplay Paul's disdain for it, and at the same time are not affected by the above-mentioned necessary conditions at all.

# DISSONANCES

## Beyond Coded Criticism

Wright and Elliott seem to imply that the subtext is an ineffective means to achieve communicative goals[27] by painting a picture in which the conceivable reason for why Paul is not being more explicit with his criticism is that he was forced by looming persecution to keep a low profile. However, it is not at all obvious to me why blurting things out would have been a more effective means of communication. Indeed, Paul's narration in general is marked by the abundant use of hints and potential story-lines in order to encourage specific behavior among his readers.[28] Moreover, it is notable that Paul's style of narration is extremely dense and presupposes that he and his audience share knowledge about the events to which he alludes.[29] For Paul to be ambiguous (to us modern readers!) is thus not something peculiar that needs to be explained. It should be our default expectation whenever we approach his letters.[30]

Accordingly, the expectation that we will find in Paul's letters phrases that reflect his unease with the Roman Empire seems quite expected—and not something that would require elaborate justification. Paul might not have expanded on these remarks in greater detail simply because there was no need for him to do so—because everybody understood the relevance anyway. Or he just did not judge it conducive to his communicative aims to hammer away at the topic. The subtle redirection of the intentions of his readers by definition needs to be carried out with care. And perhaps he also just did not want to spoil a good joke by explaining it—especially if we are dealing only with a sarcastic undertone, whose explication would have shifted away the attention from concerns that were even more relevant for the discourse.

Many of the phenomena that Wright had identified in his 1994 article seem actually explicable in such a way, without the subsequent recourse to Scott's notion of a "hidden transcript"—at least not if this category is reinterpreted *monolithically* as "coded criticism." After all, Scott's work could indeed be heuristically fruitful if we allow it to sensitize us to the *fuzzy* borders between public and hidden transcripts.[31] Statements can seem out of place in the public transcript because people simply misjudge the protocol that applies in a certain situation, or because the border of the public transcript is itself flexible to some extent, through time and geographically. And sometimes, the hidden transcript even "storms the stage"[32] in the heat of passion, with the calculation of consequences being as difficult for the ancient actors as their reconstruction is for us historians.

I have tried to demonstrate that the dynamics mentioned in the last section are indeed at play in several passages in Paul's letters, focusing in particular on 2 Cor 2:14.[33] This verse contains a Rome-critical dimension—which, however, has not been "veiled." There is no *code* that needs to be decoded. Rather, it has simply been *overlooked* in the past.

In this passage, Paul calls up the image of a Roman triumphal procession and portrays himself and his coworkers as captives, i.e., in a role as miserable as they must have looked to the Corinthians due to their chaotic travel movements. This perception is challenged because ultimately, in an ironic twist, the captives of course contribute to the glory of the triumphator. Paul does not criticize the Roman Emperor but the Corinthians, for the fact that they take issue with his ministry. But he does so specifically by means of a metaphor that invokes the emperor in the clearest possible way—only to then push him out of his quadriga by having God take his spot. In Corinth, there was a yearly cultic celebration of Claudius's victory over Britannia.[34] The Corinthians would have been confronted with this celebration for a decade and would also have been aware of the gossip surrounding this event, which deviated from the public protocol. Therefore, Paul's metaphor would have come as a welcome gleeful reminder of the fact that neither that victory nor its celebration in Rome had been particularly triumphant. It is a joke about the recently diseased emperor that is actually quite in line with the public protocol as witnessed by Seneca's *Apocolocyntosis* (though of course totally at odds with the earlier Claudian propaganda as we find it in the *Laus Caesaris*).[35]

## Crucifixion

The subversive potential of 2 Cor 2:14 becomes most obvious if we look at it as a story and pay special attention to narrative dimensions such as narrative characters, plot, and focalization. For this reason, I will in what follows approach Galatians in search for similar narrative fragments in order to find traces of such "counter-narratives"[36] that contrast with dominating Roman narratives. These fragments give us insights into the kind of subversive stories that undoubtedly will have played a role in early Christianity but which in Paul's letters are only recorded fragmentarily, as small and cloudy windows through which we can peek into the "most hidden" levels of the hidden transcript of the circle around Paul.

One aspect that has received some attention but might require closer examination is the motif of the cross. In Gal 3:1 Paul underlines how "vividly" the

Messiah had been presented *as crucified* to the Galatians (οἷς κατ᾽ ὀφθαλμοὺς Ἰησοῦς Χριστὸς προεγράφη ἐσταυρωμένος;). Commentators usually focus on the question of Paul's presentation.[37] But one might also ponder to what extent the Galatians might have witnessed crucifixions firsthand, which would have contributed significantly to how they would have imagined this scene.

Moreover, in light of the executions (though most certainly by means of decapitation) under Pliny it also seems advisable to re-read the statements concerning crucifixion with a greater sensitivity for the anxieties that the Galatians might have had for their own security. This is an area where historically oriented exegesis might still learn a lot from postcolonial interpretation, which can draw our attention to the sheer fear of death that many subordinated people experience on a daily basis.[38] Especially for the slaves (cf. Gal 3:28!), crucifixion will have constituted a real horror to be reckoned with.[39]

We, as modern exegetes, must be careful not to be misled by the fact that Paul reinterprets the historical event of the crucifixion theologically and that we can witness an emphasis on Jewish involvement in Jesus's death even within the NT writings. Both rhetorical tendencies must be seen as such. They are testament to the fact that *of course* everybody knew that crucifixion was a Roman method of execution so that portrayals that deviated from this norm required special interpretive efforts.

Keeping this in mind, it is noteworthy that Paul—in his quoted speech to Peter[40]—says that at the time of speaking he *is* in a state of co-crucifixion with Christ (Gal 2:19: Χριστῷ συνεσταύρωμαι; note the resultative aspect; in Rom 6:6, Paul uses the perfective aspect). It is the same verb that is also used in the New Testament for those who were crucified next to Jesus (Matt 27:44; Mark 15:32; John 19:32). As people who no longer need to fear execution by crucifixion,[41] I think we may be overlooking a *comforting* aspect here; namely, the idea that the horror of this prospect might be weakened by the idea that one has already experienced a life-shattering, death-like, event of similar proportions (cf. Rom 6 for baptism and burial language).

In Gal 6:14 we find the verb without prefix but again in the perfect indicative. It of course follows immediately after the talk about "persecution" in v. 12. We cannot know for sure what was in view, but even if we do not agree with the interpretation by Hardin/Winter, it seems plausible that this notion would have triggered awareness of the ever-present danger of being subjected to Roman sanctions.

Moreover, it is noteworthy that in v. 14 the "cross of our Lord Jesus Christ" (. . . ἐν τῷ σταυρῷ τοῦ κυρίου ἡμῶν Ἰησοῦ Χριστοῦ) is presented as the instrument through which Paul "is crucified" with respect to the world—and the world to him (δι᾽ οὗ ἐμοὶ κόσμος ἐσταύρωται κἀγὼ κόσμῳ). We must not miss the strangeness of the idea that the world—and that was, especially with regard to the notion of crucifixion, basically the *Roman Empire*—has undergone a crucifixion too.

Furthermore, it seems possible that the evocation of such an idea might have contributed toward activating the political domain associated with καινὴ κτίσις in the next verse, v. 15. With the whole Empire immobilized at the cross (and its leaders paraded around on it in a triumphal procession?),[42] it is those who are connected with Christ who, after their burial and resurrection in baptism (cf. Rom 6 with Gal 3:27), are now establishing new settlements.

In Gal 6:14 Christ and the Christians are at least no longer the only ones who must deal with crucifixion. Gal 5:24 is similar in that here they are more than just the passive recipients of this cruel Roman method of execution. Paul recounts a story about "those of Christ,"[43] in which they "crucified" their flesh together with their passions and desires. We must take care that this abstract language does not blind us to the again stunning fact that the Christians are now portrayed themselves as nothing less than *agents of crucifixion*, a role that is otherwise reserved for Roman soldiers!

All that being said, it must of course be noted that the fragmentary state of our sources precludes any definitive judgments. We just do not have any concrete evidence for executions for the relevant region and timeframe.[44] It is, however, at least notable that inscriptional evidence (*CIL* III 6799) from Lake Trogitis—which is located right in the middle of Paul's route (cf. Acts 13–14), between Perga and Pisidian Antioch in the west and Derbe in the east—shows that the governor M. Annius Afrinus visited this very remote region in the south of the province during his term (49–54 CE).[45] Similarly, for his successor, Q. Petronius Umber—who held the post while the reign was transitioning from Claudius to Nero—an imperial estate is documented at Düğer in Pisinia (see SEG 19:765,b).[46] *If* Galatians were written to the south of the province of Galatia, this would at least be an argument for the recipients suddenly being able to witness Roman rule from a front row seat, with all kinds of anxieties coming to the forefront.

## A Counternarrative about Nero's Adoption?

The conditional nature of the last sentence already points us to a fundamental problem with respect to *any* inquiry about traces of interaction with contemporary Roman discourses in Galatians; namely, that the location of the addressees is hotly debated and, hence, when it was composed. If Galatians was addressed to the churches founded during the first missionary journey,[47] this opens up the possibility for a date as early as right before the apostolic council in 48 CE.[48] The range of suggested dates goes up to 57 CE, after the composition of Romans. The dominating view in German literature is that

Galatians was written late but not quite as late as the latter; namely, it was written sometime between 2 Corinthians and Romans.[49] This broad range of suggested dates makes the identification of specific historical backgrounds much more difficult. This becomes especially clear in comparison to 2 Cor 2:14, where we are even in position to reconstruct contact between Paul and potential eyewitnesses of Claudius's triumphal procession as well as to speculate with good reason that Claudius might have been a subject of their conversations.[50]

In what follows, I want to examine one further, Gal 4:1–2, where the date of Paul's letter seems to have a huge impact on the plausibility of a reading as a narrative that critically interacts with dominant Roman stories. At first sight, these two verses seem to be a quite innocent narrative, as far as potential counter-imperial overtones are concerned. On its most basic level, the passage is a story about heirs in general, i.e., it does not speak about specific events but states what is typically the case, sketching social regularities, expressing whole "event bundles" (which is why others would classify this as a description).[51] The mention of a "date set by the father" in v. 2 has caused some to suggest that this story about heirs is influenced by what Paul is going to tell about the Galatians in 4:3–6, i.e., the notion of the "fulness of time" in v. 4. For example, Moo speaks about a "backreading of the application into the illustration."[52] Others have argued that the story that influences Gal 4:1–2 is not to be found in the immediate literary context but that it is, rather, the exodus narrative (in which we find both the motifs of liberation and adoption) which stands behind the entire section of 4:1–7. What then about the possibility of *contemporary Roman stories* having left their mark on Paul's narration in Gal 4:1–2?

If we presuppose the current German majority opinion concerning the date, this implies that when Paul writes Galatians, Nero has already replaced Claudius as emperor—quite recently perhaps (Claudius died, poisoned or not, on October 13, 54 CE). Given the sensitivities that Paul has demonstrated in 2 Cor 2:14 for discourses associated with this transition, an intriguing argument can be made about contemporaneous stories that involved the emperor, his heir, and even adoption—the topic that is introduced to the mix in vv. 3–7.

On February 25, 50 CE, Nero was adopted at the age of twelve years, having an advantage of three years over Britannicus, Claudius's biological son from his marriage with Messalina.[53] At this point in time, Nero was still under a *tutor* because it was only in 51 CE that he took on the *toga virilis,* thus officially becoming an adult. It is notable that this transition happened even though Nero had not yet celebrated his fourteenth birthday, the usually required age, "so that he should appear qualified for a political career" (Tacitus, *Ann.* 12.41). Gal 4:2 fits this rather unique situation shockingly well. For with respect to Nero it was indeed the case that he was "under guardians and managers until the 'date set by his father'" (Gal 4:2; ὑπὸ ἐπιτρόπους ἐστὶν καὶ οἰκονόμους ἄχρι τῆς προθεσμίας τοῦ πατρός)![54]

Against this backdrop and keeping in mind that κύριος as a title for the emperor was just gaining traction at that time,[55] the designation of the prototypical heir in Gal 4:1 as "lord of everything" (κύριος πάντων) takes on striking connotations! The same is true for the hyperbolic claim that there is no difference between the minor heir and a *slave*. If Betz can state, as if a matter of fact, that this exaggeration is due to the fact that "Paul coordinates the terms because of the equation of the pre-Christian situation of Christians with slavery,"[56] one might just as well be justified in assuming that Paul could not resist indulging in the memory of a time when the new Emperor was still lacking significant powers and wanted to paint this scene in the most drastic way possible.[57]

All that of course presupposes a context of utterance, in which the adoption of Nero might have been an issue in the first place. And indeed, Claudius's elevation of Nero was highly controversial and the adoption an object of debate. Britannicus himself (who would later be murdered by Nero shortly before reaching his fourteenth birthday) reportedly addressed Nero after his adoption as "Domitius," i.e., by his old family name (Tacitus, *Ann.* 12.41). And it is in any case noteworthy that the adoption of Nero caused significant legal troubles (cf. Tacitus, *Ann.* 12.25) because a *datio in adaptionem* was not possible, as it required the biological father to carry out a fictitious sale before the praetor and Nero's biological father had already been dead for a decade (he died in 40 CE). A regular adoption by *adrogatio* was also not possible for several reasons, one of which being the fact that Claudius already had a biological heir.[58] Even leaving that aside, the adoption was seen by contemporaries as being extraordinary. For it put an end to a supposed five-hundred-year tradition of "no trace of an adoption in the patrician branch" of the Claudian house (Tacitus, *Ann.* 12.25). Suetonius even claims that Claudius himself was well aware of this and views the whole matter as a symptom of the Emperor's mental confusion: "Just before his adoption of Nero, as if it were not bad enough to adopt a stepson[59] when he had a grown-up son of his own, he publicly declared more than once that no one had ever been taken into the Claudian family by adoption" (*Claud.* 39.2).

## CONCLUSION

Parallelomania? Well, maybe. But it is hard to deny that given a very specific context, it is difficult not to see the parallels. If Paul did not think of these stories when writing the letter, perhaps at least some of the early readers of the letters, turning to the writing after having just exchanged the latest gossip about the imperatorial family, would have giggled. To be honest, I am ultimately not convinced of this parallel myself. However, this makes this questionable counternarrative actually a fitting conclusion for this study. For against some tendencies in current exegesis, I want to close by emphasizing that it is not a problem that we cannot reach certainties on such matters. The quest for aspects in Paul's letters—including Galatians—that give us insights into the apostle's unease with the Roman Empire can be heuristically fruitful even if we only come up with possible or plausible counternarratives. We are, after all, moving here from interpretation proper (what did Paul mean?) to using the text as evidence for more far-reaching reconstructions (what did Paul think?).[60] Reconstructing authorial intent is difficult enough; trying to break through small windows that give us a glance at the most private "hidden transcript" of the Pauline circle will naturally be fraught with even more complications. But all this is no reason to despair. While we may not be in the position to make definitive conclusions on any *particular* proposed dissonance with Roman ideology in isolation, our establishing a *multitude* of such possible-to-likely readings will inevitably lead to the conclusion that something is actually there and that we are not merely chasing an illusion. After all, probability theory (I need to invoke it once more) teaches us that just as we cannot always be right when following probable tracks, analogously one of many improbable paths will ultimately lead us to our goal.[61] The exercise of our creative, even speculative, imagination in searching for counternarratives to the dominant Roman ideology in Galatians should thus be encouraged— not as an alternative but as a means to serve historical reconstruction.

## NOTES

1. Justin K. Hardin, *Galatians and the Imperial Cult*, WUNT 2/237 (Tübingen: Mohr Siebeck, 2008) is in my view the most important one among these.

2. See Christoph Heilig, "Das Neue Testament im Schatten des Imperiums," *VF 68 (2023): 14–23* for a comparative assessment of such volumes from different perspectives.

3. James C. Scott, *Domination and the Arts of Resistance: Hidden Transcripts* (New Haven: Yale University Press, 1990). Cf. in particular Richard A. Horsley, "Introduction: Jesus, Paul, and the 'Arts of Resistance': Leaves from the Notebook of James C. Scott," in *Hidden Transcripts and the Arts of Resistance: Applying the Work of James C. Scott to Jesus and Paul,* ed. Richard A. Horsley, SemeiaSt 48 (Atlanta: Scholars Press, 2004), 1–26.

4. Neil Elliott, "Strategies of Resistance and Hidden Transcripts in the Pauline Communities," in *Hidden Transcripts and the Arts of Resistance: Applying the Work of James C. Scott to Jesus and Paul,* ed. Richard A. Horsley, SemeiaSt 48 (Atlanta: Scholars Press, 2004), 97–122. For a critique, cf. Christoph Heilig, *Hidden Criticism?*

*The Methodology and Plausibility of the Search for a Counter-Imperial Subtext in Paul*, WUNT 2/392 (Tübingen: Mohr Siebeck, 2015; 2nd ed.: Minneapolis: Fortress, 2017), 55–58.

5. Richard B. Hays, *Echoes of Scripture in the Letters of Paul* (New Haven: Yale University Press, 1989); see N. T. Wright, *Paul: In Fresh Perspective* (Minneapolis: Fortress, 2005), and Neil Elliott, "'Blasphemed among the Nations': Pursuing an Anti-Imperial 'Intertextuality' in Romans," in *As It Is Written: Studying Paul's Use of Scripture,* ed. Stanley E. Porter and Christopher D. Stanley, SBLSymS 50 (Atlanta: Scholars Press, 2008), 213–33.

6. Cf. recently Joseph R. Dodson, "The Convict's Gibbet and the Victor's Car: The Triumphal Death of Marcus Atilius Regulus and the Background of Col 2:15," *HTR* 114 (2021): 182–202.

7. In particular in Christoph Heilig, "Methodological Considerations for the Search of Counter-Imperial 'Echoes' in Pauline Literature," in *Reactions to Empire: Proceedings of Sacred Texts in Their Socio-Political Contexts,* ed. John A. Dunne and Dan Batovici, WUNT 2/372 (Tübingen: Mohr Siebeck, 2014), 73–92, and Heilig, *Hidden Criticism?,* chapter 2. For a short summary, see now Christoph Heilig, *The Apostle and the Empire: Paul's Implicit and Explicit Criticism of Rome,* with a foreword by John M. G. Barclay (Grand Rapids: Eerdmans, 2022), 5–6.

8. For an introduction to this topic, see Theresa Heilig and Christoph Heilig, "Historical Methodology," in *God and the Faithfulness of Paul: A Critical Examination of the Pauline Theology of N. T. Wright,* ed. Christoph Heilig, J. Thomas Hewitt, and Michael F. Bird, WUNT 2/413 (Tübingen: Mohr Siebeck, 2016; 2nd ed.: Minneapolis: Fortress, 2017), 115–50. Right now, an interdisciplinary online research seminar is being carried through, which focuses on this issue. For details and instructions on how to participate, see https://theologie.unibas.ch/en/departments/new-testament/bayes-and-bible/.

9. Cf. Heilig, *Apostle,* 6.

10. John M. G. Barclay, "Why the Roman Empire Was Insignificant to Paul," in *Pauline Churches and Diaspora Jews*, ed. John M. G. Barclay, WUNT 275 (Tübingen: Mohr Siebeck, 2011), 363–87. On the backstory, cf. Heilig, *Apostle,* 5–7.

11. Cf. Heilig and Heilig, "Historical Methodology," 146. I suggested the addition of the fifth criterion recently in Heilig, *Apostle*, 42. With this addition I try to do justice to the critique of Laura Robinson, "Hidden Transcripts? The Supposedly Self-Censoring Paul and Rome as Surveillance State in Modern Pauline Scholarship," *NTS* 67 (2021): 55–72. Indeed, just because Paul *could have* written something does not mean that he actually *did* so (either explicitly or between the lines). Moreover, with respect to issues that might have been associated with the potential of disturbing Roman sensitivities but that were also of a largely uncontested nature among the believers, Paul could have simply entrusted the letter carriers to discuss these matters in person. This could have been done without exposing his communities to potential danger by expressing such matters in writing.

12. Bruce W. Winter, "The Imperial Cult and the Early Christians in Pisidian Antioch (Acts 13 and Galatians 6)," in *Actes du 1er Congrès International sur Antioche de Pisidie,* ed. T. Drew-Bear, M. Tashalan, and C. M. Thomas (Lyon:

Université Lumière-Lyon, 2002), 67–75, which is reprinted in modified form in Bruce W. Winter, *Divine Honours for the Caesars: The First Christians' Responses* (Grand Rapids: Eerdmans, 2015), chapter 9. The most elaborate and in some ways more nuanced proposal is, of course, offered by Hardin, *Galatians*.

13. A. Andrew Das, *Paul and the Stories of Israel: Grand Thematic Narratives in Galatians* (Minneapolis: Fortress, 2016), chapter 7.

14. James Corke-Webster, "Trouble in Pontus: The Pliny-Trajan Correspondence on the Christians Reconsidered," *TAPA* 147 (2017): 371–411. Roy K. Gibson, *Man of High Empire: The Life of Pliny the Younger* (Oxford: Oxford University Press, 2020) follows him closely.

15. Das, *Paul,* 189.

16. Heilig, *Apostle,* 30

17. Robinson, "Hidden Transcripts?"

18. Lynn H. Cohick, "Philippians and Empire: Paul's Engagement with Imperialism and the Imperial Cult," in *Jesus Is Lord, Caesar Is Not: Evaluating Empire in New Testament Studies,* ed. Scot McKnight and Joseph B. Monica (Downers Grove, IL: IVP Academic, 2013), 176.

19. Similarly unconvincing are attempts to shift any real risks after 64 CE. David G. Horrell, *Becoming Christian: Essays on 1 Peter and the Making of Christian Identity,* LNTS 394 (London: Bloomsbury, 2013), chapter 6, and Udo Schnelle, *Die ersten 100 Jahre des Christentums: 30–130 n. Chr.* 3rd ed., UTB 4411 (Göttingen: Vandenhoeck & Ruprecht, 2019) are prime examples of such an approach. These scholars correctly recognize that scholars like Joachim Molthagen, *Der römische Staat und die Christen im zweiten und dritten Jahrhundert,* 2nd ed., Hypomnemata 28 (Göttingen: Vandenhoeck & Ruprecht, 1975) were wrong when postulating on the basis of Pliny's execution of Christians a specific existing law against Christianity, but they still share their assumption that "it"—i.e., persecution of Christians—must have had a beginning because they stay within the problematic paradigm of these events having to do with religious politics in the first place.

20. N. T. Wright, "Gospel and Theology in Galatians," in *Gospel in Paul: Studies on Corinthians, Galatians and Romans for Richard N. Longenecker,* ed. L. Ann Jervis and Peter Richardson, JSNTSup 108 (Sheffield: Sheffield Academic, 1994), 222–39. Cf., e.g., Judith A. Diehl, "Empire and Epistles: Anti-Roman Rhetoric in the New Testament Epistles," *CurBR* 10 (2012): 217–63. To be sure, the act of referencing this parallel has a long tradition. See already G. Adolf Deissmann, *Licht vom Osten: Das Neue Testament und die neuentdeckten Texte der hellenistisch-römischen Welt* (Tübingen: Mohr, 1908), 266–67.

21. Cf. above on the metacriterion of likelihoods, and keep in mind that we always have to assess apparently "good" explanatory potential *in comparison* to the predictive power of its competing hypotheses.

22. On the passage, cf. Christoph Heilig, *Paulus als Erzähler? Eine narratologische Perspektive auf die Paulusbriefe,* BZNW 237 (Berlin: de Gruyter, 2020), chapter 9, section 5 and chapter 17, section 4.2.2.

23. Heilig, *Paulus,* 29–30.

24. Hardin, *Galatians,* 111. Emphasis added.

25. Hardin, Galatians, 111.

26. Robinson, "Hidden Transcripts," 66. Cf. now Heilig, *Apostle,* chapter 2 for an exploration of the consequences.

27. Heilig, *Hidden Criticism?,* chapter 5.

28. Heilig, *Paulus,* chapters 9–14. It takes me more than three hundred pages to merely scratch the surface of Paul's manifold and nuanced use of different linguistic means.

29. Cf. Heilig, *Paulus,* chapter 8, for some basic considerations.

30. Heilig, *Apostle,* 51–52.

31. For what follows, cf. Heilig, *Apostle,* 37–38 and 51.

32. Scott, *Domination,* 6.

33. Christoph Heilig, *Paul's Triumph: Reassessing 2 Corinthians 2:14 in Its Literary and Historical Context,* BTS 27 (Leuven: Peeters, 2017), and Heilig, *Apostle,* chapters 3 and 4.

34. Tiberius Claudius Dinippus was the priest of this cult of Victoria Britannica, as the inscription West no. 86 demonstrates (lines 3–4: SACERDOTI VICTORIAE | BRITANN). He had begun to hold that post around 45 CE. Cf. Giles Standing, "The Claudian Invasion of Britain and the Cult of Victoria Britannica," *Britannia* 34 (2003): 281–88.

35. Cf. for more details and more implications, Heilig, *Apostle,* 98–101.

36. Klarissa Lueg, Ann Starbæk Bager, and Marianne Wolff Lundholt, "Introduction: What Counter-Narratives Are: Dimensions and Levels of a Theory of Middle Range," in *Routledge Handbook of Counter-Narratives,* ed. Klarissa Lueg and Marianne Wolff Lundholt (London: Routledge, 2021), 4.

37. Cf., e.g., Douglas J. Moo, *Galatians,* BECNT (Grand Rapids: Baker Academic, 2013), 181–82.

38. Heilig, *Apostle,* 103–16.

39. See John Granger Cook, *Crucifixion in the Mediterranean World,* WUNT 327 (Tübingen: Mohr Siebeck, 2014), chapter 6, on the legal background.

40. See Heilig, *Paulus,* 509.

41. See Cook, *Crucifixion,* 398–416 on its abolishment.

42. Cf. Heilig, *Apostle,* 125–26, on Col 2:15.

43. Cf. Archibald T. Robertson, *A Grammar of the Greek New Testament in the Light of Historical Research,* 3rd ed. (London: Hodder & Stoughton, 1919), 767, on the article. There are many different means for creating such general narratives, which require the audience to fill in the concrete reference. There is a smooth transition to forms of potential *dis*narration, i.e., cases in which it is not at all clear if there even is a reference to happenings in the real world. Cf. Heilig, *Paulus,* chapter 12.

44. For a list of attested crucifixions, see John Granger Cook, "Roman Crucifixions: From the Second Punic War to Constantine," *ZNW* 104 (2013): 1–32.

45. Cf. Robert K. Sherk, "Roman Galatia: The Governors from 25 B.C. to A.D. 114," *ANRW* 7.2: 976, and W. M. Ramsay, "Studies in the Roman Province Galatia: III. Imperial Government of the Province Galatia," *JRS* 12 (1922): 159.

46. Sherk, "Roman Galatia," 978.

47. I am still wondering whether διαμένω in Gal 2:5 does not settle the question. Cf. Heilig, *Apostle,* 595–98.

48. Ignoring the possibility of an even earlier date if one dates the first missionary journey to 34–40 CE.

49. Jörg Frey, "Galatians," in *Paul: Life, Setting, Work, Letters,* ed. Oda Wischmeyer, trans. Helen S. Heron, with revisions by Dieter T. Roth (London: T&T Clark, 2012), 212.

50. Heilig, *Apostle,* chapter 3.

51. On the distinction, cf. Heilig, *Paulus,* 116 and 355.

52. Moo, *Galatians,* 923.

53. Cf. Hugh Lindsay, *Adoption in the Roman World* (Oxford: Oxford University Press, 2009), 201.

54. Cf. Tacitus, *Ann.* 13.10, where an otherwise unknown Asconius Labeo is mentioned as the tutor of Nero.

55. Cf. Heilig, *Apostle,* 125n62.

56. Hans Dieter Betz, *Galatians* (Philadelphia: Fortress, 1979), 203.

57. To be sure, such a thought must be a travesty to those who assume that Rom 13:1–7 still reflects Paul's optimism about the young Nero, a positive attitude that would only be crushed in 64 CE. But Rom 13 does not prove such a naivity. Rather, such a stance must be presupposed—against all odds—in order to read the passage in such a way. Cf. Heilig, *Apostle,* 113–16.

58. Cf. Rudolf Leonhard, "Adrogatio," PW 1.1: 419–21, and "Adoption 2," PW 1.1: 399–400.

59. In 53 CE, Claudius had additionally become the stepfather of his adopted son Nero by marrying him to his daughter Octavia in order to promote his position.

60. Heilig, *Apostle,* 53.

61. Imagine you are a textual critic and for each variation unit you are 90% certain that you chose the right variant. After only seven such decisions, it is already more likely than not that in at least one case you made the wrong decision. Conversely, it is more likely than not that one of seven hypotheses concerning dissonances with Roman ideology will be correct, even if they each have only an independent 10% probability of being true.

## BIBLIOGRAPHY

Barclay, John M. G. "Why the Roman Empire Was Insignificant to Paul." In *Pauline Churches and Diaspora Jews*, edited by John M. G. Barclay, 363–87. WUNT 275. Tübingen: Mohr Siebeck, 2011.

Betz, Hans Dieter. *Galatians.* Hermeneia. Philadelphia: Fortress, 1979.

Cohick, Lynn H. "Philippians and Empire: Paul's Engagement with Imperialism and the Imperial Cult." In *Jesus Is Lord, Caesar Is Not: Evaluating Empire in New Testament Studies*, edited by Scot McKnight and Joseph B. Monica, 166–82. Downers Grove, IL: IVP Academic, 2013.

Cook, John Granger. "Roman Crucifixions: From the Second Punic War to Constantine." *ZNW* 104 (2013): 1–32.

———. *Crucifixion in the Mediterranean World.* WUNT 327. Tübingen: Mohr Siebeck, 2014.

Corke-Webster, James. "Trouble in Pontus: The Pliny-Trajan Correspondence on the Christians Reconsidered." *TAPA* 147 (2017): 371–411.

Das, A. Andrew. *Paul and the Stories of Israel: Grand Thematic Narratives in Galatians.* Minneapolis: Fortress, 2016.

Deissmann, G. Adolf. *Licht vom Osten: Das Neue Testament und die neuentdeckten Texte der hellenistisch-römischen Welt.* Tübingen: Mohr Siebeck, 1908.

Diehl, Judith A. "Empire and Epistles: Anti-Roman Rhetoric in the New Testament Epistles." *CurBR* 10 (2012): 217–63.

Dodson, Joseph R. "The Convict's Gibbet and the Victor's Car: The Triumphal Death of Marcus Atilius Regulus and the Background of Col 2:15." *HTR* 114 (2021): 182–202.

Elliott, Neil. "'Blasphemed among the Nations': Pursuing an Anti-Imperial 'Intertextuality' in Romans." In *As It Is Written: Studying Paul's Use of Scripture*, edited by Stanley E. Porter and Christopher D. Stanley, 213–33. SBLSymS 50. Atlanta: Scholars Press, 2008.

———. "Strategies of Resistance and Hidden Transcripts in the Pauline Communities." In *Hidden Transcripts and the Arts of Resistance: Applying the Work of James C. Scott to Jesus and Paul*, edited by Richard A. Horsley, 97–122. SemeiaSt 48. Atlanta: Scholars Press, 2004.

Frey, Jörg. "Galatians." In *Paul: Life, Setting, Work, Letters*, edited by Oda Wischmeyer; translated by Helen S. Heron, with revisions by Dieter T. Roth, 199–222. London: T&T Clark, 2012.

Gibson, Roy K. *Man of High Empire: The Life of Pliny the Younger.* Oxford: Oxford University Press, 2020.

Hardin, Justin K. *Galatians and the Imperial Cult.* WUNT 2/237. Tübingen: Mohr Siebeck, 2008.

Hays, Richard B. *Echoes of Scripture in the Letters of Paul.* New Haven: Yale University Press, 1989.

Heilig, Christoph. "Methodological Considerations for the Search of Counter-Imperial 'Echoes' in Pauline Literature." In *Reactions to Empire: Proceedings of Sacred Texts in Their Socio-Political Contexts*, edited by John A. Dunne and Dan Batovici, 73–92. WUNT 2/372. Tübingen: Mohr Siebeck, 2014.

———. *Hidden Criticism? The Methodology and Plausibility of the Search for a Counter-Imperial Subtext in Paul.* WUNT 2/392. Tübingen: Mohr Siebeck, 2015. 2nd ed. Minneapolis: Fortress, 2017.

———. *Paul's Triumph: Reassessing 2 Corinthians 2:14 in Its Literary and Historical Context.* BTS 27. Leuven: Peeters, 2017.

———. *Paulus als Erzähler? Eine narratologische Perspektive auf die Paulusbriefe.* BZNW 237. Berlin: de Gruyter, 2020.

———. *The Apostle and the Empire: Paul's Implicit and Explicit Criticism of Rome.* With a foreword by John M. G. Barclay. Grand Rapids: Eerdmans, 2022.

————. "Das Neue Testament im Schatten des Imperiums." *VF* 68 (2023): 14–23.

Heilig, Theresa, and Christoph Heilig. "Historical Methodology." In *God and the Faithfulness of Paul: A Critical Examination of the Pauline Theology of N. T. Wright*, edited by Christoph Heilig, J. Thomas Hewitt, and Michael F. Bird, 115–50. WUNT 2/413. Tübingen: Mohr Siebeck, 2016; 2nd ed.: Minneapolis: Fortress, 2017.

Horrell, David G. *Becoming Christian: Essays on 1 Peter and the Making of Christian Identity.* LNTS 394. London: Bloomsbury, 2013.

Horsley, Richard A. "Introduction: Jesus, Paul, and the 'Arts of Resistance': Leaves from the Notebook of James C. Scott." In *Hidden Transcripts and the Arts of Resistance: Applying the Work of James C. Scott to Jesus and Paul*, edited by Richard A. Horsley, 1–26. SemeiaSt 48. Atlanta: Scholars Press, 2004.

Leonhard, Rudolf. 1893a. "Adoption 2." PW 1.1: 399–400.

————. 1893b. "Adrogatio." PW 1.1: 419–21.

Lindsay, Hugh. *Adoption in the Roman World.* Oxford: Oxford University Press, 2009.

Lueg, Klarissa, Ann Starbæk Bager, and Marianne Wolff Lundholt. "Introduction: What Counter-Narratives Are: Dimensions and Levels of a Theory of Middle Range." In *Routledge Handbook of Counter-Narratives*, edited by Klarissa Lueg and Marianne Wolff Lundholdt, 1–14. London: Routledge, 2021.

McKnight, Scot, and Joseph B. Modica, eds. *Jesus Is Lord, Caesar Is Not: Evaluating Empire in New Testament Studies.* Downers Grove, IL: IVP Academic, 2013.

Molthagen, Joachim. *Der römische Staat und die Christen im zweiten und dritten Jahrhundert.* 2nd ed. Hypomnemata 28. Göttingen: Vandenhoeck & Ruprecht, 1975.

Nanos, Mark D. *The Irony of Galatians: Paul's Letter in First-Century Context.* Minneapolis: Fortress, 2002.

Ramsay, W. M. "Studies in the Roman Province Galatia: III. Imperial Government of the Province Galatia." *JRS* 12 (1922): 147–86.

Robertson, Archibald T. *A Grammar of the Greek New Testament in the Light of Historical Research.* 3rd ed. London: Hodder & Stoughton, 1919.

Robinson, Laura. "Hidden Transcripts? The Supposedly Self-Censoring Paul and Rome as Surveillance State in Modern Pauline Scholarship." *NTS* 67 (2021): 55–72.

Schnelle, Udo. *Die Ersten 100 Jahre des Christentums: 30–130 n. Chr.* 3rd ed. UTB 4411. Göttingen: Vandenhoeck & Ruprecht, 2019.

Scott, James C. *Domination and the Arts of Resistance: Hidden Transcripts.* New Haven: Yale University Press, 1990.

Scott, James M. *Adoption as Sons: An Exegetical Investigation into the Background of ΥΙΟΘΕΣΙΑ in the Pauline Corpus.* WUNT 2/48. Tübingen: Mohr Siebeck, 1992.

Sherk, Robert K. "Roman Galatia: The Governors from 25 B.C. to A.D. 114." *ANRW* 7.2: 954–1052.

Standing, Giles. "The Claudian Invasion of Britain and the Cult of Victoria Britannica." *Britannia* 34 (2003): 281–88.

West, Allen Brown. *Latin Inscriptions: 1896–1926*. Vol. 8.2 of *Corinth: Results of Excavations Conducted by the American School of Classical Studies at Athens*. Cambridge, MA: Harvard University Press for the American School of Classical Studies at Athens, 1931.

Winter, Bruce W. "The Imperial Cult and the Early Christians in Pisidian Antioch (Acts 13 and Galatians 6)." In *Actes du 1er Congrès International sur Antioche de Pisidie*, edited by T. Drew-Bear, M. Tashalan, and C. M. Thomas, 67–75. Lyon: Université Lumière-Lyon, 2002.

———. *Divine Honours for the Caesars: The First Christians' Responses*. Grand Rapids: Eerdmans, 2015.

Wright, N. T. "Gospel and Theology in Galatians." In *Gospel in Paul: Studies on Corinthians, Galatians and Romans for Richard N. Longenecker*, edited by L. Ann Jervis and Peter Richardson, 222–39. JSNTSup 108. Sheffield: Sheffield Academic, 1994.

———. *Paul: In Fresh Perspective*. Minneapolis: Fortress, 2005.

# PART II

# Paul's Engagement with Scripture in 1 Thessalonians

*Chapter 11*

# Scripture as Paul's Foundational Ethic in 1 Thessalonians 4.1–12

## Jeffrey A. D. Weima

What is the background or determining influences of Paul's exhortations in 1 Thess 4:1–12? The possibility that the apostle's vocabulary, ethical concepts, and theological framework in this passage are indebted to the Jewish scriptures initially seems undermined by a couple of key facts. This first letter to the Thessalonians, as well as the second, in sharp contrast to most of Paul's other existing letters, does not contain even one explicit quotation from the Old Testament. Additionally, as 1 Thess 1:9 makes clear ("you turned to God from idols"), the apostle in 1 Thessalonians is writing to a predominantly Gentile congregation for whom the Jewish scriptures were a foreign and unknown source.

It is understandable, then, that some contemporary scholars assert that Paul was impacted primarily by the Greco-Roman setting of his world and that of his mostly Gentile readers in Thessalonica, and so have stressed the parallels between his exhortations here and those found in Cynic and Stoic thought. Wayne Meeks, for example, makes the following observation about 1 Thessalonians and especially the ethical exhortations in chapter 4:

> There is much about the kind of life advocated here that would be familiar to the readers from their pre-Christian experience and from the world around them: "a quiet life," "minding one's own business," monogamy and sexual purity, special affection toward brothers (*philadelphia*), composure and the ability to comfort one another in the face of death (ch. 4)—all these are commonplaces in philosophical speeches and letters of the time.[1]

But even though Paul was clearly familiar with the ethical ideas and moral values of the Greco-Roman world in which he lived and ministered, the apostle also remained indebted to the Jewish faith in which he was raised and for many years was trained. This indebtedness manifests itself at multiple places in 1 Thess 4:1–12. Some of these instances involve only a general allusion to the OT that accounts for the origin and meaning of Paul's choice of a particular word. These general allusions may not be the most significant exegetically, but they do provide important contextual evidence that Paul in this passage is, in fact, influenced by the Jewish scriptures. There are four additional instances within 1 Thess 4:1–12, however, where the allusion to the OT is quite specific and reveals an important theological conviction about the way in which Paul views his Thessalonian readers and the perspective from which he issues to them the ethical exhortations contained in this passage. A careful examination of these specific OT allusions demonstrates that Paul's exhortations in 4:1–12 are grounded in his conviction that the predominantly Gentile Jesus-followers in Thessalonica are part of the end-time people of God who already possess the gifts of holiness, the Holy Spirit, and divine instruction, which are all anticipated blessings of the new covenant in the messianic age.

## GENERAL OLD TESTAMENT ALLUSIONS IN 1 THESSALONIANS 4:1–12

### Three Verbs in 1 Thessalonians 4:1–2

The first evidence of Paul's indebtedness to the Jewish scriptures in 1 Thess 4:1–12 is found in a cluster of three verbs in the opening unit of verses 1–2 where the apostle issues a general appeal for the Thessalonian believers to increase in conduct that pleases God. Paul includes within this general appeal two parenthetical καθώς clauses where the three verbs that are important for our interest are found:

> "And so, brothers and sisters, we ask you and appeal in the Lord Jesus that—just as you *received* from us how you must *walk* and so *please God*, just as you are indeed *walking*—that you increase more and more." (4:1–2)[2]

The first verb "you received" is a technical term in Paul's letters for the reception and passing on of traditional material—important teachings that do not originate with the apostle but that he first received and subsequently handed down to his converts (cf. 1 Cor 11:23; 15:3; 2 Thess 2:15). Although this technical use of the verb "to receive" occurs in some Greco-Roman writings to refer to instruction passed on from a philosopher to his students,[3] it has a stronger parallel in the rabbinic tradition, which was an essential part of Paul's pre-Christian training.[4] The apostle's word choice adds weight to what follows: the ethical teachings found in 4:1–12 and summarized by the exhortation that this is how the Thessalonian believers "must walk and so please God" are not merely the personal instructions of Paul. Instead, they are teachings that ultimately go back to God's will expressed already in the Old Testament that have been accepted as such and have been passed on by the broader church community.

The second verb "walk," emphasized both by its repetition in the second καθώς clause and by the *inclusio* formed by these two occurrences with its third use in 4:12, has the metaphorical sense of "to conduct one's life" (BDAG 803.2). This use of the verb "to walk" to describe moral conduct and an ethical way of life has its roots in Paul's Jewish background, as roughly 200 of the 1,547 occurrences of the Hebrew verb *halak* in the Old Testament have this metaphorical meaning. The widespread familiarity with this OT metaphorical sense of the verb "walk" can be seen in the name that Jewish rabbis gave to their collection of moral writings: *halakah*. Paul's threefold occurrence of the verb "to walk" in 4:1–12 to refer to his ethical exhortations in this passage, therefore, clearly originates from his Jewish background and education.[5]

The third verb and its direct object—"please God"—is the most obvious of the cluster of terms in 4:1–2 to reveal the influence of the OT on Paul's word choice and thoughts in this introductory section. This is because the concept of pleasing God as the goal of human conduct occurs repeatedly in the Jewish scriptures (see, e.g., Num 23:27; 1 Kgs 14:13; Job 6:9; 34:9; Pss 19:14; 69:31; 104:34; Prov 15:26; 16:7; Mal 3:4). The notion of pleasing God, however, is not only found frequently in the OT but more significantly is also one of Paul's favorite expressions for proper moral conduct (Rom 8:8; 1 Cor 7:32–34; Gal 1:10; 1 Thess 2:4, 15; 4:1; see also 2 Cor 5:9; Eph 6:6; Col 1:10; 3:22). As part of the defense of his integrity, Paul earlier in 1 Thessalonians claims that he and his fellow missionaries speak "not as those who please people but those who please God" (2:4). Paul also labels those Jews who were responsible for his forced early departure from Thessalonica as those "who do not please God" (2:15). The gravity in the apostle's mind of this charge of not pleasing God is suggested by the fact that this description comes immediately after his damning accusation that certain Jews "killed both the Lord Jesus and the prophets." Now in the opening unit of 4:1–2, Paul uses a cluster of three verbs with OT allusions to remind his Thessalonian readers that the traditional material—the ethical exhortations—which they "received" from him during his mission-founding visit has the ultimate goal of causing them to "walk" in a way that "pleases God."

## The "Avenger" in 1 Thessalonians 4:6b

Paul makes an even clearer allusion to the OT in 1 Thess 4:6b. This is the first of three causal statements that reads: "because the Lord is an avenger concerning all these things" (διότι ἔκδικος κύριος περὶ πάντων τούτων, καθὼς καὶ προείπαμεν ὑμῖν καὶ διεμαρτυράμεθα). These words likely echo those of Ps 93:1 LXX (94:1 MT/ET): "The Lord is a God of vengeance" (θεὸς ἐκδικήσεων κύριος). This probability is supported not only by the use of the key word "avenger/one who issues vengeance" in both texts but also the word order of both texts where this key word is located at the head of the sentence for emphasis. If Paul is not echoing this specific OT text, then he is likely picking up the idea of God as a judge who exacts vengeance, which is a concept that occurs frequently in both the OT (e.g., Exod 7:4; 12:12; Deut 32:35; Pss 18:47; 79:10; 99:8; Jer 11:20; Amos 3:2, 14; Mic 5:15; Nah 1:2) and Jewish writings from the Second Temple period (e.g., T. Reu 6.6; T. Levi 18.1; T. Gad 6.7; T. Jos 20.1; T. Benj 10.8–10; Jos Asen 23.13).

The precise identity of the "avenger" that Paul has in view is debated: does this figure refer to God or Jesus? The fact that the apostle is alluding either specifically to Ps 93:1 LXX or more generally to multiple OT texts where God is described as the judge who exacts vengeance, as well as the four references to "God" in the immediately surrounding verses (4:3, 5, 7, 8), might suggest that the noun "Lord" (κύριος) here refers to God. Nevertheless, there are three reasons why this interpretation is almost certainly wrong. First, the noun "Lord" has occurred twelve times in the letter thus far (1:1, 3, 6, 8; 2:15, 19; 3:8, 11, 12, 13; 4:1, 2) and each of them refers to Jesus. This, of course, is hardly surprising, since the noun "Lord" is Paul's favorite designation by far for Jesus. Second, the subject of the immediately following clause in 4:7 is identified as "God" ("For God did not call . . . "), and such an explicit identification of the subject would not be necessary, if, in fact, the "Lord" in the preceding clause also referred to God. Rather, the shift from the "Lord" (= Jesus) as the avenger to "God" who did not call the Thessalonians to a life of impurity but of holiness required that the new subject of this action be explicitly identified. Third, there are several places in both letters to the Thessalonians which highlight the future coming of Jesus either generally as the agent of God's judgment on the wicked (1 Thess 1:10; 5:1–11; 2 Thess 1:7–10; 2:8–10; see also Rom 12:19; Col 3:23–25; 2 Tim 4:1) or more narrowly as an avenger (2 Thess 1:7b–8 "at the revelation of the Lord Jesus from heaven with the angels of his power in a flame of fire, exacting *vengeance* [ἐκδίκησιν] on those who do not know God and on those who do not obey the gospel of our Jesus").

Since the "avenger" in 1 Thess 4:6b refers almost certainly not to God but to Jesus, this text reveals how Paul attributes to Jesus a role that the OT attributed to God. Paul's allusion in 4:6b to Ps 93:1 LXX, therefore, reflects his Christological reinterpretation of this OT passage such that it now refers to Jesus instead of God.

### The Exhortation to Love One Another in 1 Thessalonians 4:9–10

Yet another allusion to the OT within 1 Thess 4:1–12 is found in Paul's exhortation to the Thessalonian church that they must manifest to an even greater degree love toward fellow believers (4:9–10). A specific echo of the OT exists in Paul's use, or more likely, creation, within this exhortation of the term "God-taught" (4:9b)—an echo that will be carefully considered in the discussion below. Here we briefly note that a general echo of the OT may well exist in the key word that Paul uses to introduce this new section, "Now about φιλαδελφία" (4:9a). The apostle's thinking here likely can be traced back ultimately to Lev 19:18: "You shall love your neighbor as yourself." This likelihood gains strength not only from the use of the striking term "God-taught" stemming from Isa 54:13 LXX in the immediately following clause but also from the fact that this Leviticus text was a foundational one in Paul's ethics. The apostle explicitly cites Lev 19:18 in both his letters to the Galatians (5:14) and the Romans (13:9) as the primary way in which Christ-followers can fulfill the keeping of the whole law of God. And although Paul does not cite this OT text explicitly in his letter to Philemon, he uses the concept of love for others (in distinction from love for God and/or Jesus) grounded in Lev 19:18 no less than five times to support theologically his appeal for the runaway slave in this very brief letter (Phlm 1, 5, 7, 8, 16).

### THE THEME OF "HOLINESS" (1 THESSALONIANS 4:3, 4, 7, 8)

The OT allusions in 1 Thess 4:1–12 reviewed thus far are important for demonstrating in a general way Paul's indebtedness in this passage to the Jewish scriptures. There are four additional OT allusions in 4:1–12, however, which go beyond showing the influence the Jewish scriptures had on the apostle's word choices and moral standards, and also reveal an important theological conviction about the way in which Paul views his Thessalonian readers and the perspective from which he issues to them the ethical exhortations contained in this passage.[6] The first of these important additional OT echoes involves the apostle's emphasis on the theme of "holiness" (ἁγιασμός) in the subunit of verses 3–8 dealing with sexual conduct.

Paul does not merely make a brief allusion to this OT theme of holiness but he stresses it in a variety of ways. The apostle opens his discussion of sexual conduct by equating holiness with the will of God (v 3: "For this is the will of God—your *holiness*"). He instills further importance to the theme of holiness by including in this subunit two additional references to the noun "holiness" (v 4: "that each one of you know how to control his own vessel in *holiness* and honor"; v 7: "For God did not call us for impurity but in *holiness*"). A yet additional means of emphasizing the theme of holiness within the discussion of sexual conduct is often overlooked and not captured in any of the major translations: Paul deviates from his typical description of the Holy Spirit in order to stress the "holy" character of God's Spirit (v 8b: "God, who indeed gives his Spirit, who is *holy*, into you"). The apostle skillfully foreshadows the importance of the holiness theme in 4:3–8 in the transitional prayer of 3:13, where he asks the Lord to strengthen the hearts of the Thessalonian believers so that they will be "blameless in *holiness*" when Jesus comes again "with all his *holy* ones." The theme of holiness is emphasized one final time at the end of 1 Thessalonians where Paul adapts an epistolary convention from the closing so that it looks back and echoes a major theme developed previously in the body of the letter. The apostle replaces the simple and expected closing peace benediction, "May the God of peace be with you" (see Rom 15:33; 2 Cor 13:11; Phil 4:9b), with the expanded prayer, "May the God of peace himself *make you holy* through and through; and may your whole spirit, soul, and body *be kept blameless* at the coming of our Lord Jesus" (1 Thess 5:23).

Paul's stress of the OT theme of holiness provides an important window into the thinking of the apostle with regard to how he views the predominantly Gentile converts in Thessalonica and the theological perspective in which his exhortations to holiness in sexual conduct ought to be understood. Holiness was one of the foundational features by which Israel, God's covenant people, was to be distinguished from every other nation. This nation-defining characteristic of holiness is mandated by God at Mount Sinai where he establishes Israel as his chosen covenant people: "And now if you indeed obey my voice and keep my covenant, you will be to me a *distinctive* people out of all the nations. For the whole earth is mine. You will be to me a kingdom of priests and a *holy* nation" (Exod 19:5–6 LXX). It is important not to miss here the correlation between Israel being a "holy" nation and thus a "distinctive" people. The same emphasis on holiness as a distinguishing feature of Israel is found in the later renewal of the Sinai covenant: "And the Lord has chosen you today that you may be to him a *distinctive* people, as he promised, that you may keep his commandments, and that you may be above all the nations, as he has made you renowned and a boast and glorious, in order that you may be a *holy* people to the Lord your God, as he promised" (Deut 26:18–19 LXX). The idea that holiness must be Israel's unique identification mark viz-à-viz all other nations is also stressed in the book of Leviticus, which contains multiple commands for God's chosen people to imitate the holiness of their God: "You shall be sanctified/made holy, and you shall be holy, because I, the Lord your God am holy" (Lev 11:44 LXX; see also 11:45; 19:2; 20:7, 26; 22:32).

The fundamental idea connected with God's call to holiness is that of "separation," that is, of the requirement for Israel as God's holy people to "come out" and be "distinct" from all the other nations.[7] Holiness, therefore, functions as the boundary marker that distinguishes God's people from the surrounding people groups:

> "And do not follow the practices of the nations whom I am driving out before you. . . . I am the Lord your God who has *separated you from the all the nations*. You shall therefore make a distinction between clean and unclean. . . . And you will be holy to me, because I, the Lord your God, am holy, the one who *separated you from all the nations* to be mine." (Lev 20:23–26 LXX)

Any first-century Jew—and thus obviously Paul too—would have been familiar with all of this. As Frank Thielman notes: "The pictures of Israel in solemn assembly at the foot of Mount Sinai entering into a covenant with God and then receiving instruction from Moses on their election and sanctification while poised at the border of the Promised Land were deeply etched in the Jewish religious consciousness."[8] The contents of Lev 17–26—the so-called Holiness Code due to the highly repeated use of the word "holy" and the frequent exhortation for Israel to imitate the holiness of their God—contain a collection of important laws and regulations by which the nation of Israel must separate itself from the practices of the rest of the world, and these were well-known among Jews in both Palestine and the Diaspora.[9] Paul was not merely familiar with but strongly committed to the idea of holiness as involving the kinds of distinctive practices exhorted in Lev 17–26. This is clear from his being an active and influential member of the Pharisees, a religiously conservative group within Judaism whose name, "the separated ones" (the Greek Φαρισαῖος comes from the Aramaic and Hebrew verb פרשׁ, meaning "separate, make distinct"), captured well their commitment to keep themselves apart not just from their pagan neighbors but also from their fellow Jews who did not faithfully follow the Torah's call to holiness. It is not at all surprising, therefore, that Paul viewed holiness as God's desired purpose for and distinguishing feature of Israel, his covenant people.[10]

What is surprising, however, and also of great theological significance, is that Paul applies this OT standard of holiness to the predominantly Gentile Jesus-followers in Thessalonica. The holiness that previously has been the unique divine calling of Israel has now also become God's purpose for

Gentiles in Thessalonica who have "turned to God from idols to serve the living and true God" (1:9). The holiness that has previously been the key feature that marked out Israel as a people distinct from all the other nations has now also become the boundary marker that separates the Gentile believers in Thessalonica from "the Gentiles who do not know God" (4:5), those who are "outside" of God's holy people (4:12). The natural conclusion from these observations is that Paul no longer views his predominantly Gentile converts in Thessalonica according to their former pagan status but instead sees them as the renewed Israel, as those who constitute God's covenant people just as fully as the minority of Jewish converts to Christ in that city do. As Richard Hays observes:

> In 1 Thessalonians, Paul appears to assume without argument that his Gentile Christian converts at Thessalonica have become participants in the covenant community of Israel. . . . (T)he extraordinary implications of these texts for his ecclesiology are rarely noted. Paul writes as if this Gentile Christian community is "Gentile" no longer: though they remain uncircumcised, he has transferred to them the communal ascriptions appropriate to Israel.[11]

It is on the basis of this new status of being the renewed Israel that the apostle issues his exhortations in 4:3–8 and calls upon his converts at Thessalonica—both Gentile and Jew—to exhibit in their sexual conduct the holiness that God has always called his people to possess.

## "THE GENTILES WHO DO NOT KNOW GOD" (1 THESSALONIANS 4:5)

The second OT allusion in 1 Thess 4:1–12 which similarly reveals Paul's understanding of the predominantly Gentile church of Thessalonica as the renewed Israel lies in an important contrast he makes between his Christian converts and their unbelieving fellow citizens. The apostle exhorts the Christ-followers in 4:4–5 to learn to control their sexual desires and conduct,[12] doing this "in holiness and honor" (thereby stressing again the OT standard of holiness that ought to characterize God's people) and not "in lustful passion." Paul continues to contrast the sexual conduct of the Thessalonian believers with their pagan neighbors with a comparative clause that not only explicitly identifies the latter group but also provides the theological reason for their acting in lustful passion: "just as also the Gentiles who do not know God" (4:5: καθάπερ καὶ τὰ ἔθνη τὰ μὴ εἰδότα τὸν θεόν).

Paul's description of unbelievers as "the Gentiles who do not know God," an expression used in his other letters as well (Gal 4:8–9; 2 Thess 1:8; cf. 1

Cor 1:21), likely originates from the OT. The apostle may have been thinking about a couple of OT texts that describe the Gentiles or the unrighteous as "those who do not know you/the Lord" (Ps 79:6 [78:6 LXX]; Job 18:21). The most probable source of Paul's expression in 4:5, however, is Jer 10:25, which not only parallels almost exactly the words of the apostle but also the word order and grammatical construction (the substantive use of the attributive participle): "Pour out your wrath on *the Gentiles who do not know you*" (ἔθνη τὰ μὴ εἰδότα σε). Paul's expression "the Gentiles who do not know God" also immediately places this verse in a covenant context, for "to know God" is a technical reference in the OT, especially in Jeremiah (see 31:34), to the covenant relationship.[13]

The strong contrast that Paul creates by setting his Thessalonian readers—the vast majority of whom were themselves Gentiles—over against "the Gentiles who do not know God" is striking and raises a perplexing question: How can the apostle exhort *Gentile* Christians in Thessalonica not to act in their sex life like Gentiles? The answer is that Paul no longer views his converts in Thessalonica as Gentiles but as those with a new theological identity: they are now members of God's covenant people. In responding to the issue of how Paul here can tell the Gentiles not to act like Gentiles, Nijay Gupta comments:

> It could be that Paul is comparing "Gentiles who do not know God" with "Gentiles who *do* know God." But I think Paul's thought runs deeper than this point. The idea is that they have been written into a new story through Jesus, the story of Israel; they do not literally become "Jews," but they are adopted into the family of Yahweh through Jesus and they live out a different set of values (see Rom 11:17).[14]

Paul's use of an OT expression in 4:5, therefore, provides further evidence for the two important claims made above about the theme of holiness in 4:3–8. First, it reveals that the apostle views the Gentile believers in Thessalonica as members of the renewed Israel, the covenant people of God. Second, it demonstrates that Paul understood the OT notion of holiness to be a distinguishing sign or boundary marker that sets Jesus-followers apart from the rest of humanity, from "the Gentiles who do not know God."

## "GOD, WHO INDEED GIVES HIS SPIRIT, WHO IS HOLY, INTO YOU" (1 THESSALONIANS 4:8B)

The third OT allusion in 1 Thess 4:1–12 which provides yet another important window into Paul's theological framework in the ethical exhortations of this passage is found in the final phrase of the subunit of vv. 3–8 dealing with holiness in sexual conduct: "God, who indeed gives his Spirit, who is holy, into you" (4:8b). The apostle here echoes the language of the OT prophets, especially Ezek 36:27, 37:6, and 37:14, about the gift of God's Spirit as one of the anticipated blessings of the "new" or "everlasting" covenant by which God's people will finally be able to obey his law and be the holy nation that he had originally called them at Mt. Sinai to be (Exod 19:5–6). Once again, what is surprising and significant is not that Paul's words echo this OT expectation for the coming of God's Spirit nor even that he sees this future promise as something currently fulfilled but rather that the apostle applies this new covenant blessing for eschatological Israel to the predominantly Gentile believers in Thessalonica. It is important to recognize that Paul is not explicitly teaching this truth here; rather, as Gordon Fee observes, the logic of his argument "assumes far more than it actually says."[15] This explains why a good number of Thessalonian commentators either miss the echo of the OT in 4:8b and/or fail to appreciate its significance.

There existed in Paul's day among his Jewish people a widespread expectation that God would one day pour out his Spirit on his chosen people as one of the key blessings of the new covenant to be enjoyed in the coming messianic age. This gift of God's Spirit would empower Israel to obey his law and so live according to the standard of holiness that God had mandated when he first established his covenant with them at Mt. Sinai. A number of OT prophets express an eschatological hope for living a holy and Torah-obedient life made possible through the presence of God's Spirit but none do it as clearly as Ezekiel.[16] In words that appear to have influenced Paul's statement in 4:8b, God speaks through this prophet to his covenant people:

> "I will sprinkle clean water on you, and you will be purged from all your uncleanness and from all your idols, and I will cleanse you. And I will give you a new heart, and *I will put a new spirit in you* (πνεῦμα καινὸν δώσω ἐν ὑμῖν); and I will take away the heart of stone out of your flesh, and I will give you a heart of flesh. And *I will put my Spirit in you* (τὸ πνεῦμά μου δώσω ἐν ὑμῖν) and will cause you to walk in my commands and to keep my judgements and do them." (Ezek 36:25–27 LXX)

The promise made here that God will give his Spirit as one of the blessings of the eschatological age is emphasized in Ezekiel's prophecy by its presence elsewhere in this OT book (11:19; 39:29) but especially by its double repetition in the immediately following chapter. In fact, the parallel with Paul's words is even closer in Ezek 37:6 and 37:14 LXX, where it is twice stated: "I will put my Spirit into you" (δώσω πνεῦμά μου εἰς ὑμᾶς).[17] And while other prophets do not refer to the end-time gift of God's Spirit quite as explicitly as Ezekiel does (but see Isa 32:15; 44:3; 59:21; Joel 2:28–29; Zech 12:10), Jeremiah and Isaiah do speak about a "new" or "everlasting" covenant, in which God will be present in and among his people in such a personal way that they will obey his commands and live holy lives (see, e.g., Jer 31:31–34 [38:31–34 LXX]; 32:40; 50:5; Isa 55:3; 59:21).

What is of most significance for our purposes is that Paul takes this eschatological promise about the gift of God's Spirit originally given to OT members of ethnic Israel and applies it to the NT believers in Thessalonica who are predominantly Gentile. The parallels with Ezek 36:25–27 are especially striking. For as Ezekiel prophesied (36:25: "You will be purged from all your uncleannesses, . . . and I will cleanse you"), God has cleansed the Thessalonian believers from their "uncleanness" (1 Thess 4:7) so that their sexual conduct can instead now be controlled by "holiness" (4:3, 4, 7). And as Ezekiel prophesied (26:25: "and from all your idols"), God has purged Paul's converts at Thessalonica from their idolatry, with the result that they have now "turned to God from idols to serve a living and true God" (1:9). Furthermore, as Ezekiel prophesied (26:27: "I will cause you to walk in my commands and to keep my judgments and do them"), God has now enabled Gentile Christians at Thessalonica to "walk" (περιπατεῖν) according to his commands (4:1 [2x], 12). But most significant of all, as Ezekiel prophesied (36:27: "I will put my Spirit in you"; repeated twice in 37:6, 14 but with the prepositional phrase "into you"), Paul can now say to Gentile believers at Thessalonica that God is the one "who indeed gives his Spirit, who is holy, into you" (4:8).

Confirmation that Paul is indeed echoing the words of Ezekiel lies in the fact that the apostle does not merely repeat this prophet's prediction about God giving his Spirit as an anticipated blessing of the new covenant, but Paul also uses exactly the same prepositional phrase that the prophet uses to refer to the recipients of God's gift: "into you" (εἰς ὑμᾶς). This particular prepositional phrase is a bit awkward with the verb "I will give," since the more natural and expected way to refer to the recipients of God's gift of the Spirit would be to use either the dative of indirect object (ὑμῖν: "to you") or the preposition "in" with the dative (note the prepositional phrase ἐν ὑμῖν in Ezek 36:26, 27).[18] But as Fee observes:

> This unusual usage [εἰς ὑμᾶς instead of the expected ὑμῖν or ἐν ὑμῖν] is most likely an intentional echo on Paul's part of the Septuagint of Ezekiel 37:6 and 14 ('I will give my Spirit into you'), which probably means something like, 'I will *put* my Spirit in you.' This usage reflects a Pauline understanding of the gift of the Spirit as the fulfillment of Old Testament promises that God's own Spirit will come to indwell his people.[19]

Paul does not follow Ezek 37:6 and 14 exactly, however: he changes the future indicative "I will give" (δώσω) to a present participle (διδόντα). While the gift of God's Spirit was for Ezekiel and other OT prophets a future hope, for Paul this has become a present reality.[20]

Paul's echo or "near citation"[21] of Ezek 36:6 and 14 in the final phrase of 4:3–8 sheds light on the theological framework by which the apostle issues in this paragraph his exhortations to holiness in sexual conduct. Paul interprets what God has done among these former pagans in Thessalonica as a fulfillment of the eschatological promises made to Israel. The members of the Thesssalonian congregation, despite being ethnically mainly Gentile, are no longer "Gentiles who do not know God" but now are members of the renewed Israel, the covenant people of God. This new privileged status means that their sexual behavior must no longer be characterized by "uncleanness" (4:7) but by the standard of holiness that the new covenant marks out for them. This new privileged status also means that they are the recipients of God's gift of his Spirit, and because the essential character of that divine spirit is "holy," the present and ongoing working of God's Holy Spirit will equip them to live according to the standard of holiness that ought to set God's covenant people apart from the rest of humanity.

## "GOD-TAUGHT" (1 THESSALONIANS 4:9B)

The fourth OT allusion in 1 Thess 4:1–12 which helpfully reveals Paul's theological framework in the ethical exhortations of this passage is found in the apostle's use, or perhaps even invention, of the striking term "God-taught" in 4:9b. The first half of 4:9 marks the shift away from the topic of holiness in sexual conduct (vv. 3–8) to the new topic of φιλαδελφία (vv. 9–12)—a topic that, as noted above, can likely be traced back in Paul's thinking ultimately to Lev 19:18. The second half of 4:9 provides the reason for the superfluous nature of the apostle writing to the Thessalonian church about this topic: "For you yourselves are taught by God (θεοδίδακτοι) to love one another." The term θεοδίδακτοι, a passive verbal adjective meaning "God-taught," is indeed striking, since this is the first time the term appears in any extant Greek text— a fact that leads many commentators to conclude that the term was likely coined by Paul himself.[22] The absence of the term anywhere else in the NT and only rarely in later Christian literature strengthens the remarkable nature of this compound word.[23]

Although a number of diverse proposals have been forwarded as to the origin and significance of this term,[24] the majority opinion is that Paul's use or invention of θεοδίδακτοι involves an allusion—"a shorthand reference"[25]—to Isa 54:13 LXX: "And I will cause all your sons to be taught of

God (διδακτοὺς θεοῦ)." That the apostle is familiar with this chapter from Isaiah is confirmed by his explicit citation of the opening verse of Isa 54 in his earlier letter to the Galatians.[26] The context of Isa 54 involves a variety of future blessings that the Lord will bestow to his covenant people who are currently suffering under exile in Babylonia. One of these eschatological blessings is that God will live so intimately in and among his people through his Spirit that they will no longer need to be taught by human intermediaries but will instead be "taught of God."

This end-time promise of divine instruction occurs elsewhere in texts from the OT, Second Temple Judaism and the NT, and so it was a more widely held expectation than commentators typically recognize.[27] Jeremiah similarly describes one of the key blessings of the future "new" covenant as a time when God will write his law on the hearts of his people such that "no longer will they teach their neighbor, or say to one another, 'Know the Lord,' because they will all know me, from the least of them to the greatest" (Jer 31:33–34 [38:31–34 LXX]). Isaiah describes a future age when the nations of the earth will come to Mount Zion and the temple of God to receive divine instruction: "He [God] will teach us his ways, so that we may walk in his paths" (Isa 2:3). The fact that Isaiah's vision of 2:2–4 is repeated almost verbatim in the later prophecy of Micah (Mic 4:1–3) reflects the widespread expectation for divine instruction as an end-time blessing enjoyed by God's people. This eschatological hope reappears yet again in Psalms of Solomon 17:32, which identifies the coming king who will rule in the messianic age as one who is "taught by God" (διδακτὸς ὑπὸ θεοῦ). The end-time promise of divine teaching may lie behind Paul's claim to the Corinthians that the instruction he and his fellow missionaries shared with them was "not in words taught us by human wisdom but in words taught by the Spirit" (1 Cor 2:13). The Gospel of John records Jesus's explicit citation of Isaiah 54:13: "It is written in the prophets, 'They will all be taught by God'" (John 6:45)—a claim that the messianic age has now come and that, in fulfillment of Isaiah's prophecy, God is now teaching his people directly through Jesus. The eschatological blessing of divine instruction also likely lies behind the assertion of 1 John 2:27 that, due to the enlightening work of the Holy Spirit, "you do not need anyone to teach you" and that "his [the Spirit's] anointing teaches you all things" (note also the earlier words of 1 John 2:20).

The significance of the term "God-taught," therefore, should no longer be missed: Paul is alluding in this striking word either specifically to Isa 54:13 or more generally to the widespread expectation of divine instruction as an eschatological blessing. The fact that this OT allusion occurs immediately after Paul's echo or "near citation" of Ezekiel's description of the gift of God's Spirit in the messianic age suggests that here too the apostle views the Thessalonians' practice of φιλαδελφία, or mutual love, as an end-time blessing of God's covenant people.[28] Though this eschatological gift of divine teaching was originally intended primarily for Israel (but see the reference to "all nations" in Isa 2:2 and "many nations" in Mic 4:2), Paul believes that it extends also to the predominantly Gentile Christians in Thessalonica. His use of the term "God-taught," therefore, provides further evidence for the main assertion of this chapter; namely, Paul's exhortations in 1 Thess 4:1–12 are grounded in his conviction that the Gentile Jesus-followers in Thessalonica are included in the renewed Israel, the eschatological people of God who enjoy both the blessings and challenges of that privileged relationship.

## CONCLUSION

Paul professed to have great flexibility in his missionary preaching and practice in order to win converts to the gospel (1 Cor 9:19–23). But even though the apostle apparently "became like one not having the law" so as to establish the predominantly Gentile church of Thessalonica, he did not completely abandon his Jewish heritage. The ongoing influence of the OT writings on Paul's thought as a Jesus-follower can be seen in his ethical exhortations in 1 Thess 4:1–12. The apostle's appeal for the Thessalonian believers to walk in a way that pleases God (vv. 1–2) by being holy in their sexual conduct (vv. 3–8) and by demonstrating love for others (vv. 9–12) is not grounded in pagan philosophical thought but in the OT writings. This passage contains several OT allusions that reveal not only his indebtedness to the Jewish scriptures but also an important theological conviction about the way in which Paul views his Thessalonian readers and the perspective from which he issues to them his exhortations. The apostle interprets what God has done among former pagans in Thessalonica as a fulfillment of the eschatological promises made to Israel. The majority of the Thesssalonian congregation, despite being ethnically Gentile, are no longer "Gentiles who do not know God" but now are members of the renewed Israel, the covenant people of God. This new privileged status means that their conduct—whether in matters of sexual activity or demonstrating love for others or, it can be concluded, any other behaviors—ought to be characterized by the standard of holiness that the new covenant marks out for them. This new privileged status also means that they are the recipients of God's gift of his Spirit, and because the essential character of that divine spirit is "holy," the present and ongoing working of God's Holy Spirit will equip them to live according to the standard of holiness that ought to set God's covenant people apart from the rest of humanity. This new privileged status further means that they are "God-taught"—they have received divine instruction which reliably and authoritatively gives these former pagan worshippers all that they need to know to live in a manner that pleases "the living and true God" (1:9).

## NOTES

1. Wayne A. Meeks, *The Moral World of the First Christians* (Philadelphia: Westminster Press, 1986), 127. Meeks similarly states: "All through Paul's letter [1 Thessalonians] there are elements, including even its general form, which are typical of pagan moral rhetoric" (p. 126); "The specific moral expectations that Paul expresses, of the sort that one could state as moral rules, are hardly different from those widely accepted as 'decent' in Greco-Roman society" (p. 128).

2. All the translations in this chapter, unless noted otherwise, are mine.

3. Gerhard Delling, "παραλαμβάνω," *TDNT*, 4:11–12.

4. See, e.g., William D. Davies, *Paul and Rabbinic Judaism* (London: SPCK, 1948), 247–50; Birger Gerhardsson, *Memory and Manuscript: Oral and Written Transmission in Rabbinic Judaism and Early Christianity*, trans. E. J. Sharpe; ASNU 22 (Uppsala: Gleerup, 1961) 265, 290–96.

5. So, e.g., George P. Carras, "Jewish Ethics and Gentile Converts: Remarks on 1 Thess 4,3–8," in *The Thessalonian Correspondence*, ed. Raymond F. Collins (Leuven: Leuven University Press, 1990) 306–7; Brian S. Rosner, "Seven Questions for Paul's Ethics: 1 Thessalonians 4:1–12 as a Case Study," in *Understanding Paul's Ethics. Twentieth Century Approaches*, ed. Brian S. Rosner (Grand Rapids: Eerdmans, 1995), 351–60, here 352–53. The metaphorical meaning of "walk" also occurs in nonbiblical Greek writings, but with much less frequency and normally with a different verb—πορεύομαι instead of περιπατέω: Heinrich Seesemann, *TDNT*, 5:940–45; Joseph O. Holloway, *Peripateō as a Thematic Marker for Pauline Ethics* (San Francisco: Mellen Research University Press, 1992), 1–27.

6. The subsequent discussion of these four additional OT allusions draws heavily from some of my previous publications that involve an analysis of 1 Thessalonians 4:1–12: see Jeffrey A. D. Weima, "'How You Must Walk to Please God': Holiness and Discipleship in 1 Thessalonians," in *Patterns of Discipleship in the New Testament,* ed. Richard N. Longenecker (Grand Rapids: Eerdmans, 1996), 98–119, esp. 101–3; Jeffrey A. D. Weima, "1–2 Thessalonians," in *Commentary on the New Testament Use of the Old Testament*, ed. Greg K. Beale and Donald A. Carson (Grand Rapids: Baker Academic, 2007), 876–80; Jeffrey A. D. Weima, *1–2 Thessalonians*, BECNT (Grand Rapids: Baker Academic, 2016), 246–300, esp. 264–66, 273–74, 280–83, 286–89.

7. Norman H. Snaith, *The Distinctive Ideas of the Old Testament* (New York: Schocken, 1944), 24–32.

8. Frank Thielman, *Paul & the Law. A Contextual Approach* (Downers Grove, IL: IVP Academic, 1994), 75.

9. Robert Hodgson Jr., "1 Thess 4:1–12 and the Holiness Tradition (HT)," *SBL 1982 Seminar Papers*, ed. Keith H. Richards, *SBL Seminar Papers* 21 (Chico, CA: Scholars Press, 1982), 199–215.

10. Ernest Best, *A Commentary of the First and Second Epistles to the Thessalonians* (London: Black, 1977): "There are good *a priori* grounds for accepting the idea of the presence in the early church of moral exhortation based on 'holiness' as a central concept and derived ultimately from the O.T. holiness code" (p. 179). See also Timothy A. Brookins, *First and Second Thessalonians* (Grand Rapids: Baker Academic, 2021): "For this reason, it has often been suggested that the background for 1 Thess. 4:3–8 is the holiness codes of the OT" (p. 86).

11. Richard B. Hays, "Crucified with Christ: A Synthesis of the Theology of 1 and 2 Thessalonians, Philemon, Philippians, and Galatians," in *Pauline Theology I: Thessalonians, Philippians, Galatians, Ephesians*, ed. Jouette M. Bassler (Philadelphia: Fortress, 1991), 227–46, here 235–36.

12. The precise meaning of the second command in 4:4 is, of course, one of the most disputed issues in the Thessalonian letters. For a full discussion and evaluation of the three possible interpretations, see Weima, *1–2 Thessalonians*, 267–72.

13. T. J. Deidun, *New Covenant Morality in Paul*, AnBib 89 (Rome: Biblical Institute Press, 1981), 19n61.

14. Nijay K. Gupta, *1–2 Thessalonians* (Eugene, OR: Cascade, 2016), 82. Note also the observation of Deidun (*New Covenant Morality*, 62): "That Paul should place the Thessalonian Christians (themselves ἔθνη, cf. 2,14; cf. Rm. 11,13) in antithesis to τὰ ἔθνη is incomprehensible *except* in the light of their self-understanding as God's People, true Israel."

15. Gordon D. Fee, *The First and Second Letters to the Thessalonians* (Grand Rapids: Eerdmans, 2009), 153.

16. Thielman (*Paul and the Law*, 76) notes: "No prophet understood better than Ezekiel the failure of God's people to follow the standards of purity found in Leviticus, and no prophet looked more hopefully to the eschatological day when God would, by a powerful movement of his Spirit, restore the purity and sanctity of his people."

17. Note the change in the prepositional phrase from "in you" (ἐν ὑμῖν) in 36:27 to "into you" (εἰς ὑμᾶς) in 37:6, 14—the latter of which is also found in Paul's statement in 4:8b. The significance of the prepositional phrase "into you" will be highlighted below.

18. James E. Frame notes the following about the prepositional phrase: "The εἰς is for dative or for ἐν"; *A Critical and Exegetical Commentary on the Epistles of St. Paul to the Thessalonians*, ICC (Edinburgh: T&T Clark, 1912), 156.

19. Fee, *Thessalonians*, 154.

20. The present tense of the participle does not technically convey present time but rather stresses the ongoing nature of the action: "God who indeed *continues to give* his Spirit, who is holy, into you." Nevertheless, the change from the future form in Ezek 37:6 and 14 (also twice in 36:25–27), as well as the context (Paul is referring to his readers' present experience of God's Holy Spirit), supports seeing this as an action occurring in the present.

21. The closeness of the parallel between Paul's words in 4:8b and Ezekiel 36:27 and/or 37:7, 14 causes Deidun to find here not just an "allusion" but a "near citation"; *New Covenant Morality*, 19.

22. See esp. Stephen E. Witmer, "θεοδίδακτοι in 1 Thessalonians 4.9: A Pauline Neologism," *NTS* 52 (2006): 239–50.

23. Most of the few occurrences of θεοδίδακτοι in later Christian literature involve references to 1 Thess 4:9: Barn. 21.6; Athenagoras, *Leg.* 11, 32; Theophilus, *Autol.* 2.9; Tatian, *Or.* 29; Clement of Alexandria, *Paed.* 1.6.27; 1.20.98; 2.11.48; 2.18.84; 6.18.166; *Quis div.* 20.2.

24. For a synopsis and evaluation of four alternative explanations of Paul's intended meaning or use of the term "God-taught," see Weima, *1–2 Thessalonians*, 286–88.

25. Gary S. Shogren, *1 & 2 Thessalonians* (Grand Rapids: Zondervan, 2012), 168.

26. Paul does not merely allude to but explicitly cites Isa 54:1 in Gal 4:27. Paul's letters as a whole contain some twenty-seven citations of Isaiah, involving thirty-two different verses from this OT prophecy; Douglas A. Oss, "A Note on Paul's Use of Isaiah," *BBR* 2 (1992): 105–12, here 105n1.

27. An important exception is Stephen E. Witmer, *Divine Instruction in Early Christianity*, WUNT 2/246 (Tübingen: Mohr Siebeck, 2008).

28. Deidun emphasizes the point that the *combination* of the two prophetic texts of Jer 31:34 (38:34 LXX) and Ezek 37:14 (also 36:27) "is widely attested in Jewish tradition in contexts concerning messianic times, and with particular reference to the immediacy of God's teaching"; *New Covenant Morality*, 20.

# BIBLIOGRAPHY

Best, Ernest. *A Commentary of the First and Second Epistles to the Thessalonians.* London: Black, 1977.

Brookins, Timothy A. *First and Second Thessalonians.* Grand Rapids: Baker Academic, 2021.

Carras, George P. "Jewish Ethics and Gentile Converts: Remarks on 1 Thess 4,3–8." In *The Thessalonian Correspondence*, edited by R. F. Collins, 306–15. Leuven: Leuven University Press, 1990.

Davies, William D. *Paul and Rabbinic Judaism.* London: SPCK, 1948.

Deidun, T. J. *New Covenant Morality in Paul.* AnBib 89. Rome: Biblical Institute Press, 1981.

Fee, Gordon D. *The First and Second Letters to the Thessalonians.* Grand Rapids: Eerdmans, 2009.

Frame, James E. *A Critical and Exegetical Commentary on the Epistles of St. Paul to the Thessalonians.* Edinburgh: T&T Clark, 1912.

Gerhardsson, Birger. *Memory and Manuscript: Oral and Written Transmission in Rabbinic Judaism and Early Christianity.* Translated by E. J. Sharpe. ASNU 22. Uppsala: Gleerup, 1961.

Gupta, Nijay K. *1–2 Thessalonians.* Eugene, OR: Cascade, 2016.

Hays, Richard B. "Crucified with Christ: A Synthesis of the Theology of 1 and 2 Thessalonians, Philemon, Philippians, and Galatians." In *Pauline Theology I: Thessalonians, Philippians, Galatians, Ephesians*, edited by J. M. Bassler, 227–46. Philadelphia: Fortress, 1991.

Hodgson, Robert, Jr. "1 Thess 4:1–12 and the Holiness Tradition (HT)." In *SBL 1982 Seminar Papers*, edited by K. H. Richards, 199–215. *SBL Seminar Papers* 21. Chico, CA: Scholars Press, 1982.

Holloway, Joseph O. *Peripateō as a Thematic Marker for Pauline Ethics.* San Francisco: Mellen Research University Press, 1992.

Meeks, Wayne A. *The Moral World of the First Christians.* Philadelphia: Westminster Press, 1986.

Oss, Douglas A. "A Note on Paul's Use of Isaiah." *BBR* 2 (1992): 105–12.

Rosner, Brian S. "Seven Questions for Paul's Ethics. 1 Thessalonians 4:1–12 as a Case Study." In *Understanding Paul's Ethics. Twentieth Century Approaches*, edited by B. S. Rosner, 351–60. Grand Rapids: Eerdmans, 1995.

Shogren, Gary S. *1 & 2 Thessalonians.* Grand Rapids: Zondervan, 2012.

Snaith, Norman H. *The Distinctive Ideas of the Old Testament.* New York: Schocken, 1944.

Thielman, Frank. *Paul & the Law. A Contextual Approach.* Downers Grove, IL: IVP Academic, 1994.

Weima, Jeffrey A. D. "'How You Must Walk to Please God': Holiness and Discipleship in 1 Thessalonians." In *Patterns of Discipleship in the New Testament*, edited by R. N. Longenecker, 98–119. Grand Rapids: Eerdmans, 1996.

———. "1–2 Thessalonians." In *Commentary on the New Testament Use of the Old Testament*, edited by G. K. Beale and D. A. Carson, 871–89. Grand Rapids: Baker Academic, 2007.

———. *1–2 Thessalonians.* BECNT. Grand Rapids: Baker Academic, 2016.

Witmer, Stephen E. "θεοδίδακτοι in 1 Thessalonians 4.9: A Pauline Neologism," *NTS* 52 (2006): 239–50.

———. *Divine Instruction in Early Christianity.* WUNT 2/246. Tübingen: Mohr Siebeck, 2008.

*Chapter 12*

# Called to Consecration

*Jewish Holiness, Roman Piety, and Moral Discourse in 1 Thessalonians*

## Nijay K. Gupta

"No writer writes alone." That sentiment reflects the fact that writing normally involves a network in conversation, learning from and leaving a mark on each other. I have experienced that as a writer, and it is clearly true for the Apostle Paul as well. Throughout the majority of his letters, he leaves "hyperlinks," which connect his ideas to that of others, intertextual crossing points that bring pleosemantic value to the conversation. Occasionally, Paul will reference the Jesus tradition and popular sayings in culture. But in the majority of cases, when he adds a textual "hyperlink," he appeals to Scripture, grounding key arguments in the sacred Jewish tradition. Galatians 3:8 is illuminating for how Paul viewed the Word of God as an entity worth acknowledging: "Scripture foresaw that God would justify the Gentiles by faith, and announced the gospel in advance to Abraham."[1] Here Scripture is personified, interfacing with God, showing independent intuition, and speaking of its own voice, as if some kind of sentient being. For all intents and purposes, Scripture was alive to Paul, a heavenly organism given to humanity to offer insight, to guide the way. It is no surprise, then, that Paul would quote Scripture as support and illumination for his understanding of the gospel and its mission. What *is* surprising is that in some letters, like Galatians, we find a flurry of explicit and extended Scripture quotations, and in other letters we don't find explicit citation at all. This is a much studied phenomenon, many a monograph has been written on Paul's use and non-use of Scripture.[2] This book series (and the seminar on which it is based) is devoted to just these sorts of issues.

What can we say about Paul's first letter to the Thessalonians? The natural thing to do—which I will *not* do—is to scratch around 1 Thessalonians looking for fragments of Scripture, discerning "echoes and allusions." That work has been done, and I don't have anything interesting to add to that. Echoes of Scripture are all over the place in Paul; that does not resolve the question of why there are no explicit citations in this case, and I am not sure a whole lot is achieved in the end by collecting a dozen faint echoes here and there, except to satisfy a bit of academic curiosity. So, I want to propose a different approach to the question of Scripture and 1 Thessalonians. Rather than looking for verbatim strings, long or short, I want to reflect on something a bit more obvious, and yet underexplored: *where do we see in 1 Thessalonians Jewish religious discourse clearly influenced by the Septuagint, and how would that have been processed and received by Romanized Thessalonians?*[3] Put another way, what are the most *obvious* indicators that 1 Thessalonians was written by a Jewish writer who thought and wrote in a distinctly Jewish way? How do these Jewish distinctives intersect with, inform, and perhaps even provoke non-Jewish (specifically Romanized) readers?[4]

As I have analyzed 1 Thessalonians over the last decade or so, probably the most consistently and strikingly *Jewish* feature is Hebraic piety language.[5] When Paul frames life in terms of ἁγιασμός, he was drawing primarily from Hellenistic Jewish religious discourse about a life devoted to God, a life of consecration. Romans were as "pious" as Jews and Christians (in their own minds), but in a different way. They too believed in the fundamental importance of devotion—in Latin, *pietas*, in Greek, εὐσέβεια, but they meant something very specific. Part of Paul's responsibility as apostle to the Gentiles was catechizing his churches into a *Jewish* framework of religion, devotion, and holiness, with Jesus at the center. What a pagan-turned-Jesus-follower would come away with when reading 1 Thessalonians was a whole new way of looking at how to honor the Divine, a distinctively *Jewish* way. That Greek Scripture would have played an essential formative role in how Paul articulates this will become obvious.

Before we jump into Roman versus Jewish piety discourse, it is important to address the noticeable absence of Scripture citations in 1 Thessalonians. We will do this only in a brief and cursory way, but it should be addressed nonetheless.

## THE QUESTION OF SCRIPTURE CITATIONS IN PAUL

Paul cites Scripture verbatim and explicitly over one hundred times in his letters.[6] If we take Galatians and 1 Thessalonians as written relatively close in time (e.g., a few years apart), as many scholars assume, the difference between them is striking in terms of explicit reference to Scripture. Galatians 3 and 4 are basically Paul's eschatological Messianic interpretation of key passages from the Pentateuch, with a special focus on Abraham. Whether or not the Galatian recipients of the letter could comprehend his Scriptural reasoning is unclear—we moderns have a hard time following Paul, even with Accordance Bible Software open.[7] Audience comprehensibility aside, the stark contrast between the flood of quotations in Galatians and the entire lack of explicit citation in 1 Thessalonians is remarkable, or at least striking to anyone holding both letters side-by-side.[8] One might be tempted to think that these are two different authors. Of course, 1 Thessalonians, as much as Galatians, reflects a writer whose mind was saturated in Jewish Scripture. Hans Hübner offers extensive analysis of echoes of Scripture in 1 Thessalonians in his *Corpus Paulinum.*[9] Jeffrey Weima also presents careful analysis in his section on this letter in the *Commentary on the New Testament Use of the Old Testament.*[10] The formative role of Scripture on Paul's thought is not in question. What is more relevant and profitable is considering the question of why he uses explicit quotes in some texts and not others. In a 1993 essay evaluating Richard Hays's "echoes" approach to Paul, J. C. Beker critiqued Hays for treating Paul's letters indiscriminately. Beker accused Hays of erasing clear differences between letters, prioritizing "coherence" at the cost of letter-specific "contingency." In the end, Beker reasons, Hays cannot explain why Paul quotes Scripture in some letters and not others, if Hays sees Scriptural echoes everywhere. Alternatively, Beker asserts that *not* quoting Scripture verbatim was probably Paul's normal mode of discourse, and then Paul chose to include Scriptural quotations *only* when the circumstances deemed it necessary—for example, when engaging in polemics with opponents or giving a teaching requiring Scriptural support.[11] That doesn't tie up all loose ends of the conversation, but it does shed some light. The two main letters where we find no explicit Scriptural citations—1 Thessalonians and Philippians—are warm in tone, encouraging in approach, and are not written specifically to engage false teaching.[12]

## PAUL'S ἍΓΙΟΣ LANGUAGE IN 1 THESSALONIANS

Now, let us turn back to 1 Thessalonians and look at Paul's written discourse more carefully and specifically. The first two chapters of this letter are relational, the very kinds of things you read in ancient personal letters—salutations and warm greetings, words of thanks and praise, and sometimes even explanations and self-defensive statements as we read in 2:1–12. It is not until 3:11–13. that we start to see more distinctive, direct, and continuous religious teaching and instruction from Paul. In 3:12–13, Paul exhorts them, ὑμᾶς δὲ ὁ κύριος πλεονάσαι καὶ περισσεύσαι τῇ ἀγάπῃ εἰς ἀλλήλους καὶ εἰς πάντας, καθάπερ καὶ ἡμεῖς εἰς ὑμᾶς, ¹³ εἰς τὸ στηρίξαι ὑμῶν τὰς καρδίας ἀμέμπτους ἐν *ἁγιωσύνῃ* ἔμπροσθεν τοῦ θεοῦ καὶ πατρὸς ἡμῶν ἐν τῇ παρουσίᾳ τοῦ κυρίου ἡμῶν Ἰησοῦ μετὰ πάντων τῶν ἁγίων αὐτοῦ.

Now, may the Lord multiply and overflow love that you show to each other and everyone else, just as we to you; this love is part of the Lord's plan to give you strong hearts that are blameless and *holy* before our God and Father in view of the appearance or our Lord Jesus along with all the holy ones.¹³

As the first bit of "liturgy" in the letter, you might say, there would be a lot here that Romans would find odd or out of place in religious discourse. *Love? Hearts?* But the most distinctive language, I think, would be ἁγιωσύνη (and any other term that is part of the ἅγιος word family, which appear frequently throughout 1–2 Thessalonians). It is not that Romans did not have a sense of the sacred. They were constantly and keenly aware of the need to honor the divine and maintain the *pax deorum* (peace with the gods). But what is notable is that Paul was preferencing this *specific* terminology (ἅγιος). According to an important study by Ralph Bruckner and Martin Vahrenhorst in the *Historical and Theological Lexicon of the Septuagint*, ἅγιος was rarely used in Greek literature before and outside of Hellenistic Jewish texts.¹⁴ Pagan texts—and by "pagan" I simply mean non-Jewish/non-Christian— much preferred forms of ὅσιος and ἱερός when writers wanted to talk about sacred places, objects, rituals, and events. When it comes to religious purity and purification, pagan texts defaulted to ἁγνός language. It is really with the Septuagint that we start to see ἅγιος used as a dominant cultic term by a particular group. This would be an intentional choice on the part of the authors of the Septuagint, since ἅγιος language does not appear at all in Homer, Hesiod, or the Greek tragedians. In contrast, the ἅγιος word group appears over a thousand times in the Septuagint, and this verbal preference left a clear impact on Hellenistic Jewish literature more broadly as a result. Put simply, when Jews wanted to talk about religion, purity, and the sacred, they were going to use ἅγιος language as their default or preferred terminology.¹⁵

In the Septuagint, what exactly does ἅγιος mean? It is obvious that this terminology relates to proximity to the divine (LXX Exod 19:22; Sir 36:12), but more can be said. Bruckner and Vahrenhorst point to occasions where ἅγιος is paired with ἀφορίζω, identifying holiness with separation, set apart from what is common or profane, and dedicated to divine service (LXX Exod 19:23; 29:27).¹⁶ In Jewish Scripture, it is not only the priests who are holy to God, but the whole nation, dedicated to reflecting and representing the Holy God in the world (LXX Exod 19:6; Deut 28:9; Isa 62:12; 63:18; Wis 10:15, 17; 2 Macc 15:24; 3 Macc 2:6). It is interesting to note that, while the verb ἁγιάζω is found commonly through the LXX (including the so-called OT Apocrypha), the OT Pseudepigrapha, and Philo, it is not found at all in Josephus.[17] This is not because Josephus was less of a Jewish thinker; rather, Bruckner and Vahrenhorst are right to assume that Josephus was sensitive to his non-Jewish readers, translating his historical study of the Jewish people into language and idiom that would make sense to pagans.

As we turn to the New Testament, there is no question that this same ἅγιος preference is present, reflecting the impact of the Septuagint on the apostolic writers and Evangelists. As we consider Paul, ἅγιος appears everywhere in his letters, not least in his very frequent reference to τὸ πνεῦμα τὸ ἅγιον and to the people of God as ἅγιοι. In 1 Thessalonians Paul makes a number of statements affirming the status of believers as "holy people," and also the need to grow in holiness. How can this be? How can Paul call believers to be holy when he also says they are already holy? I have heard a sports analogy that may offer some insight, despite the natural limitations of parallels or metaphors: imagine a rookie recruited to play for a premier team. In one sense, they are truly and fully part of that team—they wear the exact same jersey as the rest, including the veterans. At the same time, these rookies are called and urged to live up to the high expectations of the team. In one sense (team status), everyone is the same and has the same privileges and access to coaching, training, and resources; in another sense, clearly team members are different in capability and experience.[18] However we choose to explain this phenomenon, there was a sense of "already-not yet" when it came to holiness for Paul. *Already* set apart for God because of Jesus Christ, and *not yet* fully sanctified as a process continues on. Time and again, then, Paul calls believers to *consecration*, committing their whole selves, mind, heart, soul, and body, to be fully devoted to God. This would have been an unusual way of looking at piety and devotion for Romans (we will return to Roman piety in a moment). Thus, Paul's repeated ἅγιος commands and affirmations would be noteworthy. Here is how this looks in 1 Thessalonians.

> Now, may the Lord multiply and overflow love that you show to each other and everyone else, just as we to you; this love is part of the Lord's plan to give you strong hearts that are blameless and holy (ἁγιωσύνῃ) before our God and Father in view of the appearance or our Lord Jesus along with all the holy ones. (3:12–13, as quoted already above)[19]

> For this is God's will, your full consecration, requiring a great distance between you and sexual impurity. Each one of you ought to know how to control your "vessel" (i.e., your body) with holiness (ἁγιασμῷ) and respectability. (4:3–4)

For God did not call us to be impure, but instead to be fully consecrated (ἐν ἁγιασμῷ). So, whoever rejects this teaching is not rejecting human instruction, but the very God who gives his Holy Spirit to you. (4:7–8)

Now, may the God of peace himself make you completely holy (ἁγιάσαι), and each part of you—spirit, soul, and body—kept blameless in view of the appearance of our Lord Jesus Christ. (5:23)

Greet all the brothers and sisters with a holy kiss (φιλήματι ἁγίῳ). (5:26)

For Paul, there was an urgent and important need for believers to live blameless and holy lives in the pursuit of honoring and pleasing God. This is expressed in terms of perfection and purity, not because God has impossibly high standards, but because from a Jewish perspective those who are holy must live in a certain way in the presence of a holy God. And because God is everywhere—and inside through the Holy Spirit—then there is nowhere where this human holiness can be neglected. Believers are called to maintain a state of consecration to God, and all the more in view of the coming judgment of the Lord Jesus Christ.


## ROMAN *PIETAS*

The average Roman did not think or talk in terms of "holiness" (*sanctificatio*) the way that Jews did. They might have used that language occasionally in relation to sacred rituals, locations, and religious traditions. But when it came to the religious commitments of the regular individual, Romans more commonly referred to *pietas*. This was a crucially important virtue and commitment in Roman society, but hard to sum up in brief. It did not mean *only* religious activity like praying or oath-making. As a virtue, it first and foremost reflected a strong sense of duty and commitment. And in its most ancient usage, it was not assumed that it was directed to the gods. It was more so a general reinforcement of the stratified nature of Roman society, where everyone had someone they report to, a superior, and many had subordinates; *pietas* was about doing right by those above as well as those below. *Pietas* toward someone above you means obedience and service without question or competition. Toward inferiors and subservients, it means attention and concern.

In its earliest usage amongst Romans, *pietas* was employed in a family context (see table 12.1).[20] In fact, traces of this are reflected in a famous statement by Cicero: "The part of virtue displayed in society is called justice (*iustutia*), and that manifested towards the gods religion (*religio*), towards parents piety

**Table 12.1: Roman *Pietas* in Relationship**

| Pietas from | Pietas toward | Reference |
|---|---|---|
| Child | Father | Vergil, *Aeneid* 3.480 |
| Slave | Master | Ovid, *Metamorphoses* 1.204 |
| Child | Mother | Cicero, *Tusc.* 1.113 |
| Brother | Brother | Ovid *Met.* 9.460 |
| Spouse | Spouse | Ovid *Met.* 6.635 |
| Parents | Children | Ovid *Met.* 6.629 |
| Client | Patron | CIL VI 1.200; CIL VI 1.089 |

(*pietas*), or in general goodness, in matters of trust good faith, in moderating punishment mercy, in benevolence friendliness" (*Part. or.*, 22.78).[21]

Though Cicero categorizes *pietas* here as a family virtue, elsewhere he calls it "the foundation of all virtues" (*fundamentum est omnium virtutum*; *Planc.* 29).[22] Therefore, it could be the driving commitment to honor the gods and preserve the *pax deorum*.[23] Seneca, similar to Cicero, writes that "nothing is greater than true piety" (*nulla vis maior pietate vera est: Thy.* 549).[24] It includes fidelity to the gods but functions as an all-encompassing call for each Roman to find their place in the community, wherever their place is in the chain of command: "Roman piety unites in one whole, reverence for the gods, devotion to the Emperor, affection between the Augusti or between the Augustus and the people, tenderness of parents to sons, respect or affectionate care of the latter for their parents, and in general, love of one's neighbor, or in one word 'Religion.'"[25]

Historians of the Roman world are in agreement that Virgil was formative for conceptions of *pietas* as it shifted toward devotion to the Roman gods, and especially to Caesar as savior of the people and guardian of the state. In the *Aeneid*, Virgil cast a vision, not just for *pietas* as a universal virtue but one tied specifically to Rome. Whereas, in the past, Roman people thought primarily (though not exclusively) in terms of *pietas* toward family, especially parents, now they were shaped to apply their affections to the whole state.[26] Thus, it is no wonder that *pietas* is often paired with *iustitia*, both of these mottos of the Rome state, frequently appearing on coinage and both venerated as attribute-deities in themselves.[27] With the *Aeneid*, we see the hero Aeneas putting nation before self, expressing *pietas* toward the gods who guide his path.

Many scholars detect a shift in Roman moral philosophy over time away from *humanitas* and towards *pietas*. Whereas *humanitas* can be seen as the innate desire to care for other human beings (one might say, an "egalitarian" impulse), *pietas* emphasizes obedience to the will of the gods and reinforces hierarchy. We can see this clearly in Cicero's *On the Nature of the Gods*: "It seems probable to me that if piety towards the gods disappears, also loyalty and the community of the human race—humanity (*humanitas*)—and that particularly excellent virtue, righteousness (*iustitia*), will disappear" (*Nat. d.* 1.2.4).[28] At this time, Cicero almost certainly had in mind Caesar as one such supreme magnate, and as *pontifex maximus*, a key agent of expressing the divine will to the people. The respected historian Hendrik Vagenvoort argues that this new emphasis on piety in the writings of the Roman elite offered a justification for both Roman conquest[29] and the reign of Augustus, a kind of "manifest destiny" principle.[30] Vagenvoort detected propaganda statements that played on the fears of the people, and offered them a hero who would preserve the state, a singular fixation for their *pietas*, a leader to revere and obey to carry them out of a crisis. Cicero's statement in *De Republica* appears to be just this kind of legitimation of focusing *pietas* on an emperor-savior:

> [I]n matters of government there are curious cycles and, as it were, periods of change and vicissitudes. To know these changes is the task of the philosopher, but to see them in the distance while steering the ship of state, when the course can still be regulated and controlled—that is unquestionably the work of a great citizen and a man almost divine (*Rep.* 1.29.45; in the voice of Scipio).[31]

It is time to sum up our brief discussion of Roman *pietas*. Again, it was not a specifically religious term in its original use. It reflected a strong sense of duty to the whole system that exists around oneself, and especially toward parents and family (and by association, then, the gods connected to that system). Over time, *pietas* became more attached to devotion to the Roman state, the Roman gods, and to the emperor.[32] Duty and devotion became intertwined with reflecting the ideals of Romanness and preserving the supremacy of Rome. In the modern era, "piety" has often been conceived as an internal disposition and dynamic, but that probably developed out of Christian theology and spirituality. A distinctly *Roman* understanding of religious piety is a social virtue that may originate from within as devotion to others, but must be manifested in the expression of duty and allegiance, especially to supreme leaders like sovereign men and deities.

## CALLED TO CONSECRATION TO CHRIST

Paul, as with the rest of the New Testament writers, wrote in Greek, so he would not have chosen to use or not use the Latin word *pietas*. We know that the Greek equivalent is εὐσέβεια (and its cognates).[33] This was a common word group in the Hellenistic world in relation to worship and devotion to the gods. We have already noted above that the Septuagint prefers ἅγιος holiness language when it comes to piety, but εὐσέβεια is not absent and reflects the

Hebrew יָרֵא (e.g., Job 1:9; Isa 11:2). Sometimes, it stands for the "pious" in a binary formulation over and against the "wicked." In these cases, "pious" runs parallel to the Hebrew צַדִּיק ("righteous"), as in devout in relationship to the covenant (Isa 24:16).[34] In 4 Maccabees, we see how εὐσέβεια reflects Jewish Torah-oriented piety, using Greek language that would make sense to gentiles. In chapter 5, Eleazar speaks openly to the tyrant Antiochus about Jewish devotion:

> When he had received permission to speak, he began to address the people as follows: "O Antiochus, we who have been persuaded to adopt a way of life in accordance with divine law do not consider any compulsion more powerful than our ready obedience to the law. Therefore we do not deem it right to transgress the law in any way. Even if, as you suppose, our law were in truth not divine and we wrongly considered it to be divine, not even so would it be possible for us to invalidate our reputation for piety (εὐσεβείᾳ). Therefore do not suppose that it would be a petty sin if we were to eat defiling food. To transgress the law in matters small or great is of equal seriousness, for in either case the law is equally despised. You scoff at our philosophy (φιλοσοφίαν) as though our living by it were not sensible. But it teaches us self–control so that we overcome all pleasures and desires, and it also exercises us in courage so that we endure all pain willingly; it trains us in justice so that in all our dealings we act impartially, and it teaches us piety (εὐσέβειαν) so that we worship (σέβειν) the only living God in a way that befits his greatness. (4 Macc 5:16–24 NETS)

When we turn to the New Testament, a couple of patterns are interesting and worth noting. First, εὐσέβεια occurs rarely in the Gospels (σέβω does appear in Matt 15:9/Mark 7:7, quoting LXX Isa 29:13). There are several occurrences in Acts, including references to "devout" persons or "God-fearers," gentiles who had some form of reverence for the God of Israel (e.g., Acts 16:14; 18:7). In general, though, this language was used in generic ways to talk about respect for and devotion to the divine (Acts 18:13; 19:27).

In Paul, in the undisputed letters εὐσέβεια is not found and σεβάζομαι only in Rom 1:25 in reference to idol worship. But in the Pastoral Epistles, there are a dozen occurrences, all in relation to Christian piety and devotion. Now is not the place to explain why this preference for εὐσέβεια in the Pastorals; I will just point to the helpful study by Chris Hoklotubbe.[35] But one thing should be made clear—contrary to most English translations, εὐσέβεια does not mean "godliness." Given our discussion of *pietas* and our brief engagement with εὐσέβεια, this language is about respect, duty, and commitment to the gods, i.e., proper devotion. It is not a character trait per se but an observable loyalty to the divine. This is not about *being* like God—quite the opposite, it is acknowledging that God is God alone and mortals must know their place and role in honoring those who have authority over them.

Turning again to 1 Thessalonians we can appreciate that Romans would notice the absence of the language of εὐσέβεια for religious piety and the preference for ἅγιος language, a Jewish preference at that. What would this have signaled for a Roman? I want to make two suggestions. First, Paul's call to consecration (ἁγιασμός) is connected to his understanding of the Christian body *as* sacred space, and therefore the believer is called to a kind of sacred priesthood. The Septuagint tends to use ἁγιασμός in relationship to the temple and priesthood (LXX Amos 2:11; Sir 7:31; 2 Macc 2:17; 14:36; 3 Macc 2:18). LXX Ezekiel 45:4 is a good example of this—the context involves the vision given to the prophet Ezekiel for the building of a new temple according to a heavenly prototype. In Ezekiel 45, we read:

> From the land, it shall belong to the priests who minister in the holy place, and it shall belong to those who come near to minister to the Lord, and it shall be to them a place for houses set aside for their *consecration*. (Ezek 45:4; adapted from NETS)

> ἀπὸ τῆς γῆς ἔσται τοῖς ἱερεῦσιν τοῖς λειτουργοῦσιν ἐν τῷ ἁγίῳ, καὶ ἔσται τοῖς ἐγγίζουσι λειτουργεῖν τῷ κυρίῳ· καὶ ἔσται αὐτοῖς τόπος εἰς οἴκους ἀφωρισμένους τῷ <u>ἁγιασμῷ</u> αὐτῶν.

When Paul explains to the Thessalonians that God's will is their ἁγιασμός (1 Thess 4:3), this would express a setting apart for unique service to the divine in a sacred place. We have seen how there would be Septuagintal resonances for readers who had some familiarity with Judaism, but for pagans I think that they might have thought of something like the famous Vestal Virgins of Rome. In Roman religion in general, public priests were typically elite men who were intertwined with high Roman politics; they were not called to celibacy or separated from the common community. But the Vestal Virgins were completely cut off from their own *paterfamilias* and required to live with a pure devotion to the goddess Vesta for the sake of protecting Rome, a sacred and serious privilege. According to Plutarch, their virginity reflected the purity and incorruptibility of the eternal sacred fire that they were meant to tend (Plutarch, *Numa* 9.5).

Paul's call for the Thessalonians' holy consecration would have seemed both familiar and strange. Romans understood the concept of personal consecration, but it was meant for very specific people for a limited period of time (even the Vestal Virgins retired after thirty years, after which time they received a pension and could marry, though many chose not to). In 1 Thessalonians, Paul was exhorting all the Thessalonians to a devoted and sacred life, and especially the men who might not fully realize that a calling to please the one God and Lord Jesus Christ includes sexual purity. It is well-known how permissive Greco-Roman culture was when it came to male pursuits of sexual gratification.[36] Wives were expected to turn a blind eye to their husbands going to brothels and gratifying their urges with their slaves. Paul explained that their holy consecration means that Christian men distance themselves from πορνεία, another term that was rarely used in classical texts. In ancient usage, it referred to sex with prostitutes, but with Jewish and Christian usage it was expanded to include a broader category of marital infidelity. A text like the *Testament of the Twelve Patriarchs* uses πορνεία as a general category of sin whereby the person (usually a man) allows themself to be carried away by lust and desire, giving in to pleasure at the cost of respect for God, wife, family, and self.[37] This is very similar to the way Paul uses πορνεία throughout his letters and in 1 Thessalonians. He was reinforcing with the Thessalonian Christians that this consecration to God—of *all* of them, not just a select few—was meant to be applied to all areas of life, including the mastery of sexual desires and protection of the marriage relationship. In 1 Thess 4:4, Paul offers further explanation of what believers are meant to do regarding sexual desire. This verse has generated intense discussion amongst interpreters for many years going back to the Patristic period. Space does not permit a full breakdown of the options and their relative merits and problems; suffice to say I have laid out elsewhere in great detail the state of the discussion and my preference for the σκεῦος ("vessel") as body (or phallus) view.[38] What that means is that Paul was explicating sexual consecration as men knowing how to control their bodies with holiness and honor, not being carried away with their passions and desires as the godless pagans.[39] Many Romans would have felt a sense of superiority and pride in their privilege of forcing themselves upon their slaves, or hiring prostitutes at will. Paul turns their focus to what is pleasing to God, the divine will, which demands purity, as God is holy and pure. Many Romans would have been raised in a world where the gods revel and satisfy their desires at will, and thus humans aim to achieve a status level similar to their freedoms and luxuries. But Jews had long seen God differently, not as a cosmic master whose desires have no limits, but a being of purity, light, and truth, the Holy One of Israel.

## BLAMELESS OFFERINGS

Above we have looked at 1 Thess 4:3–4 in terms of consecration, along the lines of a priest being dedicated to divine service. Jews would have been very familiar with this concept, though obviously not every man was a priest. Romans also had priesthood, though priests in public service were not separated out from the community with purity restrictions; we looked at the case of Rome's Vestal Virgins as much closer to the Jewish concept of priesthood. Now I want to look at a second aspect of how holiness language is used in 1 Thessalonians in a distinctively Jewish way—believers as sacrifice and offerings that are acceptable to the Lord. The two passages this relates to are the parallel wish-prayers (1 Thess 3:11–12; 5:23).

> Now may our God and Father himself and our Lord Jesus direct our way to you. [12] And may the Lord make you increase and abound in love for one another and for all, just as we abound in love for you. [13] And may he so strengthen your hearts in holiness that you may be blameless before our God and Father at the coming of our Lord Jesus with all his saints. (1 Thess 3:11)

> May the God of peace himself sanctify you entirely; and may your spirit and soul and body be kept sound and blameless at the coming of our Lord Jesus Christ. [24] The one who calls you is faithful, and he will do this. (1 Thess 5:23)

Both of these wish-prayers look at the formation of believers with a view toward a moment of judgment of inspection at the coming of the Lord Jesus Christ. The language of "sound/whole" and "blameless" has a ring of the perfect form of an animal sacrifice, i.e., without blemish. According to Romans 15:15–16, Paul conceived of his apostolic mission as a kind of "priestly" (ἱερουργοῦντα) ministry, whereby he was responsible for ensuring that "the offering of the gentiles (ἡ προσφορὰ τῶν ἐθνῶν) may be acceptable (ἡγιασμένη), sanctified by the Holy Spirit." So, in light of this, it makes good sense that Paul would pray that God himself would purify these Galatian gentiles.

Now, in the Septuagint, this term for "blameless" (ἀμέμπτως) was not used for sacrifices. When applied to animal offerings, the language of ἀμώμος ("spotless") was preferred (e.g., LXX Exod 19:21). But this term (ἀμώμος) could be applied to, not just physical defects, but moral problems as well—like sacrificing goods that one obtained through cheating or stealing (Sir 34:21). In early Christian tradition, the self-sacrifice of Jesus is portrayed as a perfect, "unblemished" (ἀμώμος; 1 Pet 1:19; Heb 9:14; Eph 5:27; Phil 2:15), offering. "Blameless" (ἀμέμπτως) is, then, a similar image, a morally pure life given over to God. Philo of Alexandria uses ἀμέμπτος in reference to Cain's mistaken assumption that he offered to the Lord "blameless sacrifices" (θυσίας ἀμέμπτους; *Agr.* 127).

Romans probably would have picked up on and understood the metaphor of sacrifice here (1 Thess 5:23); what was new to their conception of religion would be this notion Paul presents of inward holiness, not just bodily purity; Paul was indicating a consecration and purity that included inner soul and spirit. Few Romans made much of inner purity before God, though this was sometimes a conversation point among moral philosophers.[40] The average Roman understood *pietas* primarily through a social and political lens of duty. The master virtue behind exercise of duty is *fides*, loyalty. And things like war, violence, and revenge could be justified by *pietas*, as is found in many cases in Roman texts. According to the *Aeneid*, the general Marcellus is praised for his heroism: "Alas for goodness (*pietas*), alas for chivalrous honor, and his sword arm unconquerable in the fight!" (6.880).[41] Marcellus fights for Rome with praiseworthy *piety*. Similarly, in Ovid's *Fasti*, Augustus's vengeance against the murderer of his father is praised as *pietas*, the fruit of fidelity and necessity of duty in warfare (*Fasti* 3.707–10).

In contradistinction, Paul directs holiness toward what is pleasing to *this* God, the God of Israel. This requires inner purity and social respect that often defies Roman power systems. Lustful passion is unholy, no matter whom the man penetrates (1 Thess 4:3–4). No brother or sister may be wronged or exploited (4:6). The ultimate value is *love* (4:9), and the Christian community shall be marked by peace (5:13), kindness toward the weak (5:14), forgiveness (5:15a), and goodness toward all (5:15b).

As we conclude our discussion of consecration in 1 Thessalonians, I want to mention briefly Paul's exhortation to share a "holy kiss" (ἐν ἁγίῳ φιλήματι) with one another (1 Thess 5:26). As far as we can tell, this was a distinctive ritual of early Christianity, combining holiness (signaling purity) and physical contact (signaling affection).[42] Part of the Christian call to consecration was experiencing belonging and intimacy with a *corpus mixtum*, circumcised together with uncircumcised, Greeks and "barbarians," men and women, slaves and free. This disrupted, even defied "Roman" *pietas* and reshaped the Thessalonians' imagination for what God was calling this people to become together.

## CONCLUSION

Our goal in this chapter has been to answer the question—*How has Jewish Scripture left its mark most clearly on Paul's first letter to the Thessalonians?* While Paul did not quote the Old Testament explicitly, it is tempting to look for places where we find strong allusions or "echoes" of Scripture. We have taken a different tactic: *if a Roman read 1 Thessalonians, what would seem unnatural or confusing insofar as it uniquely draws from Jewish religious discourse?* We have argued that one such element in 1 Thessalonians would be Paul's ἅγιος language, and what is meant for these (mostly gentile) believers to be *called to consecration* to God through Jesus Christ. Paul clearly adopts Hellenistic Jewish language to convey a religious disposition that is different from Roman conceptions of *pietas*. While Jews, Christians, and Romans would all have had some common appreciation for the need to respect and show honor to those who were above them, including the Divine, a Jewish conception of human holiness was more comprehensive; it required a deeper level of personal purity of those who will have contact with the Holy. And for Paul, Christians, as a result of the indwelling of God's own Spirit, are all called to be holy as a kind of whole priest-people. This has deep implications for how Christians live, including their sexual life and how they treat others.

## NOTES

1. All English translations of Scripture are from the NRSV unless otherwise noted.

2. Richard B. Hays, *Echoes of Scripture in the Letters of Paul* (New Haven, CT: Yale University Press, 1989); also Craig A. Evans and James A. Sanders, *Paul and the Scriptures of Israel* (Sheffield: JSOT Press, 1993); Stanley E. Porter and Christopher D. Land, ed., *Paul and Scripture*, PAST (Leiden: Brill, 2019).

3. I will sometimes refer to the Thessalonians as "Romans." In those cases, I am not referring to ethnicity, race, or citizenship, but people that are "Romanized" in culture and perspective.

4. By the middle of the first century, when Paul was writing to the Thessalonians, the city of Thessalonica was Roman, and its inhabitants "Romanized." By that I am not talking about ethnicity of the population, but initiation into a certain culture. Romanized people are taught and compelled to conform to "Roman-ness."

5. For my own work on 1 Thessalonians, see Nijay K. Gupta, *1 & 2 Thessalonians*, Zondervan Critical Introductions to the New Testament, ed. Michael F. Bird (Grand Rapids: Zondervan, 2019); also *1–2 Thessalonians*, New Covenant Commentary Series (Eugene, OR: Cascade Books, 2017).

6. See Roy E. Ciampa, "Old Testament in Paul," in *Dictionary of Paul and His Letters,* 2nd ed., ed. Scot McKnight, Lynn H. Cohick, and Nijay K. Gupta (Downers Grove, IL: IVP Academic, 2023), 722–39.

7. See Christopher D. Stanley, *Arguing with Scripture: The Rhetoric of Quotations in the Letters of Paul* (London: T&T Clark, 2004).

8. Whenever I refer to "explicit" citation, I mean quotation of Jewish Scripture that is extensive and/or obvious enough that the vast majority of readers will know Paul is quoting another text (usually with some kind of introductory formula like "as it is written").

9. Hans Hübner, *Vetus Testamentum in Novo: Band 2, Corpus Paulinum* (Göttington: Vandenhoek & Ruprecht, 1997), 549–1568.

10. Jeffrey A. D. Weima, "1–2 Thessalonians," in *Commentary on the New Testament Use of the Old Testament*, ed. G. K. Beale and D. A. Carson (Grand Rapids: Baker, 2007), 871–89.

11. J. C. Beker, "Echoes and Intertextuality: On the Role of Scripture in Paul's Theology," in *Paul and the Scriptures of Israel*, ed. Craig A. Evans and James A. Sanders (Sheffield: Sheffield Academic Press, 1993), 64–69, at 66.

12. Paul's letter to Philemon also lacks explicit Scripture citation, but I consider this a different kind of Pauline letter altogether, the most "personal" of his corpus.

13. Trans. Gupta.

14. Ralph Bruckner and Martin Vahrenhorst, "ἁγιάζω," "ἁγιασμός," "ἅγιος" in *Historical and Theological Lexicon of the Septuagint*, Volume 1, ed. Eberhard Bons and Jan Joosten (Tübingen: Mohr Siebeck, 2020), 82–106 (abbreviated hereafter *HTLS*).

15. Bruckner and Vahrenhorst observe that in Greek antiquity, the verb ἁγιάζω is *only* ever used in Jewish texts (*HTLS* 1.82).

16. Meaning in LXX: "If someone or something is designated as holy to God, it is separated from everyday life" (*HTLS* 1.83).

17. *HTLS* 1.104.

18. I credit this analogy to Anthony Thiselton, but I cannot remember whether it was from a video or an essay.

19. All translations here are my own.

20. Bryan Natali offers a helpful list for how *pietas* is used in various Roman relationships. I have organized that data into a chart. See Bryan Natali, "*Pietas*: Gods, Family, Homeland, Empire" (PhD dissertation, University of Calgary, 2014), 25.

21. Translation: Cicero, *De Oratore III, De Fato, Paradoxa Stoicorum, De Partitione Oratoria*, trans. H. Caplan, LCL, vol. 4 (Cambridge, MA: Harvard University Press, 1968), 369.

22. Translation from Natali, "*Pietas*," 8.

23. See Carlos Noreña, *Imperial Ideals in the Roman West: Representation, Circulation, Power* (Cambridge: Cambridge University Press, 2011), 72.

24. Translation: James D. Garrison, *Pietas from Vergil to Dryden* (University Park, PA: Penn State University Press, 1992), 10.

25. Francesco Gnecchi, *The Coin Types of Imperial Rome: With 28 Plates and 2 Synoptic Tables* (London: Spink & Son, 1908), 55.

26. Some of this language is borrowed from Dan Hammer, *Roman Political Thought: from Cicero to Augustine* (Cambridge: Cambridge University Press, 2014), 215.

27. See Christopher Hoklotubbe, *Civilized Piety: The Rhetoric of Pietas in the Pastoral Epistles and the Roman Empire* (Waco, TX: Baylor University Press, 2017) 33–35.

28. Translation: Hendrik Wagenvoort, *Pietas: Selected Studies in Roman Religion* (Leiden: Brill, 1980), 11.

29. Iliones, companion of Aeneas, says of this hero, "No one was more just in piety, nor greater in war and arms" (*Aeneas . . . quo iustior alter/nec pietate fuit, nec bello maior et armis*; 544–45, M 766–68); for English translation, Christine G. Perkell, *Reading Vergil's Aeneid* (Norman: University of Oklahoma Press, 1999), 36.

30. Wagenvoort, *Pietas*, 12.

31. Translation: Wagenvoort, *Pietas*, 12.

32. Natali, "*Pietas*," 29; cf. Perkell, 37–38.

33. A good affirmation of this parallel comes from translations of the *Res Gestae*, where *pietas* is rendered in Greek as εὐσέβεια without exception. See *RG* 34: "*clupeusque aureus in curia Iulia positus, quem mihi senatum populumque*

*Romanum dare virtutis clementiae iustitiae pietatis caussa testatum est per eius clúpei inscriptionem*/ὅπλον τε χρυσοῦν ἐν τῶι βουλευτηρίωι ἀνατεθὲν ὑπό τε τῆς συνκλήτου καὶ τοῦ δήμου τῶν Ῥωμαίων διὰ τῆς ἐπιγραφῆς ἀρετὴν καὶ ἐπείκειαν καὶ δικαιοσύνην καὶ *εὐσέβειαν* ἐμοὶ μαρτυρεῖ/a golden shield was placed in the Curia Julia whose inscription testified that the senate and the Roman people gave me this in recognition of my valour, my clemency, my justice, and my *pietas*."

34. Ben Sira models this use on a number of occasions (Sir 11:22; 12:2, 4; 13:7, 24; 27:11; 33:14).

35. Hoklotubbe, *Civilized Piety.*

36. For more details, see Nijay K. Gupta, "Did Early Christians Give Dignity and Honor to Female Slaves?" in *The Biblical World of Gender: The Daily Lives of Ancient Women and Men*, ed. Celina Durgin and Dru Johnson (Eugene, OR: Cascade Books, 2022), 71–84.

37. T. Reu. 3.3; 4.6, 11; 5.3, 5; 6.1, 4; T. Levi 9.9; T. Jud. 12.2; 13.3; 14.2; 15.2; 18.2.

38. Gupta, *1–2 Thessalonians*, 90–148.

39. εἰδέναι ἕκαστον ὑμῶν τὸ ἑαυτοῦ σκεῦος κτᾶσθαι ἐν ἁγιασμῷ καὶ τιμῇ, ⁵ μὴ ἐν πάθει ἐπιθυμίας καθάπερ καὶ τὰ ἔθνη τὰ μὴ εἰδότα τὸν θεόν.

40. Seneca, in classic Stoic manner, emphasized that self-centered prayers should not be made to the gods through sacrifice and vows, because the noble thing is to accept fate as it comes; *Ep.* 31.5. Epictetus held a similar view, but made the qualification that sacrifice must still be done with piety and sincerity: according to local custom, in keeping with purity, with care, in generous portion and frequency, and in alignment with one's ability and opportunity (*Enchir.* 31.5).

41. *heu pietas, heu prisca fides invictaque bello dextera!*

42. Robert Jewett, *Romans,* Hermeneia (Minneapolis: Fortress Press, 2002), 973. For a helpful analysis, see Anthony Thiselton, *The First Epistle to the Corinthians,* NIGTC (Grand Rapids: Eerdmans, 2000), 1346.

# BIBLIOGRAPHY

Beker, J. C. "Echoes and Intertextuality: On the Role of Scripture in Paul's Theology." In *Paul and the Scriptures of Israel*, edited by Craig A. Evans and James A. Sanders, 64–69. Sheffield: Sheffield Academic Press, 1993.

Bruckner, Ralph and Martin Vahrenhorst. "ἁγιάζω," "ἁγιασμός," "ἅγιος." In *Historical and Theological Lexicon of the Septuagint*, volume 1, edited by Eberhard Bons and Jan Joosten, 82–106. Tübingen: Mohr Siebeck, 2020.

Caplan, H., translator. Cicero, *De Oratore III, De Fato, Paradoxa Stoicorum, De Partitione Oratoria.* Loeb Classical Library. Cambridge, MA: Harvard University Press, 1968.

Ciampa, Roy E. "Old Testament in Paul." In *Dictionary of Paul and His Letters*, 2nd ed., edited by Scot McKnight, Lynn H. Cohick, and Nijay K. Gupta, 722–39. Downers Grove, IL: IVP Academic, 2023.

Evans, Craig A., and James A. Sanders. *Paul and the Scriptures of Israel.* Sheffield: JSOT Press, 1993.

Garrison, James D. *Pietas from Vergil to Dryden.* University Park, PA: Penn State University Press, 1992.

Gnecchi, Francesco. *The Coin Types of Imperial Rome: With 28 Plates and 2 Synoptic Tables.* London: Spink & Son, 1908.

Gupta, Nijay K. *1 & 2 Thessalonians.* Zondervan Critical Introductions to the New Testament. Grand Rapids: Zondervan, 2019.

———. *1–2 Thessalonians.* New Covenant Commentary Series. Eugene, OR: Cascade Books, 2017.

———. "Did Early Christians Give Dignity and Honor to Female Slaves?" In *The Biblical World of Gender: The Daily Lives of Ancient Women and Men*, edited by Celina Durgin and Dru Johnson, 71–84. Eugene, OR: Cascade Books, 2022.

Hays, Richard B. *Echoes of Scripture in the Letters of Paul.* New Haven, CT: Yale University Press, 1989.

Hoklotubbe, Christopher. *Civilized Piety: The Rhetoric of Pietas in the Pastoral Epistles and the Roman Empire.* Waco, TX: Baylor University Press, 2017.

Hübner, Hans. *Vetus Testamentum in Novo: Band 2, Corpus Paulinum.* Göttington: Vandenhoek & Ruprecht, 1997.

Jewett, Robert. *Romans.* Hermeneia. Minneapolis: Fortress, 2002.

Natali, Bryan. "*Pietas*: Gods, Family, Homeland, Empire." PhD dissertation. University of Calgary, 2014.

Noreña, Carlos. *Imperial Ideals in the Roman West: Representation, Circulation, Power.* Cambridge: Cambridge University Press, 2011.

Perkell, Christine G. *Reading Vergil's Aeneid.* Norman: University of Oklahoma Press, 1999.

Porter, Stanley E., and Christopher D. Land, eds. *Paul and Scripture.* PAST. Leiden: Brill, 2019.

Stanley, Christopher D. *Arguing with Scripture: The Rhetoric of Quotations in the Letters of Paul.* London: T&T Clark, 2004.

Thiselton, Anthony. *The First Epistle to the Corinthians.* NIGTC. Grand Rapids: Eerdmans, 2000.

Wagenvoort, Hendrik. *Pietas: Selected Studies in Roman Religion.* Leiden: Brill, 1980.

Weima, Jeffrey A. D. "1–2 Thessalonians." In *Commentary on the New Testament Use of the Old Testament*, edited by G. K. Beale and D. A. Carson, 871–89. Grand Rapids: Baker, 2007.

# Index

# Index of Ancient Sources

## OTHER ANCIENT SOURCES (JEWISH, CHRISTIAN, GRECO–ROMAN)

# About the Editors and Contributors

**Roy E. Ciampa** is the S. Louis and Ann W. Armstrong Professor of Religion and chair of the Department of Biblical & Religious Studies at Samford University. Previously he was professor of New Testament and chair of the Division of Biblical Studies at Gordon-Conwell Theological Seminary (Massachusetts) and manager for Biblical Scholarship and Integrated Training with the Nida Institute for Biblical Scholarship at American Bible Society. He is the author of *The Presence and Function of Scripture in Galatians 1 and 2* (1998) and coauthor, with Brian Rosner, of *First Corinthians* in *The Pillar New Testament Commentary* (2010), as well as numerous essays and articles.

**Ernest P. Clark** is director of global training with United World Mission. He was previously classics consultant at South Asia Institute of Advanced Christian Studies in Bangalore, India, and leader of the Learning Design Team with Development Associates International. He completed his PhD at the University of St Andrews. Ernest is the author of *Romans* in the Really Useful Guides series (2022) and of *Weak Elements, Weak Flesh: Reading Galatians in Conversation with Philo and Greek Medical Discourse* (Fortress Academic 2023).

**Channing L. Crisler** is associate professor of New Testament at Anderson University and the Clamp School of Divinity in Anderson, South Carolina. In addition to various articles and essays, he authored *A Synoptic Christology of Lament: The Lord Who Answered and the Lord Who Cried* (Lexington 2023); *Echoes of Lament and the Christology of Luke* (2020); *Reading Romans as Lament: Paul's Use of OT Lament in His Most Famous Letter* (2016); *An Intertextual Commentary on Romans*, 4 vols. (2021–2022); *Paul's Theology as Agonizing Struggle*; coedited *Always Reforming: Reflections on Martin Luther & Biblical Studies* (2021); coauthored *The Bible Toolbox* (2019); and contributed to *New Studies in Intertextual Interplay* (2020).

**A. Andrew Das** is Niebuhr Distinguished Chair and professor of religious studies at Elmhurst University. Along with numerous essays and articles, he has written or edited eleven books, including a major commentary on *Galatians*, and from Fortress Academic: *Solving the Romans Debate* (2007); *Paul and the Stories of Israel: Grand Thematic Narratives in Galatians* (2016); *Scripture, Texts, and Tracings in Romans* (2021); and *Scriptures, Texts, and Tracings in 2 Corinthians and Philippians* (2022). His *Remarriage in Early Christianity* is forthcoming in 2024. He is a member of the Studiorum Novi Testamenti Societas, served on the editorial board of the *Journal for the Study of Paul and His Letters,* the Christian Standard Bible translation oversight committee, and has cochaired the SBL's Scripture and Paul Seminar.

**Nijay K. Gupta** is professor of New Testament at Northern Seminary. He has written fifteen books including *Paul and the Language of Faith* (2020) and *A Beginner's Guide to New Testament Studies* (2020), as well as commentaries on Galatians, Philippians, Colossians, and 1–2 Thessalonians. Nijay is coeditor of *The State of New Testament Studies* (2019) and the *Dictionary of Paul and His Letters*, 2nd ed. (2023). He cochairs the Pauline theology seminar of the Institute for Biblical Research and serves as a senior translator for Pauline texts for the New Living Translation.

**Matthew S. Harmon** is professor of New Testament Studies at Grace College and Theological Seminary in Winona Lake, Indiana. He is the author of *She Must and Shall Go Free: Paul's Isaianic Gospel in Galatians* (BZNW 168, 2010) and a major commentary on Galatians (EBTC). In addition to writing commentaries on Philippians (Mentor) and 2 Peter and Jude (ESVEBC), he has also authored *Rebels and Exiles: A Biblical Theology of Sin and Restoration* (2020), *The Servant of the Lord and His Servant People: Tracing a Biblical Theme through the Canon* (2020), and *The God Who Judges and Saves: A Theology of 2 Peter and Jude* (2023).

**Christoph Heilig** is leader of an international junior research group at the LMU Munich that works on the intersection between exegesis and narratology. He is the author of *Hidden Criticism? The Methodology and Plausibility of the Search for a Counter-Imperial Subtext in Paul* (2015; Fortress 2017) and *Paul's Triumph: Reassessing 2 Corinthians 2:14 in Its Literary and Historical Context* (2017), and for these he was honored with the Mercator Award in the Humanities and Social Sciences in 2018. His *Paulus als Erzähler? Eine narratologische Perspektive auf die Paulusbriefe* (2020) was recently recognized with the Manfred Lautenschlaeger Award for Theological Promise in 2022. He has also published *The Apostle and the Empire: Paul's Implicit and Explicit Criticism of Rome* (2022).

**Craig S. Keener** (PhD, Duke University) is F. M. and Ada Thompson Professor of Biblical Studies at Asbury Theological Seminary. He is author of thirty-four books, with some 1.4 million copies in circulation; these include *The Mind of the Spirit* (2016) and two commentaries on Galatians. The books have won thirteen national or international awards. He has also authored roughly one hundred academic articles; seven booklets; and roughly two hundred popular-level articles. Craig is married to Dr. Médine Moussounga Keener, who was a refugee in her home country of Congo for eighteen months.

**B. J. Oropeza** is professor of biblical studies at Azusa Pacific University and Seminary in Azusa, California. He is the author or editor of many books and articles, including *Perspectives on Paul: Five Views*, *Exploring Intertextuality*, and *Exploring Second Corinthians,* as well as a contributor to the translation of the New Revised Standard Version updated edition. He is a member of the Studiorum Novi Testamenti Societas. He has also been an editorial board member of the Rhetoric of Religious Antiquity series, served as cochair of the SBL's Scripture and Paul Seminar, and started the Intertextuality in the New Testament section of the Society of Biblical Literature.

**Mark A. Seifrid** is senior professor of exegetical theology at Concordia Seminary, St. Louis, Missouri. He is the author of *The Second Letter to the Corinthians* (PNTC 2014) and contributor to the following volumes: *Nineteenth-Century Lutheran Theologians* (ed. Matthew Becker, 2015); *Paulinische Schriftrezeption: Grundlagen - Ausprägungen - Wirkungen— Wertungen* (ed. Florian Wilk and Markus Öhler, 2017); *Spurensuche zur Einleitung in das Neue Testament* (ed. Michael Labahn, 2017); *Bestimmte Freiheit* (ed. Martin Bauspieß et al., 2020); *Heiligen Schrift in der Kritik* (ed. Konrad Schmid, 2021).

**Nicolai Techow** earned his PhD from the University of Copenhagen. He has served as the coordinator of studies and research at Fjellhaug International University College, Copenhagen, where he is currently assistant professor of New Testament. He is the author of *Sinners, Works of Law, and Transgression in Gal 2:14b-21: A Study in Paul's Line of Thought* (WUNT II 2024).

**Jeffrey A. D. Weima** is professor of New Testament at Calvin Theological Seminary, where he has taught for thirty-one years. Jeff has published six books: *Neglected Endings: The Significance of the Pauline Letter Closings* (1994), *An Annotated Bibliography of 1 and 2 Thessalonians* (1998), two commentaries on 1 & 2 Thessalonians (2002; 2014), *Paul the Ancient Letter Writer: An Introduction to Epistolary*

*Analysis* (2016), and *The Sermons to the Seven Churches of Revelation: A Commentary & Guide* (2021). He is an active member of several academic societies; leads biblical study tours to Greece, Turkey, Israel/Jordan, and Italy; conducts intensive preaching seminars for pastors; and preaches/speaks widely in churches in both the United States and Canada.